ARABS IN THE EARLY ISLAMIC EMPIRE

The Royal Asiatic Society was founded in 1823 'for the investigation of subjects connected with, and for the encouragement of science, literature and the arts in relation to Asia'. Informed by these goals, the policy of the Society's Editorial Board is to make available in appropriate formats the results of original research in the humanities and social sciences having to do with Asia, defined in the broadest geographical and cultural sense and up to the present day.

For a full list of publications by the Royal Asiatic Society see www.royalasiaticsociety.org

ARABS IN THE EARLY ISLAMIC EMPIRE

EXPLORING AL-AZD TRIBAL IDENTITY

Brian Ulrich

EDINBURGH
University Press

For my grandparents

Edinburgh University Press is one of the leading university presses in the UK. We publish academic books and journals in our selected subject areas across the humanities and social sciences, combining cutting-edge scholarship with high editorial and production values to produce academic works of lasting importance. For more information visit our website: edinburghuniversitypress.com

First published in hardback by Edinburgh University Press 2019

Edinburgh University Press Ltd
The Tun – Holyrood Road
12 (2f) Jackson's Entry
Edinburgh EH8 8PJ

Typeset in 11/13 JaghbUni Regular by
Servis Filmsetting Ltd, Stockport, Cheshire
and printed and bound by CPI Group (UK) Ltd,
Croydon, CR0 4YY

A CIP record for this book is available from the British Library

ISBN 978 1 4744 3679 3 (hardback)
ISBN 978 1 4744 3680 9 (paperback)
ISBN 978 1 4744 3681 6 (webready PDF)
ISBN 978 1 4744 3682 3 (epub)

Contents

Acknowledgements

This book began as my doctoral dissertation at the University of Wisconsin. For ably guiding my studies while allowing me the freedom to explore a multitude of different issues, I thank my advisor, Michael Chamberlain. David Morgan also played a crucial role during my graduate studies, so much so that I think of him as a co-advisor. The other members of my dissertation committee, André Wink, Thomas Spear and Samer Alatout, also provided useful feedback and welcome support at different stages of the process.

As a graduate student, my work was supported by various grants of the University of Wisconsin History Department, as well as a Lemoine-Midelfort Fellowship from the University of Wisconsin Medieval Studies Program. The George L. Mosse Program in History allowed me to spend two academic years at Hebrew University in Jerusalem, where I benefited particularly from Michael Lecker's generosity with his time, knowledge and materials. A general research grant from the Gerda Henkel Stiftung allowed me to significantly revise the project during the summer and fall of 2014. For calling my attention to this funding source, I thank my Shippensburg University colleague Mark Spicka. Further revisions enabled by a Fall 2017 sabbatical moved the manuscript to almost its final form. I thank Shippensburg's Sabbatical Leave Committee for their support.

Antoine Borrut, Jens Scheiner, and Jérémie Schiettecatte each read portions of the manuscript and offered valuable feedback. Peter Webb generously allowed me to cite his forthcoming work. The anonymous reviewers selected by the Royal Asiatic Society monograph series and Edinburgh University Press both made many valuable suggestions and succeeded in performing the peer reviewers' legerdemain of making me appear smarter than I actually am. I also thank Alison Ohta of the Royal Asiatic Society and their monograph board for their support. At Edinburgh University Press, Nicola Ramsey and Kirsty Woods provided useful assistance during the commissioning and manuscript preparation processes, while Rebecca

Mackenzie, Eddie Clark, Sarah Foyle and Emma Rees ably handled other pre-publication matters. Helen Johnston of Saying and Beyond was a capable copy editor.

At all stages of the project I have benefited from conversations with and favours from others, and so would like to thank Ovamir Anjum, Giovanna Benadusi, Michael Bonner, Lawrence Conrad, Michael Decker, Fred Donner, Aisha al-Harthi, Hugh Kennedy, Derek Kennet, Robert LaFleur, Ella Landau-Tasseron, Sterenn Le Maguer-Gillon, Walter Müller, Hassan al-Naboodah, Molly Patterson, David Robinson, Ihab el-Sakkout, Scott Savran, Uli Schamiloglu, Jonathan Skaff, and Paul Yule. Shippensburg University's Department of History and Philosophy has provided a collegial professional environment since 2009, as did Colgate University's Department of History during the 2008–9 academic year. The interlibrary loan staff at Shippensburg University, first Diane Kalathas and more recently Rebecca 'Alexx' Purcell, both ably filled many complicated or challenging requests.

Portions of Chapter 1 are adapted from 'The Azd Migrations Reconsidered: Mālik b. Fahm and ᶜAmr Muzayqiya in Historiographic Context', *Proceedings of the Seminar for Arabian Studies* 38 (2008): 311–18. I thank Archaeopress for permission to reuse this material.

Notes on the Text

In accordance with house style, diacritics meant to indicate Arabic letters in the Latin alphabet are omitted from the text and notes, but do appear in the bibliography and index. However, '*ᶜayn*' and '*hamza*' are represented by 'ᶜ' and 'ᵓ' respectively. The exception is for those Arabic technical terms which remain in the text, which are fully marked. In addition, AH dates have generally been converted to the single CE year with which they most overlap.

In order to eliminate redundancy, the definite article from 'al-Azd' and similar terms is omitted whenever the English seems to benefit from having 'the'. In addition, while 'Yemen' is used for the country, the tribal block is referred to as 'al-Yaman' to avoid confusion. Similarly, 'Baḥrayn' occasionally appears to denote the historic region, as opposed to the archipelago which is the modern country. Finally, authors of Arabic primary sources appear in the notes with a commonly recognised brief form of their name which usually omits definite articles; however, the definite articles remain with modern authors of secondary sources.

Introduction

Explanation and Historiography of the Problem

Classical Arabic writers frequently portrayed the Arabs as a tribally defined people. During the 1200s, Ibn Manzur's *Lisan al-ᶜArab* quoted numerous prior authorities as saying that an *ᶜarabī* was anyone descended from the *ᶜarab*.[1] Peter Webb, however, notes that in al-Khalil b. Ahmad al-Farahidi's dictionary *Kitab al-ᶜAyn*, which was finalised by a colleague after his death in 791, 'Arab' (*ᶜarab)* was defined on the basis of purity of speech without reference to language, and was thus the opposite of *ᶜajam*, characterised by impure speech. Genealogical definitions of Arabness rose to the forefront during the ninth century, though one suspects they drew upon earlier antecedents.[2] It was in the early ninth century that Hisham b. Muhammad Ibn al-Kalbi (d. 819) wrote his works on genealogy, which drew on earlier material from a culture in which descent was a common way of characterising identity. Particularly in *Nasab Maᶜadd wa al-Yaman al-Kabir*, Ibn al-Kalbi presents what came to be the two branches of the Arabs, often called 'northerners' (Qays or Nizar) and 'southerners' (al-Yaman).[3]

Al-Khalil b. Ahmad would have had reasons for finding congenial the linguistic definitions of '*ᶜarab*' circulating in his day. Born in Oman, he belonged to a tribal grouping called al-Azd.[4] In Ibn al-Kalbi's influential genealogical work, al-Azd was a name applied to Diraᵓ b. al-Ghawth, one of the descendants of Qahtan, progenitor of al-Yaman.[5] As Webb demonstrates, 'Arabness' was a fluid and contested idea during the early caliphate. On the basis of pre-Islamic Arabic poetry, he argues that no one self-identified as an Arab in late pre-Islamic Arabia, and that the major ethnic grouping for the poets was actually Maᶜadd, later turned into a key ancestor of the northerners.[6] Robert Hoyland has argued that Webb underestimated both the epigraphic and poetic evidence for a potentially language-based Arab identity prior to Islam, saying 'he operates with the notion that either we have a coherent all-embracing Arab identity or no identity, whereas a much more nuanced approach is needed.'[7] Regardless of the degree to which Arab identity existed prior to Islam, however, it certainly gained prominence in the wake of the conquests which brought those of Arabian heritage to political and cultural power, and what it entailed became a subject of contestation and debate, with the southerners generally and often the Azd specifically denied the status of an Arabness constructed on a Maᶜadd base.[8]

The central argument of this book is that al-Azd identity existed from pre-Islamic times into the Abbasid period, though the meaning of that identity shifted in different contexts across time and space. This persistence is seen not only through the use of tribal ties as political and economic assets under certain conditions, but also through the composition and preservation of narratives which reveal a concern with tribal reputation and heritage. As a contribution to the literature on tribes and states in Middle Eastern history, this work problematises concepts of both tribe and state in arguing that the incorporation of tribally organised populations into the caliphate should be viewed as a long-term process of incorporating and redeploying both material and cultural resources. As a work of early Islamic history, it argues that the continuity of development between late antiquity and early Islam that scholars have observed in other areas is also shown in the behaviour of tribespeople and the relationship between tribes and states in the region.[9] This means, in part, that tribes continued to be a useful form of social organisation in ways more similar to those of pre-Islamic Arabia than has sometimes been supposed.

This study also has implications for several larger issues. The first is of concern to anthropologists as well as historians, and involves tribes and states as overlapping forms of social relations. The argument herein is that while Bedouin perceived tribe in terms of a network of assets, options and obligations, tribal groups often depended upon key leaders who served as guarantors of those assets and options. As the configurations of power took on more statelike qualities, state policies shaped the elite world inhabited by those leaders, leading to shifts in the nature of such leadership and the function of tribal identity. Another issue involves ethnicity in the early Islamic Middle East and the role played by tribal ties in forming a more general sense of Arab identity, as described above. Not only was Arabian descent an important part of the status claims of urban notables, but also tribal ties were a means of establishing solidarity with substantial rural populations which could serve as military and economic resources.

Historiographic Background

Much of the early work on tribes in early Islamic history focused on the origins of the division between the 'northern' and 'southern' Arabs mentioned above. Some scholars, such as W. Robertson Smith, claimed these represented 'two great races' into which Arabs had been divided 'from time immemorial'.[10] However, in his crucial study of Ibn al-Kalbi's genealogical work, Werner Caskel found that there was no evidence for this division prior to Islam, though one could perhaps discern the conditions for its development in the cultural differences between the settled agricultural civilisation of south Arabia and the pastoralists and oasis dwellers further north.[11] M. A. Shaban argues that Qays and al-Yaman were actually political parties, which he goes so far as to compare to the Whigs and Tories of seventeenth-century England.[12] Partially following Shaban, Fukuzo Amabe sees the two groups as tribal confederations with different duties, and attributes the enmity between the two to their favouring different policies based on those duties. However, Amabe himself notes numerous exceptions where groups of the Qays and al-Yaman performed the duties generally associated with the other group.[13] Shaban's idea of political parties was definitively refuted by Patricia Crone.[14] There has, meanwhile, been some movement toward arguing that the larger confederations of al-Yaman, Mudar, and Rabi^{c}a, the latter two subdivisions of the 'northerners', may in fact have origins in the sixth century, with their consolidation during the seventh and eighth representing a continuation of pre-Islamic developments.[15]

More recently, scholars have focused attention on the social, economic and political factors which contributed to changes in the tribal structure. Fred Donner has examined the effect on the Arabian tribes of the formation of the early Islamic polity, arguing that the state provided means of tying individuals to itself through the payment of military stipends and shares from state-owned lands, while simultaneously using tribal ties as mechanisms of classification and enforcement.[16] Crone's *Slaves on Horses* has been another influential interpretation. In this work, Crone 'presents an explanation of how and why slave soldiers came to be a central feature of the Muslim polity.'[17] One major component in her explanation is that the early caliphal state destroyed the Arab tribal structure, replacing it with newly created military administrative units in the garrison towns that simply bore tribal names and were ruled indirectly through a class of *ashrāf* (notables) from the leading families among the tribes.[18] A further development took place during the Marwanid period, in which these moieties in turn became purely military units, and the conflicts between them an example of military factionalism.[19] Although she highlights differences between Central Asian and Arab conquests, on the issue of tribal military units Crone may have been influenced by Chinggis Khan's reorganisation of the Central Asian tribes into an ordered military structure, the elements of which bore tribal names.[20]

Crone's factionalism model has much to recommend it as a means of understanding Marwanid politics. It is, however, inadequate as a means of understanding relations between the Arab tribes and the early Islamic state apart from the military realm, and her account of its evolution needs revisiting in light of more recent understandings of pre-Islamic Arabia and the evolution of Arab identity. For Crone, the Arabs 'enjoyed an ethnic and cultural homogeneity quite without parallel in Central Asia or Europe' and 'had lived in freedom from ethnic and social disturbance from very ancient times.'[21] A characteristic of the Arabian Peninsula was thus 'tribal immutability'.[22] None of this can now be accepted. Arab identity prior to Islam, if it existed at all, definitely did not extend to the entire peninsula and was probably of little importance, while states had long been involved with the politics of the peninsula and its tribes.

Crone's model of the interaction of tribes and states in the region is also flawed. Her definition of 'tribe' is 'a descent group which constitutes a political community' and, specifically, 'that descent group within which control of pasture land is vested, within which particular rules regarding blood-money and other aspects of behavior apply, which is endowed with a chief, and within which most of social life is conducted.'[23] She sees these tribes as a completely alternative method of social organisation to states, which as superior socio-political structures undermine and ultimately destroy them.[24] As Richard Tapper has pointed out, the last assertion seems to run contrary to the history of the Middle East in which tribes and states coexisted for long periods, and tribes sometimes gained ascendancy over and even conquered states.[25] It does, however, apparently lie behind her view of the Arab tribes in the early caliphate.

Most recently, Eva Orthmann has examined the Arab tribes from the last years of the Umayyad period into the 800s and the rise of Turkish soldiery during the reign of al-Maʾmun. In a book that ranges widely through source criticism, case studies of events, Arabic terminology, tribal structure, and more, Orthmann concludes that contrary to Crone, Arab tribes continued to play a role in political and economic life in cities, towns and the steppe throughout the period under study. The Abbasid caliphs faced many tribal revolts, and tried various strategies for managing the tribes, including co-option, the appointment of leaders, and dividing and conquering.[26] She concludes that rivalry between Qays and al-Yaman did not motivate actions, but was instead one of the tools which groups in certain times and places used to promote their interests.[27]

Orthmann's view that membership in a broad tribal confederation could serve as a situational asset will be mentioned again below. Another implication of her work focuses attention on studies of smaller tribal groups which held more regular significance. M. J. Kister's doctoral dissertation, 'Tamim in the Period of the Jahiliyya: A Study in Tribal Traditions', uses poetry, *akhbār* reports and genealogical literature to compile a valuable picture of how the Tamim represented their pre-Islamic past, while also calling attention to that tribe's important links with both Mecca and the Sasanians.[28] Michael Lecker published a prosopographical study of the Banu Sulaym, a tribe near Mecca during the life of Muhammad, partly to establish that 'dedicating a monograph to a single tribe is a feasible and useful project'. [29] Ella Landau-Tasseron drew upon her earlier work concerning the Wars of the Ridda in publishing a brief study of Asad during that period, concluding that the term 'Asad' in the sources usually represented only part of the tribe as outlined by Arab genealogists.[30] Donner has come to similar conclusions regarding the Bakr b. Waʾil.[31] ᶜAbd Allah Ibrahim al-ᶜAskar has written an examination of B. Hanifa's transition into the Umayyad period, and Mohammad Rihan has studied the history of the ᶜAmila of Lebanon under the Umayyads.[32] Rasheed Hosein has written about Thaqif, and particularly their relationship with Quraysh.[33] Most recently, Georg Leube has taken a prosopographical approach to the study of Kinda during the first three Muslim generations.[34] As a contribution to the history of Arab and Arabian tribes, this work seeks to go beyond the others by taking a broad chronological scope and offering a new model for understanding the ongoing dynamic interaction between structures identified as those of tribe and state.

Conceptual Approaches: Genealogy and Identity

The historiography above has noted definitions of 'tribe', and in fact scholars have produced multiple definitions for that term, with implications for any group such as al-Azd to which it is applied. Often 'tribe' has been used to connote primitiveness and denigrate certain societies and their history, leading scholars of most regions to abandon it altogether. It remains current, however, in Middle Eastern Studies. 'Nation' and 'ethnicity', which have replaced 'tribe' among those studying the Americas and Africa, must in Middle Eastern usage go with linguistic groups such as the Arabs and Kurds, and so 'tribe' translates the Arabic *qabīla* and sometimes *ᶜashīra*, much as it does the largest component groups of ancient Israel, for which it was used in English long before colonialism. However, an implication of this varied use is that scholars must avoid lumping together all societies labeled 'tribal', as social structures vary widely between the Middle East and, say, Central Asia, where the political economy is quite different. In addition, especially in the Arab world, the term should not be associated with nomadism.[35]

For the authors of our primary sources, al-Azd was defined through genealogy, particularly that of Ibn al-Kalbi, in which, as noted above, the Azd are all those descended from Dira᾿ b. al-Ghawth, who was sometimes known as 'al-Azd' because he displayed the courage of a lion (*al-asad*). Ibn al-Kalbi's works became standard; the work of his most prominent successor, Abu Muhammad ᶜAli b. Ahmad Ibn Hazm (d. 1064), was largely built upon them.[36] However, the Ibn al-Kalbi corpus, and by extension other extant genealogical texts from the ninth century, should be seen in the context of the articulation of an Arab identity embracing all cultural groups with real or claimed roots in the Arabian Peninsula.[37] Webb has ably charted the way genealogical texts are one source illustrating debates over inclusion and primacy within Arabness.[38] Furthermore, there is clear evidence of alternative schemes specific to al-Azd in the *Kitab al-Tijan fi Muluk Himyar*, which in its extant form is by Ibn al-Kalbi's contemporary ᶜAbd al-Malik b. Hisham (d. 833). Not only is there a Hamdan b. al-Azd who became the ancestor of some al-Azd in Iraq (specifically at Babylon), but many of the Azd of the Sarat Mountains are tied to a Hubayr b. al-Hubur b. al-Azd.[39] Despite the prominence of being sons of the al-Azd eponym himself, neither figure features in Ibn al-Kalbi's work.

In place of viewing al-Azd as a descent group traceable through genealogical literature, this study adopts a definition of tribe from William and Fidelity Lancaster: 'a definition of identity against other similar units of self-definition acting in a moral arena'. These tribes are not corporate entities, and in fact may be widely dispersed.[40] They have reputation, and tribespeople partake of that reputation in assuming and being accepted into the identity, as well as gaining access to any economic resources belonging to the tribe either through communal rights to land use or government stipends. Tribes are also formed by individuals and sub-groups who conceive of themselves as freely in association with each other.[41] This definition allows not only for the groups' decentralised organisation and dispersal throughout the Muslim lands, but also for the consistency in conceptual associations, both personal, as when individuals use the al-Azd label to move around the caliphate, and with the perception of common heritage seen in the Oman-related insults directed at al-Azd in different times and places.

For those who adhere to them, tribal identities and the relationships they involve provide assets, options and obligations.[42] These pertain not only to the material realm, but to the ideological one as well. The 'reputation' described by the Lancasters is similar to Michael Meeker's concept of 'segmentary *sharaf*'. With this term, Meeker referred to the deeds of ancestors which brought honour to their clan, deeds the power of which derived in significant ways from their recognition by other clans.[43] The concept is strikingly similar to the modern Jordanian tribal histories studied by Andrew Shryock, who writes, 'Ancestral ties to men of renown, or the lack thereof, were offered as proof of a tribesman's social standing', though in the context of his research different tribal histories were kept apart to avoid social division.[44] Here, too, we see the potential theoretical significance of tribes using higher identity levels as assets, such as with Orthmann's conclusion about Qays and al-Yaman.

The Lancasters' definition of tribe provides a framework which resonates with our sources, but as a corrective to views which emphasise an egalitarian ideal, this work occasionally references the idea of 'aristocratic orders' postulated by David Sneath. These aristocratic orders were composed of individual houses which over a period of generations mobilised genealogy to claim social and legal privilege and access to resources. Thus problematising the distinction between classically conceived states and stateless societies, and in our terminology tribal societies, Sneath goes on to suggest that aristocratic orders could provide 'a common mode and language of power that could allow rapid incorporation' into larger state structures.[45] Sneath's broader view of 'headless states' has been criticised, however, and there is no evidence it is relevant to Arabia. In addition, kinship probably plays more of a role than he allows, and the dynamics between kinship and leadership need to be handled sensitively in different historical contexts.[46]

Although Sneath addresses Arab societies only briefly, we have an indication that there could be aristocratic orders in the term '*sharīf*', which for Ibn Manzur was a noble status one could only get through one's ancestors.[47] Christian Robin shows that even in ancient times, Yemen had a highly stratified society dominated by noble lineages.[48] J. C. Wilkinson has identified tribal formation around loyalty to local shaykhs as a recurring pattern in Oman's history.[49] Ibn Khaldun's view of nomadic tribes, informed by North Africa and the Middle East, also emphasised the role of tribal leaders more than scholars have generally noted.[50] Aziz al-Azmeh has highlighted the ways in which pre-Islamic Arabia was clearly hierarchical: 'There existed a very decided reality to hierarchy and social differentiation, to the prerogatives of noble lineages and, within these lineages, to their chiefs . . . Pre-Islamic poetry is replete with a vocabulary of hierarchy, dominance and superordination, as it celebrated feats of arms.'[51] This study will frequently note the status of leaders among al-Azd and their significance for their followers, as well as the way that significance factored into the incorporation of the tribes into the caliphate.

Amidst this corrective, however, we should bear in mind that shaykhs in much of Arabia had far less control over their followers than did those in Central Asia, perhaps as a consequence of the fact there were fewer resources for them to extract and use to develop coercive potential. There is much in the sources to suggest that among their own followers, leaders acted in ways parallel to the modern ethnographic observations of Lancaster that shaykhs maintained their influence through reputation, persuasion and mediation.[52] The key point, however, is that egalitarianism was an idea, not a reality. Al-Azmeh explains: 'Individual honour, ferocious as it may have been, being dependent upon the collectivity, was, by some perennial covenant, deposited in the chief, the *sayyid*.'[53] Again, tribespeople perceived tribal identity in terms of assets, options and obligations. The power of the tribal leader, however, guaranteed the resources which gave rise to the assets, and he led during the reputational conflicts which could be a significant obligation.

In order to understand the relationship of tribe and state in the early caliphate, this work is also influenced by scholarship on comparative empires. Even though the Middle East was home to the first societies scholars describe as empires, the caliphate has seldom merited more than a passing mention in the scholarship dedicated to the theme.[54] The most in-depth discussion is that of S. E. Finer, who draws a distinction between an 'Empire Mark I', characterised by the domination of one identity group over others, and an 'Empire Mark II', in which the evolution of a common imperial culture served as the common marker of a porous ruling class. Finer specifically cites the difference between the Umayyad and Abbasid caliphates as an example of this distinction, along with the development of China between the Han and Song dynasties.[55] As with all pre-modern states, the caliphate ruled through cooperation with local notables, the nature of which varied across time and space but could include *ᶜulamāᵓ*, tribal leaders and wealthy landowners.[56] The present work will highlight ways in which the shifting types of intermediary between state and society had an impact on the signification of al-Azd identity, while the incorporation of that identity into the common imperial culture shows how elite Azdis helped to shape that culture while finding a place within it.

Searching for al-Azd Identity

The present work, then, focuses on the development and meaning of al-Azd identity and its role in the development of the early Islamic polity. It remains to understand the methods of working with the source material, which consists almost exclusively of Arabic texts containing information about the times and places under investigation. Apart from papyri and inscriptions, our earliest Arabic sources date from the ninth century, much later than the period for which most critical points of this study will be developed. While it is true that these writers primarily compiled and edited for their own purposes accounts from earlier generations of scholars, with *isnads* showing the purported chains of transmission, the main bulk of those accounts dates from only the eighth century. Such source material behind our extant works included written works from earlier authors, notes for or from lectures, and perhaps 'sourcebooks', meaning here distinct but related materials which were combined organisationally in ways Sarah Bowen Savant compares to packets of reading for modern university courses.[57] Part of the historical investigation, then, shall involve understanding the texts themselves and the ways in which we can use them to understand periods before their composition. The approach favoured in the present work is what Fred Donner calls 'tradition criticism', distinguished by an emphasis on the means and context of the transmission of information within the texts.[58]

Our approach to the texts recognises that they contain what James Fentress and Chris Wickham call 'social memory', which in their description 'identifies a group, giving it a sense of its past and defining its aspirations for the future'.[59] Social memory, because of its role for the group, is reflected upon and contested. As the authors say, 'This means that we must situate groups in relation to their own traditions, asking how they interpret their own "ghosts", and how they use them as a source of knowledge.'[60] Many of the characteristics of social memory comport well with the observations of scholars analysing the Arabic source material. For example, social memory is not only articulated in words, but also in images and rituals. These images, however, are both simplified to aid in transmission and conventionalised so as to achieve meaning for the entire group.[61] This, of course, recalls the frequent use of *topoi* in ancient and medieval literary sources, which may also have been linked to memorisation techniques. Noth and Conrad have identified a number of *topoi* in early Islamic history which one must understand in order to properly assess the source material.[62]

The Arabs eventually remembered themselves as a genealogical family, and the genealogical works produced from the ninth century on often served to record not only what were believed to be the relations among tribes, but also the deeds of generations past which could serve as the heritage of the Arab people. Writers of genealogies often wrote works refuting those they called *shuᶜūbīs*, a term which should probably be read as simply connoting anti-Arab bigotry.[63] One recurring source throughout this work is a genealogical text called either *al-Ansab* or *Ansab al-ᶜArab.* Although attributed to Salama b. Muslim al-ᶜAwtabi, who authored some Ibadi religious works, it is probably the work of an anonymous Omani author from the mid-tenth century, albeit with later emendations, and so referenced herein as ps.-al-ᶜAwtabi.[64] As Hinds notes, this work is probably more profitably regarded as an Omani heritage project than that of a particular tribe, but the significance of al-Azd in Oman means that they dominate the second volume.[65]

Scholars have debated the degree to which information in these genealogies goes back to pre-Islamic times.[66] The present work generally follows the views of Zoltan Szombathy, who sought to trace the method by which scholars developing the genealogies worked. A key part of Szombathy's argument is a distinction between general claims of descent or relationship and the systematic tracing of lines of ancestors and kinship connections, or genealogy.[67] The concept of *nasab* among Bedouin before and during the early days of Islam was simply that of relationship.[68] The pre-Islamic *nassāba* was someone who knew the heroes, legends and dishonorable relations of the tribes with which he was concerned, knowledge that served both to create group heritage and to attack the honour of rivals.[69] Bedouin in the desert had no reason to be interested in the *nasab* of tribes far afield, though elites in areas close to societies with more developed literate cultures have left inscriptions showing that they, at least, maintained longer and more comprehensive genealogies.[70] In addition, pre-Islamic Arabs seem not to have had the belief that all tribes were composed of descendants of a common ancestor, as opposed to what became the general if not universal assumption during the Abbasid period. Southern Arabia in particular had tribes whose names derived from toponyms.[71] Robertson Smith noted that as late as Umayyad times, some tribes were represented in poetry as having female eponyms.[72] Asad Ahmed and Webb have both seen a decline in the significance of matrilineal lines during the eighth century.[73] Because of these shifts, the present work will, particularly in dealing with earlier periods, privilege as most likely older accounts which do not conform to the patterns expected in the Abbasid period.

Szombathy describes the macro-genealogy as composed of 'patches' and 'filling stuff'. A 'patch' was the name of one or more real or legendary figures drawn from the source material. Thus, the prophet Muhammad and his immediate family represented 'patch number one'. The 'filling stuff' was scholarly conjecture, such as names added to a genealogy to push a figure further into the past or relationships between patches that seemed to the genealogists to belong together.[74] In addition, scholars felt compelled to provide all manner of details, both to secure their scholarly reputations and out of a sense that not knowing the answer to a question was an intolerable failure.[75] The 'patches' for the systematised genealogy came from tribal tales and poems, accounts of local relationships among tribes, hadith, and the official registers for the tribally organised stipend system in the garrison towns. Although some of this information was collected among Bedouin in the desert, far more stemmed from Bedouin or their immediate descendants in the cities of Iraq, especially the market west of Basra. Poetry from pre- and early Islamic times also had information which the developers of Arabic genealogy integrated into their scheme.[76]

However, although adopting Szombathy's model for the formation of the genealogies, as well as his terminology, the present work resists drawing too firm a distinction between pre-Islamic Bedouin and Arabs in the early caliphate, for the former were also impacted by elites and state structures. Aziz al-Azmeh believes overarching genealogies were articulated under the Jafnids and Nasrids drawing upon 'ancient ethnological lore prevalent in the steppe and desert'.[77] Ibn al-Kalbi, for example, drew in his works on material from al-Hira, where history was produced during the reign of al-Nuᶜman III.[78] In other words, the 'patches' might often be larger than Szombathy appears to allow, and as with the critique of Crone's view of Arab tribal identity discussed in the introduction, a view of pristine desert tribes is misleading.

Because genealogies can still serve as a useful reference for orientation, this work will note how different al-Azd groups mentioned fit into them. The thrust of reconstruction, however, will rely on other material. One important source is poetry, which survives even from the pre-Islamic period.[79] Although there was some forgery of poetry, most is now accepted as authentic, but unfortunately the bulk of the pre-Islamic Arabic poetry comes from northern Arabia and the Hijaz, and there is little from the pre-Islamic Azd.[80] One possible reason for this is a lack of the Bedouin themes that appealed to Abbasid-era collectors influenced by what Webb has called the 'Bedouinisation of memory', an issue which will also figure into Chapter 1.[81] The same may account for why al-Azd is so little referenced in the *adab* literature, material delineating the attributes necessary to become a cultured member of Abbasid urban society,[82]

Many sections of this work will rely heavily on prosopography, defined by Lawrence Stone as, 'the investigation of the . . . characteristics of a group of actors in history by means of a collective study of their lives.'[83] Crone, springing off her deep scepticism about the reliability of the sources' narratives, argued that 'early Islamic history has to be almost *exclusively* prosopographical'.[84] As noted above, Lecker and Leube use prosopography in studies of the Banu Sulaym and Kinda respectively.[85] Our extant sources are, to put it mildly, filled with lots and lots of names, and these usually have *nisbas*, such as al-Azdi, from which we can see their tribal identity. The imperfections of this technique are obvious, for only a small percentage of individuals appear in written texts, and there is a significant bias towards groups involved in events which caught the attention of later chroniclers, such as the life of Muhammad and the conquests. Nonetheless, from these names, we can discern useful patterns of geographic concentrations and what levels of identity existed and were most important in certain times and places.

Particularly for the period after the conquests, the histories produced by medieval Islamic society also become useful sources of information on general developments. Meaning can also be teased from the specific narratives they contain. As noted above, our extant sources from the ninth century and later drew on earlier material, and through the *isnads* we have chains of sources whom we can identify from biographical dictionaries. Scott Savran notes how narratives are a 'bridge linking collective memory and identity construction, to the extent that narrative serves as the vehicle by which a group imagines *its* history.'[86] In addition to origin stories, the didactic structure of narratives allows us to consider issues of relevance to those to whom they can be traced, such as a group for which segmentary *sharaf* is being claimed and defended.[87] This is not to say that we can 'reconstruct lost texts', as we are at the mercy of decisions made in later recensions and different ways the authorities themselves may have presented material at different times.[88] However, the material of different authorities often has clear patterns and themes which vary by time and place. In this way, the book also contributes to ongoing scholarship into historical memory in early Islamic history and our understanding of the sources on which our knowledge is based, including the work of individual transmitters of historical traditions.[89]

Al-Azd

Al-Azd is a particularly useful tribe for the purposes of this study. First, it includes populations from both Oman and the Sarat Mountains in western Arabia, allowing us to highlight the differences between those two areas.

It played a significant role in key events of early caliphate, and was well represented in the conquests of the east. One of its leading families, that of al-Muhallab b. Abi Sufra and his descendants, were pivotal players on the Umayyad political scene at a point when Arab and tribal identities were very much in flux, and thus al-Azd became a key element of the broader al-Yaman grouping. Finally, the availability of sources by and about people continuing to use the al-Azdi *nisba* well into Abbasid times allows us to consider what the identity contained in the *nisba* meant for them and how it fits the broader society of which they were a part.

In Ibn al-Kalbi's system, al-Azd included not only the groups known as the Azd Sarat, Azd ʿUman and Azd Shanuʾa (or Shanuʿa), but also the Ghassanids and the Ansar of Medina. However, there is good reason to omit the latter two groups from this study. The Ansar, for example, are treated separately from al-Azd in virtually every context except for genealogical works and accounts of the 'Scattering of al-Azd', which will feature in Chapter 1. An exception is two lines of poetry attributed to both Hassan b. Thabit and Saʿd b. al-Husayn al-Khazraji, both poets from Muhammad's time, in which both the Ansar and Ghassan are said to be al-Azd, and Ghassan is described as a watering place.[90] However, there is much poetry falsely attributed to Hassan b. Thabit, and the fact these lines are so unmoored from authorship suggests they may have been written much later.[91] In his mid-eighth-century *Tafsir*, Muqatil b. Sulayman al-Azdi lists the Azd as migrating to Bahrayn and Oman, with the Ansar and Ghassan listed as separate groups moving to Medina and al-Sham.[92] Ghassan was also separate from al-Azd in pre-Islamic inscriptions.[93] Despite the historically tenuous relationship, however, Ibn al-Kalbi's concern with tribes of historical or religious significance means that in *Nasab Maʿadd wa al-Yaman al-Kabir*, roughly half of the al-Azd material involves the Ansar or the Ghassanids. Nothing at all is said of many of the influential clans found in the *Taʾrikh al-Mawsil* of Abu Zakariyya al-Azdi (d. 945), and the Azd ʿUman, supposedly the most numerous, are squelched together in just four pages.[94]

That leaves us with the three groups which have 'Azd' in their name above. Szombathy saw the identification of the Azd Sarat and Azd ʿUman as a single tribe as comparable to a fallacy described by hadith scholars in which persons or groups with the same name were conflated.[95] Caskel also suggests that the two groups seem forced together to create a single tribe where none had previously existed. At the same time, given the degree to which they are mixed together genealogically, he does wonder if there may in fact have been some sort of pre-Islamic unity.[96] Caskel also suggests that the sheer height of the al-Azd eponym in the genealogical scheme testifies to its artificiality.[97] In discussing the important al-Azd subgroup of Daws, Caskel notes that the Tarif and Sulaym b. Fahm still lived in the Sarat mountains when Ibn al-Kalbi undertook his genealogical work, that the Munhib had lived there previously, and then argued that the large Malik b. Fahm grouping from Oman had been added to the line in Basra.[98] This, however, depends on his incorrect claim that the Azd in Basra prior to the arrival of Malik b. Fahm groups in the city had mostly been Daws. He also argued that further answers to the joining of the al-Azd branches probably lay in Kufa.[99] The belief in an early Daws primacy among al-Azd comes from Julius Wellhausen; however it is supported only by Wellhausen's errant belief that the Huddan were Daws.[100] In fact virtually all of the Azd in Basra during the early Islamic period were from Oman, and all those of Kufa were from western Arabia. All of the Azd of Basra who have entries in Ibn Saᶜd for his first five generations are from Omani tribes. In Khalifa b. Khayyat's ninth-century *Kitab al-Tabaqat*, the only western Azd in Basra is ᶜUqba b. Wassaj al-Bursani, a descendant of the Ghitrif.[101] There is nothing in the al-Azd settlement in Basra to account for the way Oman's al-Azd fit into the genealogical tables.

Focusing solely on the Azd ᶜUman and Azd Sarat also ignores the Azd Shanuᵓa, the division of the tribe which is most intermingled between the two sides of Arabia. Wilkinson claims that the difference between the Azd ᶜUman and Azd Shanuᵓa was based on different organisational structures in Oman prior to Islam combined with a special association of the Azd ᶜUman with the Muhallabids.[102] He identifies Azd Shanuᵓa with the Omani tribes of ᶜUthman b. Nasr, the most famous of which were the Maᶜwala, the Huddan and the Yahmad.[103] However, there were also tribes identified as Azd Shanuᵓa found entirely in western Arabia. According to Abu al-Faraj al-Isfahani (d. 967), the Azd Shanuᵓa were the Azd who settled in the Sarat Mountains after the flood which followed the breaking of the Maᵓrib dam.[104] Ps.-al-ᶜAwtabi included the Daws as an Azd Shanuᵓa group, as well as the ᶜUthman b. Nasr.[105] Both Abu ᶜUbayd al-Bakri and Yaqut (d. 1229) included an account naming as the Azd Shanuᵓa the tribes of Ghamid, Bariq and Daws, tribes which drove the Khathᶜam out of much of the Sarat Mountains running between Mecca and Yemen.[106] A stray reference to the B. Lihb as Azd Shanuᵓa may relate to their association with the Ghamid.[107] Yaqut also traced the Azd Shanuᵓa to a Shanuᵓa region of Yemen 42 farsakhs from Sanᶜaᵓ.[108] The early Umayyad poet Suraqa b. Mirdas al-Bariqi identified the Azd Shanuᵓa as his own people (*qawm*).[109] Also, during the Wars of the Ridda, Humayda b. al-Nuᶜman al-Bariqi and his followers fell back on a place called Shanuᵓa.[110] This region is today identified with the region of the B. Rizam near Abha in Saudi Arabia's ᶜAsir province.[111] Ibn Hisham's *Kitab al-Tijan* also links the Azd Shanuᶜa with a place called Shanᵓ (sic), and places ancestors of the Ghamid and Bariq prominently among them.[112]

The Azd Shanuᵓa were thus not a strictly genealogically defined grouping, though they did include the dominant al-Azd subgroups during the first half of the eighth century.[113] Chapter 1 will make the case that they had a common highland valley lifestyle in both Oman and western Arabia, and that their rise to prominence and geographic spread occurred in conjunction with the defeat of the Kinda during the sixth century. However, they were not the only divided grouping. Ibn al-Kalbi also placed descendants of ᶜAmr b. al-Azd in both Oman and the Hijaz, though mostly the former.[114] Caskel and Strenziok's register, however, mentions that some were no longer al-Azd, such as the al-Saᶜiq b. ᶜAmr and Saᶜd b. ᶜAmr becoming part of ᶜAbd al-Qays.[115] Caskel and Strenziok also believed that ᶜImran b. ᶜAmr Muzayqiya, an important figure in one branch of the Azd ᶜUman, was originally ᶜImran b. ᶜAmr b. al-Azd.[116] Abu Muhammad al-Hamdani (d. 945) noted groups of al-Asd b. ᶜImran in the Sarat Mountains.[117]

Preview of the Chapters

Chapter 1 deals with al-Azd origins in pre-Islamic Arabia. The first section of this chapter reviews the evidence of pre-Islamic inscriptions and archaeology, arguing for the existence of one or two al-Azd tribal kingdoms during the third century CE which are dimly reflected in later historical memory and which represent the earliest known basis of the al-Azd identity. It also examines the accounts of al-Azd origins from the early Islamic written tradition, concluding that while they contain some pre-Islamic elements, they represent the issues of the early caliphate, and are thus a product of that period in Iraq. Information on the Azd in both Oman and the Sarat Mountains is then reviewed in detail, which allows for conclusions about tribal groups and leadership on the eve of Islam and how they were impacted by the development of the Islamic state. This chapter also introduces a distinction between a directly controlled western Arabia and an eastern Arabia that was at best loosely allied with the early Islamic state, a distinction which will extend further into discussions of the expansion of the Arabs into the greater Middle East.

Chapter 2 focuses on the conquests and the establishment and society of the garrison towns in lower Iraq. It begins by arguing that whereas the conquests of Syria and those which resulted in the foundation of

Kufa were centrally directed from the Hijaz, Basra resulted from a more independent tribal movement which only slowly saw increasing levels of administration on behalf of the caliphate. It establishes that military factionalism played an early role in tribal political alignments which explains the alignment of the tribes in the Battle of the Camel during the First Civil War, including an alliance of Oman's al-Azd with Thaqif and the Umayyads that persisted through the end of the seventh century. It also examines the shifts in identity in Iraq as larger identity groupings such as 'al-Azd', which seem to have played little practical role in Arabia, became significant due to their use as administrative units under the early Umayyads, though it highlights ways in which this process had far more continuity with pre-Islamic Arabia than is sometimes supposed.

Chapter 3 deals with the Muhallabids, the most important al-Azd family during the eighth century. A key theme is the changing nature of elite status during the period, changes which impacted the types of figures seen as assets and options by Azdis. The Muhallabids were of non-Arab origin, but after rising to prominence on the eastern frontier both presented themselves and were presented by later al-Azd sources as a long-standing shaykhly family. They also represent a transition from independent tribal generalship in the east to central control of the conquests, with al-Hajjaj's rivalry with the Muhallabids marking the end of the al-Azd-Umayyad alliance and potentially the rise of opposition between 'northern' and 'southern' Arabs in the caliphate. Throughout, the chapter shall highlight ways in which the Muhallabids served as 'sites of memory' the textual commemoration of which allows us to see the shifting nature of tribal identity in later times.

Chapter 4 focuses on the conquests during the first half of the eighth century and the role of the Azd in the society of the eastern frontier. One key point developed is that whereas some scholars have posited that the commercial interests of Omani Azdis were a driving force behind the conquest of Sind under al-Hajjaj, a careful look at the sources reveals that Omanis were already present in the region at that time, and that al-Hajjaj probably attempted to centralize control over movements which began long before him. This also suggests a pattern, seen also in Yazid b. al-Muhallab's conquests south of the Caspian Sea, according to which factions avoided conquering regions from which they were already benefiting commercially, regions which were then conquered by others. The last part of this chapter examines al-Azd settlement in Khurasan and significance of tribal identification in the province

Finally, Chapter 5 will explore the Azd in the al-Jazira region of northern Iraq under the early Abbasids. This area had a significant tribal population, and much of the conflict in the area took the form of tribal *ᶜaṣabiyya*. The Abbasid period, however, saw new types of intermediary between state and tribal population in the form of the learned classes and locally important leaders who were co-opted with estates and appointments to official offices. These city-based elites often relied on rural reserves of manpower to actualise local authority, especially when the central government was weakened by the civil war of the early 800s. The sources on this period show evidence of a living genealogical idiom, but also new ways of deploying the pre-Islamic heritage and identities which had been reified in writing since the formation of the garrison towns' administrative units.

Notes

1. Ibn Manzur, *Lisan al-ᶜArab*, I, p. 537.
2. Peter Webb, *Imagining the Arabs: Arab Identity and the Rise of Islam*, pp. 178–87. See also Jan Retsö, *The Arabs in Antiquity: Their History from the Assyrians to the Umayyads*, pp. 24–30.
3. Hugh Kennedy, 'From Oral Tradition to Written Record in Arab Genealogy', pp. 540–1.
4. Rafael Talmon, *Arabic Grammar in Its Formative Age: Kitab al-ᶜAyn and Its Attribution to Ḫalil b. Aḥmad*, p. 14.
5. Caskel and Strenziok, I, p. 176; Ibn al-Kalbi, *Nasab Maᶜadd wa al-Yaman al-Kabir*, pp. 362–3.
6. Webb, *Imagining the Arabs*, pp. 77–85.
7. Robert G. Hoyland, 'Reflections on the Identity of the Arabian Conquerors of the Seventh-Century Middle East', pp. 126–30.
8. Retsö, *Arabs*, pp. 31–7; Webb, *Imagining the Arabs*, pp. 209–13. As Webb notes, Suliman Bashear previously noted an increase in the significance of Arabness in hadith from the eighth century, though he did not question a pre-existent Arab ethnos. Suliman Bashear, *Arabs and Others*, pp. 118–21.
9. This trend toward highlighting continuities between the two periods was launched in earnest by Michael Morony, *Iraq After the Muslim Conquest*. A recent synthesis of much of this scholarship is found in Jonathan Berkey, *The Formation of Islam: Religion and Society in the Near East, 600–1800*.
10. W. Robertson Smith, *Kinship and Marriage in Early Arabia*, p. 7.
11. Werner Caskel, *Gamharat an-Nasab: Das Genealogische Werk des Hisam Ibn Muhammad al-Kalbi*, I, pp. 20–1.
12. M. A. Shaban, *Islamic History* AD *600–750 (*AH *132): A New Interpretation*, pp. 120–2.
13. Fukuzo Amabe, *The Emergence of the ᶜAbbasid Autocracy: The ᶜAbbasid Army, Khurasan and Adharbayjan*, pp. 23–5.
14. Patricia Crone, 'Were the Qays and Yemen of the Umayyad Period Political Parties?'

15. Wilferd Madelung, 'Rabi'a in the Jahiliyya and in Early Islam'.
16. Fred Donner, *The Early Islamic Conquests*, pp. 256–9.
17. Patricia Crone, *Slaves on Horses: The Evolution of the Islamic Polity*, p. 3.
18. Crone, *Slaves*, pp. 30–2, 38–9.
19. Crone, *Slaves*, pp. 38–9, 42–5.
20. Crone refers to Central Asia as 'the paradigmatic home of barbarian conquerors', and describes a pattern of Central Asian tribal state formation that involves redistribution of the people into new military and administrative units. Crone, *Slaves*, pp. 18–20; David Morgan, *The Mongols*, pp. 89–90. Timothy May, *The Mongol Art of War*, p. 31.
21. Crone, *Slaves*, pp. 24–5.
22. Crones, *Slaves*, p. 23.
23. Patricia Crone, 'The Tribe and the State', pp. 51, 55.
24. Crone, 'Tribe', p. 69.
25. Richard Tapper, 'Anthropologists, Historians, and Tribespeople on Tribe and State Formation in the Middle East', pp. 63–4. The same article subjects her entire argument to a strong critique, mainly on theoretical grounds.
26. Orthmann, *Stamm und Macht: Die arabischen Stämme im 2. und 3. Jahrhundert der Higra*, pp. 344–413.
27. Eva Orthmann, *Stamm und Macht*, esp. pp. 79–136, 344–7. Despite its title, there is very little of the third century in it. Of the thirty-four cases of tribal conflict listed at the end, thirty-one are in the second century, probably an indicator that tribes became less significant after the introduction of Turkish soldiery.
28. M. J. Kister, 'Tamim in the Period of the Jahiliyya: A Study in Tribal Traditions'.
29. Michael Lecker, *The Banu Sulaym: A Contribution to the Study of Early Islam* (Jerusalem: Hebrew University of Jerusalem, 1989), p. IX.
30. Ella Landau-Tasseron, 'Asad from Jahiliyya to Islam', p. 5.
31. Fred McGraw Donner, 'The Bakr b. Wa'il tribes and politics in northeastern Arabia on the eve of Islam', p. 37.
32. Abd Allah Ibrahim al-ᶜAskar, 'Migrations of the Banu Hanifa to Other Islamic Regions During the Umayyad Period', pp. 1–40; Mohammad Rihan, *The Politics and Culture of an Umayyad Tribe: Conflict and Factionalism in the Early Islamic Period.*
33. Rasheed Hosein, 'Tribal Alliance Formations and Power Structures in the Jahiliyah and Early Islamic Periods: Quraysh and Thaqif (530–750 CE)'.
34. Georg Leube, *Kinda in der frühislamischen Geschichte: Eine prosopographische Studie auf Basis der frühen und klassischen arabisch-islamischen Geschichtsschreibung*. I regret that this book was published too late to have much influence on the present work.
35. Thomas Barfield, 'Tribe and State Relations: The Inner Asian Perspective', pp. 160–70; Kurt Franz, 'Resources and Organizational Power: Some Thoughts on Nomadism in History', pp. 62–7; Stefan Leder, 'Nomadic

and Sedentary Peoples – A Misleading Dichotomy? The Bedouin and Bedouinism in the Arab Past', pp. 401–16; Crone, *Slaves*, pp. 18–19.

36. Ibn Hazm, *Jamhara Ansab al-ᶜArab*.
37. J. C. Wilkinson, *The Imamate Tradition of Oman*, p. 75; Webb, *Imagining the Arabs*, pp. 194–7.
38. Webb, *Imagining the Arabs*, pp. 205–22.
39. Ibn Hisham, *Kitab al-Tijan fi Muluk Himyar*, p. 289.
40. William Lancaster and Fidelity Lancaster, 'Tribal formations in the Arabian Peninsula', p. 146.
41. Lancaster and Lancaster, 'Tribal formations', pp. 155–6; William Lancaster, *The Rwala Bedouin Today*, pp. 76–7.
42. Lancaster, *Rwala*, passim.
43. Michael Meeker, 'Meaning and Society in the Near East: Examples from the Black Sea Turks and the Levantine Arabs (I)', pp. 246–54.
44. Andrew Shryock, *Nationalism and the Genealogical Imagination: Oral History and Textual Authority in Tribal Jordan*, p. 14.
45. David Sneath, *The Headless State: Aristocratic Orders, Kinship Society and Misrepresentations of Nomadic Inner Asia*, p. 203.
46. Peter B. Golden, review of *The Headless State: Aristocratic Orders, Kinship Society and Misrepresentations of Nomadic Inner Asia*; İsenbike Togan, 'The Use of Sociopolitical Terminology for Nomads: An Excursion into the Term *Buluo* in Tang China'.
47. Sneath, *Headless*, pp. 133–4 is the only place where Arabs are mentioned. Ibn Manzur, *Lisan*, V, p. 575.
48. Christian Julien Robin, 'Matériaux pour une prosographie de l'Arabie antique: les noblesses sabéenne et ḥimyarite avant et aprés l'Islam', pp. 133–4.
49. Wilkinson, *Imamate Tradition*, p. 108.
50. As al-Azmeh highlights, Ibn Khaldun had a premodern view of history that focused on the ruling powers of settled domains as emblematic of entire peoples, and the social organisation of nomadic peoples mattered only insofar as its role in the production of states. For Ibn Khaldun, history was an unending struggle for power in which groups dominated each other and only a small number of individuals and families gradually accrued power and influence based on their roles as group leaders, ultimately becoming kings whose descendants were nonetheless destined to fall to a new rising power. The key to gaining dominance was *ᶜasabiya*, or group solidarity. Individuals in cities were restrained by laws, and as such people grew into adults they became used to bowing before others. Nomads were restrained by respect for their leaders, who gained stature because the strength of their small units' *ᶜaṣabiya* allowed them to rise to prominence over other, similar units in the broader tribe. Nomads' way of life meant they also had superior military attributes, and their living in descent groups means they had greater *ᶜasabiya* than do those in cities. This was true even though the kinship of

desert tribes is often imagined rather than real. See Aziz al-Azmeh, *Ibn Khaldun: An Essay in Reinterpretation*, pp. 12–14, 27–33; Ibn Khaldun, *The Muqaddimah: An Introduction to History*, I, pp. 247–310.

51. Aziz al-Azmeh, *The Emergence of Islam in Late Antiquity: Allah and His People*, p. 126.
52. Lancaster, *Rwala*, pp. 80–9.
53. Al-Azmeh, *Emergence*, p. 128.
54. Exceptions are Eric Cline and Mark Graham, *Ancient Empires: From Mesopotamia to the Rise of Islam*, pp. 319–40; Chris Wickham, 'Tributary Empires: Late Rome and the Arab Caliphate', pp. 205–13; S. E. Finer, *The History of Government from the Earliest Times*, pp. 665–727; Timothy Parsons, *The Rule of Empires: Those Who Built Them, Those Who Endured Them, and Why They Always Fall*, pp. 65–110; Jane Burbank and Frederick Cooper, *Empires in World History: Power and the Politics of Difference*, pp. 78–80; Garth Fowden, *Empire to Commonwealth: Consequences of Monotheism in Late Antiquity*, pp. 138–68.
55. Finer, *History*, pp. 8–9.
56. Finer, *History*, pp. 682–4.
57. For the uses of writing to transmit historical and other information up through the early Abbasid period, see Gregor Schoeler, *The Oral and the Written in Early Islam*. On 'sourcebooks', see Sarah Bowen Savant, 'Genealogy and Ethnogenesis in al-Mas^cudi's *Muruj al-dhahab*', pp. 123–5.
58. Fred Donner, *Narratives of Islamic Origins: The Beginnings of Islamic Historical Writing*, pp. 13–19.
59. James Fentress and Chris Wickham, *Social Memory*, p. 25.
60. Fentress and Wickham, *Social*, p. 26.
61. Fentress and Wickham, *Social*, pp. 47–8.
62. Albrecht Noth, *The Early Arabic Historical Tradition: A Source-Critical Study*. 2nd ed. in collaboration with Lawrence I. Conrad.
63. Majied Robinson, 'Prosopographical Approaches to the Nasab Tradition: A Study of Marriage and Concubinage in the Tribe of Muhammad (500–750 CE)', pp. 77–9; Sarah Bowen Savant, 'Naming Shu^{c}ubis'. Tarif Khalidi notes that the period when the old tribal elite was losing its social and political position was also when Arab genealogy reached its fullest development. Khalidi, *Arabic Historical Thought in the Classical Period*, p. 50.
64. Ḥassan al-Naboodah, 'Kitab "al-Ansab" li-l-^{c}Awtabi: Ishkalat fi al-Nisba wa-al-ta$^{\circ}$lif', *Majalla Dirasat al-Khalij wa-al-Jazira al-^{c}Arabiyya* 32 (2006), pp. 139–72.
65. Martin Hinds, *An Early Islamic Family from Oman: al-^{c}Awtabi's Account of the Muhallabids*, p. 9.
66. Goldziher, for example, believed pre-Islamic Arabs were 'concerned with genealogical questions' but 'had no science of genealogy'. By this he

means that they had ideas of relationship to past heroes and glories, but did not keep extensive genealogical trees such as we find in the works written under the caliphate. He describes them instead as 'loose and fragmentary traditions'. Goldziher, *Muslim Studies*, I, pp. 164–5. Webb's view seems similar to this in *Imagining the Arabs*, pp. 194, 229 n. 76. For Kister and Plessner, on the other hand, Arab genealogical lore was a topic of 'uninterrupted transmission' from before Islam through the Umayyad period and even into Abbasid times. M. J. Kister and M. Plessner, 'Notes on Caskel's Ǧamharat an-Nasab', pp. 30–1.

67. Zoltan Szombathy, *The Roots of Arabic Genealogy: A Study in Historical Anthropology*, pp. 26–8.
68. Szombathy, *Arabic Genealogy*, pp. 62–6.
69. Szombathy, *Arabic Genealogy*, pp. 67–71.
70. Szombathy, *Arabic Genealogy*, pp. 74–5.
71. Szombathy, *Arabic Genealogy*, pp. 83–8.
72. Robertson Smith, *Kinship*, p. 20.
73. Asad Ahmed, *The Religious Elite of the Early Islamic Hijaz: Five Prosopographical Case Studies*, pp. 135–6; Webb, *Imagining the Arabs*, pp. 197–205.
74. Szombathy, *Arabic Genealogy*, pp. 139–42.
75. Szombathy, *Arabic Genealogy*, pp. 36–9.
76. Szombathy, *Arabic Genealogy*, pp. 105–25. For an examination of how such material was collected, see Zoltan Szombathy, 'Fieldwork and Preconceptions: The Role of the Bedouin as Informants in Medieaval Muslim Scholarly Culture (Second–Third/Eighth–Ninth Centuries)'.
77. Aziz al-Azmeh, *Emergence*, p. 125. Fisher has also advocated a concept of Arab identity supported by court patronage of poetry and the use of Arabic in monumental inscriptions. Greg Fisher, *Between Empires: Arabs, Romans, and Sasanians in Late Antiquity*, pp. 128–72.
78. Philip Wood, 'Al-Ḥira and Its Histories', pp. 785–99.
79. Aziz al-Azmeh, *The Arabs and Islam in Late Antiquity: A Critique of Approaches to Arabic Sources*, pp. 101–11.
80. Munt et al., 'Arabic and Persian Sources for Pre-Islamic Arabia', p. 480; Strenziok, EI2, I, p. 812.
81. Webb, *Imagining the Arabs*, p. 337
82. Francesco Gabrieli, art. 'Adab,' in *EI2*, 1:175–6
83. Lawrence Stone, 'Prosopography', *Historical Studies Today*, ed. Felix Gilbert and Stephen R. Graubard (New York: W. W. Norton & Company, 1972), p. 107.
84. Crone, *Slaves*, p. 17.
85. Lecker, *Banu Sulaym*.
86. Scott Savran, *Arabs and Iranians in the Islamic Conquest Narrative: Memory and Identity Construction in Islamic Historiography, 750–1050*, p. 7. See also Fentress and Wickham, *Social*, pp. 49–75.

87. On narrative choices as interpretation and narrative in the general styles of sources relevant to this study, see Hayden White, *The Content of the Form: Narrative Discourse and Historical Representation*, pp. 1–57. See also al-Azmeh, *Arabs and Islam*, pp. 55–86; Robert Hoyland, 'History, Fiction, and Authorship in the First Centuries of Islam', pp. 16–46.
88. Lawrence Conrad, 'Recovering Lost Texts: Some Methodological Issues', pp. 258–60, 262; Ella Landau-Tasseron, 'On the Reconstruction of Lost Sources', pp. 48–57.
89. In different ways, a focus on memory as seen in historical narratives has become an important element of research into early Islamic history. For examples in addition to those already cited, see Julie Scott Meisami, 'The Past in Service of the Present: Two Views of History in Medieval Persia'; Sarah Bowen Savant, *The New Muslims of Post-Conquest Iran: Tradition, Memory, and Conversion*; Jacob Lassner, *The Middle East Remembered: Forged Identities, Competing Narratives, Contested Spaces*; Hugh Kennedy, *The Great Arab Conquests: How the Spread of Islam Change the World We Live In*, pp. 24–7; Antoine Borrut, *Entre mémoire et pouvoir: L'espace syrien sous les derniers Omeyyades et les premiers Abbassides (v. 72–193/692–809)*.
90. Isfahani, *Kitab al-Aghani*, XVI, p. 43; Ibn al-Kalbi, *Ma^c^add wa al-Yaman*, p. 363.
91. Munt et al., 'Sources', p. 487.
92. Ibn Sulayman, *Tafsir*, III, p. 530.
93. Robin, 'Ghassan et Arabie', p. 108.
94. Abu Zakariyya Yazid b. Muhammad al-Azdi, *Ta'rikh al-Mawsil*; Ibn al-Kalbi, *Ma^c^add wa al-Yaman*, pp. 362–533, with Malik b. Fahm on pp. 488–92.
95. Szombathy, *Arabic Genealogy*, p. 152.
96. Caskel and Strenziok, *Gamharat an-Nasab. Das Genealogische Werk des Hišham ibn Muḥammad al-Kalbi*, II, p. 41.
97. Caskel and Strenziok, *Gamharat*, II, p. 43.
98. Caskel and Strenziok, *Gamharat*, II, p. 41.
99. Caskel and Strenziok, *Gamharat*, II, p. 41.
100. Julius Wellhausen, *The Arab Kingdom and Its Fall*, p. 399; Brian Ulrich, 'The Azd Migrations Reconsidered: Narratives of 'Amr Muzayqiya and Malik b. Fahm in Historiographic Context', p. 314.
101. Ibn Khayyat, *Kitab al-Tabaqat*, p. 205.
102. Wilkinson, *Imamate Tradition*, p. 75.
103. Wilkinson, *Ibadism: Origins and Early Development in Oman*, p. 33.
104. Isfahani, *al-Aghani*, XXII, p. 110.
105. ^c^Awtabi, *al-Ansab*, II, p. 662.
106. Bakri, *Mu^c^jam*, I, p. 63; Yaqut, *Mu^c^jam al-Buldan*, I, p. 380.
107. Isfahani, *al-Aghani*, XXI, p. 235.
108. Yaqut, *Buldan*, III, p. 418.

109. Suraqa b. Mirdas al-Bariqi, *Diwan*, p. 61.
110. Tabari, *The History of al-Tabari*, X, p. 161; Tabari, *Ta'rīkh al-Rusul wa al-Muluk*, I, p. 1985. Both this and the 'Shan[c]' below might be the same as the Jabal Shann mentioned by al-Hamdani as near Jabal Bariq, *Sifa Jazira al-Arab*, pp. 125, 173.
111. Muhammad b. [c]Ali b. Husayn al-Hariri, *Qabila al-Azd min Fajr al-Islam ila Qiyam al-Dawla al-Sa[c]udiya al-Awla*, p. 11.
112. Ibn Hisham, *Kitab al-Tijan*, pp. 288–9.
113. Sam[c]ani does assert that Shanu'a was a name for an [c]Abd Allah b. Ka[c]b b. [c]Abd Allah b. b. Ka[c]b b. Malik b. Malik b. Naṣr b. al-Azd. However, his genealogies are usually idiosyncratic, unsourced, and late enough that they are mostly dismissed in this study. He does, however, include western Arabians under the label. Sam[c]ani, *al-Ansab*, III, pp. 477, 479.
114. Caskel and Strenziok, *Gamharat*, II, p. 41.
115. Caskel and Strenziok, *Gamharat*, II, pp. 492, 535.
116. Caskel and Strenziok, *Gamharat*, II, p. 43.
117. Al-Hamdani, *Sifa*, p. 70.

1

The Azd in Pre- and Early Islamic Arabia

Most of the Arab population of the early Islamic empire claimed roots in the Arabian Peninsula. That Arabian past, however, became an important site of heritage construction for the Arab elite. As Donner describes, already during the first Islamic century, accounts of pre-Islamic Arabia were in circulation, which he attributes to a competition for status and leadership based on tribes' pre-Islamic heritage.[1] During the Abbasid period, such accounts, especially as associated with Bedouin or Bedouinising poetry, became an important touchstone in Arab ethnic identity.[2] Webb has written of the 'Bedouinisation of memory' of pre-Islamic Arabia, and Peter Heath and Isabel Toral-Niehoff have looked at how narratives of pre-Islamic battles were passed down over the centuries.[3] The development of Arab identity also involved an implicit belief among Arabic traditionists in a unified Bedouin Arab culture which scholars could construct in text on the basis of accounts from Bedouin sources of their own time, as well as accounts passed down from the past. Significantly, however, they also saw each tribe as the best source of information on its own past.[4]

Because of these circumstances surrounding the production of our extant Arabic source material, reconstruction of pre-Islamic Arabian history is challenging, and conclusions are inevitably tentative. Nonetheless, the material on al-Azd is sufficient to explore multiple issues in the early development of an al-Azd identity and the situation of many al-Azd groups on the eve of Islam. This chapter will first examine the most solid evidence of al-Azd origins: early South Arabian inscriptions mentioning kings of al-Azd which one can relate to archaeological evidence of major settlements and ancient traditions found in the genealogical works. Then it will take on the early Islamic literary account of the 'Scattering of al-Azd', deconstructing the story so as to provide insight into the formation of the early Islamic al-Azd genealogy and posit certain elements as reflective of late pre-Islamic Arabia. Finally, it shall provide an overview of information on groups in both eastern and western Arabia which either were al-Azd at the time or became so during or soon after the conquests, with an understanding that such distinctions are difficult to make given the source material. This creates at least a partial portrait of the tribal organisation in each region in the early seventh century and the ways in which that organisation was influenced by the rise of the Islamic polity. This material will also allow us to see what sorts of identity material were carried from Arabia during the seventh century to become part of the al-Azd heritage as it would develop in later periods.

Al-Azd in Pre-Islamic Inscriptions

Several ESA (Epigraphic South Arabian) inscriptions contain references to a group called ᵓsd, sometimes with the definite article and sometimes without. Scholars have argued extensively over the referents of these inscriptions and their relationship with Arab tribal groups known especially from sources describing the sixth and seventh centuries. They also mention individuals by the root '*mlk*', which originally denoted the leader of a particular tribe.[5] The argument here is that these inscriptions refer to an al-Azd tribal 'kingdom' in the Wadi Bisha and the highlands to the west during the third and fourth centuries, as recently identified by Jérémie Schiettecatte and Mounir Arbach, and that the Azd of the Islamic period exist in a continuity of historical memory with that kingdom.[6] One vague historical memory of this is found in Ibn Hisham's *Kitab al-Tijan*, according to which al-Azd from the Sarat Mountains were led by a woman from Ad through a rocky area called Tarb and a place called Karaᵓ to the Wadi Bisha, where they made their dwellings.[7] In addition, memories of the Wadi Bisha kingdom are found in the genealogies of the Nasr b. al-Azd, who inhabited those lands in later centuries. However, this al-Azd identity played no demonstrable role in tribal alliances as reflected in the Arabic historical tradition.

The root ᵓsd, by assimilation, gives rise to 'Azd'. Walter Müller credits one of his students with the observation that in Arabic, 'al-Azd' always carries the definite article but 'Asad' never does.[8] As Jan Retsö has pointed out, however, this observation is incorrect, and might not hold true for Sabaic if it were.[9] There are also cases when a *sīn* is used in place of a *zayn* with the definite article for the group which is the subject of this monograph.[10] The strong tendency to use the article in 'al-Azd' but not 'Asad' could easily have emerged through the Abbasid-era genealogists' desire for etymological distinctions. Furthermore, some of the purported 'Asad' references show a degree of involvement in the affairs of South Arabian kingdoms that is difficult to credit across the length of the peninsula. A more probable reading of 'ᵓsd' without the article would be its meaning of men who can fight, what A. F. L. Beeston translated as 'soldiers' in military contexts, but simply the opposite of 'women' in non-military ones.[11] The presence of the root 'mlk', however, renders this unlikely.

The inscription Ja 635, from the reign of Shaᶜr ᵓAwtar in the early third century, records a battle against rebels 'at the border of the territory of ᵓl-ᵓsd, at the crossing-place of the two wells of Dhu Thumal'.[12] Hermann Von Wissmann has suggested that this referred to the oasis of Thumal in the Wadi Bisha, and that al-Azd was a large Bedouin confederation west of the territory of the Kinda, who were based in Qaryat al-Faw.[13] M. D. Bukharin believes the inscription refers to a battle pitting Sabaᵓ against an alliance of the Romans under Emperor Macrinus and the Kinda, presumed to be controlling Thumal during a movement from the Red Sea coast toward Hadramawt.[14] Muhammad ᶜAbd al-Qadir Bafaqih identifies Thumal as a form of the name for the al-Azd clan Thumala, and took Ja 635 as a whole as confirmation that al-Azd were present not only in the southern Sarat Mountains, but also the fertile plain to the east.[15] Ps.-al-ᶜAwtabi, in his 'Scatting of al-Azd' tradition (see below), locates the B. Thumala between Najd and al-Taᵓif.[16] This could refer to the Wadi Thumala, another possible referent for the inscription.[17]

Inscription Ja 2110 (Aden Museum 848) references an al-Harith b. Kaᶜb, *Malik* of Asd, who along with Malik b. Badd, *Malik* of Kinda, Madhhij and the Arabs was involved with King ᵓIlsharah Yahdub of Sabaᵓ (c. 235–55). Although Doe and Jamme translate the inscription as indicating a military campaign by Sabaᵓ's ruler against the named leaders, Müller believes it refers to a diplomatic mission northward.[18] It is presumably the same al-Harith b. Kaᶜb who appears in the inscription Ja 660, where he and Sud (or Saᶜd) b. ᶜAmr are rebels captured in the late third century by Sabaᵓ's Himyarite conqueror Shammar Yuhariᶜsh. The two rebels are here identified as 'ᵓsdn', which in this grammatical context certainly means soldiers.[19] In their initial publication of Ja 2110, Doe and Jamme identified 'ᵓAsd' as 'Asad', who lived in the city of al-Tanhab, though they also identified their king with B. al-Harith b. Kaᶜb in the city of Huban.[20] Retsö has here pointed out that, in addition to the uncertainty in the linguistic argument that 'Azd' can never take the definite article, the accounts of the tribe of al-Harith b. Kaᶜb, which at some point in history identified with al-Azd before re-identifying themselves as Madhhij, represent a positive argument on historical grounds to accept that 'ᵓsd' here is al-Azd.[21]

Another inscription (Sharafaddin 44) from the reign of Shammar Yuhariᶜsh in the early fourth century describes a diplomatic mission to Malik b. Kaᶜb, *Malik* of al-Azd, and then onward to the Sasanian royal cities of Seleucia and Ctesiphon, as well as the land of Tanukh, which was almost certainly southwest of the Euphrates. Although here the inscription has a definite article, Malik b. Kaᶜb and the earlier al-Harith b. Kaᶜb were probably both rulers of the same group. Müller believes that al-Azd here refers to the Azd ᶜUman, and that the mission proceeded from Najran to al-Yamama and then took a Gulf route between Oman and Mesopotamia.[22] Retsö, however, argues that it is more likely this inscription refers to the same place as Ja 635, the Wadi Bisha. He also made a connection to the Nasr b. al-Azd of the Islamic genealogies and the Namara inscription.[23] We can draw the genealogical connection in more detail. Nasr b. al-Azd, who again is the progenitor of most al-Azd in the area later, had one son named Malik, described as being among the most generous kings of the pre-Islamic Arabs, known for provisioning rest stops for travellers.[24] This purported king had a great-grandson named al-Harith b. Kaᶜb, and al-Harith b. Kaᶜb in turn had a grandson named Malik b. Kaᶜb.[25] The names are common, but the pattern high up on the genealogical tree is striking, and it is possible that the genealogies were constructed from locally preserved memories of the kings from the ESA inscriptions.

This possibility that the men named in the inscriptions could correlate with the early figures of the Nasr b. al-Azd should be set beside the possibility that the ancient al-Harith b. Kaᶜb was the eponym of the tribe of that name. Often known simply as Balharith, the al-Harith b. Kaᶜb were the dominant tribe of Najran, and although considered part of Madhhij, several authorities said it had originally been part of al-Azd.[26] One source, for example, explains Madhhij as a height in Yemen where groups would gather and eventually be called after it, and implies this happened with the al-Harith b. Kaᶜb.[27] As another alternative, Christian Robin suggests that the tribal name B. al-Harith b. Kaᶜb was actually applied to groups under the authority of descendants of the al-Harith b. Kaᶜb who was martyred by the Himyarites in 523.[28] It is of course often impossible to know what stories or genealogical machinations are represented in our extant Arabic sources, and another possibility is that al-Harith b. Kaᶜb was effectively double-purposed, with a group claiming descent from him becoming part of Madhhij, but a recollection of an al-Azd *malik* by that name leading to his appearance under Nasr b. al-Azd.

The term ᵓsd also occurs in three inscriptions found at al-ᶜUqla, where the kings of Hadramawt were crowned during the third century. Jamme dated these texts to the late third century, though they are now seen as roughly contemporary with Ja 2110.[29] The most important, Ja 957, mentions an ᶜAmr b. ᶜAwf of *ᵓsd* who was a father-in-law of Yadaᶜᵓil Bayyin (c. 225–55) and in charge of provisioning the important ceremonial centre of ᵓAnwadum. Jamme, who interpted *ᵓsd* as the tribe Asad, saw two other named figures, Dadad from Ja 939 and ᶜAwd b. Bakr from Ja 962, as associates of this ᶜAmr b. ᶜAwf.[30] As ᶜAmr b. ᶜAwf was a contemporary of al-Harith b. Kaᶜb, I conclude that this was potentially a separate, perhaps ancestrally related al-Azd polity, and that together it and the one centred in the Wadi Bisha were the two mentioned in the Namara inscription.[31] The latest relevant inscription, from about the year 360, was found at ᶜAbadan, between Hadramawt and Dathina. It refers to the land of al-Azd, where the king Thaᵓran Yunᶜim fought Rasan and Suday, which Robin identifies as al-Azd subgroups.[32] This was about the time of the first breaking of the Maᵓrib dam found in inscriptions.[33]

Arabian political history before the twentieth century is mostly the story of leaders in fertile settlement areas along trade routes developing force projection capacity and using it to extract tribute from nomads and nearby areas of strategic interest.[34] The Epigraphic South Arabian inscriptions provide evidence that a group called al-Azd exercised power from settlements in the Wadi Bisha. One city that may have served as an al-Azd capital is Jurash, where excavations have shown signs of commercial activity similar to that at the Kinda capital of Qaryat al-Faw.[35] Although Arabs of later centuries had no concrete knowledge of this hegemony, knowledge of its existence persisted in southern Arabian sources such as ps.-al-ᶜAwtabi and Ibn Hisham as a genealogical 'patch' and remembered glory, and connection with it formed the basis of the al-Azd tribal identity in the centuries after its decline.

The Scattering of al-Azd

The 'Scattering of al-Azd' is the literary account of al-Azd origins found in somewhat different versions in multiple sources from the early Islamic period and forming part of the broader complex of stories offering explanations for the dispersion of tribes across Arabia.[36] These al-Azd migration accounts can be neatly separated into two parts, one concerning the flight of ᶜAmr Muzayqiyaᵓ from the great flood which followed the bursting of the Maᵓrib dam, which led to the 'Scattering', and the other involving Malik b. Fahm's migration from south-western Arabia to become Oman's first Arab settler. Ps.-al-ᶜAwtabi, for example, ties a long account of Malik b. Fahm's migration with an earlier account of the flight from Maᵓrib led by ᶜAmr Muzayqiyaᵓ by means of a brief tradition from other sources which tells of Malik's decision to leave the Sarat Mountains when descendants of his brother ᶜAmr killed the dog of a man under his protection. This tradition briefly mentions the scattering of the Azd and the flood as events prior to Malik's residence in the Sarat.[37] In the *Ta'rikh al-Mawsil*, Abu Zakariyya al-Azdi has a very similar story recounted through a different chain of authorities, these seemingly local to al-Jazira, which omits Ma'rib altogether; al-Azdi himself mentions it fleetingly in his introduction to the report.[38] Meanwhile, of the ᶜAmr Muzayqiya' traditions, those in the *Futuh al-Buldan* of Ahmad b. Yahya al-Baladhuri (d. 892) and al-Hamdani's *al-Iklil* make no mention of Malik b. Fahm, while ps.-al-ᶜAwtabi mentions only his name alongside that of ᶜAmr Muzayqiya' as leading the Azd from Ma'rib and again as the leader of the Azd ᶜUman in a stylised list of all al-Azd groups.[39]

This split is also seen in the classical genealogical scheme largely associated with Ibn al-Kalbi. The eponym al-Azd had several sons, but the two most important were Mazin and Nasr. Mazin, sometimes called Ghassan, was the ancestor of ᶜAmr Muzayqiya', who links together a number of prominent groups such as the Jafnids and Ansar. What is striking is that, of these groups, only the Bariq and the Muhallabids and their relatives among the B. ᶜImran seem recognisably al-Azd during the Umayyad period. The other significant al-Azd groups, the Azd ᶜUman, Azd Sarat and Azd Shanu'a, are descendants of Nasr.[40] The traditions surrounding ᶜAmr Muzayqiya' as we have them clearly belong to the Islamic period, and were probably deployed to promote the Ansar by linking them with pre-Islamic Arabian kings.[41] Other sources also emphasise the Ansar's connections to southern Arabia through the ᶜAmr Muzayqiya' tradition. In *Futuh al-Buldan*, for example, al-Baladhuri incorporates it into his account of the history of Medina, concluding that the Ansar became great during the Jahiliyya so that they could later support Muhammad.[42]

In his *al-Ishtiqaq*, a work dedicated to explaining the origin of Arabic names, Ibn Durayd (d. 933) largely follows Ibn al-Kalbi in using ᶜAmr Muzayqiya' to link together diverse groups. According to Ibn Durayd, ᶜAmr Muzayqiya' got his byname because he tore up his clothes every day so that no one could wear them after him. Among his sons, Jafna was the ancestor of the Ghassanids, and his name came perhaps from a vine, perhaps a sword, or perhaps a famous person. Ibn Durayd agrees with other sources, however, in claiming that the name Ghassan derives from a watering hole. Al-Harith was called 'Muharriq' because he was the first to torment people with fire. Thaᶜlaba, ancestor of the Ansar, was called al-ᶜAnqa' because of his long neck. Dhuhl was the ancestor of the bishops of Najran who sent a delegation to Muhammad. A final son, Kaᶜb, was the ancestor of Samawᶜal b. Hayya, a Jew who ruled Tayma and became arabicised. Al-Harith's descendants included another Jew, al-Fityawn,

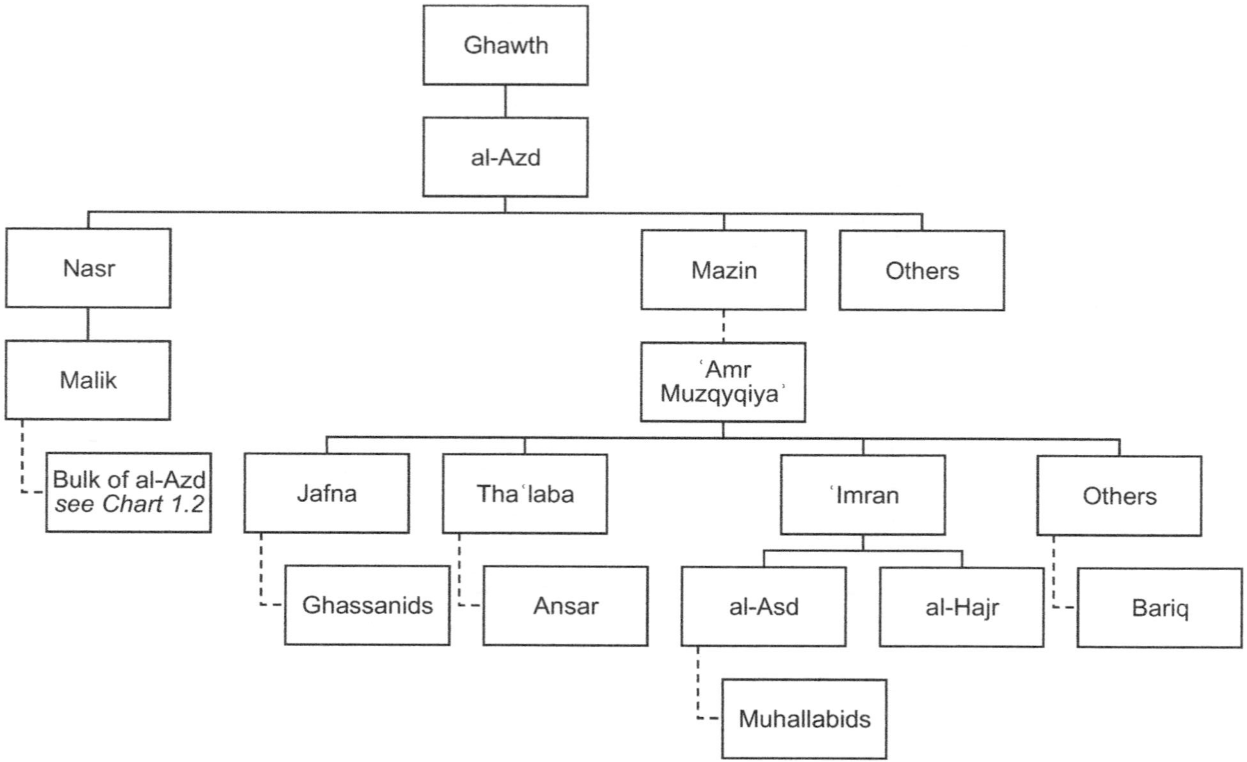

Chart 1.1 Simplified al-Azd genealogical chart showing the difference between descendants of Nasr and Mazin. Dashes indicate omitted generations and/or transition into groups.

who was King of Yathrib before being killed by the Ansar; some of his descendants fought at Badr.[43]

One important extant version of the ᶜAmr Muzayqiyaᵓ traditions is in ps.-al-ᶜAwtabi. This account is sourced to an Abu ᶜAbd Allah al-Mawsili, coming via Ibn Ishaq (d. 760s), Wahb b. Munabbih and Ibn al-Kalbi, a clearly scrambled sequence with Wahb, who died in the 720s or 30s and was known for his accounts of Jewish and Yemeni history, as the actual oldest source.[44] Parts of this text are identical to the parallel account in al-Masᶜudi (d. 956).[45] It begins with Sabaᵓ, his progeny, and the prosperity of Maᵓrib, including a detailed description of the dam. When the people forsook God, they were warned of an impending catastrophe by ᶜImran, ᶜAmr Muzayqiyaᵓ's brother and a soothsayer who foresaw the ruin of the land if the people did not return to a monotheism they had once practised. Before his death, he summoned ᶜAmr and urged him to marry the soothsayer Turayfa, of the people of Radaman from Himyar. One day Turayfa divined the imminent bursting of the dam and warned her husband. ᶜAmr's first instinct was to conceal the fact and sell his property in the region, but he then feared people might think ill of him if he did that. Instead, he invited the people of Maᵓrib to a feast, where by prior arrangement he staged an argument with one of his sons who wound up striking him. This led the shocked people to want to buy his property, in the expectation that he would soon leave because of the insult. His property thus sold, he departed with his sons, accompanied by Malik b. Fahm and the other Azd.[46]

The Azd then travelled north passing through several countries, in each of which they fought against the inhabitants and left behind some of their number. ᶜAmr Muzayqiyaᵓ died early on in the land of the ᶜAkk, and was replaced as king by his son Thaᶜlaba. There is also a brief reference to al-Azd driving the Khathᶜam and Bajila from Tabala and the Wadi Bisha. Finally the Azd reached Mecca, where they drove out the Jurhum before scattering in different directions in search of better lands, leading to the different groups such as the Ghassanids which are linked together as al-Azd in the genealogies. In some ways, this represents a second distinct 'scattering'. Thaᶜlaba's own descendants, Aws and Khazraj, came to occupy Yathrib, where in early Islamic times they became the Ansar.[47]

Another account of ᶜAmr Muzayqiyaᵓ is found in ᶜAbd al-Malik b. Hisham's *Kitab al-Tijan*. Most of this work goes back to Wahb b. Munabbih, but for this material the source is Muhammad b. Abi Bakr b. Muhammad, the son of a hadith compiler important during the reign of ᶜUmar II (717–20). Its description of ᶜImran b. ᶜAmir and his family positions them more overtly as proto-Muslims carrying on the tradition of Sulayman rather than as simply soothsayers. In addition to the bursting of the dam as God's punishment, ᶜImran also predicts the Ethiopian invasion, though he says it will be matched by the coming of the prophet Muhammad al-Tihami. Turayfa's prediction of the flooding is more protracted and dramatic. Beyond such differences, however, it is close to the version in ps.-al-ᶜAwtabi, and so Wahb b. Munabbih may be its ultimate source, as well.[48] In his *al-Iklil*, al-Hamdani has a brief account of ᶜImran which is much as same as Ibn Hisham's.[49]

These accounts display several features that suggest they originated in the early Islamic period. The most obvious is the prominence given to Mecca and Medina, as well as the Ansar. In addition, they are a perfect example of the *iftirāq* theme identified by Caskel as a means by which tribes were linked into a unified people through recourse to a common ancestor, whose descendants were then scattered throughout the peninsula.[50] As part of al-Yaman, the ᶜAmr Muzayqiyaᵓ group was traced back to the ancient South Arabian kingdoms, exemplified in the person of Sabaᵓ, one of the descendants of Qahtan, progenitor for the southern Arabs. One intention of these traditions is to promote the Ansar within Islam. Guillaume calls attention to the massacre of al-Husayn and his followers at Karbalaᵓ and the sack of Medina in which 10,000 Ansar were killed at the start of the Second *Fitna*, and suggests the poetry in Ibn Ishaq's biography connecting them to al-Yaman belongs to a world shaped by those events: 'Its aim is to set forth the claims of the Ansar to prominence in Islam not only as men who supported the prophet when the Quraysh opposed him, but as men descended from kings.'[51]

Shorn of their tenuous links to the migration of ᶜAmr Muzayqiyaᵓ and his descendants, the accounts of Malik b. Fahm include little of what one might expect if they were primarily from the early Islamic period. Al-Azdi's account in *Taᵓrikh al-Mawsil* has received little attention. It features under the year 129 (747) as part of a special history of leading al-Azd clans in the al-Jazira region, almost all of which traced their descent to Malik b. Fahm, and it comes via sources from that area. In this version, the Azd Shanuᵓa lived in the Sarat Mountains and multiplied, after which some of them went to Oman and became the Azd ᶜUman. Malik b. Fahm was the first of these, and the reason for his migration was the disrespect shown to his neighbour by the people of his brother in the matter of that neighbour's dog.[52] The identification of the Azd ᶜUman as stemming from the Azd Shanuᶜa reflects their attachment to the Azd Shanuᶜa tribe of Daws in Ibn al-Kalbi's macro-genealogy. This version is also similar to what was very briefly summarised by al-Yaᶜqubi (d. 897) in his *Ta'rikh*, including the identification of the Azd ᶜUman as originally Azd Shanu'a.[53]

In *Ta'rikh al-Mawsil*, Malik b. Fahm had fourteen sons, of whom Jadhima was the eldest and the one who gave Malik his *kunya*. One important aspect in this work is that eight of the sons are grouped according to three mothers, from Tayyi', ᶜAbd al-Qays and Kinda.[54] There are accounts that parts of those three tribes moved to Mosul under the caliph ᶜUthman, and the city had tribal quarters named for the Tayyi' and Kinda.[55] It is difficult, however, to find ᶜAbd al-Qays in the region, nor do the Azd present at that early stage seem to have been Malik b. Fahm. Those three tribes were, however, all prominent in Oman, raising the possibility that existing Omani ties either impacted the settlement of Mosul or, more likely, the historical memories thereof.[56] One further note is that 'Fakhidh al-Kalba', an Arabian toponym ostensibly explained by the dog story, seems unlikely to be an Iraqi development.

Ps.-al-ᶜAwtabi's version comes from Ibn al-Kalbi and is primarily focused not on the migration to Oman, but rather on the Battle of Salut against the Persians. Following the dog quarrel, Malik b. Fahm passed to Oman by way of Hadramawt. His followers included not only al-Azd, but also Qudaᶜa, with Malik and ᶜAmr b. Fahm b. Taymallah listed as among their leaders. Malik b. Fahm sought land from Oman's ruler, a *marzubān* under the Persian ruler Dara b. Dara b. Bahman, and wound up having to win two major battles against the Persians — one against the *marzubān*, and the other against an invasion force sent by Dara. Malik reigned as king for seventy years. This narrative, found in an Oman-centred text, served to legitimise elements of the Omani social order on the eve of Islam and the power of certain clans claiming descent from Malik b. Fahm.[57]

Jan Assmann observes a tendency of the past in cultural memory to 'be condensed into symbolic figures', with 'figure' here meaning themes such as the Hebrew Exodus or stories of patriarchs. The result, in other words, is myth, which is 'foundational history that is narrated in order to illuminate the present from the standpoint of its origins'.[58] This clearly applies to the 'Scattering of al-Azd' accounts, which seek to explain tribal relationships of a community imagined sometimes as simply tribal Arabian, but also tied into ancient Yemen and at times even monotheistic and tied to the prophetic history of the Qur'an. The tradition of ᶜAmr Muzayqiya' helped construct a foundation myth for a core portion of al-Yaman in early Islam. For versions featuring a proto-Muslim ancient Arabia, they fit well with Webb's view of the role of monotheism in constructing the Arab heritage during the Abbasid period if not earlier, with Sulayman playing the legitimising role for southerners which Ibrahim did for northerners.[59]

The Malik b. Fahm accounts serve instead as the origin story for tribal populations in Oman which later spread elsewhere in the eastern caliphate. In its eventual insertion into the larger ᶜAmr Muzayqiyaᵓ framework, we see an example in narrative of one of Szombathy's patches being combined with others to construct broader groupings and ultimately a united Arab people. Both the accounts and the idea of Malik b. Fahm were cast differently for different audiences and deployed to different ends. Thus, Ibn al-Kalbi used him to involve the Qudaᶜa and Tanukh in the broader al-Yaman grouping, and ultimately the history of the Lakhmids through Jadhima b. Malik b. Fahm.[60] In Chapter 3, we will explore further some of the circumstances under which both the ᶜAmr Muzayqiyaᵓ and Malik b. Fahm accounts could have been developed or elaborated upon.

Al-Azd in Western Arabia

For the sixth and seventh centuries, we have the most voluminous information for the Azd of western Arabia, whether Azd Sarat or Azd Shanuᵓa. In the genealogical system, these are mostly descendants of Nasr b. al-Azd, and especially al-Harith b. Kaᶜb. The sources, however, present a picture of frequent rivalry among groups regardless of where they place in classical genealogies, as well as a fluidity of identification even with major groupings. For this reason, what follows is reconstructed primarily from narrative accounts or prosopographical sources which can highlight which groups served as identities meaningful for individual designation, activity and memory. Al-Hamdani's account of the Arabian Peninsula is also useful, with the caution that much may have changed between the period under discussion here and when he wrote during the early tenth century. Dictionaries of Companions of the Prophet are also used cautiously. Many of the figures therein are ephemeral, and significantly the numbers increase dramatically over the centuries.[61] Because of this, only the works of Ibn Saᶜd (d. 845) and Ibn ᶜAbd al-Barr (d. 1071) are used below.

Strenziok's previous account of the Azd of western Arabia appeared in the second edition of the *Encyclopedia of Islam*. This account, however, needs modification in several ways. First is the reliance on later geographies, not only al-Hamdani, but also Yaqut, with an assumption of stability through the centuries which we can problematise with sources not available when he was writing. Second, Strenziok does not distinguish between the Azd Sarat and Azd Shanuᵓa. For him, the latter was simply an obscure genealogical term. Finally, he asserts that the Azd were predominantly weavers. In late pre-Islamic western Arabia, however, the work of weaving involved a significant amount of slave labour, and thus to assert

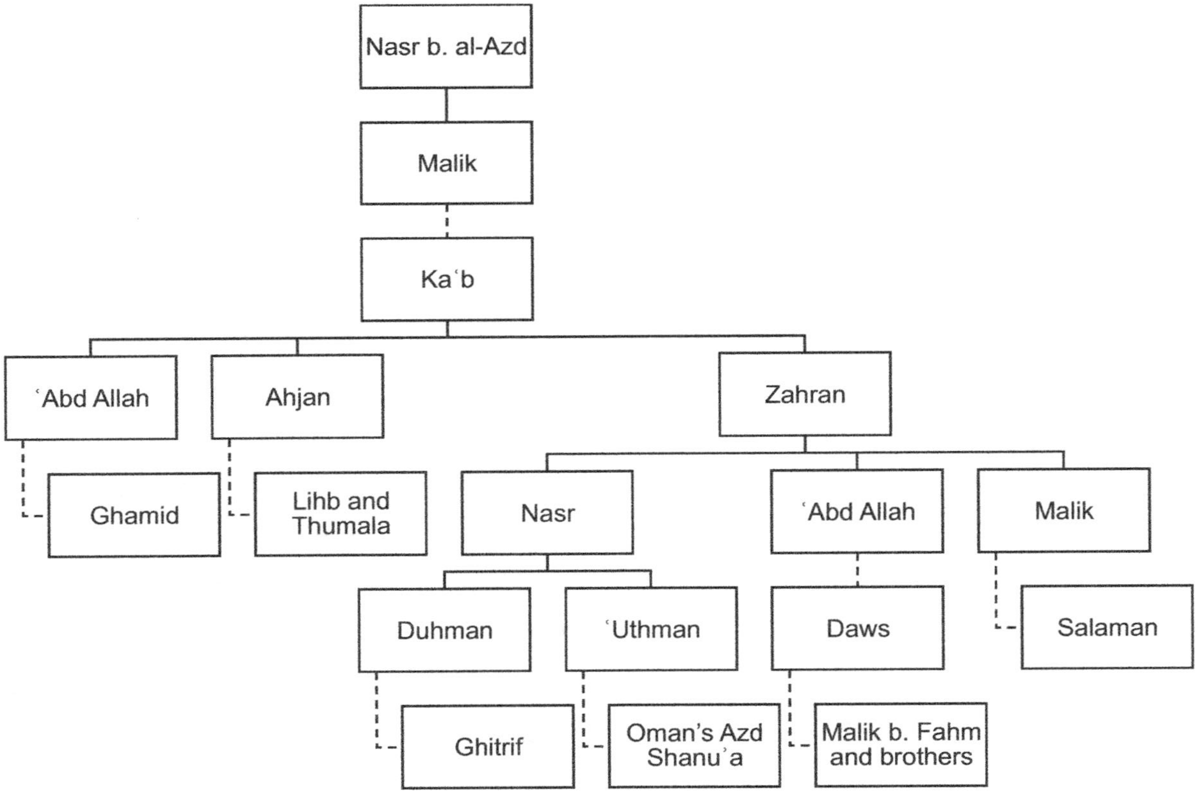

Chart 1.2 Simplified genealogical chart showing key descendants of Nasr b. al-Azd.

that a tribe was in the weaving business was an insult made by enemies, and so should not be taken at face value.[62]

In what follows, al-Azd tribal subgroups are covered in a rough procession from south to north with an inventory of information on each. The intent is to establish a picture which does not rely exclusively on genealogical works and suppositions, and which in fact can serve to illuminate the origins of groups and their alliances. Scholars under the caliphate assumed that almost all tribal names derived from eponymous ancestors, so in what follows we will regard alternative accounts as most likely older, though certainly not necessarily accurate. This material also illustrates the impact of the rise of the Islamic state both within and among the groups discussed. It is also hoped that the assembly of information will be of use to those interested in the traditions associated with a particular group or place, such as to provide context for archaeological exploration.

There is evidence in this region for a significant role of tribal leaders associated with mediation, military skill and religious rituals. Joy McCorriston has described the way pilgrimage practices in ancient southern Arabia served as a means for constituting the tribal groups participating. Rural sanctuaries held stone houses of gods where tribal leaders performed sacrifices and distributed the meat as a feast.[63] Communal sacrifice and feasting at tombs may have helped groups continue after the death of key figures.[64] Although from an earlier period, such a view of leadership and tribal identity has some similarities with the sources on the pre-Islamic Azd, suggesting that the Sarat Mountains and nearby coastal plains and wadis more closely resembled Yemen than they did the central deserts on which our understanding of pre-Islamic Arabian society is often based. In the late pre-Islamic Hijaz, an attempt to mark a sacred precinct was a sign of status and a claim to power and influence in a given region.[65]

Unfortunately, in lieu of archaeological evidence, most of our specific knowledge of the religion of western Arabia in the sixth and seventh century depends on material found in the *Kitab al-Asnam* attributed to Ibn al-Kalbi and the *Kitab al-Muhabbar* of his student Ibn Habib (d. 859).[66] Hawting has clearly demonstrated that this material, in its extant form, reflects the concerns of Islamic society, and has important parallels with other monotheistic critiques and portrayals of polytheistic societies.[67] However, Hawting also argues that many of the divine names found in the Arabic sources survived from the pre-Islamic period which were simply re-purposed for the agendas of our extant sources.[68] He also notes that information about who worshipped which gods where is often contradictory.[69] Because of this, we should not simply take at face value many of the isolated snippets we find: a group called the B. ᶜAjlan b. Thaᶜlib b.

Wabara were keepers of al-Saʿida, a deity worshipped among al-Azd and found at a place called Bahud; the Azd Sarat worshipped a deity named ʿAʾim; the Azd had a deity named Bajar who was also worshipepd by their neighbours from Tayyiʾ and Qudaʿa.[70]

We start with the Bariq, which was the main group furthest south. In the classical genealogical scheme, Bariq was the name given to Saʿd b. ʿUday b. Haritha b. ʿAmr Muzayqiyaʾ. His brother ʿAmr was the progenitor of the al-Hujn, though in practice the tribal name Bariq applied to the descendants of both.[71] Although a folk etymology had the moniker come from lightning which pursued Saʿd's people towards pasture, it was probably the name of the mountain in the Sarat which was their base.[72] Abu al-Mundhar interpreted a poem to mean that Bariq was in the Tihama. Yaqut quotes Ibn ʿAbd al-Barr's *Inbah* as saying it was a watering place in the Sarat Mountains where Saʿd and two of his nephews settled after the bursting of the Maʾrib dam, but in his compilation of Companions' biographies, Ibn ʿAbd al-Barr also calls it a mountain, as does al-Hamdani.[73] Two al-Hujn subgroups, one of whom had the same name as the nephew in Yaqut's Ibn ʿAbd al-Barr tradition, were in al-Sham.[74]

According to al-Bakri's account from Ibn al-Kalbi, this mountain had previously been one of the centres of the Khathʿam; the Azd drove them out following their flight from Sabaʾ.[75] The Bariq were apparently in a late wave of migrants from Yemen, for according to ps.-al-ʿAwtabi the Ghamid, an al-Azd group discussed below prevented them from entering the Sarat Mountains, and the Bariq entered into an alliance with (*ḥulafāʾ*) the B. Numayr (of the B. ʿAmir).[76] This alliance was in effect at the Battle of Shiʿb Jabala, which was fought between 550 and 570, and was a victory for the B. ʿAmir against an alliance led by Tamim and backed by both the Lakhmids and Kinda, who were then based in al-Yamama.[77] The Bariq fought in this battle on the side of the B. ʿAmir and B. ʿAbs, and their poet al-Muʿaqqar al-Bariqi, who later went blind, was widely quoted regarding it.[78]

The Bariq, then, would have taken their namesake height sometime after that battle, or in the second half of the sixth century. The fact it became their name shows the relevance of Yemen as a model through which to understand this region. In the Yemeni highlands, nobles who took over a particular region would take a lineage name based on their conquest, with individuals getting more such names as they acquired territory. Such lineage names would often be preceded by '*dhu*'. In the lowlands, blood relationships mattered more, but lineage names still indicated social roles. During the late pre-Islamic period, some territories started being named for their primary noble lineage, as Robin notes the transition from calling the inhabitants of Najran by that name to identifying them as al-Harith b. Kaᶜb.[79] This clearly did not apply to the Bariq, however.

The Bariq also came to control al-Hubasha, an eight-day market at Qanuna six nights' travel south of Mecca which was the largest along the Tihama. Yaqut, however, had it under the control of the Qaynuqaᶜ.[80] It is probable that the Bariq took it over at some point after Muhammad's defeat of the Qaynuqaᶜ, as it was in the territory of the Bariq during the ninth century, when the market was destroyed.[81] The change to Bariq control could have happened after ᶜUmar b. al-Khattab appointed Humayda b. al-Nuᶜman al-Bariqi as governor of the Sarat district.[82] This Humayda b. al-Nuᶜman al-Bariqi was also, according to Sayf b. ᶜUmar (d. 796), the leader of the ridda movement at Shanuʾa in Yemen.[83] Ibn Habib listed the Bariq among the '*qabāʾīl al-ḥilla min al-ᶜarab*', with *ḥilla* being one of the two cultic associations which made pilgrimage to Mecca, and the one which included most of Tamim and Rabiᶜa, but not Quraysh.[84] There is also a report of a man named Limays b. Saᶜd al-Bariqi who came to Mecca to trade early in Muhammad's adulthood and complained to the Quraysh of unjust treatment.[85] Finally, according to Sayf b. ᶜUmar, the conquest commander ᶜArfaja b. Harthama was from the Bariq, though he lived among the Bajila; Ibn al-Kalbi lists him as al-Hujn.[86]

Somewhat north of the Bariq were the Ghamid, whose territory was in the south central portion of the Sarat Mountains, associated with what is now called ᶜAqiq Ghamid. The term '*ᶜaqīq*' refers to a wide valley created by floodwater, and several places are known by the name.[87] Sabaean inscription Ja 616, from the late first century, mentions a subgroup of the tribe of Daʾa as Gh.m.d., which Bafaqih identifies with this group. He also identifies the other subgroups with different tribes known from the Islamic period, indicating a fragmented tribal system in the mountains.[88] The area stands out for its gold reserves, which were probably worked during Muhammad's lifetime. According to Gene Heck, the sites 'constitute the largest group of historic mine workings in the southern Arabian Shield'.[89] These mines could have provided the Ghamid with a significant degree of capital to invest in commerce and agricultural improvement. Certainly as they were a geographically fixed resource, control of them was important.

In Ibn al-Kalbi's genealogical system, Ghamid was the name of either ᶜAmir (or ᶜAmr) b. ᶜAbd Allah b. Kaᶜb b. al-Harith b. Kaᶜb. b. ᶜAbd Allah b. Malik b. Nasr b. al-Azd or his father. There are various attempts to explain how ᶜAmir got the name, derived from the root gh-m-d, used for covering or sheathing.[90] A pre-Islamic Ghamid poet, Firas b. ᶜUtayba, composed a bit of love poetry.[91] Other poets included ᶜAbd al-ᶜUzza b.

Suhal, ᶜAbd al-Rahman b. ᶜAwf and Rabiᶜa b. Muhrib.[92] Sakhr b. Wadaᶜa al-Ghamidi, a Companion, lived in al-Taᵓif, though perhaps was not born there.[93] Snatches of poetry of one Zuhayr al-Ghamidi suggest the Ghamid fought several battles against sections of the al-Hajr b. al-Hinw b. al-Azd.[94] Al-Hamdani placed the al-Hinw in the Sarat Mountains just south of the Ghamid.[95]

Many Ghamid, particularly those descended from al-Dul b. Saᶜd Mana'a b. Ghamid, played a role in events under the rightly guided caliphs.[96] Abu Zabyan al-Aᶜraj of the Dhubyan b. Thaᶜlaba b. al-Dul was noted in ps.-al-ᶜAwtabi as one of the three great mounted warriors of the Arabs. Before Islam he was a great raider, and it was said that the ᶜAqiq was his reclining spot because no one roused him except Husayda al-Quhafi of Khathᶜam, who went to raid Ghamid only to have Abu Zabyan kill him. There are also accounts of his conversion to Islam. According to these, Abu Zabyan received a letter from Muhammad calling him and the Ghamid to Islam, became part of the Ghamid delegation to Muhammad, carried the banner of that tribe at al-Qadisiyya, and received a stipend level of 1500.[97] This lineage also had a disputed claim to the poet ᶜAbd Allah b. Salima al-Ghamidi, whose fragmentary work features in the *Mufaddaliyyat*, a late eighth-century poetic compilation.[98]

Living in close proximity to the Ghamid and sharing in the mining wealth were the Lihb.[99] The genealogical eponym was Lihb b. Ahjan b. Kaᶜb, a nephew of ᶜAbd Allah b. Kaᶜb who was ancestor of the Ghamid, and one of several tribes considered sons of Ahjan. The tribe is described as especially renowned for their skill in avian augury.[100] Ibn Durayd defines '*lihb*' as a narrow ravine high up on a mountain.[101] Al-Waqidi (d. 823) also mentions an al-Nuᶜman b. al-Zarrafa (or al-Zaraᶜ) al-Lihbi who carried the al-Azd banner before Islam and did so again in the attack on al-Taᵓif.[102] This is undoubtedly the same as the al-Nuᶜman b. Baziya (or al-Razziya, al-Dariya) al-Lihbi reported by Ibn ᶜAbd al-Barr as an *ᶜarīf* of al-Azd in Greater Syria who carried their banner there.[103] '*ᶜArīf*' could mean a leader or manager, though by the end of the seventh century it came to be a specific role in the state management of tribal populations, as will be discussed in Chapter 2.

The Thumala were closely related to the Lihb; their eponym was Lihb b. Ahjan's nephew.[104] The proposed etymology for their name is the froth of milk, and they are mentioned in the oeuvre of the brigand-poet Taᵓabbata Sharra.[105] The Thumala's noble clan were the descendants of Ballal b. ᶜAmr.[106] The Ballal and the Rizam, another Thumala subgroup, are mentioned as interdependent neighbours (*mutajāwarīn*) in an account from Abu al-Faraj al-Isfahani (d. 967), an account which also suggests that around the time of Muhammad they were involved in conflict with the B. Hudhayl.[107] According to al-Baladhuri, the Thumala lived among the Tubba^c b. Bakr of ^{c}Adwan, an important Qays group.[108] In a tradition sourced to one of the Ibn Zubayrs, a man of Thumala complained about his treatment by a Meccan merchant.[109] Ibn ^{c}Abd al-Barr and Ibn Sa^{c}d list four Companions from this tribe: al-Hakam b. ^{c}Amr al-Thumali, who fought at the Battle of Badr, and another named Abu al-Hajjaj al-Thumali. A third Companion, ^{c}Abd Allah b. Qurt al-Thumali, played a role in the conquest of Syria, and will be dealt with in the next chapter.[110] Sa^{c}d b. ^{c}Iyad al-Thumali, who went to Kufa, is mentioned only by Ibn Sa^{c}d, though al-Sam^{c}ani knows him as a Successor.[111]

Caskel and Strenziok called the Zahran the largest al-Azd tribe, which seems in part to be because of the Omani additions.[112] I have not, however, found evidence that the Zahran participated as a unit in tribal feuding or that the name was used in early seventh-century nisbas, nor was there a Zahran embassy to Muhammad or a purported letter to such a group from him. The exception to this is Junada b. Abi Umayya al-Zahrani, a very young Companion who was a naval commander in the Mediterranean from the caliphate of ^{c}Uthman to that of Yazid I and who is also listed as al-Dawsi.[113] If Zahran did exist as a separate active identity, it may have referred to all followers of the noble clan of Ghitrif, who figured genealogically as descendants of Duhman b. Nasr b. Zahran. Saqb b. Duhman was an ancestor of Umayma bt. Abi Umayma, the mother of ^{c}Abd Allah b. al-Zubayr, who was widely recognised as caliph during the 680s. The Ghitrif, who often feature in accounts involving the Daws and Quraysh, are one of many groups who are descendants of Saqb's brother Sa^{c}b b. Duhman. As Duhman is an uncommon name that also occurs in the Daws lineage, this genealogical positioning may have been a prestige-enhancing move 'up' from an originally Daws identity to accommodate either the Zubayrids or the Ghitrif themselves.[114]

We do have evidence of one Zahran subgroup as a functioning identity in its own right during the period, and that is the Salaman b. Mufrij. They were the natal tribe of the pre-Islamic brigand-poet Hajiz b. ^{c}Awf, who was a client of the Makhzum shortly before Islam.[115] Another brigand-poet, al-Shanfara, is said in some accounts of his life to have lived among them after being given as ransom, though he was actually born among the al-Hinw b. al-Azd. However, as Suzanne Pinckney Stetkevich has pointed out, these legends serve primarily to explain his hostility to his natal tribe. In addition, based on the current study, the fact al-Azd is implied as a meaningful solidarity grouping in them also suggests the stories are relatively late, and testify only to a memory that the poet, if he even existed, may have had some connection to the Salaman.[116] There is also an account of a seven-man Salaman delegation to Muhammad led by Habib b. ᶜAmr al-Salamani.[117]

According to al-Dinawari (d. 896) and Ibn Hazm, there were also members of the Shababa b. Malik b. Fahm in the Sarat Mountains. Al-Dinawari located them specifically near al-Taᵓif in an area behind a place called Shihat where there was rugged high ground (*ḥidāb*). They were known for their region's high quality of honey, called '*ᶜasl al-durm*', which came from a plant called *nadgh*. This preference of that kind of honey may, of course, simply be a taste of the eighth century, as it is credited specifically to the caliph Sulayman b. ᶜAbd al-Malik and al-Hajjaj b. Yusuf, but is unlikely to have been unknown in the seventh, especially if the Thaqif tribesman al-Hajjaj is the one who popularised it at court.[118]

The Daws were furthest north, and their proximity to Mecca and Medina meant that they are easily the best-represented in the sources for the sixth and seventh centuries. According to al-Baladhuri and Ibn al-Kalbi, many claimed that the Daws were originally the Daws b. ᶜAdwan, part of the large Qays tribe east of the Sarat Mountains.[119] Al-Samᶜani (d. 1166) cites an Abu al-Zubayr, commenting on a hadith from Jabir b. ᶜAbd Allah al-Ansari, identifying Daws as the name of a fortress atop a mountain, and suggests as a possibility that Daws had inhabited this fortress.[120] However, al-Samᶜani also reports traditions that Daws was the name of the nursemaid of an ᶜImran b. ᶜAmr, presumably ᶜAmr Muzayqiyaᵓ, as well as the story of the Azd ᶜUman migrations which fuses al-Azd and Qudaᶜa and has been explained as relating to stories of the Tanukh.[121] In the common genealogical scheme, within al-Azd, Daws was a great-grandson of Zahran and the connecting link between the Azd ᶜUman and those of the Hijaz. Fahm, from the Malik b. Fahm traditions described above, was his grandson. The Daws in the Sarat were descendants of Sulaym b. Fahm and Munhib b. Daws, and a poem attributed to al-Tufayl b. ᶜAmr in the narrative of the Daws conversion to Islam refers to the Fahm and Munhib in ways that suggest those two identities together made up Daws.[122] It was also suggested above that the Ghitrif had an originally Daws genealogy which was pushed to a higher level so as to separate them out with an elevated status. In the *Lisan al-ᶜArab*, Ibn Manzur even says says *ghiṭrīf* is a synonym for *sayyid* and *sharīf*.[123]

At some point during the later part of the sixth century, Daws fought a war against Ghitrif. At the time, the Ghitrif were widely recognized as a pre-eminent lineage in their region. They took twice as much blood money for each man killed as they gave to others, annually collected the *itāwa* tax from the Daws, and subjected them to other humiliations. In an account credited by al-Isfahani to Abu ᶜAmr al-Shaybani, the conflict began when two Ghitrifi youths killed a Daws shaykh and the Daws took revenge by killing a Ghitrif shaykh at Qanuna. Humama b. al-Harith al-Dawsi sent his son ᶜAmr to lead the Daws fighters in the conflict, and Damad b. Mishrah al-Harithi led the Ghitrif. The Daws won at the Yawm Hadwa al-Wadi, a battle fought at a mountain called ᶜUwayra which Yaqut implicitly places in the Tihama.[124] Ibn al-Kalbi has a somewhat different account, in that upon reaching manhood ᶜAmr resented the domination of the al-Ghitrif, and on a provocation rallied the Daws against them.[125] Regarding Humama, Ibn ᶜAsakir (d. 1175) reports from Ibn Durayd and Ibn al-Kalbi that he was Humama b. Rafiᶜ b. al-Harith al-Dawsi, a handsome man who took great care with his hair, which he named after a type of clover (*al-raṭba*). His home was a place called Baruq.[126] One day he met a woman from the B. Kinana with a husband from her tribe. She asked Humama to take her with him to his home, and once they arrived, Humama cut her Achilles tendon so that she could not escape from him as she had with him. This woman was the mother of ᶜAmr b. Humama, said here to be the father of al-Tufayl b. ᶜAmr.[127]

ᶜAmr b. Humama al-Dawsi reportedly lived to the ripe old age of either 300 or 400 years, which probably indicates that this conflict was perceived as having occurred a substantial period of time before Islam.[128] ᶜAmr's son Jundab, whom Abu al-Faraj al-Isfahani reports as being of the Dhubyan b. ᶜAwf b. Daws, lived before Islam and converted.[129] This Jundab b. ᶜAmr passed through Medina on his way to Syria and left his daughter Umm Aban behind with then-caliph ᶜUmar b. al-Khattab. After her father's death, she married ᶜUthman and became the mother of four sons and one daughter.[130] At some point, Jundab may also have been a *ḥalīf* of the B. Umayya b. ᶜAbd Shams.[131] That the Ghitrif continued to have influence is shown by a tradition that Damad's son Khalid received a letter from Muhammad.[132] Both families also controlled the sanctuaries of pre-Islamic Arabian deities. Ibn al-Kalbi tells us that al-Jaluq, a sibling branch of the Ghitrif eponym, were custodians of the 'idol' Dhu al-Shara.[133] Ibn Hisham describes Dhu al-Shara as existing in a reserved territory (*ḥimā*) based around a mountain spring.[134] Ibn Habib also mentions the Ghitrif as the keepers of Manat, a deity worshipped by the shores of the sea between Mecca and Medina by people of the Ansar and Azd Shanuʾa.[135] As for ᶜAmr b. Humama, he is noted as the keeper of Dhu al-Kaffayn, identified by Ibn al-Kalbi as the god worshiped by the Munhib b. Daws.[136] The Azd in the Sarat Mountains also venerated Dhu al-Khalasa, who was worshipped at a cultic centre under the domination of the

Khathᶜam.[137] Hawting calls attention to accounts of Dhu al-Shara, Dhu al-Kaffayn, and Dhu al-Khalasa as an example of confusion in the source material, suggesting originally sparse material had been elaborated on in different ways.[138] This is certainly possible, but some of his confusion evaporates if we do not follow him in seeing the Ghitrif as a tribe distinct from the Daws and ignore the role deities play in individual conversion accounts.[139]

During the time of Muhammad, a feud erupted between Daws and Quraysh following the murder of Abu Uzayhir al-Dawsi of the Ghitrif. This Abu Uzayhir married three of his daughters to three members of Quraysh: ᶜUtba b. Rabiᶜa, Abu Sufyan b. Harb, and al-Walid b. al-Mughira of the clan of Makhzum. When al-Walid was killed, he complained that Abu Uzayhir had kept his dowry despite not letting the daughter go to him. Al-Walid's son Hisham therefore killed Abu Uzayhir in the market of Dhu al-Majaz. Fearing a conflict within the Quraysh, Abu Sufyan stopped his son Yazid from avenging Abu Uzayhir and paid blood money instead. However, Saᶜd b. Safih b. al-Harith al-Dawsi waged his own campaign for vengeance against Quraysh, killing all those of that tribe whom he could lay hands on. A poem from Dirar b. al-Khattab, brother of the caliph ᶜUmar b. al-Khattab, tells of how a woman named Umm Ghaylan, who was a personal attendant, probably to a woman of Daws, saved him when he was in the Daws country near al-Taᵓif.[140] Umm Ghaylan is described as a *mawlā*, which probably represents an anachronistic usage of that term, as in pre-Islamic Arabia the term *mawālī* both applied to collectives rather than individuals and usually indicated mutual help rather than servitude.[141] Among those Saᶜd killed was Bujayr b. ᶜAwwam, a brother of al-Zubayr whom the Dawsi encountered in al-Yamama. Ibn al-Kalbi also reports several Makhzumis as being killed in al-Yamama during the feud, so there may have been a significant incident there.[142] ᶜAtika bt. Abi Uzayhir al-Dawsi was the mother of two of Abu Sufyan's sons, ᶜAnbasa and Muhammad.[143] ᶜAnbasa was governor of Mecca and Taᵓif under Muᶜawiya.[144] The Daws were also reportedly a source of Ethiopian slaves for the Quraysh; the Quraysh are said to have sold donkeys to the Daws.[145]

The key figure in accounts of the Daws' conversion to Islam is al-Tufayl b. ᶜAmr al-Dawsi, who is often called Dhu al-Nur because of the light he possessed after his conversion. The most common is found in almost identical versions via Ibn Hisham and al-Waqidi, the latter going back to an ᶜAbd al-Wahid b. Abi Awn al-Dawsi, a *ḥalīf* of the Quraysh. According to this version, al-Tufayl came to Mecca and was warned that Muhammad had dangerous speech which was dividing the community, and so al-Tufayl sought to avoid hearing him. When he did anyway, he desired to know more, followed Muhammad to his home, and there converted upon hearing his explanation of Islam. Al-Tufayl then asked for a sign that would help him convert his people, and was granted a light between his eyes. This both startled him and caused him to become concerned that people would take it as a sign of punishment, and so the light moved to his whip. Once back among his people, he converted his father and wife, insisting that the latter had to first cleanse herself at the shrine of Dhu Shara. No others joined them, however, and so he returned to Muhammad asking that he curse the Daws; instead, Muhammad prayed for them to receive divine guidance and sent al-Tufayl back. This time al-Tufayl made converts, and returned with them to assist Muhammad at Khaybar. Then, after the conquest of Mecca, Muhammad sent him to burn Dhu al-Kaffayn, the deity of ᶜAmr b. Humama. This caused the Daws to convert en masse, and al-Tufayl returned to Medina, where he remained until Muhammad's death.[146]

Al-Isfahani's narrative comes in his biography of al-Harith b. al-Tufayl b. ᶜAmr, which makes al-Tufayl himself the grandson of ᶜAbd Allah b. Malik b. Fahm. The sources are again Ibn Durayd and Ibn al-Kalbi, though the *isnad* does not go back further. Al-Tufayl recited poetry for Muhammad about his people's fighting prowess, after which Muhammad called him to Islam and sent him back to his people upon his conversion. It was then a dark and stormy night when al-Tufayl came to Baruq, described as a large Daws settlement on the mountain of Dhu Rimaᶜ at the *Y.z.ḥ.z.ḥ* Road. The light from his whip illuminated him and dazzled the people, and he converted his father and wife, but only converted Abu Hurayra among his people. Abu Hurayra returned with him to Muhammad. Muhammad sent al-Tufayl back to his people, after which he did win converts among them.[147] The main differences between this and the al-Waqidi/Ibn Hisham account are the insertion of Abu Hurayra, role of al-Tufayl's poetry in his encounter with Muhammad, and detail about the Daws' homeland. There is also an account from the eighth-century Basrans Muhammad b. Sirin and Jarir b. Hazm (d. 786) that the Daws converted out of fear of Muslim military power after hearing Kaᶜb b. Malik's poetry about their victory over the Thaqif.[148]

Because of their proximity to Mecca and Medina, the Daws had more Companions, whether real or fictive, than any other al-Azd tribe. According to a family tradition, Saᶜd b. Abi Dhubab al-Dawsi converted to Islam and was placed in charge of his people (*qawm*) by both Muhammad and ᶜUmar b. al-Khattab. It is unclear which people this governorship referred to, however.[149] Abu al-Arwa al-Dawsi was a loyalist of the caliph ᶜUthman who transmitted hadith from Abu Bakr and lived with the Dhu Hulayfa of al-Azd, a group with a very South Arabian-style name apparently taken from a place a few miles from Medina.[150] Maᶜiz b. Malik al-Aslami, another Companion, is mentioned as a *saʾīr* of Daws.[151] Iyas b. ᶜAbd Allah al-Dawsi settled at some point in Medina and transmitted hadith.[152] Finally, Sawad b. Qarib al-Dawsi was a poet and soothsayer before Islam.[153]

Abu Hurayra al-Dawsi was among the most commonly cited Companions for the transmission of hadith. His given name is unknown; it was apparently changed when he converted to Islam, but both his old and new names were the subject of controversy. Ibn al-Kalbi reports that he was the nephew of Saᶜd b. Safih. He arrived in Medina before or during Muhammad's raid on Khaybar, and went to join Muhammad on that expedition. Al-Waqidi reports that he came to Medina with eighty families of Daws after the destruction of Dhu al-Kaffayn. Thereafter, he became one of the *Ahl al-Suffa*, a group who lived off charity in the mosque. Al-Waqidi also has him perform the Qadiyya pilgrimage and fight at Muʾta, the conquest of Mecca, the campaign against the Hawazin, and Tabuk.[154] Many of these appearances, however, relate to legal points, as also seen in his account of Abu Bakr's hajj.[155]

ᶜUmar b. al-Khattab appointed Abu Hurayra as governor of eastern Arabia (*Baḥrayn*). However, al-Thaᶜalibi gave the Companion the dubious distinction of Islam's first embezzler, because he took money from the public treasury while in that post. For this ᶜUmar dismissed him and beat him until he repaid a substantial sum. The account in which Abu Hurayra was then re-offered the post but declined it due to unworthiness is probably apologetics. He was later appointed as governor in Medina during the absences of Marwan b. al-Hakam. According to al-Thaᶜalibi, Abu Hurayra was called '*shaykh al-maḍira*' because at Siffin he would cross the lines to eat that dish which had been prepared for Muᶜawiya. Other sources, however, claim he remained in Medina after his removal from his governorship. He said the funeral prayers for Muhammad's wives ᶜAʾisha and Umm Salama, and died in the late 670s at the age of 78. After he died, his son sold his home (*dār*) in Medina, where the buyer also reached some sort of agreement with the *mawālī* of Abu Hurayra still living there.[156]

The Daws and Ghitrif were not the only al-Azd groups to have intermarried with the Quraysh in Mecca. A woman named Fatima from the B. Hidjina of al-Azd was the mother of ᶜAbd ᶜUzza b. ᶜAbd Shams.[157] Muhammad's wife Ghuziya was previously the husband of Abu al-ᶜAkr b. Sumayy al-Azdi, and called Umm Sharik after her son with him.[158] ᶜUbayd Allah b. ᶜAbd al-Dar was the son of a woman of the

B. Thumala.[159] Two Azdis among the prophet's Companions also had mothers from the B. al-Muttalib of ᶜAbd Manaf. One was Abu Hakim al-Qaᶜqaᶜ b. Hakim al-Azdi, a *ḥalīf* of the B. al-Muttalib.[160] The other was ᶜAbd Allah b. Malik al-Azdi, who was known as Ibn Buhayna after his mother. ᶜAbd Allah b. Malik's paternal genealogy was traced back to the Mihdab b. Mubashshar, a line related to the Ghitrif. He had left his people over a dispute before also becoming a *ḥalīf* of the B. al-Muttalib in order to secure protection and lived about thirty miles from Medina.[161] Such marriages in hosting alliances were a common way of cementing bonds.[162]

Muᶜiqib b. Abu Fatima al-Dawsi was another Azdi in Mecca, and converted to Islam early. Sources record him as having some sort of dependent status to the Quraysh: he was either a *ḥalīf* of the Al Saᶜid b. al-ᶜAs or one of their clients who had been taken prisoner, or perhaps a *ḥalīf* of the Al ᶜUtba b. Rabiᶜa. Muᶜiqib either emigrated to Ethiopia or left Mecca for the land of his people, presumably the Sarat Mountains, and then returned to fight at Khaybar with Abu Musa al-Ashᶜari. ᶜUmar b. al-Khattab later put him in charge of the treasury. He was also a leper and died during the caliphate of ᶜUthman.[163] The Daws, like other tribes in the vicinity of Mecca and Medina, do not seem to have had a *ridda* movement, which may testify to their close relationship with the ruling elites of early Islam.[164]

Apart from the Daws, other al-Azd were around Mecca and Medina as *ḥulafāʾ*. Khalid al-Qasri, who was governor of Mecca before becoming governor of Iraq in the 720s and 730s, purchased some small houses in Mecca that had belonged to the al-Barahima, Azd Sarat *ḥulafāʾ* of the Harb b. Umayya. The Hibar of al-Azd also lived as *ḥulafāʾ* of the B. Makhzum.[165] Hudhayfa b. Mihsan al-Bariqi was a *ḥalīf* of the Ansar whose role in the early Islamic history of Oman we will describe below.[166] According to Ibn ᶜAbd al-Barr, Mikhnaf b. Sulaym al-Ghamidi was also a *ḥalīf* before Islam, though he does not say of whom.[167] ᶜAbd Allah b. al-Harith b. Sakhbara al-Azdi lived in Mecca before Islam as a *ḥalīf* of the future caliph Abu Bakr, who later married his wife Umm Ruman of the B. Kinana.[168]

Several other random Azdis are worth mentioning. Muhammad supposedly wrote a letter to one Junada al-Azdi, mentioned in a report which also mentions 'his people and those who had become his dependents'.[169] This may be the Junada b. Malik al-Azdi al-Kufi whom Ibn ᶜAbd al-Barr knows through a family *isnad* for a hadith on the end of feuds from before Islam.[170] Umim b. al-Harith al-Azdi of the B. Saqᶜab was among the husbands of Umm Farwa bt. Abi Quhafa.[171] Ibn Saᶜd and Ibn ᶜAbd al-Barr also both have accounts of a Dimad al-Azdi, who served as a source for hadith transmitted by Ibn ᶜAbbas. This Dimad was a member of the Azd Shanuᶜa known for magical healing and a companion (*ṣadīq*) of Muhammad before Islam. When the Quraysh told him that Muhammad was mad, Dimad went to cure him, but converted to Islam after hearing him.[172]

The story found under the heading of the deputation of al-Azd to Muhammad is really the story of the al-Azd conquest of Jurash and defeat of the Khathᶜam. Ibn Saᶜd provides it with the isnad of al-Waqidi < ᶜAbd Allah b. ᶜAmr b. Zuhayr al-Kaᶜbi < Munir b. ᶜAbd Allah al-Azdi, while another version is found in Ibn Hisham and Ibn Ishaq; the recension of Ibn Ishaq by al-Tabari (d. 923) gives the latter's source as ᶜAbd Allah b. Abi Bakr al-Ansari. According to the story, Surad b. ᶜAbd Allah al-Azdi led a deputation of ten to Muhammad, and they embraced Islam. Muhammad then put Surad in command of a battle against non-Muslim al-Yaman tribes, and Surad went to lay siege to Jurash, described as a '*madīna ḥaṣīna mughalliqa*'. After about a month of this siege, Surad feigned a retreat and waited at a mountain called Shakar, then fell upon the Jurash army which was sent to pursue him. The people of Jurash then sent a deputation to Muhammad to profess Islam, and he granted them a reserved pasture (*ḥimā*) around the city.[173] Al-Baladhuri has a different account going back to al-Zuhri according to which the people of Tabala and Jurash both accepted Islam without fighting, and Muhammad appointed Abu Sufyan as their governor.[174]

Jurash was a city at the head of the Wadi Bisha along the caravan route which connected southern Arabia and Mecca to the east of the mountains. It was dominated by the Himyar, and in Ibn al-Kalbi's genealogy Jurash was actually the name of a clan of Himyar with the eponym Munabbih b. Aslam.[175] An al-Azd poem provided by Ibn Hisham implies the campaign in Muhammad's time involved the pursuit of Khathᶜam in particular, and that it constituted a livestock raid until they came to 'Himyar with its forts', presumably a reference to the fortified Jurash.[176] 'Shakar' is most likely the Jabal Hamuma across the Wadi Bisha from Jurash.[177] In the ninth century, al-Hamdani reported Jurash as controlled by a Himyar noble clan called the al-ᶜAwasij. At the same time, nearby was a spring called Tandaha around which lived the B. Usama of al-Azd.[178] Because the chains of authorities for the account of its al-Azd conquest do not go back earlier than the start of the eighth century, it may represent a retrospective islamisation of a conflict completely unrelated to Muhammad, an islamisation which served to justify temporary al-Azd rulership of the city.

The information presented above allows for several conclusions. First is that the al-Azd groups on which the most information survives are those which played a role in early Islam and the conquered territories. With three of these, Bariq, Ghamid and Daws, there is also the common factor that they are Azd Shanu'a, but the same is not true of the Thumala, Lihb or Salaman. At the same time, many of the prominent early Islamic figures from these tribes are not clearly related to the named heroes of the past. These points not only confirm that the literary sources dealing with pre-Islamic Arabia reflect the preoccupations of emigrant population centres further north under the caliphate, but that those who settled in the cities of Syria and Mesopotamia passed down primarily not direct family stories or visions of a united al-Azd confederation, but rather accounts important to groups at this level, which would therefore also have represented the most important layer of identity. The stories they told, repositories of Meeker's 'segmentary *sharaf*', were anchored in poetry, usually poetry about conflict.

The figures who played an important role in the early caliphate also seem to have come by their influence not through their own tribes, but through their connections to Mecca and Medina. Jundab b. ᶜAmr al-Dawsi was from the leading clan of the Daws, but it was Abu Hurayra who became a governor. Jundab himself was the father of a daughter who married ᶜUthman. The most prominent Bariqi in the early caliphate was not Humayda b. al-Nuᶜman al-Bariqi, who if he led a *ridda* movement was perhaps among the tribe's leaders, but the Ansar client Hudhayfa b. Mihsan. Among the Ghamid, Abu Zabyan may have participated in the conquests, but the general and governor was Mikhnaf b. Sulaym, also a client, quite probably of either the Ansar or Quraysh. The Islamic state was built by co-option, as Donner and Power describe, but the elite in the Hijaz was always fully in charge, and rising to the elite depended on connections with them.[179]

The patterns of settlement and genealogy were clearly fluid. Any residual al-Azd identity left over from the kingdoms of the ESA inscriptions seems to have been stronger among the Azd Sarat than the Azd Shanu'a, and was perhaps most important to the Ghitrif lineage and those who followed it. The Daws and the Bariq may in fact have adopted al-Azd identity only a few decades prior to Islam. The theory of segmentation is utterly worthless for explaining the pattern of alliance and conflict among that level of grouping. One prominent non-al-Azd group in the mountains, the Khathᶜam, was also in a position of decline. The Ethiopian general Abraha may have attempted to build a tribal client state around them during his invasion, giving a position of prominence they were slowly losing, as with the capture of Jurash.[180] Chiefly lineages often combined control of religious sanctuaries with military power, and the latter was subject to challenge and required continual demonstration.[181]

The Azd in Eastern Arabia

The region of Arabia where al-Azd was most dominant was Oman. The account of Malik b. Fahm analysed above highlights immigration from Yemen across southern Arabia and conflict with the Persians. However, there is no firm date to which we can tie an al-Azd arrival into Oman. The name Dara b. Dara was almost certainly provided by Ibn al-Kalbi himself for reasons related to his handling of the Tanukh.[182] For this reason, we must reject Paul Yule's interpretation of the appearance of the Samad archaeological culture as the al-Azd migrations, which he bases on the confluence of its 300 BCE date with a late Achaemenid al-Azd arrival.[183] J. C. Wilkinson correctly sees the story of Malik b. Fahm as representing a mashing together of patterns over centuries, both in terms of the penetration of Oman by Yemeni cultural elements and Persian influences and attempts at control.[184] Both Wilkinson and Isam al-Rawas find the first two or three centuries CE as the most likely period for a significant immigration of what became the Malik b. Fahm tribes, while Mouton and Schiettecatte suggest that the Arabian campaigns of Ardashir and Shapur II in the early Sasanian period destroyed Parthian-period coastal settlements and led to new prominence of pastoral nomads.[185]

Wilkinson has also amply explained the al-Azd settlement patterns in Oman, and what follows for both the Malik b. Fahm tribes and other al-Azd groups largely relies upon his work. The Malik b. Fahm generally occupied the periphery of the main settled agricultural areas, initially in the Sharqiyya region of southeastern Oman before dispersal northward. Some members of the most numerous branch within Oman, the al-Harith b. Malik b. Fahm, were found in the Sharqiyya around the city of Ibraᵓ, but the largest concentration was around the market port of Daba, which today straddles the border between Oman's exclave on the Musandam Peninsula and the United Arab Emirates. This Daba concentration was probably the source for migrations along the Batina coast.[186] The most famous al-Harith b. Malik clan, the Laqit, ruled over Daba, a fact which will figure below in discussion of the *ridda* in Oman. The Laqit was also the clan to which ps.-al-ᶜAwtabi attached al-Tufayl b. ᶜAmr al-Dawsi attempting to make him into an Omani.[187] Kaᶜb b. Sur al-Laqiti was a Christian before converting to Islam, suggesting they were influenced by the Nestorian Christianity found throughout the Gulf.[188] The ᶜAmr b. Malik b. Fahm were a similarly large and scattered group, with most of them in Dhofar, but others in northern Oman west of the Hajar Mountains.[189]

Much of the al-Azd power structure on the eve of Islam is found in the story of Salima b. Malik b. Fahm. According to the account of ps.-al-ᶜAwtabi, Salima was both Malik's youngest son and the one his father favoured most, which led to jealousy among his brothers. These brothers accused Salima of slacking off on guard duty; while Malik rebuked them, a seed of doubt led him to check. When he crept up on Salima in the dark of night, Salima, who was not slacking, fatally shot him with an arrow before realising who he was. Although Hinaᵓa b. Malik tried to mediate between Salima and the other sons, the enmity of Maᶜn b. Malik in particular led him to flee across the sea. Salima arrived on Jask along the Iranian coast opposite Oman, where he took a wife and had a son who became the progenitor of the al-Isfahiyya, named after the mother. Salima then went to Kirman, where he won the right to settle by telling his story to the leaders (*mulūk*), one of whose daughters he married.[190]

When Salima arrived, Kirman was ruled by a tyrant. Salima agreed to kill this tyrant, an act which made him a popular hero and the region's new ruler. As time passed, however, some of the people came to resent being ruled by an Arab (*ᶜarabī*), and began opposing him at the frontiers of his realm. Salima then wrote to his brother Hinaᵓa for help. Hinaᵓa came with a significant force which propped up his rule. There was, however, dissension among his sons which people took advantage of to restore the rule of that area to the Persians (*al-ᶜajam*). Salima's descendants then scattered around Fars, Kirman, the islands of the Persian Gulf, and the area behind Qalhat in Oman and along the Batina coast.[191]

Ps.-al-ᶜAwtabi's version of this story is filled with vivid storytelling, and if Wilkinson is correct that it references the descent of the Saffarids, then it was probably told in their circles.[192] As an account of the generation following Malik b. Fahm, it suggests a continuation of eastward migration at Persian expense and Arab political power in southern Iran. However, it could just as easily be a legend built around a Salima who was not originally attached to Malik b. Fahm at all. His sojourn in Jask, which was probably Larak Island, is clearly designed to provide a suitable lineage for the al-Isfahiyya.[193] Both the account and associated poetry link the deposed ruler of Kirman to the family of Dara b. Dara, a connection which for reasons noted above must be a late development. The clearest significance regards the relationship of the 'sons' of Malik b. Fahm, with Hinaᵓa closely allied with Salima and Maᶜn opposed.

The Hinaᵓa were actually the leading Malik b. Fahm group, and found mainly west of the northern Hajar Mountains.[194] Ps.-al-ᶜAwtabi states that

Hina'a followed his father as ruler and had three sons: Aslam, Jahman and Sa'ida. One of their pre-Islamic shaykhs was Tha'laba b. Bakr b. Aslam, who raided the B. Hanifa-ruled al-Yamama for horses and livestock, defended that livestock from the B. ʿAmir b. Saʿsaʿa, and became part of the al-Azd movement further up the Gulf. Another shaykh was Rubkha b. Harith b. ʿA'idh of the Aslam b. Hina'a, which seems to have been the primary branch. Ps.-al-ʿAwtabi's account of him describes how he averted a crisis by paying the blood money owed by another lineage.[195] Al-Samʿani also lists as a *nisba* Bajli, said to be from Bajla bt. Hina'a b. Malik. This Bajla was the mother of a Sulaym b. Mansur of Qays and used for his immediate band, which would later include ʿAmr b. ʿAnbasa, an early convert to Islam.[196]

The Farahid, whose name may have meant 'young sheep', 'lion cubs', or 'kid goats', were allies of the Hina'a.[197] Their shaykhly sections were found along the Batina coast, but the bulk of them were in the southeast between the Sharqiyya region and Dhofar.[198] For pre-Islamic times, one al-Hurr b. al-Hurr was counted among the great horse warriors of his day.[199] This leadership coalition of Hina'a, Farahid and Salima was opposed by the al-Harith, described above, and also by the Maʿn, in parallel with the account of Salima. The Maʿn lived mainly in the highlands stretching between Oman and the country of the Mahra. Ps.-al-ʿAwtabi records a figure named Humaym b. ʿAmir of the B. Shartan b. Maʿn who conducted a famous livestock raid on a Kharaja b. ʿAmr, perhaps one of the Mahra. The Shartan may have been their main shaykhly section, as it also gave rise to Masʿud b. ʿAmr, an al-Azd leader in Basra whom we will deal with in detail in the next chapter.[200] Of the Shababa b. Malik b. Fahm, the Hummam lived around the oasis of Tu'am, as did the Sulaym, a leading clan of the previously mentioned ʿAmr. The B. Jahdam occupied Samad al-Sha'n in the Sharqiya region.[201] Of the other Malik b. Fahm groups we know little. Al-Hamdani also mentions unspecified groups of Nasr b. al-Azd living in the environs of al-Shihr and Raysut and the edges of Fars.[202]

The ʿImran group of al-Azd, which like the Malik b. Fahm counted among the Azd ʿUman, entered the country via the north, and were still concentrated in that area; though some had penetrated further, others remained in the Sarat, and yet others were in Fars. ʿImran's two sons were al-Asd, who in genealogical legend married Hind bt. Sama b. Lu'ayy of Quraysh, and al-Hajr, for whom ps.-al-ʿAwtabi claims the city of al-Hajar in al-Yamama was named. Al-Asd is the father of ʿAtik, the clan to which belonged both the Muhallabids and the leading al-Azd family in Marwanid Basra, Ziyad b. ʿAmr and his descendants. Within Oman, the al-Hajr were along the Batina coast while the al-Asd were across the mountains in the Jawf and northward.[203] According to Ibn al-Kalbi, the Azd claimed that ᶜAmr b. al-Hajr b. ᶜImran was a prophet.[204] The ᶜImran were also apparently in Baḥrayn, as members of the B. ᶜAwdh b. Sud b. al-Hajr were conspicuously active there in the days of al-Hajjaj.[205]

The most powerful al-Azd groups at the dawn of Islam belonged to the Azd Shanuᵓa, and particularly the B. Maᶜwala. According to ps.-al-ᶜAwtabi, the first Maᶜwala king in Oman was ᶜAbd ᶜIzz b. Maᶜwala, who also collected the taxes from al-Yamama and Bahrayn and raided maritime coastal communities (*ahl al-ᶜubab*), from whom he took 1,000 horses. As his governor in al-Yamama he appointed a grandson of al-Yahmad, who like Maᶜwala was the eponym of one of Oman's Azd Shanuᵓa tribes.[206] The Maᶜwala of his day were clearly an ascendant Bedouin tribe who probably extended their influence amidst the collapse of Kinda power. Wilkinson placed the eastward Azd Shanuᵓa migrations in the fifth and early sixth centuries.[207] During the middle and late fifth century, the Kinda ruler Hujr b. ᶜAmr Akil al-Murar ruled al-Yamama, as did his son Muᶜawiya al-Jawn after him. The latter's descendants still reigned there at the time of the Battle of Shᶜib Jabala, which we have described above as being in the third quarter of the sixth century. That battle marked their final defeat and withdrawal from central Arabia to Hadramawt.[208] An early date for that battle fits plausibly with a rough estimate of the time of ᶜAbd ᶜIzz. The other significant Azd Shanuᵓa groups in Oman, the B. Huddan and the B. Yahmad, lived in sections of the Hajar Mountains named after them, and the bulk of the B. Maᶜwala lived in a stretch of mountains that bordered the sea between the Baṭina coast and Qalhat.[209] This, too, seems to imply a continuity of lifestyle given their probable origins with the Azd Shanuᵓa of the Sarat Mountains, a lifestyle based on small livestock and limited cultivation in the wadis.[210]

At some point the Sasanians established a presence in Oman, and granted the title 'Al-Julanda' to the Arabian leaders through whom they sought to control the region.[211] Its holders included a descendant of ᶜAbd ᶜIzz, called by the Arabic sources al-Julanda b. al-Mustakbir, who died around 630, and whose two sons, ᶜAbd and Jayfar, jointly ruled the country after him, though Jayfar may have had some primacy.[212] According to ps.-al-ᶜAwtabi, the Sasanians ruled the coast via a *marzubān* while the Al al-Julanda controlled the interior mountains and desert. During the life of Muhammad, the *marzubān* was either named Badhan or al-Fastkhan, and left the country to consult with the Sasanian ruler over the matter of Muhammad.[213] The use of ps.-al-ᶜAwtabi's account to argue for significant Sasanian administration linked with a supposed economic prosperity has been sharply critiqued, but the presence along the coast of ethnicities associated with the Sasanian Empire is likely, and some attempt at a Persian governor would fit the context of the early seventh century in parallel to developments further up the Gulf.[214] The discovery at Fulayj of a Sasanian fort, possibly one of a chain of forts guarding the coastal plain, supports ps.-al-ᶜAwtabi's general picture.[215] The departure of the *marzubān* at the time of Muhammad shows Sasanian control slipping away as the empire fell into internal turmoil in the aftermath of its defeat in a protracted war against the Byzantines, suggesting the arrangement was short-lived.

Accounts of the Omani conversion to Islam harmonise well with the view that Sasanian power in the country was retreating. In al-Baladhuri's account, the sons of al-Julanda are based in Suhar.[216] At the same time, according to ps.-al-ᶜAwtabi, they were in the desert when ᶜAmr b. al-ᶜAs arrived with a letter from Muhammad to call them to Islam, and then went to Dastgerd, the old Sasanian fortified section of Suhar.[217] This implies that the Maᶜwala had continued a nomadic or semi-nomadic lifestyle from the previous century, and used Suhar as a central gathering place rather than a permanent seat of power. ᶜAmr b. al-ᶜAs was successful in winning the conversion of ᶜAbd and Jayfar, who may have imposed Islamic rule on the entire country. Ps.-al-ᶜAwtabi even credits them with spreading Islam to Mahra and al-Shihr. In ps.-al-ᶜAwtabi, their campaigns led to the expulsion of the Sasanians, an event commemorated by Thabit Qutna al-ᶜAtaki, a poet associated with Yazid b. al-Muhallab during the early 700's.[218] This affiliation with the Islamic state likely represented finding a patron to replace the Sasanians, with the establishment of the family's control extending into what later Islamic authors cast as the Omani ridda.[219]

Wilkinson has identified three distinct accounts of the Omani *ridda*.[220] One, found in ps.-al-Waqidi, suffers from geographical implausibility. It states that when ᶜIkrima b. Abi Jahl began fighting Kinda rebels in Maʾrib, tribes around Daba revolted in sympathy with their fellow Yamanis. They threw out Abu Bakr's governor Hudhayfa b. Mihsan al-Bariqi. Abu Bakr then ordered ᶜIkrima to immediately suppress the revolt in Daba, which he did, with a final engagement that saw the deaths of the local leaders and the sending of several hundred prisoners to Medina. ᶜIkrima then proceeded to Haḍramawt; a problem with the account is that it involves a passage from Maʾrib to Daba that had to go through *ridda* country.[221] In addition, although Wilkinson believes tribal solidarity did lead to a revolt in Daba, this account relies on a solidarity between Kinda and al-Azd which is not otherwise in evidence for this period.

The second version goes back to Sayf b. ᶜUmar and is preserved most fully in al-Tabari. According to this account, Laqit b. Malik Dhu al-Taj, an enemy of the family of al-Julanda, claimed prophecy and drove ᶜAbd and Jayfar out of Oman to the mountains and sea. Jayfar then wrote to Abu Bakr, who dispatched Hudhayfa b. Mihsan and ᶜArfaja b. Harthama al-Bariqi to retake the country. To these forces he later added those of ᶜIkrima b. Abi Jahl. The Muslim armies gathered at Suhar and Laqit's at Daba. The Muslims then pried some followers away from Laqit before marching on Daba, where they won, killing 10,000 and plundering its marketplace. Hudhayfa remained behind to govern the area, while prisoners were sent to Medina.[222] The third account is found in the Omani sources, especially ps.-al-ᶜAwtabi. According to this local version, Hudhayfa b. Mihsan was Abu Bakr's governor in Oman, and while in Daba found himself in dispute with a woman of the al-Harith b. Malik b. Fahm over her tax assessment. When tribesmen from the area took her side a conflict ensued, which Hudhayfa appears to have won, since he sent prisoners to Medina. A delegation of local tribal leaders then went to Medina and won their release.[223]

Wilkinson argues convincingly that Sayf's account is an overdramatisation which appealed to al-Tabari mainly because it fitted the Omani events into a larger Wars of the Ridda framework.[224] He also believes that Hudhayfa b. Muhsin, central to all three accounts, was genuinely Medina's representative in the area, and involved in a tax dispute. This, too, seems sound. I am less convinced by his argument that Laqit b. Malik al-Azdi is simply a garbled recollection of the tribal name for the Laqit b. al-Harith b. Malik b. Fahm.[225] First, Laqit appears in al-Baladhuri, who never used Sayf b. ᶜUmar as a source.[226] Al-Tabari's Persian 'translator' al-Balᵓami (d. 990s) also appears to have independent information, stating that Laqit's family formerly held the al-Julanda title, but that he had become a retainer of Jayfar b. al-Julanda.[227] This of course explains both his prominence and his rivalry with the rulers in Suhar.

An understanding of the place of Daba and Suhar in the early seventh century provides important context for these events. According to an account passed on through the Tamim, both were locations presided over by al-Julanda b. Mustakbir and which formed part of an annual cycle of markets around the Arabian Peninsula.[228] What is striking is that Daba was a much bigger market than Suhar. Both markets took place during the spring, when ships sailing with the monsoons arrived from India.[229] The market at Daba was purportedly frequented by merchants from India and as far away as China. The accounts say almost nothing about Suhar, however, which may have been a more regional affair.[230] Sayf b. ᶜUmar also referred to Daba as Oman's chief delimited settlement area (*miṣr*) and marketplace.[231] An older elite could easily have been asserting themselves at Daba against the Suhar-based sons of al-Julanda.[232] The defeat of this movement, with the accompanying death of its leadership and destruction within the city, would then have led to the eclipse of Daba by Suhar and the B. al-Harith of the area to seek new fortunes with the Islamic conquests, as shall be detailed in the next chapter.[233]

Conclusion

Epigraphic South Arabian inscriptions testify to the existence of at least one and perhaps a second al-Azd tribal kingdom in the third century, one in the Wadi Bisha, and the other somewhere further east near Hadramawt. The rulers of these kingdoms passed into legend and provided a claimed ancestral identity for the Azd of the century before Islam, surviving as a genealogical patch in the macro-scale Arab genealogies of later centuries. However, there is no evident connection between those traditions and the 'Scattering of al-Azd' legends, which are products of the Islamic period concerned with the internal tribal politics of the caliphate and the elaboration of identities relevant to that period. The likely oldest element of those legends, the migration of Malik b. Fahm as the progenitor of the Azd ᶜUman and his battles with the Persians, is unrelated to the inscriptions, but revealing of the tribal politics of Oman in the decades prior to Islam.

There is no evidence that a division between northern and southern Arabs structured al-Azd political relationships prior to Islam. Tribal alliances and identity shifts routinely cross the Qays/al-Yaman boundary known from the eighth century. This does not mean that tribes might not at times have had some sense of such a division or a past linked to southern Arabia's ancient kingdoms, only that such memories did not influence their behaviour in any detectable way. The al-Azd identity may have mattered more, particularly to those tribes whose own smaller group was less powerful, but again, it did not routinely predict alliance or enmity, and its membership shifted with relations of clientship or new alliances due to migration. In Oman, al-Azd's numerical preponderance was too great for it to matter in competition over resources. In the west, the one possible line of division involving the al-Azd as a group was with the Khathᶜam, perhaps because that had in the days of the Ethiopian invasion acted as a meaningful block from which al-Azd was excluded.

Although equality may have been an ideal, pre-Islamic Arabia had a clear hierarchy, with known chiefly lineages. These could be akin to Sneath's 'aristocratic orders', in that they involved influence built up over generations so that claims to resources were in part genealogical. However, there is evidence of significant flux in which lineages were most dominant, as shaykhly positions were subject to continual challenge. Reputation always had to be continuously defended in the present. As al-Azmeh puts it, 'A primus inter pares asserted authority by wielding superior wealth and force unsentimentally.'[234] Group identity was also paramount as a tool for individuals. As Crone notes, 'in pre-Islamic Arabia, dependent relationships were formed between groups, or between individuals and groups, not between individuals.'[235]

The political impact of the rise of the Islamic state differed between Oman and the west. In both regions, leadership was co-opted into the Islamic state, though certainly this is an area where later generations would have an interest in claiming to have become Muslims as early as possible. In the west, however, the existing tribal elites were in the shadow of the Hijaz's dominance. In Oman, on the other hand, the Islamic state's elite was comfortably distant, and Islam could be a way to gain effective power through alliance with an outside patron to replace the weakened Sasanians. Wilkinson observes that representatives of the early Islamic state must have depended upon the Julandas for any administrative and bureaucratic organisation.[236] Certainly in the events portrayed in Oman under the theme of '*ridda*', the Julandas eliminated rivals both political and mercantile, setting themselves up for several more generations of rulership.[237]

In considering this material, however, we must bear in mind that while there is memory, there is also forgetting. As Aleida Assmann notes, 'Acts of forgetting are a necessary and constructive part of internal social transformations.'[238] The rise of the caliphate and migrations to the garrison towns mean that our sources were produced by people for whom over time the Bedouin past became paramount. Thus we read more of livestock raids than village irrigation rights. What was useful for those recounting the pre-Islamic Arabian past is what would conform to the expectations and value system which came to underpin ideas of Arabness, expectations which fit the Bedouinising theme mentioned at the beginning of this chapter. The tribal traditions most likely to survive thus became those which comported with the broader metanarrative by which polytheistic Bedouin Arabs became Muslims and spread Islam into the broader Middle East.

Notes

1. Fred Donner, *Narratives*, pp. 196–8. See also Peter Webb, 'Al-Jahiliyya: Uncertain Times of Uncertain Meanings'.
2. Rina Drory, 'The Abbasid Construction of the Jahiliyya: Cultural Authority in the Making', p. 34; Peter Webb, 'Al-Jahiliyya'.
3. Webb, *Imagining the Arabs*, p. 337; Peter Heath, 'Some Functions of Poetry in Premodern Historical and Psuedo-Historical Texts: Comparing *Ayyam al-ᶜArab*, al-Tabari's *History*, and *Sirat ᶜAntar*', pp. 40–4; Isabel Toral-Niehoff, 'Talking about Arab Origins: The Transmission of the *ayyam al-ᶜarab* in al-Kufa, al-Baṣra and Baghdad', pp. 47–75.
4. Szombathy, 'Fieldwork and Preconceptions', pp. 142–4.
5. Joy McCorriston, *Pilgrimage and Household in the Ancient Near East*, p. 74.
6. Jérémie Schiettecatte and Mounir Arbach, 'The Political Map of Arabia and the Middle East in the third century AD revealed by a Sabaean inscription', pp. 179–81.
7. Ibn Hisham, *Kitab al-Tijan*, p. 292.
8. Walter Müller, 'Eine Sabaische Gesandtschaft in Ktesiphon und Seleucia', p. 159.
9. Retsö, *Arabs*, p. 571, n. 109.
10. Ibn Durayd, *al-Ishtiqaq*, p. 435; Hamdani, *Sifa*, p. 70.
11. A. F. L. Beeston, *Warfare in Ancient South Arabia (2nd–3rd Centuries A.D.)*, p. 11.
12. A. Jamme, *Sabaean Inscriptions from Mahram Bilqis (Marib)*, pp. 137–8. The reading given here is that from Schiettecatte and Arbach, 'Political Map', p. 180.
13. Hermann von Wissmann, *Zur Geschichte und Landeskunde von Alt-Südarabien*, p. 185.
14. M. D. Bukharin, 'Towards the Earliest History of Kinda', p. 76.
15. Muhammad ᶜAbd al-Qadir Bafaqih, *L'Unification du Yemen Antique*, pp. 308–9.
16. ᶜAwtabi, *al-Ansab*, II, p. 710.
17. Schiettecatte and Arbach, 'Political Map', p. 180.
18. D. B. Doe and A. Jamme, 'New Sabaean Inscriptions from South Arabia', pp. 15–16; Walter Müller, 'Eine Sabaische Gesandtschaft in Ktesiphon und Seleucia', p. 160.
19. Jamme, *Mahram Bilqis*, pp. 164–6; Beeston, *Warfare*, p. 58. I thank Jérémie Schiettecatte for explaining the reasons for the translation.
20. Doe and Jamme, 'New Sabaean Inscriptions', p. 16.
21. Retsö, *Arabs*, pp. 500, 571 n. 108, 109, 110.
22. Müller, 'Gesandtschaft', p. 159.
23. Retsö, *Arabs*, p. 500, n. 157.
24. ᶜAwtabi, *al-Ansab*, II, p. 661.

25. Caskel and Strenziok, *Gamhara*, Table 210; ᶜAwtabi, *al-Ansab*, II, p. 662; Ibn Ḥazm *Jamhara*, p. 376; Ibn al-Kalbi, *Maᶜadd wa al-Yaman*, p. 479.
26. Irfan Shahid, *Byzantium and the Arabs in the Fifth Century*, p. 400; ᶜAwtabi, *Ansab*, II, p. 696.
27. Ibn ᶜAbd al-Barr, *al-Inbah ᶜala Qabaʾil al-Ruwat*, p. 112.
28. Christian Julien Robin, 'Matériaux', p. 146
29. Albert Jamme, *The al-ᶜUqlah Texts*, pp. 13–14; Schiettecatte and Arbach, 'Political Map', p. 180.
30. Jamme, *al-ᶜUqlah*, pp. 21, 51.
31. The Kinda hegemony of the fifth and sixth centuries was not a united monarchy, rather a loose coalition, as leaders placed their sons in charge of particular cities which evolved in autonomous directions.
32. Christian Julien Robin and Iwona Gajda, 'L'Inscription du Wadi ᶜAbadan', pp. 115, 118, 123; Christian Robin, 'Du Nouveau sur les Yaz'anides', pp. 182–3.
33. Retsö, *Arabs*, p. 556.
34. al-Azmeh, *Emergence*, p. 117.
35. David F. Graf and Salem Tairan, 'Jurash, cité caravanière sur la route de l'encens', pp. 24–9.
36. This section, as well as the opening paragraphs under 'The Azd in Eastern Arabia', are modified from material previously published in Ulrich, 'Azd Migrations'. On the theme of migration, see Munt et al., 'Sources', pp. 440–3.
37. ᶜAwtabi, *al-Ansab*, II, pp. 715–16.
38. Azdi, *Taʾrikh al-Mawsil*, pp. 96–7.
39. ᶜAwtabi, *al-Ansab*, II, pp. 686, 694–5, 708.
40. Ibn al-Kalbi, *Jamharat al-Nasab*, pp. 615–21; Caskel and Strenziok, *Gamharat*, I, tables 176, 210.
41. Ulrich, 'Azd Migrations', p. 312.
42. Baladhuri, *Futuh al-Buldan*, p. 18.
43. Ibn Durayd, *al-Ishtiqaq*, pp. 435–6.
44. Fuat Sezgin, *Geschichte des Arabischen Schriftums*, I, pp. 305–6.
45. Masᶜudi, *Muruj al-Dhahab*, II, pp. 193–207.
46. ᶜAwtabi, *al-Ansab*, II, pp. 687–94.
47. ᶜAwtabi, *al-Ansab*, II, pp. 694–715.
48. Ibn Hisham, *Kitab al-Tijan*, pp. 273–97.
49. Hamdani, *al-Iklil*, pp. 217–18.
50. Caskel and Strenziok, *Gamharat*, I, pp. 41–4.
51. Ibn Hisham, *Life of Muhammad*, pp. xxvii.
52. Azdi, *Tarikh al-Mawsil*, pp. 97–100.
53. Yaqᶜubi, *Tarikh*, I, p. 204.
54. Azdi, *Tarikh al-Mawsil*, pp. 98–9.
55. Huriya ᶜAbduh Sallam, *Iqlim al-Mawsil fi al-Asr al-Umawi: Dirasa Hadariya*, pp. 32, 72.

56. Isam al-Rawas, *Oman in Early Islamic History*, p. 31; Wilkinson, *Water and Tribal Settlement in South-East Arabia: A Study of the Aflaj of Oman*, pp. 244–7.
57. ᶜAwtabi, *al–Ansab*, II, pp. 715–25.
58. Jan Assmann, *Culture and Early Civilization: Writing, Remembrance, and Political Imagination*, pp. 37–8.
59. Webb, *Imagining the Arabs*, pp. 261–5.
60. Wilkinson, *Water and Tribal Settlement*, p. 128; Wilkinson, *Ibadism*, pp. 26–8.
61. Fuad Jabali, *The Companions of the Prophet: A Study of Geographical Distribution and Political Alignments*, p. 13.
62. Heck, *The Precious Metals of Western Arabia and Their Role in Forging the Economic Dynamic of the Early Islamic State*, p. 164. In Umayyad times, assertions that someone was a weaver were used to imply non-Arab descent. See Michael Lecker, 'Judaism among Kinda and the *Ridda* of Kinda', p. 641.
63. McCorriston, *Pilgrimage*, pp. 65–6.
64. McCorriston, *Pilgrimage*, p. 120.
65. Al-Azmeh, *Emergence*, p. 130.
66. For an evaluation of Ibn Habib's work, see Monika Springberg-Hinsen, *Die Zeit vor der Islam in arabischen Universalgeschichten des 9. bis 12. Jahrhunderts*, pp. 20–3.
67. G. R. Hawting, *The Idea of Idolatry and the Emergence of Islam: From Polemic to History*, pp. 88–110.
68. Hawting, *Idea of Idolatry*, pp. 111–19, in which he also expresses reservations about allowing information from Arabic sources equal weight with earlier material, most prominently epigraphy.
69. Hawting, *Idea of Idolatry*, pp. 119–22.
70. Ibn Habib, *Kitab al-Muhabbar*, p. 316; Ibn al-Kalbi, *Kitab Asnam*, pp. 40, 63.
71. Ibn al-Kalbi, *Maᶜadd wa al-Yaman*, pp. 463–5; Ibn ᶜAbd Rabbih, *al-ᶜIqd al-Farid*, III, p. 327.
72. ᶜAwtabi, *al-Ansab*, II, p. 600; Bakri, *Muᶜjam*, I, p. 63; Ibn Durayd, *al-Ishtiqaq*, p. 480; Samᶜani, *al-Ansab*, I, p. 265.
73. Yaqut, *Buldan*, I, pp. 379–80; Ibn ᶜAbd al-Barr, *Inbah*, p. 112; Ibn ᶜAbd al-Barr, *Istyaᶜab fo Maᶜrifa al-Ashab*, III, 175; Hamdani, *Sifa*, p. 125.
74. ᶜAwtabi, *al-Ansab*, II, pp. 603, 612–13; Ibn Durayd, *al-Ishtiqaq*, p. 481.
75. al-Bakri, *Muᶜjam*, I, p. 63. There is a place of the same name near Kufa which results in the confusion of al-Bakri, *Muᶜjam*, I, *Taʾrīkh Makkah* p. 221; Yaqut, *Buldan*, I, pp. 379–80.
76. ᶜAwtabi, *al-Ansab*, II, pp. 606–7. On pre-Islamic Arabian alliances, see Ella Landau-Tasseron, 'Alliances Among the Arabs'; Patricia Crone, *Roman, Provincial and Islamic Law: The Origins of the Islamic Patronate*, pp. 51–63; Orthmann, 'Als Yaman und Rabiᶜa ihre Stirnlocken abschnitten.

Kritische Anmerkungen zu einem Hilf-Bund in Hurasan aus der späten Umaiyadenzeit', pp. 156–9.

77. Irfan Shahid, 'Shi^{c}b Djabala, *EI* 2, IX, pp. 525–5.
78. ^{c}Awtabi, *al-Ansab*, II, pp. 602, 606–7, 609–12; Ibn ^{c}Abd Rabbih, *al-^{c}Iqd*, V, pp. 128–30; Marzubani, *Mu^{c}jam al-Shu^{c}ara*, p. 204; Isfahani, *al-Aghani*, XI, pp. 137, 159–61; Abu Ubayda, *Naqaʾid*, pp. 659, 675–6; Ibn Qutayba, *Fadl al-^{c}Arab wa-al-Tanbih ^{c}ala ^{c}Ulumiha*, p. 132; Amidi, a*l-Muʾtalif wa al-Mukhtalif*, p. 92.
79. Robin, 'Matériaux', pp. 135–46.
80. Bakri, *Mu^{c}jam*, I, p. 418; Yaqut, *Buldan*, II, p. 243.
81. Hamdani, *Sifa*, p. 181; Sa^{c}id al-Afghani, *Aswaq al-^{c}Arab fi al-Jahiliya wa al-Islam*, p. 259.
82. Donner, *Early Islamic Conquests*, p. 211.
83. Tabari, *History* X, p. 161; Tabari, *Taʾrīkh*, I, p. 1985.
84. Ibn Habib, *Muhabbar*, p. 179; al-Azmeh, *Emergence*, p. 196. Ya^{c}qubi says '*qabāʾil min al-Azd*' belonged to *al-ḥilla*. *Taʾrikh*, I, p. 257.
85. Isfahani, *al-Aghani*, XVII, p. 298
86. Tabari, *Taʾrīkh*, I, 2,186; Tabari, *History*, XI, pp. 199–200; Ibn al-Kalbi, *Ma^{c}add wa al-Yaman*, p. 465; Boaz Shoshan, *The Arabic Historical Tradition and the Early Islamic Conquests*, p. 36.
87. ^{c}Abd Allah Yusuf al-Ghunaym, *al-Ashkal Sath al-Ard fi Shibh al-Jazira al-^{c}Arabiya fi al-Masadir al-^{c}Arabiya al-Qadima*, p. 390.
88. Bafaqih, *Unification*, pp. 300–2; Jamme, *Mahram Bilqis*, pp.114–15.
89. Gene Heck, *Precious Metals*, pp. 295–303.
90. Caskel and Strenziok, *Gamharat*, I, p. 218; Ibn al-Kalbi, *Ma^{c}add wa al-Yaman*, p. 481; Ibn Durayd, *al-Ishtiqaq*, p. 492; Ibn Hazm, *Jamhara*, p. 377; ^{c}Awtabi, *al-Ansab*. II, 680–1, 714; Dabbi, *The Mufaddaliyat: An Anthology of Ancient Arabian Odes According to the Recension*, I, p. 182.
91. ^{c}Awtabi, *al-Ansab*, II, p. 681; Marzubani, *Mu^{c}jam*, p. 319.
92. Ibn al-Kalbi, *Ma^{c}add wa al-Yaman*, pp. 481–4; Ibn Durayd, *al-Ishtiqaq*, p. 492; ^{c}Awtabi, *al-Ansab*, II, p. 683.
93. Ibn ^{c}Abd al-Barr, *al-Isti^{c}ab*, II, p. 272.
94. Khalid b. ^{c}Ali al-Mardi al-Ghamidi, *Qabila Ghamid: Ansabha wa-Tarikhha*, p. 117.
95. Hamdani, *Sifa*, p. 119.
96. Caskel and Strenziok, *Gamharat* p. 218; Ibn al-Kalbi, *Ma^{c}add wa al-Yaman*, pp. 482–3.
97. Ibn Durayd, *al-Ishtiqaq*, pp. 493–4; ^{c}Awtabi, *al-Ansab*, II, pp. 681–2; Ibn Hazm, *Jamhara*, p. 378; Ibn Sa^{c}d, *al-Tabaqat al-Kubra*, I, p. 135; Ibn al-Kalbi, *Ma^{c}add wa al-Yaman*, p. 483.
98. Dabbi, *Mufaddaliyat*, I, pp. 182–94.
99. Heck, *Precious Metals*, pp. 295–6.
100. Caskel and Strenziok, *Gamharat*, I, p. 210; Ibn al-Kalbi, *Ma^{c}add wa al-Yaman*, p. 480; ^{c}Awtabi, *al-Ansab*, II, pp. 679–80; Ibn Hazm, *Jamhara*,

p. 376; Ibn Durayd, *al-Ishtiqaq*, pp. 491; Isfahani, *al-Aghani*, IX, p. 34; Baladhuri, *Ansab*, V, p. 470; Sam^c^ani, *al-Ansab*, I, p. 84; Ibn Qutayba, *^c^Uyun al-Akhbar*, I, p. 148.

101. Ibn Durayd, *al-Ishtiqaq*, p. 491; ^c^Awtabi, *al-Ansab*, II, p. 680.
102. Waqidi, *Kitab al-Maghazi*, p. 923; Waqidi, *The Life of Muhammad*, p. 453; Ibn ^c^Asakir, *Ta^ɔ^rikh Madinat Dimashq*, XXV, p. 17.
103. Ibn ^c^Abd al-Barr, *Isti^c^ab*, IV, p. 60. See also Sam^c^ani, *al-Ansab*, V, p. 29.
104. Caskel and Strenziok, *Gamharat*, I, p. 210; Ibn al-Kalbi, *Ma^c^add wa al-Yaman*, p. 481; ^c^Awtabi, *al-Ansab*, II, p. 684; Ibn Ḥazm, *Jamhara*, p. 377; Sam^c^ani, *al-Ansab*, II, p. 15.
105. Ibn Durayd, *al-Ishtiqaq*, p. 492; ^c^Awtabi, *al-Ansab*, II, p. 684; Isfahani, *al-Aghani*, XXI, pp. 143, 147.
106. Caskel and Strenziok, *Gamharat*, II, p. 222; Ibn Hazm, *Jamhara*, p. 377; Sam^c^ani, *al-Ansab*, I, p. 445, V, p. 28.
107. Isfahani, *Aghani*, XXI, pp. 216–17; Mubarrad, *Kamil*, II, p. 182; Amidi, *al-Mu^ɔ^talif*, p. 68.
108. Baladhuri, *Ansab*, VII/2, Beirut, p. 143.
109. Isfahani, *al-Aghani*, XVII, p. 297.
110. Ibn ^c^Abd al-Barr, *al-Isti^c^ab*, I, p. 415, III, p. 102, IV, p. 196; Ibn Sa^c^d, *Tabaqat*, VII, p. 198.
111. Ibn Sa^c^d, *Tabaqat*, VI, p. 451; Sam^c^ani, *al-Ansab*, II, p. 16.
112. Caskel and Strenziok, *Gamharat*, II, pp. 43, 599. For an example of a later *nasab* work with Zahran and Daws well-stocked with Omanis, see Ibn Mubarrad, *Nasab ^c^Adnan wa Qahtan*, pp. 67–8, where the subgroups of Malik b. Fahm are downgraded to *arhaṭ*.
113. Ibn ^c^Abd al-Barr, *al-Isti^c^ab*, I, pp. 318–20; Sam^c^ani, *al-Ansab*, III, p. 200; Ibn ^c^Asakir, *Ta^ɔ^rikh*, XI, pp. 292–3.
114. Caskel and Strenziok, *Gamharat*, I, p. 217, Ibn Hazm, *Jamhara*, p. 385; Sam^c^ani, *al-Ansab*, III, p. 47. Caskel and Strenziok considered the Ghitrif the dominant lineage of the Zahran, and possibly of all Azd Sarat. Caskel and Strenziok, *Gamharat*, II, p. 44.
115. Caskel and Strenziok, *Gamharat*, I, p. 210, II, p. 292; ^c^Awtabi, *al-Ansab*, II, p. 663; Ibn Hazm, *Jamhara*, p. 386; Sam^c^ani, *al-Ansab*, III, p. 373.
116. Caskel and Strenziok, *Gamharat*, II, p. 43; ^c^Awtabi, *al-Ansab*, II, pp. 663–76; al-Isfahani, *al-Aghani*, XXI, pp. 179–95; Ibn Hazm, *Jamhara*, p. 386; Dabbi, *al-Mufaddaliyat*, I, pp. 194–207; Suzanne Pinckney Stetkevich, 'Archetype and Attribution in Early Arabic Poetry: al-Shanfara and the Lamiyyat al-^c^Arab', pp. 367–71; Alan Jones, *Early Arabic Poetry: Select Poems*, pp. 157–222.
117. Ibn Sa^c^d, *Tabaqat*, I, p. 160; Ibn ^c^Abd al-Barr, *al-Isti^c^ab*, I, p. 385.
118. Ibn Hazm, *Jamhara*, p. 380; Dinawari, *Kitab al-Nabat*, pp. 264, 266; Ibn Manzur, *Lisan*, V, p. 414; Sam^c^ani, *al-Ansab*, III, p. 417.
119. Baladhuri, *Ansab*, VII/2, Beirut, p. 141; Hisham b. Muhammad Ibn al-Kalbi, p. 471.

120. For Jabir b. ʿAbd Allah, known as the last Companion to die in Medina, see Ibn ʿAbd al-Barr, *Istiʿab*, I, pp. 292–3; Ibn Saʿd, *Tabaqat*, III, p. 292; Ibn Hajar, *Tahdhib al-Tahdhib*, I, pp. 42–3; For Abu al-Zubayr Muhammad b. Muslim b. Tadrus al-Asadi, see Kamaruddin Amin, 'Nasiruddin al-Albani on Muslim's Sahih: A Critical Study of His Method', pp. 164–5; F. Sezgin, *Geschichte*, I, pp. 86–7.
121. Samʿani, *al-Ansab*, II, p. 568, p. 141, IV; Wilkinson, *Water and Tribal Settlement*, p. 128; Wilkinson, *Ibadism*, pp. 26–8. An Abu Zubayr who died in 128 AH is mentioned in Dhababi, I, pp. 126–7.
122. Caskel and Strenziok, *Gamharat*, I, pp. 210, 214, 215; Isfahani, *al-Aghani*, XIII, p. 218.
123. Ibn Manzur, *Lisan*, V, p. 667.
124. ʿAwtabi, *al-Ansab*, II, pp. 823–31; Yaqut, *Buldan*, II, p. 313; Isfahani, *al-Aghani*, XIII, pp. 220–3. For Abu ʿAmr al-Shaybani, see Ibn ʿAbd al-Barr, *Istiʿab*, IV, p. 283; Samʿani, *al-Ansab*, III, p. 498.
125. Isfanani, *al-Aghani*, XIII, pp. 223–5.
126. This amends the printed text slightly to bring it closer to one of the manuscript variations mentioned in a note and in line with a settlement name from other sources.
127. Ibn ʿAsakir, *Taʾrikh*, XXV, pp. 9–10. According to the isnad, the tradition was reported by ʿAbd al-Rahman b. Mughraʾ Abu Zuhayr al-Dawsi to Abu Miskin, from whom Ibn al-Kalbi had it.
128. Sijistani, *Kitab al-muʿammarin min al-ʿarab*, p. 22; Mubarrad, *al-Fadl*, ed. ʿAbd al-ʿAziz al-Maymani, p. 12.
129. Isfahani, *al-Aghani*, XIII, pp. 219–20.
130. Isfahani, *al-Aghani*, I, pp. 396–8; Ibn Habib, *al-Muhabbar*, pp. 381–2; Baladhuri, *Ansab*, IV/1, pp. 497, 601; Tabari, *Taʾrīkh*, I, p. 3056; Tabari, *History*, XV, p. 254; Ibn Shabba, *Kitab Taʾrikh al-Madina al-Munawwara*, II, pp. 111–13. Ahmed, *Religious Elite*, pp. 115–31.
131. Ibn ʿAsakir, *Taʾrikh*, XI, pp. 317–18.
132. Ibn Saʿd, *Tabaqat*, I, p. 129.
133. Ibn al-Kalbi, *Kitab al-Asnam*, pp. 37–8; al-Azmeh notes *shara* is Arabic for the *Citrullus colocynthis*, *Emergence*, p. 212 n. 306. As Dhu Shara was highly popular with Nabataeans outside their homeland, it is probable they brought him to the region at some point in the past. Peter Alpass, *The Religious Life of Nabataea*, pp. 234–7.
134. Ibn Hisham, *Sira al-Nabawiya*, p. 257; Ibn Hisham, *Life*, p. 176. For a discussion of different types of sacred and reserved space in late pre-Islamic western Arabia, see Harry Munt, *The Holy City of Medina: Sacred Space in Early Islamic Arabia*, pp. 23–31.
135. Ibn Habib, *al-Muhabbar*, p. 316. See also Ibn al-Kalbi, *Kitab al-Asnam*, pp. 13–14.
136. Ibn al-Kalbi, *Kitab al-Asnam*, p. 37; Ibn Hisham, *Sira*, p. 257; Ibn Hisham, *Life*, p. 177.

137. Michael Lecker, 'Was Arabian Idol Worship Declining on the Eve of Islam?', pp. 22–3; Ibn al-Kalbi, *Kitab al-Asnam*, pp. 35–6.
138. Hawting, *Idea of Idolatry*, pp. 122–8.
139. Hawting, *Idea of Idolatry*, p. 123.
140. Ibn Hisham, *Sira*, pp. 275–9; Ibn Hisham, *Life of Muhammad*, pp. 187–90; Baladhuri, *Ansab*, I, pp. 135–6, *Ansab*, V, pp. 270, 580–1; Ibn Sallam al-Jumahi, *Tabaqat Fuhul al-Shu^{c}araʾ*, pp. 251–2; Ibn Habib, *al-Muhabbar*, p. 434.
141. A. J. Wensick, "*Mawla*", *EI*, VI, pp. 874–5; Crone, *Roman*, pp. 43–4. For studies of the term's change over time, see Crone, *Roman*, and Elizabeth Urban, 'The Early Islamic Mawali: A Window onto Processes of Identity Construction and Social Change'.
142. Baladhuri, *Ansab*, V, pp. 31, 45, 304.
143. Baladhuri, *Ansab*, IV/1, p. 6.
144. Baladhuri, *Ansab*, IV/1, pp. 39, 159.
145. Patricia Crone, *Meccan Trade and the Rise of Islam*, p. 123.
146. Ibn Hisham, *Sira*, pp. 255–7; Ibn Hisham, *Life*, pp. 175–7; Ibn Sa^{c}d, *Tabaqat*, IV, pp. 439–40; Ibn ^{c}Asakir, *Taʾrikh*, XXV, pp. 10–15. See also Baladhuri, *Ansab*, I, p. 382; Ibn al-Kalbi, *Asnam*, p. 37; Waqidi, *al-Maghazi*, pp. 870, 923; Waqidi, *Muhammad*, pp. 428, 452–3. Ibn Habib claims ^{c}Amr b. Humama destroyed Dhu al-Kaffayn himself in al-Muhabbar, pp. 318–19. On destroying deities as proof of loyalty to Islam, see Konstantin Klein, 'The Silence of the Gods: Some Observations on the Destruction of Pagan Temples, Shrines and Statues in the Late Antique East (from Constantine to Muhammad'), pp. 65–7.
147. Isfahani, *al-Aghani*, XIII, pp. 218–19; Ibn ^{c}Asakir, *Taʾrikh*, XXV, pp. 17–18.
148. Ibn Qutayba, *Fadl*, p. 180. For Muhammad b. Sirin al-Ansari, see Ibn Hajar, *Tahdhib*, IX, p. 336. His student Jarir b. Hazm will be discussed more fully in the next chapter.
149. Ibn Sa^{c}d, *Tabaqat*, IV, p. 488.
150. Ibn Sa^{c}d, *Tabaqat*, IV, p. 488; Ibn ^{c}Abd al-Barr, *Isti^{c}ab*, IV, p. 158; Yaqut, *Buldan*, II, pp. 339–40.
151. Ibn Sa^{c}d, *Tabaqat*, IV, p. 479.
152. Ibn ^{c}Abd al-Barr, *Isti^{c}ab*, I, p. 215.
153. Ibn ^{c}Abd al-Barr, *Isti^{c}ab*, II, pp. 233–4.
154. Ibn Sa^{c}d, *Tabaqat*, IV, pp. 479–83; Ibn ^{c}Abd al-Barr, *Isti^{c}ab*, IV, pp. 332–4; Waqidi, *al-Maghazi*, pp. 636, 683, 709, 733, 760–5, 801, 824, 936–41, 1006–7, 1038; Waqidi, *Muhammad*, pp. 313, 336, 349, 361, 374–7, 395, 406, 459–61, 493, 509; Ibn Shabba, *Taʾrikh al-Madina*, I, p. 119; Sam^{c}ani, *al-Ansab*, II, pp. 568–9; Dhahabi, *Tadhkira al-Huffaz*, I, pp. 32–7.
155. Waqidi, *al-Maghazi*, p. 1078; Waqidi, *Muhammad*, p. 528.
156. Ibn Sa^{c}d, *Tabaqat*, IV, pp. 484–5; Ibn ^{c}Abd al-Barr, *Isti^{c}ab*, IV, pp. 334–5; Tha^{c}alibi, *Curious*, pp. 45–6; Ibn Qutayba, *al-Ma^{c}arif*, pp. 277–8; Ibn

Shabba, *Ta'rikh al-Madina*, I, p. 156; Ibn Qutayba, *ᶜUyun al-Akhbar* I, pp. 53–4.

157. Baladhuri, *Ansab*, IV/1, p. 2.
158. Ibn Habib, *al-Muhabbar*, pp. 191, 411.
159. Baladhuri, *Ansab*, V, p. 215.
160. Ibn Habib, *al-Muhabbar*, p. 407.
161. Ibn Habib, *al-Muhabbar*, p. 407; Ibn Saᶜd, *Tabaqat*, IV, p. 488; Ibn Saᶜd, *Tabaqat*, V, p. 90.
162. Ella Landau-Tasseron, 'Status of Allies in Pre-Islamic and Early Islamic Arabian Society', pp. 8–11.
163. Baladhuri, *Ansab*, I, pp. 200–1; ᶜAwtabi, *al-Ansab*, II, p. 793; Ibn Saᶜd, *Tabaqat*, IV, pp. 377–8.
164. Elias Shoufani, *al-Riddah and the Muslim Conquest of Arabia*, p. 78.
165. Azraqi, *Ta'rikh Makkah*, pp. 647, 658.
166. ᶜAwtabi, *al-Ansab*, II, pp. 613, 799.
167. Ibn ᶜAbd al-Barr, *Istiᶜab*, IV, p. 30.
168. Baladhuri, *Ansab*, V, p. 169.
169. Ibn Saᶜd, *Tabaqat*, I, p. 131.
170. Ibn ᶜAbd al-Barr, *Istiᶜab*, I, p. 318. The only Junada al-Azdi in Ibn al-Kalbi is the Syrian military commander Junada b. Abi Umayya, who is probably too late to have plausibly received such a letter. Ibn al-Kalbi, *Maᶜadd wa al-Yaman*, p. 506.
171. Ibn Habib, *al-Muhabbar*, p. 452.
172. Ibn ᶜAbd al-Barr, *Istiᶜab*, II, p. 303; Ibn Saᶜd, *Tabaqat*, IV, p. 440.
173. Ibn Saᶜd, *Tabaqat*, I, p. 163; Ibn Hisham, *Sira*, pp. 1008–9; Ibn Hisham, *Life*, p. 642.
174. Baladhuri, *Futuh*, p. 59; See also Ibn Sulayman, *Tafsir*, II, p. 166.
175. Caskel and Strenziok, *Gamharat*, II, p. 266; I, p. 278; Ibn al-Kalbi, *Maᶜadd wa al-Yaman*, p. 545.
176. Ibn Hisham, *Sira*, p. 1009; Ibn Hisham, *Life*, p. 642.
177. Muhammad Ahmad Muᶜabbir, *Madina Jurash: min al-marakiz al-hadariya al-qadima*, pp. 18–20.
178. Hamdani, *Sifa*, pp. 117–19
179. Donner, *Early Islamic Conquests*, pp. 259–63; Timothy Power, *The Red Sea from Byzantium to the Caliphate: AD 500–1000*, pp. 89–92.
180. Al-Azmeh, *Emergence*, p. 120.
181. Donner, *Early Islamic Conquests*, pp. 28–37, who however sees the military and religious lineages as separate.
182. Ulrich, 'Azd Migrations', pp. 314–15.
183. Paul Yule, 'The Samad Period in the Sultanate of Oman', pp. 123–4.
184. Wilkinson, *Ibadism*, pp. 37–40; D. T. Potts, *The Arabian Gulf in Antiquity*, I, p. 399.
185. Wilkinson, *Ibadism*, p. 40; Isam al-Rawas, *Oman*, pp. 27–8; Michael Mouton and Jérémie Schiettecatte, *In the Desert Margins: The Settlement*

Process in Ancient South and East Arabia, pp. 98–9. Al-Rawas's dating of the migration to the second century, however, is inconsistent with his belief it followed Ardashir's reported defeat of an Omani king.

186. Wilkinson, *Ibadism*, p. 41; Wilkinson, *Water and Tribal Settlement*, pp. 244–5.
187. ʿAwtabi, *al-Ansab*, II, pp. 791–3.
188. Tabari, *Taʾrikh*, I, p. 3178; Tabari, *History*, XVI, p. 118; Baladhuri, *Ansab*, II, p. 216; Hamad Bin Seray, 'The Arabian Gulf in Syriac Sources', pp. 207–9.
189. Wilkinson, *Ibadism*, pp. 41–2; Wilkinson, *Water and Tribal Settlement*, pp. 244–5
190. ʿAwtabi, *al-Ansab*, II, pp. 732–8.
191. ʿAwtabi, *al-Ansab*, II, pp. 738–44; Wilkinson, *Ibadism*, p. 44; Wilkinson, *Water and Tribal Settlement*, pp. 244–5.
192. ʿAwtabi, *al-Ansab*, II, pp. 743–4. Wilkinson, *Ibadism*, p. 44
193. Daniel T. Potts, 'Jask', *Encyclopedia Iranica.*
194. Wilkinson, *Water and Tribal Settlement*, pp. 244–5.
195. ʿAwtabi, *al-Ansab*, II, pp. 775–8.
196. Samʿani, *al-Ansab*, I, p. 299.
197. Lughawi, *Kitab al-Maratib al-Nahwiyin*, p. 44; Talmon, *Arabic Grammar*, p. 5. There are reports that some Persians claimed the Farahid were descendants of Sasanian soldiers from the expedition to conquer Yemen, apparently an attempt to claim Persian ancestry for al-Khalil b. Ahmad. See Talmon, *Arabic Grammar*, pp. 6–13.
198. Wilkinson, *Ibadism*, p. 43; Wilkinson, *Water and Tribal Settlement*, pp. 244–5.
199. ʿAwtabi, *al-Ansab*, II, p. 782.
200. ʿAwtabi, *al-Ansab*, II, p. 794.
201. Wilkinson, *Ibadism*, p. 43; Wilkinson, *Water and Tribal Settlement*, pp. 244–5.
202. Hamdani, *Sifa*, p. 211.
203. ʿAwtabi, *al-Ansab*, II, pp. 621–2, 711–13; Wilkinson, *Ibadism*, pp. 46–7; Wilkinson, *Water and Tribal Settlement*, pp. 244–5; Ibn al-Kalbi, *Maʿadd wa al-Yaman*, pp. 566–71. Samʿani has ʿAtik as the son of Nasr b. al-Azd, *al-Ansab*, IV, p. 129.
204. Ibn al-Kalbi, *Maʿadd wa al-Yaman*, p. 470.
205. Baladhuri, *Ansab*, VI, pp. 604–6.
206. ʿAwtabi, *al-Ansab*, II, pp. 806–7. Wilkinson interprets the 'people of the waves' as Persian settlements along the coast, though they could just as easily have been settled Arabic speakers. J. C. Wilkinson, 'The Julanda of Oman', p. 97. Samʿani has ʿAbd and Jayfar as descended from Ziyad b. Shums rather than Maʿwala b. Shums, III, *al-Ansab*, pp. 235, 473.
207. Wilkinson, *Ibadism*, pp. 49–50.
208. Gunnar Olinder, *The Kings of Kinda of the Family of Akil al-murar*,

pp. 42, 47; Gunnar Olinder, 'Al al-Gaun of the Family of Akil al-murar', pp. 208–15, 228–9; Sidney Smith, 'Events in Arabia in the 6th Century A.D.', pp. 445–6; Wilkinson, *Ibadism*, pp. 13–14, 49–50.

209. Wilkinson, *Water and Tribal Settlement*, pp. 244–5.
210. Wilkinson, *Ibadism*, pp. 51, 55.
211. Wilkinson, 'Julanda', p. 99.
212. Jayfar's primacy is in Ibn Sa^cd, *Tabaqat*, I, p. 127 and, by implication, Bal^cami, *Tarikh-i Bal^camī*, p. 412. There is, however, no clear reason to claim the title was held by earlier members of the family.
213. ^cAwtabi, *al-Ansab*, II, pp. 762–3.
214. J. C. Wilkinson has most advocated a strong Sasanian presence, beginning in 'Arab-Persian Land Relationships in Late Sasanid Oman'. See also Wilkinson, *Water and Tribal Settlement*, pp. 130–3; *Ibadism*, pp. 55–63; Potts, *Arabian Gulf*, II, pp. 335–8. For critiques of Wilkinson's work, see Derek Kennet, 'The Decline of Eastern Arabia in the Sasanian Period'; Brian Ulrich, 'Oman and Bahrain in Late Antiquity: The Sasanians' Arabian Periphery'; Harry Munt, 'Oman and Late Sasanian Imperialism'.
215. Nasser Said al-Jahwari, Derek Kennet, Seth Priestman and Eberhard Sauer, 'Fulayj: A Late Sasanian Fort on the Arabian Coast', pp. 737–8. For other evidence of Sasanian maritime interests, see Beatrice de Cardi, 'A Sasanian Outpost in Northern Oman'; Derek Kennet, 'Kush: A Sasanian and Islamic-Period Archaeological Tell in Ras al-Khaimah (U.A.E.)'.
216. Baladhuri, *Futuh*, p. 76.
217. ^cAwtabi, *al-Ansab*, II p. 764. The Arabic cognate *daskara* indicates a central manor (*qaṣr*) with smaller houses surrounding it.
218. ^cAwtabi, *al-Ansab*, II pp. 763–6; Wilkinson, *Ibadism*, pp. 72–4.
219. Shoufani, *al-Riddah*, pp. 37, 87–9.
220. Wilkinson, *Ibadism*, pp. 79–84, which includes a fuller account of how the different narratives are reflected in a variety of sources.
221. Waqidi, *Kitab al-Ridda*, pp. 199–200; See also Ibn A^ctham al-Kufi, *Kitab al-Futuh*, I, pp. 73–5.
222. Tabari, *History*, X, pp. 152–5; Tabari, *Ta^ɔrīkh*, I, pp. 1977–80.
223. ^cAwtabi, *al-Ansab*, II, pp. 713–14, 799–801.
224. Implicit here is the idea that 'ridda' is a theme of Islamic historiography to which distinct accounts could be attached. Noth/Conrad, pp. 28–30.
225. Wilkinson, *Ibadism*, pp. 84–6.
226. Baladhuri, *Futuh*, p. 76.
227. Bal^cami, *Tarikh*, p. 412. For al-Bal^cami's use of sources other than al-Tabari in his 'translation', see A. C. S. Peacock, *Mediaeval Islamic Historiography and Political Legitimacy: Bal^cami's Tarikhnama*, pp. 90–105. In the case of al-Bal^cami, it would also be useful to know whether information appears only in certain manuscripts. On this issue, see Peacock, *Mediaeval Islamic Historiography*, pp. 52–66; Elton Daniel, 'Manuscripts and Editions of Bal^cami's Tarjamah-i Tarikh-i Tabari'.

228. Michael Bonner, 'Commerce and Migration in Arabia before Islam: A Brief History of a Long Literary Tradition'.
229. Michael Bonner, '"Time Has Come Full Circle": Markets, Fairs and the Calendar in Arabia before Islam', p. 29.
230. Ibn Habib, *al-Muhabbar*, pp. 265–6; Crone suggests Daba may have been the port mentioned by Procopius in his account of the Persian monopoly of the silk trade in Crone, *Meccan Trade*, p. 81. Suhar was, however, mentioned in a poem of the late sixth century in the sense of a place distant from the poem's action. Dabbi, *Mufaddaliyat*, I, p. 668.
231. Tabari, *History*, X, p. 154; Tabari, *Taʾrīkh*, I, p. 1979.
232. Shoufani, *al-Riddah*, p. 157.
233. That Suhar arose as a rival to Daba was also the interpretation of al-Afghani, *Aswaq*, p. 264.
234. Al-Azmeh, *Emergence*, p. 126.
235. Crone, *Roman*, p. 43.
236. Wilkinson, *Ibadism*, p. 87.
237. For *ridda* as a distinct historiographic theme, see Noth/Conrad, pp. 28–30; Donner, *Narratives*, pp. 200–2.
238. Aleida Assmann, 'The Dynamics of Cultural Memory between Remembering and Forgetting', p. 98.

2

The Azd and the Early Islamic State

The early development of the Islamic state is inextricably bound up with the conquests of its vast territories. Space does not permit a full discussion of the different approaches to either topic; however, a key issue has been to what degree the Islamic sources' image of centralisation in both the administrative and military domains holds true, and to what degree it is simply a topos.[1] One point, however, is that from the perspective of contemporary non-Muslim sources, the conquests did not begin in the aftermath of Muhammad's mission, and Arabians began violently encroaching on both Byzantine and Sasanian territory some decades before the 630s.[2] With this context, the perspective of the present work is that the conquests represented a broad, decentralised population movement out of Arabia, one which the developing Islamic polity in Medina gradually came to dominate to the point where the caliphs, presumably based upon the successes of their own armies, could install their own agents throughout the Arab-inhabited territories who could direct and administer their populations. The Islamic polity, in other words, did not only expand through the conquests, but also within them until the two became largely coterminous.[3] This chapter will analyse this process of expansion in different regions before examining how al-Azd fit into the rapidly shifting milieu as both agents and subjects.

Accounts in the Arabic sources written under the Abbasids portray the first caliphs, especially ᶜUmar, exchanging letters with agents throughout their domains, managing in detail everything from urban planning to military operation details. As Noth and Conrad have shown, however, these letters are simply a narrative device, with the exchanges often logistically impossible and filled with anachronisms. The topos's purpose is to demonstrate the authority of the caliphs over their realm as wise and far-sighted planners on whom all depended for their success. Many of these accounts are also tied to the establishment of legal principles, such as the distribution of spoils.[4] More broadly, al-Tabari in particular shaped his narrative around Sayf b. ᶜUmar, a key early source for this centralisation topos. Al-Tabari's dependence on a political conception which is anachronistic if not completely fanciful makes this period ideal grounds for Antoine Borrut's suggestion that historians make greater use of the sources 'en marge' of al-Tabari-related 'vulgate historiography.'[5]

Noth and Conrad also argue that the conquests themselves developed as a historiographic theme by combining narratives focused originally on individual local battles.[6] Donner disagrees, pointing out that based on what we know of the titles of books from the 700s, general conquest works preceded local ones. He furthermore argues that if local conquest accounts were compiled all over the Islamic empire prior to the production of the first written materials, there must have been a common impulse, which he found in the legitimisation needs of the early Islamic community.[7] However, if the conquests of areas immediately adjacent to Arabia took place over decades, then that suggests that Noth and Conrad were correct. In his own reconstruction of the development of conquest narratives, Donner posits that battle stories, which he compared to those of pre-Islamic Arabia, circulated to celebrate the deeds of individuals and specific tribes.[8] This continuation of the Arabian heritage suffices to explain the occurrence of conquest narratives throughout the territory of the caliphate, while the accounts must originally have been local since conquests occurred over a period of time and not always under the direction of central powers with a common ideological impulse.

The reliability of individual conquest accounts also poses problems. Donner suggests that people who witnessed the conquests could have survived until the Marwanid period, when we begin to have written sources.[9] However, a person whom an early historian could have interviewed in 700 would have to be around 75 years old to pass on first-hand accounts of the major conquests under ᶜUmar b. al-Khattab. That a few such people did so is possible, but it seems unlikely as an explanation for the sheer volume of conquest material we have. Furthermore, as discussed by Jan Vansina, it is not enough to witness an event and have at least a somewhat objective perspective on it; you must also have a perspective which allows you to understand what you are witnessing. The example he cites to illustrate this point is soldiers in battle, who see only a small part of a larger engagement through the confusion of combat and the haze of emotional involvement.[10] Under those conditions it is challenging for historians to use oral tradition to reconstruct battles and campaigns even shortly after the event, much less after the passage of decades or centuries, and we should expect the surviving accounts on this point to show significant confusion. The massive reinvention of tradition described by Conrad for Arwad is as good as we might expect from medieval historians trying to compile a comprehensive narrative of such an event even independent of such material's political and social uses.[11]

In Iraq, the Arabs who composed the conquering armies settled in Basra and Kufa, two of several cities called '*amṣār*' (sing. *miṣr*), often called in English 'garrison towns.' The verb *maṣṣara* meant to declare something a boundary, and 'boundary' was one meaning of *miṣr*, going with the plural *muṣūr*. According to the *Lisan al-ᶜArab*, the term for the cities came from the fact that they served as a boundary between the caliph ᶜUmar b. al-Khattab and the sea.[12] More probably, however, the term for the new conquest settlements came from an older Yemeni word for a military expeditionary force.[13] The original settlements were military camps for the conquest armies, which quickly grew into cities where Arab tribespeople were joined by kin from Arabia and those from the conquered population interested in the cities' economic opportunities.

For the tribes, two significant changes accompanied this move. One was a change in environment from a rural one where they lived in small settlements or pastoral communities to militarised urban administrative centres. The other was economic, as those who migrated to the garrison towns were enrolled on the *diwān*, or the tribal register through which the government allotted stipends. In fact, the growth of many urban centres in the Middle East was linked to this stipend system, as throughout the caliphal period, the military received its pay as minted coins rather than in land grants.[14] Some historians have additionally posited that the Arab tribal system was completely reinvented or even destroyed in these garrison towns during the Sufyanid period, as Umayyad governors created new units for military and administrative purposes, a position which we will critique below.

Syria

The Islamic conquest of Syria was primarily carried out by tribes from southern Arabia.[15] Donner has identified two major sets of traditions regarding the campaigns. One collection of accounts was passed through Ibn Ishaq, al-Waqidi and Saᶜid b. ᶜAbd al-ᶜAziz al-Tanukhi, and forms the basis for al-Yaᶜqubi's work.[16] It includes a claim through al-Tanukhi going back to Syrian authorities that the Azd represented one-third of the Muslim force at the Battle of Yarmuk. The other major set of traditions, that of Sayf b. ᶜUmar, does not address the tribal composition of forces, perhaps because of Sayf's bias toward northerners.[17] Donner also includes appendices listing individuals named in the sources he consulted as participating in specific engagements. Among al-Azd, we find mostly Daws.

Jundab b. ᶜAmr b. Humama al-Dawsi, son of the Daws tribal leader discussed in the previous chapter, died during the campaign.[18] Also listed as dying in the conquests are a son and grandson of al-Tufayl b. ᶜAmr Dhu al-Nur, the lead convert among the Daws who was himself also reported as dying at Yarmuk, al-Yamama, or Ajnadayn. The Companion Abu Hurayra al-Dawsi is also mentioned as a participant at the pivotal Battle of Yarmuk. The only non-Daws among the Azd in Syria is Habbar b. Sufyan al-Azdi, reported as dying at Ajnadayn.[19]

To this we can add material from Abu Ismaᶜil al-Azdi's *Futuh al-Sham*, which Donner referenced only for the Battle of Ajnadayn. At the time Donner wrote, Western scholars considered this work a late forgery. Since then, however, it has been rehabilitated as a text of the early ninth century, a text which drew heavily on material circulating in Kufa, especially as transmitted by Abu Mikhnaf al-Azdi of the Ghamid (d. 774).[20] In this work, al-Harith b. ᶜAbd Allah al-Azdi al-Namiri is presented as the firsthand source of several accounts of the Battle of Yarmuk, which he seems to have handed down to Sufyan b. Sulaym al-Azdi.[21] Al-Harith b. ᶜAbd Allah identified himself as a confidante (*ṣadīq*) of the general Khalid b. al-Walid.[22] This Sufyan b. Sulaym also transmitted from other Azdis, including Sufyan b. ᶜAwf al-Ghamidi, who purportedly bore a message from the commander Abu ᶜUbayda b. Jarrah in Hims to the caliph ᶜUmar in Medina.[23] Rashid b. ᶜAbd al-Rahman al-Azdi is also presented as a firsthand Yarmuk source; his transmitter was al-Muhajir b. Sayfi al-ᶜUdhri.[24] One al-Aᶜla b. Suraqa al-Azdi is mentioned as a companion of Abu Hurayra, who was mentioned above.[25]

Of the Azd, the *Futuh al-Sham* most frequently mentions ᶜAbd Allah b. Qurt al-Thumali. He is portrayed as serving frequently as a messenger and participated in several campaigns for which he is cited as a source by Sufyan b. Sulaym.[26] He was also appointed governor of Hims, either by Abu ᶜUbayda b. Jarrah or by ᶜUmar, though he may have been later relieved of that post by one or the other.[27] Ibn ᶜAsakir, however, has him as Hims's governor under Muᶜawiya and says that his house in the city was still known. According to Ibn ᶜAsakir and Ibn ᶜAbd al-Barr, the prophet had changed his name to ᶜAbd Allah, and he transmitted a few hadith. He was killed while fighting the Byzantines at a place along the coast called Burj Ibn Qurt.[28]

Tarif Khalidi believes, based on references to al-Azdi's *Futuh al-Sham* and Ibn ᶜAsakir's *Tahdhib al-Taʾrikh al-Kabir*, that the Azd were the largest single group to enter Syria in the wake of the Battle of Yarmuk, and that they may have come with the Khathᶜam. They were also favoured in Syria by the Sufyanids.[29] Fuad Jabali's prosopographical work found that around 10 per cent of the Companions of the Prophet active in Syria were al-Azd, a sample of forty-five individuals. Of those with more specific geographic information, over half lived in Hims (thirteen individuals). The largest single subgroup was the B. Thumala, which had six settlers in Hims.[30] This number may be associated with ᶜAbd Allah b. Qurt, in which case it would be part of a pattern of incoming Arabs settling in areas where they could make kinship claims upon prominent leaders while also serving as a potential base for that leader's support, a classic form of assets and options at work.

The general conclusion suggested by the above is that early al-Azd immigration to Syria came from the western tribes. We still see this pattern in the early Umayyad period, when Sufyan b. ᶜAwf al-Ghamidi was in command of several anti-Byzantine campaigns under Muᶜawiya.[31] Apart from those belonging to Daws and Sufyan b. ᶜAwf, however, the mentioned individuals do not figure into the Arabic genealogical literature. This stands out in the case of the prominent ᶜAbd Allah b. Qurt, and may have its origins in the Thumala's small role in both the life of Muhammad and early Islamic Iraq, where that literature took shape. Beyond this, however, there is little information on which to reconstruct the history of Syria's al-Azd. We are in significantly better shape for the garrison towns of southern Iraq, however, to which we now turn.

Founding the Garrison Towns

Basra developed near the site of al-Ubulla, a pre-Islamic port at the head of the Persian Gulf.[32] The site was significant because of the proximity of the *mirbad*, a pre-Islamic market.[33] The city grew up immediately east of this landmark, which in later times became an important site of both cultural and economic exchange between Basra and those Arabs who remained desert nomads in the area.[34] Abbasid-period Arabic scholars attempted to derive the name 'Basra' from aspects of the area's geology, though the tenth-century proponent of the Persian heritage Hamza al-Isfahani claimed that it was from the Persian 'Bas Rah' referring to its status as a crossroads.[35] The name may also be derived from the Aramaic for 'place of huts'.[36] According to ps.-al-ᶜAwtabi, the future Basra had a single village named al-Khurayba,[37] and became the site where many Arabs preferred to alight during campaigns against the Persians, with pitched pavilion tents and leather domes where the tribal elite would receive visitors.[38] According to al-Baladhuri, ᶜUmar b. al-Khattab appointed ᶜUtba b. Ghazwan as governor of Basra, and the latter settled at al-Khurayba. Upon his arrival, he found that many Muslims were wintering there and when not raiding, built houses from reeds. ᶜUtba himself built an administrative centre and a mosque in 14 (635).[39]

According to al-Baladhuri's *Futuh al-Buldan*, during the time of ᶜUmar b. al-Khattab, three *dastajirds* (Ar. *daskara*, pl. *dasākir*) were located in the al-Azd area of Basra, while two each were in al-Khurayba and a place called al-Zabuqa.[40] Two other accounts place the number of *dastajirds* at two in al-Azd, two in Tamim, one in al-Khurayba and two in al-Zabuqa.[41] Although known by a Persian term, the Arabic sources report that these were not abandoned Persian fortifications as often claimed, but instead were built of unfired bricks by Arabs.[42] Massignon identified the al-Azd *dastajirds* with the B. ᶜAdi and the B. Huddan; however, the B. ᶜAdi in Basra were probably not al-Azd.[43] One possibility is that there were al-Azd in the area linked to the Lakhmids, which would mean that all three or four regions with the *dastajirds* are given a pre-Islamic designation.[44]

Later, ᶜUmar b. al-Khattab assigned Abu Musa al-Ashᶜari to organise the site of Basra, with a special district for each tribe in which they could build dwellings. Abu Musa also built the brick congregational mosque in the centre.[45] The alleys between each district were initially meant for separation rather than circulation.[46] The Khuzistan Chronicle, a Syriac source from the third quarter of the seventh century, also remembers Abu Musa as the founder of Basra.[47] Although that source is at least a generation after the events in question, the witness remains striking regarding who left the early impression as the city's founder.[48] The total picture has verisimilitude with our knowledge of pre-Islamic Arabia and Hoyland's over-arching view of the first conquests. Temporary encampment at markets where elites would hold court was a common feature of Arabian life. Hoyland describes increasing Bedouin pressure on the Sasanians during the early 600s, especially when central authority collapsed with their defeat in the war against the Byzantines.[49] Settlement at Basra by Arabians raiding the Sasanians thus predates conquests by commanders owing allegiance to the Islamic state, of whom ᶜUtba b. Ghazwan was probably the first. It was Abu Musa, however, who established a permanent garrison town as that state's outpost at the head of the Persian Gulf.

Historiographic confusion comes from accounts which imply that ᶜUtba b. Ghazwan brought the first settlers as part of an army under a plan carefully directed by ᶜUmar b. al-Khattab, an example of the anachronistic central planning highlighted by Noth and Conrad.[50] Sayf b. ᶜUmar says that the caliph ordered ᶜUtba b. Ghazwan to camp at the edge of the desert and the sown so as to block Sasanian supply routes to the crucial urban centre al-Madaᵓin. Once in the region, the Muslims moved several times before settling in the desert, in a city planned by Abu al-Jarbaʾ ᶜAsim b. al-Dulaf of the B. Ghaylan b. Malik b. ᶜAmr b. Tamim. ᶜUtba had a canal dug to water the site from the Tigris.[51] In al-Dinawari, the name of the urban planner is Nafiᶜa b. al-Harith al-Thaqafi.[52] Al-Madaʾini (d. c. 840) has a similar account, which he links to the conquest of al-Ubulla.[53] Other accounts give ᶜUmar a role in selecting the exact site through an insistence on not having a river between himself and the Muslim armies.[54] Several sources have ᶜUmar in his letter to ᶜUtba calling al-Ubulla the 'land of India' (*'arḍ al-Hind'*); elsewhere he is presented as calling it 'the opening of India' (*'farj al-Hind'*).[55] This is certainly anachronistic, as from ᶜUmar's perspective, the primary ports for Indian goods would have been those in southern Arabia, such as Daba. According to al-Dinawari, when ᶜUtba arrived at the site of Basra, there were ruined dwellings and a Sasanian defensive garrison.[56]

In attempting to explain the confusion of the Arabic accounts, Charles Pellat suggests that ᶜUtba initially founded only a military camp for raids, but that ᶜUmar later ordered him to start a permanent settlement.[57] It is probable, however, that this confusion was caused by both centralising and standardising impulses in the historiography. In addition to making ᶜUmar a micro-manager, Arabic traditions were influenced by the development in Kufa, where there is a much stronger case that it was an organised military encampment from the beginning. The extant sources are unanimous that Saᶜd b. Abi Waqqas founded it in the aftermath of the Battle of al-Qadisiyya, a significant victory for the Islamic state over the Sasanians which saw the former begin to assume administration and tax collection in the central Euphrates valley.[58]

Kufa was founded where the route from central Mesopotamia to Yemen meets the Euphrates River.[59] According to Sayf b. ᶜUmar, the caliph ᶜUmar ordered the army of Saᶜd b. Abi Waqqas to move away from al-Madaʾin and the Tigris so as to maintain their health and stamina, and the site of Kufa was selected for a new settlement. At the time, the site had three monasteries and a number of scattered reed huts. According to Sayf's account, the Muslims themselves first built of reeds, but changed to bricks after a fire, a change for which they sought ᶜUmar's permission. Abu al-Hayyaj b. Malik laid out the plan for Kufa just as Abu al-Jarbaʾ had for Basra, assigning a parcel of land for each tribe. The Azd were on the south side of town across a street from the Kinda. Newcomers would come first to a *munākh* (halting spot), and remain there until Abu al-Hayyaj found a place for them. Saᶜd built a mosque, treasury and citadel.[60] Other accounts contradict Sayf on some details. Only he mentions town planners. Abu ᶜUbayda and Ibn al-Kalbi both say that the tribal quarters were determined by shooting arrows and having the tribes settle where their arrows landed. Along with al-Waqidi, however, they recount ᶜUmar's correspondence with Saᶜd much as Sayf does.[61] Al-Yaᶜqubi gives ᶜUmar an even larger role, assigning specific land grants to prominent Companions in and around the city. However, he also has tribes arrive independently and find their own place, including al-Azd, who settled between Kinda and Bajila. Al-Yaᶜqubi's account stands out also for its emphasis on tribal leaders, who may have been the commanders in Saᶜd's army.[62]

The differences between the foundations of Basra and Kufa reflect the differences between the impact of the rise of the Islamic state on eastern and western Arabia discussed in the previous chapter. Kufa was founded by tribes from western Arabia where the caliphate exercised more centralised control under the elite from Mecca and Medina. In the east, the caliphate's presence was small and depended more on the authority of local leaders whose own power was enhanced by co-option. Just as the Omani conflicts passed on historically under the theme of *ridda* reflected the interests of the al-Julanda family more than an agenda imposed from the Hijaz, so was Basra an outgrowth of existing tribal movements within which the caliphate gradually asserted control. In order to understand the Azd in Basra, we must therefore understand the ways in which the early Islamic state began asserting control, the connections of the Azd to that state, and the pattern of their immigration into Basra.[63]

Tribal Confederations

Sayf's account of Kufa is the basis for understanding one key development in the history of the garrison towns: their division into administrative units. According to Sayf b. ᶜUmar, the army at the Battle of al-Qadisiyya was divided into 'tenths', and these 'tenths' were an important element of Kufa's population settled near the town's main gathering area.[64] These grew unevenly, however, and so with ᶜUmar's permission, Saᶜd consulted genealogists and redivided them into 'sevenths'. Al-Azd formed part of a contingent with Bajila, Khathᶜam, Kinda and Hadramawt.[65] Similarly, in Basra, Ziyad b. Abihi is credited with dividing the city's Arabs into 'fifths', with the divisions bearing the names Tamim, Bakr b. Waʾil, ᶜAbd al-Qays, al-Azd and Ahl al-ᶜAliya.[66]

Crone sees the Sufyanid tribal confederations such as al-Azd and Tamim as creations of the caliphal government when they created these units. As she describes, 'The quarter or fifth was in the nature of a large semi-artificial tribe, a *qawm* or *qabīla* which could serve for the organization of army and city alike . . . with the quarters and fifths, the Arabs had got their tens, hundreds, and thousands.'[67] Hawting describes the process of settlement in the garrison towns as 'both a reconstruction and intensification of the tribal system of pre-Islamic Arabia, and a reformulation of the genealogical links which were its mythological justification.'[68] Khalid Blankinship takes an even stronger line, saying they were 'indisputably creations of the government', composed of clans which had lived in geographic proximity in the Arabian Peninsula.[69]

This idea, however, needs spelling out and perhaps adjusting. The tribal units which came to define Umayyad Basra were known prior to Islam. The previous chapter argued for a pre-Islamic al-Azd identity going back to ancient tribal kingdoms attested in ESA inscriptions. The Bakr b. Waʾil appear in sixth-century Christian sources and inscriptions, and were affiliated with the Kingdom of Kinda and later the Lakhmids.[70] The Tamim were also linked to the Lakhmids, whom they served as intermediaries in controlling other tribes and protecting caravans.[71] There does seem to be uncertainty about the ᶜAbd al-Qays, who were ruled directly by the Sasanians and inhabited the oases in eastern Arabia. The fact their genealogies have an unusually large number of gaps and inconsistencies could mean this group was a late creation out of a mixed population along the eastern shore of the Gulf, and in Kufa they were sometimes called the *Ahl al-Hajar*.[72] However, 'Abucaei' was the name of a tribe in Ptolemy's geography.[73]

Furthermore, evidence suggests the military divisions in the garrison towns were not originally meant to reorganise the tribal structure. As Michael Morony has demonstrated, no stage of the divisions in Kufa corresponded to the pattern of tribal settlement.[74] The Azd, for example, were grouped militarily with their neighbours the Kinda, as well as with the Bajila from the north side of the city.[75] Furthermore, even though al-Azd did not appear separately in the final Kufan divisions, it continued to serve as a primary *nisba* for eighth-century figures such as the historian Abu Mikhnaf. Similar evidence appears in Basra, where despite the existence of the al-Azd division, there is at least one report of al-Azd in the Ahl al-ᶜAliya.[76] Also significant is that the tribal divisions clearly grew in an unequal manner, suggesting that associations were formed by the consent of tribal authorities rather than entirely through government assignment.

One more critical reason to find in these confederations a strong, lasting imprint of peninsular origins is the way differences between them sometimes took on clearly ethnic aspects, as would be predicted by Webb's work. We see this othering in the Tamim poet al-Farazdaq's satires from the end of the seventh century, which attack al-Azd as non-Arab (*ᶜarab*).[77]

In one poem, al-Farazdaq declares that the Azd have lips and noses which are Nabataean rather than Arab. The mockery also attacks al-Azd for not being nomadic in ways that suggest there were attempts to relate Bedouinness to Arabness earlier than Webb allows. The Azd are attacked for being more familiar with ships than horses, for not knowing their genealogies, and not having lounged in large Bedouin goat-hair tents or lit campfires after wandering. Al-Farazdaq seems to see his people as Mudar, a unit that included Tamim and several other related tribes, and this is not simply as a military faction based on residence in Basra.[78]

Although in some times and places governments have created tribal systems to serve their own ends, there is no reason to draw from this universal conclusions about how tribes and states behave in relation to each other.[79] In the words of William and Fidelity Lancaster, 'Although the evidence (for such creation) seems convincing for Iran, it is not so for what is now the Arab Middle East, where language, ethnicity, and political structures did not define territorial entities, but which had a strong cultural continuity established and maintained by strong tribal links between regions.'[80] As Saleh Said Agha and Tarif Khalidi argue, the Umayyads probably influenced the top of the tribal structure, but at lower levels it may in fact have become even more malleable than in pre-Islamic times.[81] The fact the Kufan divisions were almost always given joint tribal names suggests that the government did not supersede all earlier identities, and that Basra had a simpler pattern of tribal settlement which allowed four of the five groupings to be named after just one tribe.

Developments during the Sufyanid period could be described as the consistent activation of a particular level of identity to suit conditions in the garrison towns, coupled with a government decision to keep the fighters with others from the same tribe which were then arranged according to military administrative need. As argued in the last chapter, in the Arabian Peninsula, the higher levels of tribal nomenclature were seldom if ever functional corporate bodies, instead solely serving as markers of identity linked to a distant past. The pre-Islamic Arabian tribal system allowed for this possibility through the *ḥilf* system, which involved forming what Landau-Tasseron has called 'hosting alliances' allowing newcomers access to residential quarters.[82] The organisation of the garrison towns made finding a patron to provide accommodation mandatory.[83] Alliances for protection also played a role, as Sufyanid agents in Iraq held all clans responsible for the behaviour of their members, and deducted blood money from the payments due the group from the central treasury.[84] The use of the communal lands is also interesting. According to Sayf b. ᶜUmar, the tribesmen did not wish to settle these lands directly, and instead appointed an administrator to manage them and distribute the proceeds.[85] An implication is that this crucial administrative position was filled through tribal rather than government decisions.

This is not to say, however, that the tribes thus constituted represented pre-Islamic alliances, as many smaller tribes were undoubtedly attached to larger ones. For example, the B. ᶜAmm were counted as Tamim and converted to Islam only after settling among the Tamim in Basra under ᶜUmar b. al-Khattab. The fact the B. ᶜAmm were attacked for being inauthentically Tamim indicates that other groups not so attacked could claim to have a deeper historical relationship with that grouping.[86] The B. ᶜAmm were most likely Persian speakers from Ahwaz, and their name came from the fact they fought with the Tamim as cousins. Several sources also claim that they were originally al-Azd.[87] We find some cases where an individual would be known by both an ancestral *nisba* and the name of the tribe among whom he lived in the garrison towns, such as the little-known Companion ᶜAbd Allah b. Khalid b. Salama al-Makhzumi, who in later sources was also called al-Rasibi for his Basran settlement.[88]

Evidence of *nisba* changes becomes much clearer during the Marwanid period. The eighth-century traditionist al-Qasim b. al-Fadl al-Huddani was by descent one of the B. Luhayy, but took his *nisba* from living among the Huddan in Basra.[89] A Kharijite leader named ᶜImran b. Hittan al-Shaybani reportedly shifted his tribal identity with his residence when he took shelter in Basra after the collapse of a Kharijite emirate in north-eastern Arabia during the days of the caliph ᶜAbd al-Malik.[90] Following the Second Civil War, the Marwanids increased the extent and precision of administrative control in their realm. Research using papyri shows that in Egypt, they improved property registration, rationalised administrative structures, and introduced new practices to register and monitor individuals.[91] This also involved new policies towards the tribespeople of the garrison towns whom they had defeated. This was a reason for new transfers to battle fronts, as well as the founding of the new city of Wasit, the base for a force of Umayyad loyalists from Syria.[92] A state policy of tying tribal identity more firmly to the fifths would fit this pattern of tighter control. Sayf b. ᶜUmar also describes what may be a Marwanid development when he described the Arabs of the garrison towns as divided into *ᶜirāfas*, each of which was collectively entitled to 100,000 dirhams. In Kufa, this money was given to the heads of each 'seventh', who in turn passed it on to a designated official for distribution.[93] The distribution officials were not drawn from the *ashrāf* class, and may have been a check on their power.[94] They may have actually been a replacement power structure, as the heads of the tribal divisions begin to disappear from the record. The process by which tribe became associated with residency led ultimately to the tribal names simply representing neighbourhoods of Basra where the tribes in question initially settled. This process is clear in al-Samᶜani, who says, for example, of the name 'al-Qasmali' that it was a tribe of al-Azd and that a *khaṭṭ* and *maḥalla* of Basra acquired their name as a result of their settlement there. He indicates a similar process for the nisbas al-Jahdami and al-Tahi.[95]

The Azd in Basra

There is contradictory information about the al-Azd arrival in Basra. An account from Abu ᶜUbayda (d. 824), which he takes from his teacher Yunus b. Habib al-Jarmi (d. 804)[96] and two Tamim transmitters, has been the most influential, and many have taken it to indicate definitively when the Azd ᶜUman first came to the city.[97] According to this report, many al-Azd moved into Basra near the end of Muᶜawiya's reign. Some among the Tamim wished to ally with them, but their leader al-Ahnaf b. Qays advised against it saying that if they did, they would become servants to the Azd. Then, when Bakr b. Waᵓil made such an alliance and Masᶜud b. ᶜAmr of al-Azd was its ultimate head instead of the Bakri leader Malik b. Mismaᶜ, al-Ahnaf b. Qays was able to say, 'I told you so.'[98] In what might be taken as an elaboration of this account, Abu ᶜUbayda also reports that when Malik b. Mismaᶜ and Ashyam b. Shaqiq b. Thawr were disputing the leadership of the Bakr b. Waᵓil, with the latter supported by the caliph Yazid, Malik and his followers made an alliance with al-Azd which eventually prevailed.[99]

Some scholars have questioned Abu ᶜUbayda's account, pointing out that there is plenty of mention of al-Azd in Basra during the period of the rightly guided caliphs.[100] Much of the historiographic context for the account is the tribal conflict which surrounded the death of Masᶜud b. ᶜAmr, which we will deal with extensively below. However, considering that in that feud the alliance between al-Azd and Bakr b. Waᵓil was to win a significant victory over the Tamim, and also that al-Ahnaf b. Qays was the great early Islamic hero of the Tamim and noted for his wise leadership, one must suspect that this story with its Tamim sources serves largely to massage al-Ahnaf's reputation. The import in this context is that even though they were defeated in the realm of conflict within Basra under his leadership, the Tamim did win a victory in terms of honour by retaining their independence.[101]

Beyond that, the passage poses linguistic problems which require a solution prior to any historical or literary analysis. The Leiden text says, after stating that the Mudar outnumbered Rabi^ca in Basra and that the Azd were the last to settle there, '*kānū haythu muṣṣirat al-Baṣra fa-ḥawwala ^cUmar b. al-Khaṭṭāb min tanūkh min al-muslimīn ilā-l-Baṣra wa aqamat jam^cat al-Azd lam yataḥawwalū.*' Hawting, in his role as a translator, sticks close to this text to produce, 'they were where the garrison town of al-Basrah was founded and ^cUmar b. al-Khattab moved into it those Muslims who adopted a fixed abode, while the group of the Azd remained where they were and did not move.'[102] This takes the reference to Tanukh as the verb complex '*man tanakha*'. In contrast, Martin Hinds proposes instead, 'once it (Basra) had been established'.[103] That would be an unusual reading of '*haythu*', though we could propose '*hin*' instead. More significantly, he argues for '*man bi-tawwaj*' in place of the '*in tanūkh*', noting similarities with accounts regarding the transfer of Arabs from Tawwaj, a settlement on the Bushehr Peninsula, to Basra.[104] This also, however, changes the import of the account in al-Tabari, which does not refer to the arrival of all the Azd in Basra, but instead only those from Tawwaj.

An alternate version of the Azd's arrival in Basra follows their participation in the earliest Islamic conquests of Fars.[105] As reconstructed by Hinds, the first substantial campaign in the area was led by ^cUthman b. Abi al-^cAs al-Thaqafi, who served as governor of Oman under ^cUmar; his brother al-Hakam b. Abi al-^cAs governed eastern Arabia (*Baḥrayn*). The full details of the campaign need not concern us, though it was limited mainly to the coastal plain and could not take the major cities inland. It was, however, carried by forces recruited locally, with Oman and its al-Azd serving as the biggest reserve of manpower. According to ps.-al-^cAwtabi, there were three main al-Azd divisions: Sabra b. Shayman al-Huddani commanded the Azd Shanu^ɔa; Yazid b. Ja^cfar al-Jahdami the Azd ^cUman; and Abu Sufra al-^cAtaki commanded the ^cImran or Azd Bahrayn.[106] Wilkinson, however, suggests credibly that the actual ^cImran leader was ^cAmr b. al-Ashraf al-^cAtaki, who would later appear as one of the al-Azd leaders in Basra along with Sabra.[107]

Abu Mikhnaf reports that in 19 (640) ^cUthman b. Abi al-^cAs conquered Tawwaj, built mosques there, and made of it a '*dār li-l-muslimīn*', mentioning the ^cAbd al-Qays in particular as its inhabitants. The ^cAbd al-Qays inhabitants are confirmed by al-Baladhuri's other sources, though these name al-Hakam as the founder. Hinds prefers al-Hakam as Tawwaj's founder, while also noting the likelihood that many al-Azd were also at Tawwaj, as indicated in other sources. After the defeat of the *marzubān* Shahrak, when ^cUthman b. Abi al-^cAs arrived if he was not already there, Tawwaj became an official garrison town.[108] ^cUthman led seasonal campaigns against the Sasanians from Tawwaj for a number of years, into the reign of ᶜUthman b. ᶜAffan. Hinds believes the settlement was entirely al-Azd at this stage, though the question of its tribal composition may be anachronistic.

Tawwaj was located amidst palm groves on the Bushehr Peninsula along the Shirin River north of Borazjan near the Sasanian port of Rishahr.[109] Archaeologically it has yielded only early Islamic artefacts and not Sasanian. Carter et al. believe it was not occupied until the eighth century and that it effectively replaced the Sasanian sites of Rishahr and Deh Qa'ed.[110] The only other settlements known on the peninsula during the late Sasanian and early Islamic periods are in the foothills at the eastern edge of the Angali plain south of Borazjan.[111] Based on this material record, we can question whether there was anything to actually conquer at the site, as there is a separate battle reported for Rishahr. In addition, one would ideally not use Tawwaj as a base for conquests on the mainland since the travel across the isthmus connecting the peninsula to the mainland is difficult; as Carter et al. point out, it was functionally an island.[112] We most likely have a development similar to that of Basra, where a partially nomadic population which engaged in occasional raids in the area came under the control of a governor sent by the Islamic state. The raiding and the governor were then later fused together in an account fitting the theme of conquest, with the inhabitants even seeking to enhance the status of their city by claiming garrison-town status.

Ps.-al-ᶜAwtabi is the main source for the movement of population from Tawwaj to Basra. According to him, the first al-Azd came to Basra at the time it was founded, 'claiming that the people of Basra had envied them "*manzilatahum*".'[113] Hinds translates the last word as 'their standing', but it might also refer to places of nomadic alighting.[114] Ps.-al-ᶜAwtabi says further there were 18 original Omanis in Basra, among them Kaᶜb b. Sur al-Laqiti, who went as part of a delegation to ᶜUmar from Tawwaj and was subsequently appointed the city's qadi, and his scribe Masᶜud b. ᶜAmr, the future al-Azd leader. During the caliphate of ᶜUthman, there followed, also from Tawwaj, commanders from the army of ᶜUthman b. Abi al-ᶜAs.[115]

Al-Madaᵓini says outright that al-Azd and Dabba were the bulk of ᶜAᵓisha's supporters at the Battle of the Camel, and this is definitely the impression we get from studying the names from battle accounts and the reported course of events.[116] According to Ibn Khayyat, ᶜAᵓisha and her companions Talha and al-Zubayr stayed among the Tahiya after their agreement with ᶜAli's governor, ᶜUthman b. Hunayf, but before they broke it and seized control of the city.[117] Sayf b. ᶜUmar located the Battle of the Camel in the territory of the Azd of Basra, with ᶜA'isha sheltering in the mosque of the B. Huddan.[118] Poets often noted the Azd as ᶜA'isha's defenders.[119] Ibn Khayyat reports that al-Azd casualties included thirty fighters of the B. Jahdam, as well as Kaᶜb b. Sur, ᶜAmr b. al-Ashraf and a son of Sabra b. Shayman.[120] Al-Yaᶜqubi puts the number of al-Azd killed at 1,700.[121] For Sayf b. ᶜUmar, the number is 2,000 out of a total of 10,000 killed.[122] Jarir b. Hazm's number is 1,350 al-Azd out of 2,500 killed supporting ᶜA'isha, while Ibn Aᶜtham al-Kufi puts Azd casualties at 4,000 out of about 7,000.[123] According to Sayf b. ᶜUmar, Masᶜud b. ᶜAmr and Ziyad b. ᶜAmr were leaders of al-Azd along with Sabra b. Shayman at the Battle of the Camel.[124]

The Azd most likely sided with ᶜA'isha because of their ties with the Umayyads through ᶜUthman b. Abi al-As al-Thaqafi. As noted above, the Azd of Basra were dominated by the tribal levies he had commanded from Tawwaj. One of his lieutenants, Sabra b. Shayman, appears in almost all sources as the leader of the city's al-Azd. According to Abu Mikhnaf, ᶜAmr b. al-Ashraf carried the tribal banner and was one of those who died defending ᶜA'isha's camel.[125] Hossein Rashid has demonstrated close ties between the Umayyads and the B. Thaqif, including during the First Civil War.[126] ᶜUthman b. Abi al-ᶜAs in particular had an Umayyad mother, Safiyya bt. Umayya b. ᶜAbd Shams, and an Umayyad wife, Rayhana bt. Abi al-ᶜAs b. Umayya.[127] After he was replaced as general in the Fars campaign, the caliph ᶜUthman awarded him a grant of land near Basra, where his son founded what was reputedly the city's first *ḥammām*, near what would one day be a garden.[128]

ᶜAli appointed as governor in Basra his cousin ᶜAbd Allah b. al-ᶜAbbas, ancestor of the future Abbasid caliphs. At one point, however, the two had a falling out. As a protest, Ibn al-ᶜAbbas left Basra for Mecca.[129] He took with him six million dirhams in sacks, leading people from all Basra's fifths to come after him intent on taking the wealth. In Abu ᶜUbayda's account, Sabra b. Shayman was the first to propose letting him keep the money, as the Qays threatened to fight on Ibn ᶜAbbas's behalf, and Sabra argued that future Qays support in the cause of Islam would be worth more than money.[130] Ibn ᶜAbbas later reconciled with ᶜAli and resumed the Basra governorship.[131] He was, however, not in the city when Muᶜawiya sent a man named Ibn al-Haḍrami to preach the Umayyad cause there. As Ibn al-Hadrami's influence increased, Ziyad b. Abihi, whom Ibn ᶜAbbas had left as his deputy, sought sanctuary (*jiwār*) for himself and the treasury from Sabra b. Shayman. Sabra granted his request, perhaps because Ibn al-Hadrami had declined al-Azd hospitality for that of the Tamim, despite the loyalty of the Azd in the Battle of the

Camel. Madelung suggests this raised the specter that Muᶜawiya would favour the Tamim, part of his own Mudar group, as caliph. Independent of his adoption by Muᶜawiya, Ziyad was a Thaqafi from al-Taᵓif, but it is unclear whether the Azd would have had a sense of alliance with that entire tribe independent of their connections to the Umayyads. Ziyad also moved the minbar into the mosque of the B. Huddan, where he led prayers and distributed food while trying to turn the Azd against the pro-Umayyad Tamim. The Azd stood by Ziyad and succeeded in re-establishing his power in the city, though they refused to cooperate when he burned Ibn al-Hadrami and his followers alive inside the *qaṣr* they had occupied.[132]

The above account of the early history of al-Azd in Basra suggests not only that they were present, but also that they acted politically as an ally of the Umayyads and did so for independent tribal or factional reasons rather than loyalty to an established state or religious community. Under Muᶜawiya b. Abi Sufyan, and particularly his governor Ziyad b. Abihi, state representatives would increasingly centralise administrative authority, such as with the division into fifths discussed above. We also see increasing centralisation in the appointment of the qadi. Michael Morony doubted that the earliest qadis in Basra occupied a citywide formal office, and suggested they actually resolved disputes only within their tribes or otherwise informally.[133] This supposition is most likely correct, as even in the *Akhbar al-Quda'a* of Muhammad b. Khalaf Wakiᶜ, the sequence of caliphs is muddled after Kaᶜb's death in the Battle of the Camel. This is despite Wakiᶜ's clear desire to present an orderly series of qadis for the whole city, beginning with one Abu Maryam Iyas b. Subih al-Hanafi, said to have had four stations around the city, only one of which was in his own tribal district.[134]

Kaᶜb b. Sur serves the early Islamic historiographical tradition as an ideal qadi, and as such plays a prominent role in Wakiᶜ's text. As with other sources, Wakiᶜ claims Kaᶜb b. Sur was appointed as qadi by ᶜUmar based on their interactions in Medina and continued in his office until that caliph's death. When ᶜUthman came into office, he appointed Abu Musa al-Ashᶜari as qadi as well as governor, but when ᶜAbd Allah b. Kurayz succeeded Abu Musa as governor, Kaᶜb b. Sur was reappointed as qadi, and the latter continued in that office until his death in the Battle of the Camel.[135] With Kaᶜb's death, however, the accounts become contradictory. According to al-Asmaᶜi, Kaᶜb was succeeded by another Azdi, ᶜAbd al-Rahman b. Yazid al-Huddani, a half brother of al-Muhallab b. Abi Sufra on his mother's side who continued in office until the arrival of Ziyad b. Abihi in the reign of Muᶜawiya.[136] This shows the continuing prominence of the Huddan in Basra. Other sources of Waki^{c}', however, say the qadi was Abu al-Aswad al-Duli (of the al-Dul b. Karim), ^{c}Abd Allah b. Fadala al-Laythi (of Quda^{c}a), or al-Harith b. ^{c}Abd ^{c}Awf al-Hilali (of Tamim).[137] A strong possibility is that each of these had among his own people some of the duties later associated with the qadi. Only later did the office clearly become centralised.

There are scattered references to individual prominent Azdis during the reign of Mu^{c}awiya which allow some insight to presence and potential influence. One al-Harith b. ^{c}Abd Allah al-Azdi briefly became governor.[138] According to a tradition from al-Mada'ini going back to an al-Azd shaykh named Ibn Abi ^{c}Amr, when Ziyad b. Abihi appointed sub-governors over Khurasan, his choice for Herat, Badghis, Qadis and Bushanj was Nafi^{c} b. Khalid al-Tahi. When Ziyad later turned against Nafi^{c}, imprisoning him and extracting from him either 100,000 or 800,000 dirhams, some of the leaders of al-Azd came to his defence, among them Sayf b. Wahb al-Ma^{c}wili (of the B. Ma^{c}wala). When Ziyad remembered how Sabra b. Shayman had helped him, he released Nafi^{c} and his money. Sayf b. Wahb was, according to a poem, known for his generosity, while Sabra was known for his deeds.[139] This allows us to note two tribes that were in Basra at that time. The fact that the B. Ma^{c}wala, who had been most prominent of the Azd in Oman, were in Basra and yet Sabra b. Shayman was portrayed as the leader of the Azd there just a few years before when the Huddan Mosque became a key centre of the al-Azd district suggests that they arrived in the city after the Huddan. About the other clan mentioned, the Tahiya, we shall say more below.

Al-Baladhuri passes on an account of the revolt of two Kharijites whom he names as Qurayb b. Murra al-Azdi and Zahhaf b. Zahr al-Ta'i. In this account, these events took place when Ziyad b. Abihi was in Kufa and ^{c}Ubayd Allah b. Abi Bakra was his deputy over Basra. With between sixty and eighty followers, the two Kharijis sought to put one of them in authority, though they did not decide until Ziyad sent his *shurṭa* (security force) after them, when they decided not to fight without an imam. Most transmitters claim they appointed Qurayb, though some say Zahhaf. They then went out near the cemetery of the B. Yashkur, killing those they met. They fought a man named Hakkak from the B. Dubay^{c}a whom they believed to be with the head of the *shurṭa*. They also attacked a man from the B. Qutay^{c}a and seized the doors of that tribe's mosque until the people fled. Then they rushed inside, and a man climbed the minaret, calling out, 'Oh, horses of God, ride!' However, he was brought down from the minaret and killed. Bukayr b. Wa'il al-Tahi from al-Azd then went out before them with a talisman, but they attacked him with swords, and he had to be rescued. After this, the B. Rasib came out and the Kharijites attacked them, as they did a man named Hajjar b. Abjar al-ᶜIjli who had come from Kufa on business and had to be rescued by Shaqiq b. Thawr al-Sadusi. Hajjar called to the B. Rasib that he had come to help them; they accepted, and fighting continued until 500 members of the *shurṭa* joined the B. Rasib in the battle. Eventually ᶜAbbad b. Husayn al-Habati killed Qurayb and took his head back to Ziyad. Ziyad, after crucifying the bodies of the Khaijites, was told that the B. Rasib had fought best of all the tribes.[140] Abu ᶜUbayda also mentions that during this conflict, the Kharijites passed by the B. ᶜAli, who are identified as Omani.[141]

Khalifa b. Khayyat cites an account from Wahb b. Jarir (d. 821), most of which has an *isnad* going through his father. In this version, set in the early 670s when Sumara b. Jundab al-Fazari was Ziyad's deputy over Basra, Zuhhaf and Qurayb killed a man named Ruᵓba b. al-Makhbul at the mosque of the B. Dubayᶜa before proceeding to seize the mosque of the B. Qutayᶜa, though in this version the man who climbed the minaret was killed while on it. After the Kharijites were driven from this mosque, there is a brief account of an encounter with a man and his wife who fled into their house and locked the door. After Hakkak was killed, the Kharijites scattered to different al-Azd mosques, with groups also going to the Mosque of al-Maᶜawil and the courtyard of the B. ᶜAli. Their opponents included Sayf b. Wahb (presumably the Sayf b. Wahb al-Maᶜwali mentioned above) and a number of his friends, as well as the B. ᶜAli and B. Rasib. Also in Wahb's account, Qurayb was killed by ᶜAbd Allah b. Aws al-Tahi, and also described as of the Iyad b. Sud and a cousin of Zahhaf.[142] Ibn Khayyat and al-Baladhuri also mention the B. ᶜAli fighting the Kharijites in an Abu ᶜUbayda tradition linked to a poem from an anonymous Omani.[143]

Several of the groups mentioned in this account are associated with the Bakr b. Waᵓil. Two are the B. Yashkur and B. Dubayᶜa, the first two groups attacked, suggesting that al-Azd and Bakr b. Waᵓil lived in close proximity. Shaqiq b. Thawr al-Sadusi's rescue of the man from the B. ᶜIjl might also support that if those two Bakri were near their homes. Of the non-Bakr b. Waᵓil groups, the B. Qutayᶜa are probably the tribe descended from the Malik b. Shanwa of the B. Judham, a tribe closely linked with the Azd in Basra.[144] Beyond that, however, we have a number of al-Azd groups. The B. Maᶜwala make another appearance, adding further evidence of their presence. The B. Tahiya, B. ᶜAli and B. Iyad were all known to the genealogists as sons of Sud b. al-Hajr b. ᶜImran.[145] Al-ᶜAtik b. al-Asd b. ᶜImran was the tribe of the Muhallabids, whose influence on the Azd will form the subject of Chapter 3. For now, we need only note that both the B. ᶜAtik and the Sud groups are connected to the Azd at an interesting genealogical level, with ᶜImran being cast by most genealogists as one of the sons of ᶜAmr Muzayqiyaᵓ who, as described in Chapter 1, connected al-Azd to such questionable relations as the Ghassan and Ansar.[146] By contrast, both the Nasr b. Zahran and Malik b. Fahm branches of the Azd, which included the main clans in Basra and Oman, claimed descent from Nasr b. al-Azd, whose brother Mazin was theoretically ᶜImran's great-great-great-great-grandfather.[147]

The identity of the B. Rasib is somewhat tricky, and in examining it we should also take into account the fact that in an arbitration we will discuss in more detail below, which chose Babba as governor of Basra, the Qudaᶜa representative, al-Nuᶜman b. Suhban, is described in al-Baladhuri's version of Wahb b. Jarir as 'al-Azdi *thumma* al-Rasibi'.[148] Wilkinson thought, based on Omani sources and context, that the Rasib were originally a Qudaᶜa tribe which may have also had ties to the Mahra.[149] Although Ibn al-Kalbi placed the Rasib as part of the Jarm, there are plausible traces of al-Azd links.[150] First, the group's eponym is Rasib b. Khazraj; the tribe Khazraj of Medina, of course, was genealogically considered part of al-Azd. Furthermore, Rasib's mother was Shufuf bt. Malik b. Fahm al-Azdi.[151] Caskel concluded that the Rasib was the catch-all branch of the Jarm for immigrants from Oman in Basra, a conclusion necessary to justify the opinion of an Azd ᶜUman poet who placed some of the Jarm in Oman, which Caskel doubted.[152] Regarding another famous Rasibi, the Kharijite leader ᶜAbd Allah b. Wahb, Wilkinson believes his genealogy was forged to give him plausible al-Azd ties.[153]

The Fitna *of Masᶜud b. ᶜAmr*

By far the most significant event illuminating the position of the tribes in early Islamic Basra and their capacity for action was the strife which followed the death of the al-Azd leader Masᶜud b. ᶜAmr in the early days of the Second Civil War after the 683 death of the caliph Yazid I. Many interpretations, beginning from the theory that the Azd were newcomers at that time, see it as the outcome of a disruption to the city's tribal balance. Hawting, for example, believes the arrival of Azd immigrants provided the Rabiᶜa with the chance to attack Tamim domination.[154] Much as with the Battle of the Camel, however, the clearest context is the onset of a dispute of the caliphate and the connections between tribes and political factions. For example, in his biographies of the prophet's companions and their successors, al-Tabari describes Babba, who became Basra's governor during the crisis, as coming to power amidst conflict between the city's Zubayrid and Marwanid factions.[155] It is in fact inescapable that the conflict was primarily one between one tribe, al-Azd, which was sheltering the Umayyad governor and another, Tamim, where advocates of Ibn al-Zubayr were prominent.

Masᶜud b. ᶜAmr himself was of the Malik b. Fahm tribe of Maᶜn. There is some confusion on this point, as his successor, Ziyad b. ᶜAmr, was of the ᶜAtik. However, only one of many sources says the two were brothers. Ibn Hazm has both Ziyad and Masᶜud as sons of ᶜAmr b. al-Ashraf b. al-Bukhtari of al-ᶜAtik, and reports that Masᶜud had descendants in Tabriz.[156] He also lists another brother, Waᵓil, whose grandson Tasnim b. al-Hawari fought with the Abbasid caliph al-Mansur against the rebel Ibrahim b. ᶜAbd Allah in Basra, a revolt which will figure into the next chapter. This Tasnim had descendants whom Ibn Hazm also listed. Even Ibn Hazm mentions, however, that Ibn al-Kalbi lists Masᶜud as Masᶜud b. ᶜAmr b. ᶜAbd b. Muharib of the Maᶜn.[157] Wilkinson believes that Masᶜud b. ᶜAmr was the head of a wave of migration from the Bedouin fringe of southern Oman near the end of the Sufyanid period, a wave which ultimately gave rise to the tradition that all the Azd in Basra arrived at that time.[158]

The accounts in the extant sources go back to four main authorities of the ninth century, Abu ᶜUbayda, Wahb b. Jarir, al-Madaᵓini and Ibn al-Kalbi.[159] Examining the different material in line with Donner's 'tradition criticism' makes clear how each of those authorities presented a somewhat different narrative based on their own sources and agendas. A comparison of the different accounts not only allows us to reconstruct the core of what happened, but also to comment upon how and why the accounts differ, which illuminates matters relating to identity and values at the end of the seventh century, as well as the traditionists' own time. The study begins with a comprehensive presentation of the version of Abu ᶜUbayda, which allows for a useful orientation, as well as a sense of the conflicting traditions.

Abu ᶜUbayda's account is found partially in al-Tabari, but in its fullest version in the *Naqaᵓid Jarir wa al-Farazdaq*. In fact, that work may include an entire recension of an Abu ᶜUbayda work reported by Ibn al-Nadim, 'Kitab Masᶜud b. ᶜAmr wa Maqtalihi'.[160] Abu ᶜUbayda was a *mawlā* of a Taym group, usually said to be the Taym of Quraysh.[161] Ignaz Goldziher considered him a passionate *shuᶜūbī*, whereas H. A. R. Gibb saw him as primarily a Kharijite.[162] A. A. Duri regarded him as both, while Charles Pellat found his surviving work too fragmentary to form a judgement.[163] Savran believes his reputation as a *shuᶜūbī* came from his role in integrating Persian history into the pre-history of Islam, a project seen as threatening to those who wished to preserve the privileges of Arab identity.[164] According to al-Lughawi and Ibn Qutayba, he was an Ibadi known especially for reporting the faults of the Arabs, though the idea he was Ibadi probably arose because of an interest in Kharijite poetry. His specialties included battles fought by Arabs, and his student ᶜUmar b. Shabba said that he knew the names, not only of every cavalier (*fārs*) in the Jahiliya and early Islam, but of their horses as well.[165] Wilferd Madelung's assessment is highly positive: 'Abu ᶜUbayda's historical reporting was little distorted by sectarian, political, or racial bias . . . His reports are generally as reliable or unreliable as were his informants. These he often chose, to be sure, more for their first-hand knowledge than for their impartiality.'[166]

Abu ᶜUbayda's account of events begins with a tradition from ᶜUthman al-Batti through Ghaylan b. Muhammad. The former was a Basran hadith scholar called a *ṣaḥib al-raʾy*, part of a movement which would be associated with the Hanafis.[167] In this account a man named ᶜAbd al-Rahman b. Jawshan witnessed one Salama b. Dhuʾayb al-Riyahi ride his horse into the camel market[168] carrying weapons and a banner, wearing a *sāj* or *ṭaylasān* and calling on people to follow Ibn al-Zubayr as caliph. Some began pledging allegiance to him. Al-Ahnaf b. Qays al-Tamimi offered to bring the rebel leader to the Umayyad governor ᶜUbayd Allah b. Ziyad, but upon seeing the number of people who had rallied to the Zubayrid cry, instead withdrew with his followers from the controversy, neither arresting Salama nor returning to ᶜUbayd Allah.[169]

In describing further developments, Abu ᶜUbayda, now quoting the linguist Yunus b. Habib al-Jarmi, claims that ᶜUbayd Allah b. Ziyad tried to get the Bukhariyya to fight for him against Salama's many Basran recruits, but they refused. ᶜUbayd Allah's brothers also abandoned him. The governor then feared for his life, and, remembering that his father, Ziyad b. Abihi, had found refuge with the Azd during the First Civil War, sought the aid of al-Harith b. Qays of the Jadhima b. Malik b. Fahm. ᶜUbayd Allah told al-Harith that his father, Ziyad b. Abihi, had advised him to seek out al-Harith if he ever had the need to flee. Al-Harith was less than eager to assist ᶜUbayd Allah because neither he nor Ziyad had done much for the Azd during their time as governors. However, al-Harith did agree to help him reach his maternal uncles among the B. Najiya,[170] who were pleased to see al-Harith, but displeased enough at the sight of ᶜUbayd Allah that they began firing arrows at him, at least one of which lodged in his turban. Al-Harith decided not to stop there after all, and so proceeded with ᶜUbayd Allah to the dwelling of his own people, the Jahdam b. Jadhima, before going to Masᶜud b. ᶜAmr. Masᶜud granted ᶜUbayd Allah the sanctuary, but expressed misgivings that the Azd received no good from their previous sheltering of Ziyad, and that this sanctuary would lead to strife between the Azd and others in Basra. Al-Harith, however, asserted that none can fault the Azd for fulfilling an oath of allegiance as far as granting shelter.[171]

In another tradition from Abu ᶜUbayda, which is traced back to descendants of the family of Ziyad b. Abihi, ᶜUbayd Allah did not meet Masᶜud, and sanctuary was merely granted by al-Harith b. Qays. Al-Harith came with both ᶜUbayd Allah and ᶜAbd Allah b. Ziyad, as well as 100,000 dirhams, and went to Masᶜud's wife and paternal cousin Umm Bistam. Al-Harith told her he had a proposition which would result in her becoming pre-eminent over her women and her people's nobility being secured, as well as immediate wealth for her if she would agree to take in ᶜUbayd Allah. She demurred, saying that Masᶜud would object, but al-Harith persuaded her to garb ᶜUbayd Allah in her own clothing and let them worry about Masᶜud. She did that, took the money, and then told Masᶜud what had happened. Masᶜud grew angry with her, but then ᶜUbayd Allah and al-Harith came out of her chamber and the former asked him to honour the hospitality which she had given, to which Masᶜud, after some persuasion, agreed. ᶜUbayd Allah remained there until Masᶜud died.[172]

Abu ᶜUbayda then gives an account of the selection as governor of ᶜAbd Allah b. al-Harith, more commonly known as Babba, who was of ᶜAbd al-Muttalib lineage on his father's side, and a son of Hind bt. Abu Sufyan. According to the story, Mudar and al-Yaman each chose one representative to negotiate over the leadership, and eventually the Yamani, al-Nuᶜman b. Suhban al-Rasibi, tricked the Mudari into accepting Babba, noting that he was related to both Muhammad and the Umayyads. Abu ᶜUbayda's sources disagreed, however, over whether the Azd as a group were in favour of Babba as governor.[173] The sources for this material are Yazid b. Sumayr al-Jarmi and Suwwar b. ᶜAbd Allah b. Saᶜid al-Jarmi, whom Hawting finds evidence of having family connections to al-Nuᶜman b. Suhban, suggesting this was a particular family tale about a well-known historical event.

Abu ᶜUbayda also describes, on the authority of Tamimis named Zuhayr b. Hunayd and ᶜAmr b. ᶜIsa, the arrival in Basra of news of a massacre of Bakr b. Waᵓil by Tamim in the city of Herat. In his account, fighting breaks out immediately when word arrives, but then subsides for a month before someone is killed while boasting and the Bakr b. Waᵓil demand retaliation for that. Their leader at the time was Ashyam b. Shaqiq b. Thawr al-Sadusi,[174] who had gained that headship through the intervention of Yazid b. Muᶜawiya with ᶜUbayd Allah b. Ziyad.[175] When he proposed exploring means of peaceful resolution to the conflict, the Bakr b. Waᵓil abandoned him and went to their previous leader, Malik b. Mismaᶜ, who had renewed an alliance with the Azd that had existed under Yazid b. Muᶜawiya. ᶜUbayd Allah, who as noted above was still with Masᶜud in this version, encouraged Masᶜud to work with Malik, and gave him 200,000 dirhams to help win support for a joint venture. This is also the context of Abu ᶜUbayda's material on the Azd's arrival in Basra.[176]

Because of this agreement, when tensions flared in the aftermath of ᶜUbayd Allah's deposition, the Azd were on the side of the Bakr b. Waᵓil, as were the ᶜAbd al-Qays. Continuing his account from the Ziyadids mentioned above, Abu ᶜUbayda claims that Masᶜud b. ᶜAmr asked ᶜUbayd Allah to accompany him so that he could be restored to his place, but ᶜUbayd Allah preferred to remain behind. Masᶜud b. ᶜAmr, wearing a yellow *qabaᶜ*, then entered the mosque, climbed the minbar, and exhorted people to *sunna*, while the Bakr b. Waᵓil burned the dwellings of the Tamim. A source of Abu ᶜUbayda suggests that the Azd found Babba ineffective, and one can certainly credit the sentiment, as that governor's response to the crisis was simply to declare he would not deal with it.[177]

Accounts from Abu ᶜUbayda concerning how the Tamim came to respond vary, though al-Ahnaf b. Qays's reluctance to fight is in all of them. Eventually the Tamim did rush into combat, joined by the Sasanian soldiers who had federated to the tribe during the conquest period. One report, allegedly passed on by the prominent religious figure Hasan al-Basri (d. 728), indicates that as Masᶜud was atop the *minbar* exhorting the people to avoid conflict, people who had come from the direction of the Tamim's residences killed him. With one exception mentioned below, all Abu ᶜUbayda's accounts, of which the dominant is from the Tamim source Ishaq b. Suwayd al-ᶜAdawi,[178] identify the Tamim as Masᶜud's killers in one way or another. Abu ᶜUbayda also mentions that Ashyam b. Shaqiq, the ousted leader of the Bakr b. Waᵓil, was wounded while fleeing, and that Malik b. Mismaᶜ was besieged in his residence. ᶜUbayd Allah fled to Syria.[179]

Without citing a source, Abu ᶜUbayda reports that the Azd decided upon Ziyad b. ᶜAmr al-Ataki as their new leader. There is then a description of battle formations featuring a number of non-Arab groups and, in a point of contention with other sources, the ᶜAbd al-Qays allied with the Bakr b. Waᵓil and al-Azd.[180] After some fighting, two members of Quraysh, named ᶜUmar b. ᶜAbd al-Rahman and ᶜUmar b. ᶜUbayd Allah, the latter Ibn Zubayr's governor in the city after Babba, sought to mediate the dispute, but to no avail. The account of this attempted mediation is interesting for its depiction of the relative dispositions of Malik b. Misma^c and al-Ahnaf b. Qays, which is attributed to the fact that al-Ahnaf faced opposition from his followers whereas Malik did not. Thereafter the fight resumed, broken frequently by mediation attempts, until finally they settled on that proposed by the two ᶜUmars. The result was that al-Azd received ten times the normal blood money for Masᶜud. ᶜUmar b. ᶜUbayd Allah paid 90 per cent of this amount. During the negotiations, according to Abu ᶜUbayda, the Azd and their allies met for consultations in the Dar Rufayda in the market (*sūq*), while the Tamim met in a court (*dār*) by the al-Tariq canal, which you would have passed by had you gone from the Dar Jabala b. ᶜAbd al-Rahman towards the area of the B. ᶜAdi. Al-Ahnaf b. Qays then gave a speech in which he described al-Azd as Tamim's brothers in Islam, partners in marriage arrangements, neighbours in dwelling, and their hand against enemies, and said that the Azd of Basra were dearer to him than the Tamim of Kufa, with the Azd of Kufa dearer than the Tamim of al-Sham, with attendant loyalties.[181] The entire affair lasted eight or nine months.[182]

One anecdote from Abu ᶜUbayda and Yunus b. Habib tells of a daughter of Masᶜud named Faᶜama who came upon Malik b. Mismaᶜ in the *mirbad* and demanded that the head of al-Ahnaf b. Qays be brought to her. They brought her a head, and she attacked it with her teeth and bathed her arms in its blood before departing. She later married.[183] Abu ᶜUbayda also preserved an account of how Masᶜud killed a Kharijite while returning from visiting a friend, but said this claim was false. Presumably it exists as a possible motive for Kharijites to attack Masᶜud in the mosque, which some said they did, as Abu ᶜUbayda placed it before what he said was also a false report that Masᶜud's ascent of the minbar caused everyone to ignore some Kharijites who had just escaped from prison, and who proceeded to enter the mosque and kill Masᶜud before fleeing to al-Ahwaz.[184] Both the latter accounts come simply from 'people'.

Although this account contains many fanciful and stylised episodes, especially during the battle, their presence can perhaps be explained by a philologist's interest in their literary style and poetic content.[185] Abu ᶜUbayda's sources are diverse, but there is a preponderance of the Tamim. He references no al-Azd sources, though there are several from the Jarm, who were close allies of al-Azd. His canvas deals most overtly with the context of Ibn al-Zubayr's movement, and he also includes Basra's non-Arab population in ways not preserved in the extant material from other traditionists. Abu ᶜUbayda's version of events is also unique in that it does not mention the Kharijites, an aspect found in others and which Abu ᶜUbayda seems at pains to refute with the two traditions mentioned last above.

Another long account portraying the events against a different broader canvas comes through the Basran traditionist Wahb b. Jarir al-Azdi al-ᶜAtaki,[186] usually citing his father Jarir b. Hazm and often coming through either Ahmad b. Ibrahim al-Dawraqi (d. 860)[187] or ᶜUmar b. Shabba. Jarir b. Hazm was a Basran *hadith* scholar of the mid–late eighth century known for his book on the Azraqites, a significant movement of Kharijites defeated by the Azdi general al-Muhallab b. Abi Sufra.[188] The early part of his material focuses on ᶜUbayd Allah's attempts to secure his position in Basra after Yazid's death, during which he releases some Kharijites from prison. These Kharijites then gathered around Nafiᶜ b. al-Azraq in the *mirbad*, and ᶜUbayd Allah appealed to the people of Basra for help against them in a sort of false flag operation. It is when he found no support through this scheme that he fled to the Azd.[189]

The next part of Wahb's account purportedly goes back to al-Harith b. Qays himself through the latter's kinsman Abu Labid al-Jahdami.[190] This account is similar to if shorter than that of Abu ᶜUbayda with regard to ᶜUbayd Allah's approach to al-Harith and their journey to Masᶜud (complete with the arrow lodging in ᶜUbayd Allah's turban), but does not include the discussion of al-Azd hospitality to Ziyad b. Abihi. In *Ansab al-Ashraf*, al-Baladhuri also includes a brief aside for Wahb's transmission from al-Qasim b. al-Fadl al-Huddani, a hadith scholar mentioned above, that the two passed through the place of the B. Tahiya, who captured and forced them to ransom themselves. In the end, ᶜUbayd Allah is given refuge in the home of ᶜAbd al-Ghafir b. Masᶜud, whose wife Khayra bt. Khufaf b. ᶜAmr, a possible niece of Masᶜud and thus cousin of ᶜAbd al-Ghafir, is also mentioned. A brief tradition ostensibly from Khayra claims that while in her chamber, ᶜUbayd Allah was visited by his wife Hind b. Asmaᵓ, with whom he talked and bantered before eventually helping Khayra with her sewing.[191]

Masᶜud, al-Harith and others then went around warning the Azd that Ibn Ziyad was among them and it would be best to be armed, while the other tribes noted Ibn Ziyad's absence and concluded he was most likely with the Azd. The account then shifts to another chain of authorities noting that Ziyad b. Abihi's sheltering with al-Azd is noted as a reason why ᶜUbayd Allah would flee there.[192] Wahb b. Jarir also includes an account passed through transmitters named Ghassan b. Mudar and Saᶜid b. Yazid that at ᶜUbayd Allah's request, Masᶜud summoned as a counsellor one Hadash One-Eye, who criticised ᶜUbayd Allah for his treatment of the Azd and, calling Masᶜud a 'stupid shaykh', persuaded him to send ᶜUbayd Allah away with an escort of sixty or seventy Azdis. Another version of ᶜUbayd Allah's departure from Basra puts the number at 100, though without the account of Hadash One-Eye, while a third tradition says ᶜUbayd Allah was with Masᶜud for three months.[193]

Wahb b. Jarir goes on to describe the appointment of Babba, using a version of al-Nuᶜman's trick based directly on a ruse of ᶜAmr b. al-ᶜAs's during the arbitration over the caliphate during the First Civil War.[194] In the Ibn Jarir account, there is also a claim here from Abu ᶜUyayna al-Muhallabi that this is when the Azd gathered to Masᶜud b. ᶜAmr. Then, via an account traced to Ibrahim b. ᶜAbd Allah, a supposed participant in the events, Wahb tells how the Azd and Rabiᶜa went to the minbar which Masᶜud ascended; Ahmad b. Ibrahim al-Dawraqi also indicates that he wore a yellow silk *qaba*ᵓ, though this specific tradition has no report on what he did there. Masᶜud and the Azd then leave the mosque with Masᶜud on a female mule, and his followers crowded around him until he fell at the hands of around forty Kharijites who had been instigated against him by al-Ahnaf b. Qays and were led by Ibn al-Azraq, for whom the Azraqites are named.[195]

Wahb also has an account claiming that Masᶜud exhorted people to follow the Umayyads, and the Kharijites killed him after he had left the mosque. The Azd then fought the Tamim, made an agreement, and everyone started following Babba. Another report, this one again going back to Abu ᶜUyayna al-Muhallabi, has Masᶜud's body dragged to the residences of the B. Ibrahim, which resulted in the Tamim being blamed for his death. Then, when conflict began, al-Ahnaf told the Azd that the Tamim had not killed Masᶜud, and that it was Kharijites who had done so. When the Azd protested that they had found Masᶜud's body among the Tamim's dwellings, al-Ahnaf then asked what would satisfy them, and the Azd gave three options. The first was to leave the city and return to the desert, the second was war, and the third was for the Tamim to pay ten times the normal blood money for Masᶜud. The final option, as in the other accounts, was accepted by the Tamim, and a man named Iyas b. Qatada paid the blood money for the Tamim, taking the money from both his own wealth and the stipend assigned to his people, presumably the Quraysh.[196]

In Wahb's account of the selection of Ziyad b. ᶜAmr as the new Azd leader, which goes back to al-Qasim b. al-Fadl al-Huddani citing anonymous shaykhs, the Azd chose Ziyad because al-Muhallab b. Abi Sufra was away at the time. When the Azd came to al-Muhallab afterwards, he berated them for sheltering 'this slave' (meaning ᶜUbayd Allah b. Ziyad) and making enemies of the people of their country, which caused them to stalk off. Al-Muhallab, according to this account, was then troubled, and went to join Ibn al-Zubayr. Meanwhile, the Tamim went to al-Ahnaf b. Qays complaining of the Azd, who asked them to entrust him with their affairs, which they did. He then travelled with them to the *mirbad*, where they fought against the Azd and Bakr b. Waᵓil before the matter was settled.[197] In Wahb's accounts, the blood money was not actually delivered until the later governor Qubaᶜ took it from the treasury.[198]

Wahb's account, while not as ornate as Abu ᶜUbayda's, nonetheless displays anachronisms which betray later embellishments. For example, the ᶜAbd al-Qays are allied with the Tamim rather than with the Bakr b. Waᵓil and al-Azd. Although the participation of the ᶜAbd al-Qays is not well-attested during these events, they were clearly allied with al-Azd against Tamim a few years later, and probably were here, as well.[199] The change may be either to balance the sides perceptually with two tribes on each or because these accounts were the product of a period when the key division was between Qays and al-Yaman, and while the alliance between southern al-Azd and northern Bakr b. Waᵓil is inescapable given the overall narrative and events in Khurasan, storytellers could at least preserve some order by allying the ᶜAbd al-Qays to their fellow northerners. What I believe holds the key to understanding this account, however, is the appearance of al-Muhallab b. Abu Sufra as the one who should have been the al-Azd leader but was an opponent of the Azd's actions during this period.

Despite Wahb's account's reliance on al-Azd sources, Masᶜud b. ᶜAmr appears in a bad light. The most striking example of this is that despite the fact Abu Uyayna al-Muhallabi appears as a source, the account does not include the tradition which appears elsewhere in isolation in which Masᶜud was unenthusiastic about seeing ᶜUbayd Allah, but al-Harith reminded him of the acclaim they had received for sheltering Ziyad. After expressing some concern that by sheltering the despised governor he would provoke a feud with the other tribes in Basra, Masᶜud granted shelter to ᶜUbayd Allah. In another account, this one from Ahmad b. Ibrahim al-Dawraqi, Wahb b. al-Qasim b. al-Fadl al-Huddani claimed that Masᶜud and al-Azd went to make the oath of allegiance to Babba while the Bakr b. Waᵓil stayed in the *mirbad*. The next day, the Bakr b. Waᵓil went to pledge allegiance when Kharijites from among them came and warned them not to. The Bakris were then afraid of what would happen, and sought to go to pledge alongside al-Azd. Rabiᶜa, which here clearly indicates the leaders of Bakr b. Waᵓil, discussed this with Masᶜud, who told them al-Azd had already pledged. Masᶜud ended up escorting the

Bakr, however, and was ambushed and killed by Kharijites in an open area.[200]

These al-Azd narrators were clearly at pains to pass on this account because it portrayed al-Azd as noble for their hospitality. Ibn Jarir, however, likely did not include them because he was concerned not with the virtues of al-Azd as a whole, but rather with his kinsman al-Muhallab. Ibn ᶜAsakir lists al-Mufaddal b. al-Muhallab as someone from whom Jarir heard hadith and historical accounts.[201] If Abu ᶜUbayda's main context for events is the conflict between Umayyad and Zubayrid factions, Ibn Jarir's is that between the Muslim community and the Kharijites. As noted above, Jarir b. Hazm is credited with a work on the Azraqites, whom al-Muhallab was responsible for defeating, and as we shall see in the next chapter, material which is probably from that work dwells primarily on the general's virtue. His and his son's material on these events probably formed an early section of that narrative, which was probably a paean to al-Muhallab.[202]

A third account of the conflict comes through ᶜUmar b. Shabba and al-Madaᵓini. In this version, during the governorship of Babba, a man from Medina came to the city, and Babba decided to give him the home of a *mawlā* of Ziyad named al-Fil. Al-Fil fled leaving his dwelling locked, however, and the B. Sulaym, among whom he lived, resisted the attempts of *shurṭa* chief Himyan b. ᶜAdi to seize the place. They drove him off with the aid of the Bukhariyya and the armed *malāwī* of one ᶜAbd al-Malik b. ᶜAbd Allah b. ᶜAmir b. Kurayz. The next day that man encountered one of the Bakr b. Waᵓil, and hence a kinsman of Himyan, which led to a scuffle between the Mudar, which included both the Sulaym and Tamim, and Bakr b. Waᵓil, with the latter forming an alliance with al-Azd.[203] Unlike Abu ᶜUbayda, al-Madaᵓini does not tie the Tamim-Bakr b. Waᵓil feud in Basra to events in Khurasan, at least in the extant material.

Al-Madaᵓini's account continues with the Tamim gathering around al-Ahnaf b. Qays, who dispatched Salama b. Dhuᵓayb al-Riyahi with his spear to the mosque, where the Azd and Bakr b. Waᵓil had followed Masᶜud b. ᶜAmr. There, led by the Asawira, they set upon and killed Masᶜud, though the source mentions that the Azd blamed the deed on Azraqites instigated by al-Ahnaf. Then there was strife in Basra, which was settled by two mediators, at least one of whom was from Quraysh, and an agreement by al-Azd to accept ten times the normal blood money for Masᶜud. During the conflict, Babba remained in his house, and so Ibn al-Zubayr asked the Companion Anas b. Malik to lead prayers in the city. Afterwards, Ibn al-Zubayr appointed ᶜUmar b. ᶜUbayd Allah governor over Basra, and ᶜUmar's brother ᶜUbayd Allah b. ᶜUbayd Allah led the prayers until the new appointee's arrival.[204] Al-Madaʾini cites Muhammad b. Hafs al-Bahili and Hilal b. Ahwaz for a tradition in which al-Ahnaf defended this decision as an alternative to continuing to fight or fleeing Basra.[205] Al-Madaʾini's account continues with the speech by al-Ahnaf b. Qays in which he described the Azd as brothers in Islam, partners in marriage arrangements, neighbours in dwelling, and their hand against enemies. The account, still seemingly from Muhammad b. Hafs al-Bahili, then goes on to describe how Iyas b. Qatada, one of the Quraysh whose mother was of al-Ahnaf's immediate kin, was responsible for the blood money owed to al-Azd and Rabiᶜa, and eventually died as a devout dweller in a mosque.[206]

In this account, al-Madaʾini's primary theme would seem to be the wisdom of al-Ahnaf b. Qays, and in fact much of al-Baladhuri's biography of the Tamim leader is derived from al-Madaʾini.[207] In that source, al-Ahnaf is credited with 'putting the affairs of the people in order and extinguishing the fires' in the aftermath of Masᶜud's death.[208] Al-Madaʾini's only mention of ᶜUbayd Allah b. Ziyad in what has been preserved is a statement by al-Ahnaf forbidding the Tamim from seizing the governor's house during the conflict,[209] though this indicates that al-Madaʾini still saw the events against the background of his deposition and flight. Also noteworthy is the fact that in al-Madaʾini's account of al-Muthanna b. Mukharriba al-ᶜAbdi's mission to Basra on behalf of al-Mukhtar, al-Ahnaf again appears as a peacemaker,[210] whereas he is much more aggressive in a parallel account from al-Baladhuri,[211] one which Michael Fishbein notes better explains subsequent events.[212]

The fourth major account, coming from Hisham b. Muhammad al-Kalbi's work based on that of his fellow Kalbi historian ᶜAwana b. al-Hakam, includes a claim that the Basrans rejected ᶜUbayd Allah after he failed to establish his authority over Kufa, and that after taking refuge with al-Azd but before fleeing he appointed Masᶜud as his deputy, and the latter was simply seeking to enforce his claim when he climbed the minbar. Qays and Tamim rejected these claims, and al-Ahnaf b. Qays instigated the Kharijites into taking a hand. According to Ibn al-Kalbi, one of the Kharijites – a Persian named Muslim – fired the arrow which felled Masᶜud, and the Azd then retaliated against the Kharijites before gaining wind of possible Tamim involvement.[213]

After Masᶜud's death the Azd rallied behind Ziyad b. ᶜAmr, and marched with the Bakr b. Waʾil against the Tamim. After some fighting in which many were killed, the Tamim sued for peace, saying that if there were proof of Tamim involvement in Masᶜud's death, the Azd could kill the best man among them, whereas if there were none, the Tamim would swear that they had nothing to do with it. They also offered 100,000 dirhams in blood money, and when the latter was accepted, the feud ended. Iyas b. Qatada was again responsible for paying the blood money, and the Basrans chose first Babba as their governor, before Ibn al-Zubayr replaced him with Qubaᶜ.[214] This Kufan account is primarily interested in ᶜUbayd Allah b. Ziyad's flight to Syria and the establishment of Ibn al-Zubayr's authority in Iraq. There are also differences in the chronology of events surrounding the appointment of governors.

Despite their differences, these accounts have sufficient common elements that we can propose a selection of material which must have been common to an earlier stratum of the tradition, probably dating no later than the early eighth century to account for its use by ᶜAwana, and hence close to the truth. These common elements would be ᶜUbayd Allah's fall from the governorship and flight to his al-Azd allies, Masᶜud's alliance with Malik b. Mismaᶜ of Bakr b. Waᵓil and his ascent of the minbar, Masᶜud's death, and an ensuing battle between al-Azd and Tamim and their respective allies which was settled when al-Ahnaf b. Qays agreed to pay ten times the normal blood money for Masᶜud's death, money which was actually paid by another source. In the midst of this, Babba became governor, but was unable to fully establish authority over the city.

Beyond these basics, there are a few additional conclusions we can draw with some certainty. One is that Masᶜud and the Azd were supporters of the Umayyads. Both Abu ᶜUbayda and Ibn al-Kalbi/Ibn al-Hakam link Masᶜud's going to the mosque to his relationship with ᶜUbayd Allah. Al- Madaᵓini is silent on that point, and Wahb b. Jarir claims he aspired to become governor himself. That claim may be part of Ibn Jarir's desire to paint Masᶜud as less suitable as a leader than al-Muhallab, and even if he were seeking the position for himself, it need not contradict an ultimate loyalty to the Umayyads over their rivals. Another probable conclusion is that the Tamim or one of their Persian clients killed Masᶜud, but that some Azdis preferred to blame the Kharijites so as to claim that al-Muhallab's successful war against the latter properly avenged him. Surviving poetry savages al-Azd for failing to avenge Masᶜud, suggesting that their acceptance of blood money was seen as less honourable than blood vengeance at a very early date.[215] Ibn al-Kalbi's account also indicates that some were blaming the Kharijites during the eighth century, before Jarir b. Hazm, and he or Ibn al-Hakam have tried to reconcile the two claims of responsibility. Al- Madaᵓini even says directly that it was the Azd who sought to cast blame on the Kharijites.

In addition to the conflict between Umayyads and Zubayrids, conflict over wealth undoubtedly played a role in undermining the stability achieved under the Sufyanids. The end of Muᶜawiya's reign saw several military disasters which lessened the booty upon which the Sufyanid system of clientship and payments rested.[216] The Tamim clearly had more military power than any other group within the city, so much that three of them banded together and were unable to win a decisive victory. Basra was founded at the edge of Tamim's territory, which might account for much of their power.[217] If substantial numbers of Rabiᶜa and al-Azd did come later, they might also have been counted as late in migrating out of Arabia to the garrison towns, despite their sojourn in Tawwaj. This would leave them with smaller payments. Furthermore, only the Tamim had a preponderance of nomads in their population. As noted above, the ᶜAbd al-Qays, Bakr b. Waᵓil and al-Azd were all mainly settled tribes at the time of the conquests, though the others did have at least some nomadic components. This may be significant if the Tamim's nomadic ways led them to have a significant number of horses, something that would also explain their union with Persian cavalry. Even the Muhallabid stables were among the Tamim.[218] In the Sufyanid financial system, those with horses received as much as three times the payment of those without.[219] Archaeological evidence indicates that along the Gulf coast, fields were worked with hand-held hoes, while in Oman, farmers used ards probably pulled by one or two oxen.[220] In other words, horses were not used for agriculture. The conflict was definitely settled by a large financial payment which according to the tribal value system both sides found humiliating and which may have been paid from the treasury. ᶜAbd al-Ameer ᶜAbd Dixon suggests that monetary rewards were the main incentive for Umayyad support in the al-Jufra revolt against Musᶜab b. al-Zubayr which probably took place in 689, and that al-Azd and Bakr b. Waᵓil were the core of that Umayyad support, though tribe was only a minor factor.[221] Later, however, Musᶜab was unsuccessful in retaining Basrans' loyalty through increased stipends.[222] Several sources also report that al-Ahnaf b. Qays later warned against allowing the Syrians access to the riches of Iraq.[223]

These events also have relevance for the idea that a dramatic shift in tribal identity took place in the early Umayyad period, and that al-Azd in particular was a largely artificial creation of the garrison towns. Certainly the Azd whose aid ᶜUbayd Allah sought were different from those of his father's time. Ziyad sought shelter with Sabra b. Shayman of B. Huddan Azd Shanuᵓa from the Nasr b. Zahran branch of the Azd confederation,[224] whereas both al-Harith and Masᶜud were from the Malik b. Fahm branch of Azd ᶜUman. However, despite these differences, ᶜUbayd Allah,

Mas^cud and al-Harith are all portrayed as implicitly claiming an al-Azd unity with regard to the hospitality those during the First Civil War had shown Ziyad and the expected repayment which never materialised. This indicates that as later Azdis migrated to the garrison towns, they took on the loyalties and expectations of those already present, in this case alliance with the Umayyads and their representatives.

By the end of the Sufyanid period, it is beyond doubt that there were clearly understood groups such as al-Azd, Tamim and Bakr b. Wa'il, each consisting of numerous subgroups with a genealogically expressed affiliation. These groups were 'definition(s) of identity against other similar units in a moral arena', the Lancasters' definition of tribe.[225] They were transregional in composition, claiming members in the Arabian Peninsula and the frontier as well as in Basra, yet local in leadership. There was no supreme leader of Tamim or al-Azd, only locally dominant figures such as al-Ahnaf b. Qays and Mas'ud b. 'Amr. Much like traditional Bedouin leaders, they appear primarily in relationships with other groups, and maintaining the group's autonomy was a virtue.[226] In addition, they were repositories and guarantors of tribal honor. The Azd considered Mas'ud more important than a typical tribesman, and worth greater blood money, much as the Ghitrif claimed for themselves in pre-Islamic Arabia. At the local level, competition was intense unless mediated through the central government or the Quraysh, who as the tribe of the Prophet enjoyed a special status and were acceptable to all. The external relationships, especially those in Arabia, served in part to increase the 'segmentary *sharaf*' of those present in Basra.

Although the central government showed some favouritism, it did not determine who would have supreme authority over the tribes. This is seen in both the leadership battle within the Bakr b. Wa'il and in the easy manner in which Ziyad was chosen to replace Mas'ud after the latter's death. Beyond this, the system of relations between tribal leaders and the governor resembles the model outlined by Crone.[227] In order to place this in context, however, we should consider that tribesmen conceived of themselves as free individuals whose association under a given identity was voluntary.[228] That tribesmen conceived of themselves autonomously is suggested by the fact those who participated in sectarian movements are almost exclusively and most reliably portrayed as individual actors, as were governors and other agents of the state. The exception that proves the rule here is the conflict between the Tamim and the al-Azd-Rabi'a alliance when al-Muthanna b. Mukharriba was under attack by the Tamim and others in support of the Zubayrid governor. The rhetoric surrounding the conflict makes plain that tribes were concerned with matters of sovereignty rather than ideology, a position further supported by the tribes' rejection of al-Mukhtar's attempt to win their loyalty shortly afterward.[229]

Kufa

We can say much less about the Azd in Kufa, mainly because there were fewer of them. As Azdis played only a small role at al-Qadisiyya, it is unsurprising that so few settled in Kufa.[230] Those who did were from Western Arabia, primarily the Bariq and the Ghamid, with a small number from other groups. The fact Kufa was remote from al-Azd population centres in Arabia explains why the numbers remained small, such that the tribe quickly disappeared from its administrative divisions even though individuals remained prominent.

According to the *Dīwān* of the poet Suraqa b. Mirdas al-Bariqi, during the governorship of Bishr b. Marwan, there was flooding in the neighbourhood of the Bariq and the B. Sulaym, which were possibly adjacent.[231] Although there is dispute over who was the first qadi in Kufa, several sources name ᶜUrwa b. Abi al-Jaᶜd al-Bariqi. The other names reflect a diversity of tribes much as does the qadi list for the reign of ᶜAli b. Abi Talib in Basra.[232] This ᶜUrwa was a Companion known as a sound hadith transmitter, and he had previously been the commander of horsemen at Baraz al-Ruz in Iraq.[233] The fact both Kufa and Basra had Azdis as their most prominent early qadis is probably a coincidence, but ᶜUrwa's appearance in this role does contribute to the picture of the Bariq as a crucial part of the al-Azd presence in the city. Another early Bariq resident was al-Mustazill b. al-Husayn al-Bariqi, who died in the days of ᶜAli b. Abi Talib.[234]

Multiple al-Azd appear in accounts about al-Walid b. ᶜUqba, who served his maternal brother the caliph ᶜUthman b. ᶜAffan as governor of Kufa before being removed for immoral conduct. Accounts of ᶜUthman's reign most obviously lend themselves to sectarian agendas. As Heather Keaney has pointed out, however, those involving al-Walid b. ᶜUqba also involve debates over the proper relationship between religious and political authority and how Muslims should act in the face of the moral failings of government officials.[235] The implication of this is that, as with the accounts of the *fitna* of Masᶜud b. ᶜAmr analysed above, historians must be aware of the literary strategies and purpose of the narratives before deciding how and why to use their information for the questions at hand.

The sources also show significant confusion over individuals named Jundab of al-Azd during this period.[236] Abu Mikhnaf, al-Yaᶜqubi and other sources report that a Jundab al-Azdi killed a sorcerer in either the primary mosque or al-Walid's house, for which he was imprisoned for carrying out a penalty which was the business of the government. Some accounts specify that al-Azd intervened to spare Jundab the death penalty. Authorities vary as to whether he was Jundab b. ᶜAbd Allah of the B. Zabyan of Ghamid, a *mawlā* of the B. Zabyan, or Jundab b. Kaᶜb, either one of the B. Zabyan or a *mawlā* of al-Saqᶜab b. Zuhayr al-Kabiri of the Kabir b, al-Dul of al-Azd. Because of his piety, however, the prison guard let Jundab leave Kufa for Medina, where he remained until after ᶜUthman's death. The guard, however, was executed.[237] Also according to multiple sources, when al-Walid prayed drunk, Abu Zaynab al-Azdi stole al-Walid's signet ring and went with it to ᶜUthman, who replaced al-Walid with Saᶜid b. al-ᶜAs. Abu Zaynab's name was either Zuhayr b. ᶜAwf al-Azdi (Abu Mikhnaf) or Jundab b. Zuhayr (al-Waqidi). The names here are generally confused, as Ibn Ishaq said that Jundab b. Zuhayr and Abu Zaynab were two separate members of a Kufan delegation to ᶜUthman, with Jundab having stolen the ring.[238] Jundab b. Zuhayr also appears as one of Kufa's leading figures during the governorship of Saᶜid b. al-ᶜAs.[239]

Sayf b. ᶜUmar, whose pro-ᶜUthman agenda is always evident, provides an account which is probably meant to discredit his opponents by attributing to them ulterior personal motives in bringing down al-Walid.[240] According to Sayf, Zuhayr b. Jundab al-Azdi and Shubayl b. Ubayy al-Azdi were among a gang of youths who killed Ibn Haysuman al-Khuzaᶜi, for which they were executed. Jundab b. ᶜAbd Allah al-Azdi and the fathers of the others kept watch on al-Walid hoping to find grounds against him for killing their sons. When he learned that al-Walid was involved in drinking, Jundab called it to the attention of the prominent figures in Kufa, who went to al-Walid's house and discovered it.[241]

Al-Waqidi also reports two Azdi Jundabs as opponents of ᶜUthman in Kufa, Jundab b. Zuhayr al-Ghamidi and Jundub b. Kaᶜb al-Azdi. ᶜUthman gave orders for them to be exiled to Syria.[242] Jundab b. Zuhayr later fought under Mikhnaf b. Sulaym al-Ghamidi at Siffin, where in Abu Mikhnaf's account the two discuss having to fight other Azdis.[243] He was killed by a Syrian Azdi during that battle.[244] Abu Mikhnaf also reports a Jundab from Kufa on ᶜAli's side at the Battle of the Camel.[245] Abu ᶜUbayda said two Jundabs were on ᶜAli's side at Siffin.[246] In an anonymous report that clearly reflects later religio-political disputes, Jundab b. ᶜAbd Allah is cited as telling ᶜAli that were he to die, they would follow his son al-Hasan. ᶜAli replied that he would neither order them to do so nor forbid them.[247] Jundab b. ᶜAbd Allah is reported as an adviser of al-Hasan b. ᶜAli after ᶜAli's death.[248]

Much of the Jundab material ties one or both Jundabs to the Ghamid and support for ᶜAli. That may reflect reality, or it may be later traditionists' assumptions based on the prominence of Mikhnaf b. Sulaym al-Ghamidi as Kufa's most prominent al-Azd resident and well-known supporter of ᶜAli. This Mikhnaf, the ancestor of the traditionist Abu Mikhnaf, is often called '*bayt al-Azd b-al-Kūfa*', a phrase which indicates preeminence among the tribe.[249] He served for a time as governor of Isfahan, and commanded the Kufan al-Azd at the Battle of the Camel, where he was killed.[250] His son ᶜAbd al-Rahman b. Mikhnaf was a commander against the Azraqites during the second civil war, and will feature in Chapter 3. Another member of the family was Muhammad b. Mikhnaf. In an elegy, Suraqa b. Mirdas referred to him as being saved by al-Azd, and in another elegy he refers to al-Azd's solidarity in battle (*ᶜiṣāba*) and calls an 'Ibn Mikhnaf' 'horse-warrior of my people (*farsān qawmī*)'. This Ibn Mikhnaf, either Muhammad or ᶜAbd al-Rahman, is also noted for his generosity to the Azd Shanuʾa and compared to past heroes: an Iyas who fought the Persians, Jundab who slew the sorcerer, and ᶜUrwa al-Bariqi.[251] Suraqa also refers to ᶜAbd al-Rahman b. Mikhnaf as '*sayyid al-Azd min Azd Shanūʾa wa Azd ᶜUmān*'.[252]

Many al-Azd play a prominent role in Abu Mikhnaf's accounts of revolts under Muᶜawiya. One early appearance of the Azd is during the war against the Kharijite al-Mustawrid b. ᶜUllifa in the early 660s. In the area of Kufa, ᶜUmayr b. Abi Ashaʾa al-Azdi was killed fighting against the rebel. He was apparently a commander in the Umayyad army, and was remembered for some lines of poetry composed during the battle.[253] Another man, one Wuhayb b. Abi al-Ashaʾa al-Azdi, presumably ᶜUmayr's brother, also fought on the side of the Umayyads during that campaign.[254] One Azdi is listed as giving testimony against the Shi'ite rebel Hujr b. ᶜAdi. That is Qudama b. al-ᶜAjlan al-Azdi, who owned several villages near the Tigris, including one called Daylamaya.[255]

Abu Mikhnaf also related the involvement of other Azdis in the flight and execution of Hujr b. ᶜAdi. Two members of al-Azd, Abu Sufyan b. ᶜUwaymir and ᶜAjlan b. Rabiᶜa, carried him to the home of another Azdi, named ᶜUbayd Allah b. Malik, where he hid for a time.[256] Later, when Ziyad b. Abihi decided which tribes should go to the cemetery of the Kinda to pursue Hujr, he allegedly took into account the possibility of feuding between al-Yaman and Mudar, and ended up sending many tribes of the former, including al-Azd, to the cemetery of the Saʾidiyyin. Abu Mikhnaf quoted a tradition from Muhammad b. Mikhnaf that he was one of the Yaman involved when their leaders began to discuss the matter at the cemetery, and advised them to let the tribes of Hamdan and Madhhij, who had been sent ahead, deal with the matter and spare them from having to carry out an unwanted task. The advice was accepted, though when Ziyad found out he criticised the al-Yaman, except for Hamdan and Madhhij.[257] Finally, there is a tradition that Rabi^ca b. Najid al-Azdi sheltered Hujr for one day and one night.[258] Again, the same caveats apply to this account as did the al-Mustawrid b. ᶜUllifa material, and we might also add that although Muhammad b. Mikhnaf was undoubtedly involved, Abu Mikhnaf shows a pattern of attributing wise and sometimes prophetic advice to his family members which must remain suspect.

A final episode involving al-Azd in Kufa during the period covered by this chapter is the heckling of ᶜUbayd Allah b. Ziyad by ᶜAbd Allah b. ᶜAfif al-Azdi when the former announced the slaying of al-Husayn b. ᶜAli. According to Abu Mikhnaf's account from Humayd b. Muslim al-Azdi, a pro-ᶜAlid source who is particularly important for Karbala narratives, ᶜAbd Allah b. ᶜAfif was a partisan of ᶜAli who had lost one eye fighting at the Battle of the Camel and the other at the Battle of Siffin, and he spent all his days praying in Kufa's main mosque. When ᶜUbayd Allah made his announcement in the mosque, ᶜAbd Allah shouted him down and reviled him, leading ᶜUbayd Allah to order his soldiers to seize him. ᶜAbd Allah then shouted an al-Azd battle cry, which led ᶜAbd al-Rahman b. Mikhnaf to declare that he had brought ruin on both himself and his tribe. Young Azdis present took ᶜAbd Allah to his family, but Ibn Ziyad's men went there and killed him, and he was crucified on the salt flats.[259] It is not clear what ᶜAbd al-Rahman b. Mikhnaf's prediction referred to, though it could possibly be a device to explain why he did not support a Shi'ite against the governor. In Ibn Aᶜtham al-Kufi's tenth-century version, ᶜAbd Allah b. ᶜAfif was saved by the tribal notables, and in retaliation ᶜUbayd Allah siezed ᶜAbd al-Rahman b. Mikhnaf and other al-Azd. The battle to capture him pit Mudar against al-Yaman and Jundab b. ᶜAbd Allah al-Azdi. Upon ᶜAbd al-Rahman b. Mikhnaf's release, he assured ᶜUbayd Allah of his loyalty.[260]

One conclusion from this material is that, as in Basra, al-Azd was clearly a meaningful unit of identity in Kufa by the Sufyanid period. Prominent tribal leaders used 'al-Azdi' as their *nisba*, and it is used in poetry in ways which clearly include several of the smaller groups which played the most significant role in pre-Islamic Arabia. This very use as a *nisba*, however, makes it difficult to learn more about the backgrounds of the al-Azd leaders apart from the prominent members of Bariq and Ghamid, even though the Ibn al-Kalbis of Kufa would play the most important role in the formation of the caliphate's Arab genealogical framework.

Conclusion

The filters and themes found in what Borrut calls 'vulgate' historiography have obscured the differences between the genesis of Basra and Kufa. Nonetheless, those differences left residue even in histories portraying both as the result of specific direction from Medina and central planning. As with Tawwaj, more than one person is named as the founder of Basra. Whereas Kufa was divided into administrative units in the days of ᶜUmar, Basra would not be until the Sufyanid period. The difference stems from the gradual extension in the Persian Gulf region of the reach of the Islamic state through its local representatives, who appeared amidst and began coordinating tribal movements and conflict with neighbouring powers which began independent of the caliphate.[261] Nonetheless, tribes were autonomous early on in both cities, as seen by the existence of multiple qadis.

Al-Azd from western Arabia immigrated mainly to Syria, whereas those from Oman ended up in Basra. Many of those Omanis, however, had already spread, with other Gulf tribes, throughout the Gulf littoral. In Tawwaj, retrospectively claimed as a garrison town, they came to be led by ᶜUthman b. Abi al-ᶜAs al-Thaqafi, whose authority was at least partly because of his access to state resources and successful military leadership. It was ultimately through him that the first wave of al-Azd settlers in Basra were tied to the Islamic state, and this connection dictated their support for the Quraysh/Thaqif alliance from the Battle of the Camel through to he Second Civil War. Only when the Marwanid governor al-Hajjaj b. Yusuf went to eliminate the Muhallabids as potential rivals would this alignment end.

The mutual consent by which newcomers were added to existing tribal units during the Sufyanid period entitled them to housing and a stipend, as well as the protection of the tribe's leader. It is noteworthy, for example, that prestigious al-Azd shaykhs, such as Sayf b. Wahb al-Maᶜwali, would intervene on behalf of an individual from a tribe only loosely connected to them, such as the B. Tahiya, and that such power could be exercised by tribal leaders on behalf of state appointees, with the former effectively protecting the latter, who was saved in part by his tribal identity. This system, however, meant that in tribal areas, the state controlled people rather than territory, and exercised that control only over those individuals who continued to buy into the system. The Arab tribes formed a periphery in the sense that term has been deployed in the study of empire, but a periphery that was defined socially rather than territorially, despite the segregation into the garrison towns.[262] This model of indirect control over people may also explain the conflict in the sources between claims in al-Tabari that the Sufyanids controlled Oman and those in Omani sources that they did not.[263] After all, in the not unlikely event that the B. Ma^cwala shaykhs in Basra who submitted to the Sufyanid system maintained relations with their kinsmen the Julanda rulers of Oman, the sources could be justified in seeing Ziyad's influence extending there even if the Julandas saw themselves as buying into a voluntary alliance.

Shelagh Weir examines the effect of the administration through Yemeni tribes during the Hamid al-Din period. A key element of this was the taking of members of leading Razihi clans as hostages, with payments eventually made to their families which served to bind those groups more closely to the state. As this system became more routine and central to tribal politics, it affected tribal structures. For example, an existing division of the Naziri into Thirds became more important, as one hostage was to be taken from each. In addition, that portion of the hostage stipend which was collected from within the tribe was allocated according to newly created administrative units called 'fifths'.[264] As Weir says:

> The hostage system shows how easily the tribal structure of Razih could be harnessed to new administrative purposes. It also demonstrates how social systems can be created and re-created in the collective consciousness. In time people internalise and reify new structures, and start thinking of them as 'natural' entities with obvious significance. Older Naziris, looking back on this period, clearly thought of themselves as 'members' of 'fifths', as well as of clans, Thirds, and tribes. Hostage agents also joined the ranks of tribal leaders, and began to be mentioned as representing their tribes – together with *a'yan* and *mashayikh* – at the head of agreements (D1936a). The hegemonic tool or 'technology' for this restructuring and rethinking was the centrally important tribal institution of corporate subscription, adapted, in this instance, to state purposes.[265]

Weir's research in Yemen demonstrates many of the patterns also found in the garrison towns, patterns which combine state policy with tribal institutions rather than pit them against each other. There were no hostages in the early caliphate, but levels of identity that had been functionally dormant in Arabia came to have new, practical uses. Furthermore, although the practices of leadership did not change, the scale did. Sabra b. Shayman and Mas^cud b. ^cAmr had access to far more resources in the caliphate than did tribal leaders in Oman, and also had a greater number of followers. The increasing social differentiation would mean status increasingly came from political connections rather than support from followers, and, in these urban areas, such connections would yield more assets and options to followers than would military prowess.

Notes

1. For an overview of issues, see Fred McGraw Donner, 'Centralized Authority and Military Autonomy in the Early Islamic Conquests', pp. 337–60.
2. Robert Hoyland, *In God's Path: The Arab Conquests and the Creation of an Islamic Empire*, pp. 56–7.
3. This may also explain why, as described by Parvaneh Pourshariati, accounts of the Arab conquest of Iraq and Iran required different dating if read for their references to the Sasanian context. See Pourshariati, *Decline and Fall of the Sasanian Empire: The Sasanian–Parthian Confederacy and the Arab Conquest of Iran*, pp. 161–285.
4. Albrecht Noth, *The Early Arabic Historical Tradition: A Source-Critical Study*, pp. 76–87; Boaz Shoshan, *Historical Tradition*, pp. 4–6, 69–71.
5. Borrut, *Entre*, pp. 109–66. Borrut saw Sayf b. ᶜUmar as writing during a period in which the affirmation of Abbasid political authority was historiographically paramount, but given that Sayf was a pronounced Uthmani, that was likely not his interest. Borrut, *Entre*, pp. 80–5.
6. Noth/Conrad, pp. 31–2.
7. Fred Donner, *Narratives*, pp. 175–7.
8. Donner, *Narratives*, p. 179. This view was recently elaborated upon in Shoshan, *Historical Tradition*, pp. 29–46.
9. Donner, *Narratives*, p. 205.
10. Jan Vansina, *Oral Tradition as History*, p. 4.
11. Lawrence I. Conrad, 'The Conquest of Arwad: A Source-Critical Study in the Historiography of the Medieval Near East'.
12. Ibn Manzur, *Lisan al-ᶜArab* III, p. 745.
13. Fred M. Donner, *Muhammad and the Believers: At the Origins of Islam*, p. 137.
14. Kennedy, 'Military Pay and the Economy of the Early Islamic State', pp. 155–63.
15. Donner, *Early Islamic Conquests*, p. 147.
16. On Saᶜid b. ᶜAbd al-ᶜAziz al-Tanukhi, see Ibn ᶜAsakir, *Taʾrikh*, XXI, pp. 193–213.
17. Donner, *Early Islamic Conquests*, pp. 128, 133–6, 316 n. 208.
18. Ibn ᶜAsakir, *Taʾrikh*, XI, pp. 316–18.
19. Donner, *Early Islamic Conquests*, pp. 358–9, 363–4, 368; Ibn ᶜAsakir, *Taʾrikh*, XXV, pp. 7, 18–20.
20. Lawrence I. Conrad, 'Al-Azdi's History of the Arab Conquests in Bilad al-Sham: Some Historiographical Observations'; Suleiman Mourad, 'On Early Islamic Historiography: Abu Ismaᶜil al-Azdi and his Futuḥ al-Sham'; Jens J. Scheiner, 'Grundlegendes zu al-Azdis Futuh as-Sam'. See also Shoshan, *Historical Tradition*, pp. 8–10.
21. Sufyan b. Sulaym al-Azdi was the Syrian head of al-Hajjaj's police force in Wasit. Crone, *Slaves*, p. 139.

22. Azdi, *Futuh al-Sham*, pp. 287, 292, 299–300, 302, 309–10.
23. Azdi, *Futuh*, pp. 252–4, 284; Ibn ᶜAsakir, *Taʾrikh*, XXI, pp. 347–52.
24. Azdi, *Futuh*, pp. 316, 321; Ibn ᶜAsakir, *Taʾrikh*, XVII, pp. 460–1.
25. Azdi, *Futuh*, p. 331.
26. Azdi, *Futuh*, pp. 115–16, 155, 162, 221, 228–30, 240, 244, 246, 270–1, 279–80, 283–4, 344.
27. Azdi, *Futuh*, p. 388; Ibn ᶜAbd al-Barr, *al-Istiᶜab*, III, p. 102; Ibn ᶜAsakir, *Taʾrikh*, XXXIII, p. 10.
28. Ibn ᶜAsakir, *Taʾrikh*, XXXIII, pp. 5–10; Ibn ᶜAbd al-Barr, *al-Istiᶜab*, III, p. 102
29. Tarif Khalidi, 'Tribal Settlement and Patterns of Land Tenure in Early Medieval Palestine', pp. 182–3, 186 n. 13.
30. Jabali, *Companions*, pp. 130–1, 386–403.
31. Baladhuri, *Ansab*, IV/1, pp. 86, 104, 289; Caskel and Strenziok, *Gamharat*, I, p. 218; Ibn Hazm, *Jamhara*, p. 378.
32. For a reconstructed scheme of Basra during our period, see Louis Massignon, 'Explication du Plan de Basra (Irak)', p. 65.
33. Nezar Alsayyad, *Cities and Caliphs: On the Genesis of Arab Muslim Urbanism*, pp. 46–7.
34. al-Afghani, *Aswaq*, pp. 407–8; Szombathy, *Arabic Genealogy*, p. 107.
35. Yaqut, *Buldan*, I, pp. 510–11.
36. Thabit A. J. Abdullah, *Merchants, Mamluks, and Murder: The Political Economy of Trade in Eighteenth-Century Basra*, p. 9.
37. In Sayf b. ᶜUmar's version of a letter from ᶜAli describing his victory in the Battle of the Camel, al-Khurayba is described as a *finaʾ*, or a wide open space, suggesting it may have fallen into ruins. Tabari, *Taʾrīkh*, I, p. 3228; Tabari, *History*, XVI, p. 168. Hamza al-Isfahani supplies Vaheshtabadh Ardashir as the village's Persian name. Yaqut, *Buldan*, II, p. 415.
38. ᶜAwtabi, *Ansab*, II, p. 628.
39. Baladhuri, *Ansab*, VII/2, Beirut, pp. 179–80; al-Baladhuri, *Futuh*, pp. 346–7.
40. Baladhuri, *Futuh*, p. 341. See above, Note XXX.
41. Baladhuri, *Futuh*, pp. 342, 350; Ibn Saᶜd, *Tabaqat*, VII, p. 5; Tabari, *Taʾrīkh*, I, p. 2378.
42. Baladhuri, *Ansab*, VII/2, Beirut, p. 180; Yaqut, *Buldan*, I, p. 512. Yaqut does, however, report a ruined *qaṣr* at al-Khurayba. Yaqut, *Buldan*, II, p. 415.
43. Massignon, 'Basra', p. 70.
44. Some scholars have suggested that reference to Omani in Pliny's *Natural History* refers to al-Azd at the head of the Gulf, but the Azd ᶜUman would have only gotten that name after arrival in the country, almost certainly after Pliny's time. Potts, *Arabian Gulf*, II, p. 224.
45. ᶜAwtabi, *al-Ansab*, II p. 628; al-Baladhuri, *Futuh*, p. 347.
46. Alsayyad, p. 51.
47. *Khuzistan Chronicle*, p. 43.

48. Chase Robinson points out the problems with assuming that our earliest sources are always accurate in 'The Conquest of Khuzistan: A Historiographical Reassessment', pp. 17–18.
49. Hoyland, *God's Path*, pp. 49–51.
50. Noth/Conrad, pp. 81–2.
51. Tabari, *Taʾrīkh*, I, pp. 2377–8, 2380–1; Tabari, *History*, XII, pp. 161–3, 165. Balᶜami also says that the Arabs of the area were under the King of Oman. Balᶜami, *Tarikh*, pp. 453–4.
52. Dinawari, *al-Akhbar al-Tiwal*, p. 113.
53. Tabari, *Taʾrīkh*, I, pp. 2381–5; Tabari, *History*, XII, pp. 165–8. On al-Madaʾini, see Ilkka Lindstedt, 'The Life and Deeds of ᶜAli b. Muhammad al-Madaʾini'.
54. Ibn Saᶜd, *Tabaqat*, VII, p. 5; Yaqut, *Buldan* I, p. 311.
55. Yaqut, *Buldan*, I, p. 513; Tabari, *History*, XII, pp. 15, 162.
56. Dinawari, *al-Akhbar*, pp. 112–13. For yet another account, see Ibn Khayyat, *Taʾrikh*, pp. 68–9.
57. Charles Pellat, *Le Milieu Basrien et la Formation de Gahiz*, p. 3.
58. Hoyland, *God's Path*, p. 52.
59. For a reconstructed plan, see Massignon, 'Explication du Plan de Kufa (Irak)', p. 36.
60. Tabari, *Taʾrīkh*, I, pp. 2383–94; Tabari, *History* XIII, pp. 63–75.
61. Baladhuri, *Futuh*, pp. 275–6, Yaqut, *Buldan*, IV, p. 558. See also Dinawari, *al-Akhbar*, p. 118; Ibn Khayyat, *Taʾrikh*, p. 76.
62. Yaᶜqubi, *Kitab al-Buldan*, pp. 310–11.
63. It may also be significant that the Diwan al-ᶜata gave special stipend levels to veterans of Yarmuk and al-Qadisiyya, both of which were victories won from Western Arabia, but nothing from the east. Gerd-Rüdiger Puin, *Der Diwan von ᶜUmar Ibn al-Hattab: Ein Beitrag zur frühislamischen Verwaltungsgeschichte*, p. 114.
64. Tabari, *Taʾrīkh*, I, p. 2490; Tabari, *History*, XIII, pp. 70–1.
65. Tabari, *Taʾrīkh*, I, p. 2495; Tabari, *History*, XIII, p. 76.
66. Baladhuri, *Ansab*, IVa, p. 190.
67. Patricia Crone, *Slaves*, p. 31.
68. Hawting, *The First Dynasty of Islam: The Umayyad Caliphate 661–750*, p. 36.
69. Khalid Yahya Blankinship, *The End of the Jihad State: The Reign of Hisham Ibn 'Abd al-Malik and the Collapse of the Umayyads*, p. 44.
70. Werner Caskel, 'Bakr b. Wa'il, *EI* I, p. 963.
71. Michael Lecker, 'Tribes in Pre- and Early Islamic Arabia', pp. 68–76; Isabel Toral-Niehoff, *Al-Hira: Eine Arabische Kulturmetropole Im Spätantiken Kontext*, pp. 127–8.
72. Werner Caskel, 'Abd al-Kays', *EI* I, pp. 72–4; Morony, *Iraq*, p. 241.
73. Robert G. Hoyland, *Arabia and the Arabs: From the Bronze Age to the Coming of Islam* (London and New York: Routledge, 2001), p. 26.

74. Morony, *Iraq*, pp. 243–5.
75. Tabari, *Ta'rīkh*, I, pp. 2489–90, 2495.
76. Tabari, *Ta'rīkh*, II, p. 1382; Tabari, *History*, XXIV, p. 114; al-ᶜAli, p. 82.
77. On al-Farazdaq, see Isfahani, *Aghani*, XIX, pp. 1–61; Ibn Qutayba, *Shiᶜr wa al-Shuᶜara'*, pp. 310–8.
78. Joseph Hell, 'Al-Farazdaq's Lieder auf die Muhallabiten', 1905, pp. 598–607.
79. See, for example, Richard Tapper, *Frontier Nomads of Iran: A Political and Social History of the Shahsevan*, p. 345.
80. William Lancaster and Fidelity Lancaster, 'Concepts of Leadership in Bedouin Society', p. 38, n. 25.
81. Saleh Said Agha and Tarif Khalidi, 'Poetry and Identity in the Umayyad Age', pp. 63–4.
82. Ella Landau-Tasseron, 'Status of Allies', p. 6.
83. Alastair Northedge, 'Archaeology and New Urban Settlement in Early Islamic Syria and Iraq', p. 263.
84. Morony, *Iraq*, p. 255.
85. Tabari, *Ta'rīkh*, I, p. 2469.
86. Isfahani, *al-Aghani*, III, p. 257.
87. Lecker, 'Tribes', pp. 65–6.
88. Jabali, *Companions*, p. 34; Samᶜani, *al-Ansab*, III, p. 27.
89. Samᶜani, *al-Ansab*, II, p. 221.
90. Mubarrad, *Kamil*, III, pp. 169–72.
91. Petra M. Sijpesteijn, *Shaping a Muslim State: The World of a Mid-Eighth-Century Egyptian Official*, pp. 94–6.
92. Jacob Lassner, *Middle East Remembered*, p. 151.
93. Tabari, *Ta'rīkh*, I, p. 2496; Tabari, *History*, XIII, p. 77.
94. Hugh Kennedy, *The Armies of the Caliphs: Military and Society in the Early Islamic State*, p. 22.
95. Samᶜani, *al-Ansab*, II, p. 164, IV, pp. 4, 478.
96. He was a *mawlā* of the B. Dabba. Ibn Qutayba, *al-Maᶜarif*, p. 541; Zubaydi, *Tabaqat al-Nahwiyin wa al-Lughawiyin*, pp. 51–3; Ibn al-Nadim, *Fihrist*, pp. 66–7; Ibn al-Anbari, *Nuzha al-Alibba' fi Tabaqat al-Udaba'*, pp. 31–4; Yaqut, *Muᶜjam al-Udaba'*, V, pp. 651–3.
97. See, for example, Morony, *Iraq*, pp. 248–9; Pellat, *Milieu*, p. 24.
98. Tabari, *Ta'rīkh*, II, pp. 449–50; Tabari, *History*, XX, pp. 27–8.
99. Tabari, *Ta'rīkh*, II, pp. 448–9; Tabari, *History*, XX, pp. 25–6.
100. Salih Ahmad ᶜAli, *Khitat al-basra wa-mintaqiha: dirasa fi ahwaliha al-ᶜumraniya wa-maliya fi al-ᶜuhud al-islamiya al-ula*, p. 97.
101. Al-Mada'ini also reports a tradition of this nature, in which al-Ahnaf b. Qays explains to a critic his otherwise humiliating decision to pay the blood money for Masᶜud b. ᶜAmr. The source for this is Muhammad b. Hafs al-Bahili, who was also listed in the *isnad* for the tradition discussed above.

Baladhuri, *Ansab*, IVb, pp. 113–14. Bahil was the tribe of al-Ahnaf's mother, Habba bt. ᶜAmr. Baladhuri, *Ansab*, VII/1, Beirut, p. 101.

102. Tabari, *Taʾrīkh*, II, p. 450; Tabari, *History*, XX, p. 27.
103. Martin Hinds, 'The First Arab Conquests in Fars', p. 45.
104. Hinds, 'First Arab Conquests', p. 45.
105. What follows is from Hinds, 'First Arab Conquests', pp. 29–53.
106. ᶜAwtabi, *al-Ansab*, II, p. 797.
107. Wilkinson, *Ibadism*, p. 93.
108. Baladhuri, *Futuh*, pp. 386–7. There is also a report that Tawwaj was founded earlier. Baladhuri, *Futuh*, p. 81.
109. Donald Whitcomb, 'Bushire and the Angali Canal', pp. 332–3.
110. Robert Carter et al., 'The Bushehr Hinterland: Results of the First Season of the Iranian–British Archaeological Survey of Bushehr Province, November–December 2004', pp. 72, 97–8.
111. Whitcomb, 'Bushire', p. 330; Carter et al., 'Bushehr', p. 66.
112. Robert Carter et al., 'Bushehr', p. 69.
113. ᶜAwtabi, *al-Ansab*, II, p. 628; Hinds, *Early Islamic Family*, p. 18.
114. Ibn Manzur, *Lisan*, VI, p.724.
115. ᶜAwtabi, *al-Ansab*, II, pp. 628–9; Hinds, *Early Islamic Family*, pp. 18–20. The text gives al-Thaqifi as Masᶜud b. ᶜAmr's *nisba*, but this is obviously wrong.
116. Tabari, *Taʾrīkh*, I, p. 3189; Tabari, *History*, XVI, p. 130.
117. Ibn Khayyat, *Taʾrikh*, p. 109. This is from Abu Yaqzan b. Hafs, for whom see F. Sezgin, *Geschichte*, I, pp. 266–7.
118. Tabari, *Taʾrīkh*, I, p. 3178; Tabari, *History*, XVI, p. 118.
119. Tabari, *Taʾrīkh*, I, pp. 3190, 3194, 3204; Tabari, *History*, XVI, pp. 130, 134, 144.
120. Ibn Khayyat, *Taʾrikh*, p. 114; Ibn al-Kalbi, *Maᶜadd wa al-Yaman*, p. 468.
121. Yaᶜqubi, *Taʾrikh*, II, p. 182.
122. Tabari, *Taʾrīkh*, I, p. 3224; Tabari, *History*, XVI, p. 164.
123. Tabari, *Taʾrīkh*, I, p. 3232; Tabari, *History*, XVI, p. 171; Ibn Aᶜtham al-Kufi, *Kitab al-Futuh*, II p. 342.
124. Tabari, *Taʾrīkh*, I, p. 3180; Tabari, *History*, XVI, p. 120.
125. Tabari, *Taʾrīkh*, I, p. 3201; Tabari, *History*, XVI, p. 141.
126. Rasheed Hosein, 'Tribal Alliance Formations', p. 72.
127. Lecker, 'Tribes', p. 86.
128. Hinds, 'Early Islamic Conquests', p. 47; Baladhuri, *Futuh*, p. 353.
129. Madelung, *The Succession to Muhammad: A Study of the Early Caliphate*, pp. 271–6.
130. Tabari, *Taʾrīkh*, I, pp. 3454–5; Tabari, *History*, XVII, pp. 211–12; Baladhuri, *Ansab*, II, pp. 160–1.
131. Madelung, *Succession*, p. 277.
132. Tabari, *Taʾrīkh*, I, pp. 3414–17; Tabari, *History*, XVII, pp. 166–70;

Baladhuri, *Ansab*, II, pp. 373–84; Abu ᶜUbayda, *Naqaᵓid*, p. 125; Madelung, *Succession*, pp. 279–83.

133. Morony, *Iraq*, pp. 438–9.
134. Wakiᶜ, *Akhbar al-Qudat*, I, pp. 269–74.
135. Wakiᶜ, *Akhbar al-Qudat*, I, pp. 274–5; Ibn Qutayba, *al-Maᶜarif*, p. 430.
136. Wakiᶜ, *Akhbar al-Qudat*, I, pp. 287–8.
137. Wakiᶜ, *Akhbar al-Qudat*, I, pp. 288.
138. Tabari, *Taᵓrīkh*, II, p. 71; Tabari, *History*, XVIII, p. 76.
139. Tabari, *Taᵓrīkh*, II, pp. 7–80; Tabari, *History*, XVIII, pp. 85–6.
140. Baladhuri, *Ansab*, IV/1, pp. 175–7. See also Mubarrad, *Kamil*, III, pp. 244–5.
141. Baladhuri, *Ansab*, IV/1, p. 177.
142. Ibn Khayyat, *Taᵓrikh*, pp. 135–7. Most of this material is also found in Tabari, *Taᵓrikh*, pp. 90–1. See also Wilkinson, *Ibadism*, p. 157.
143. Baladhuri, *Ansab* IVa, pp. 153.
144. Caskel and Strenziok, *Gamharat*, I, p. 245.
145. Caskel and Strenziok, *Gamharat*, I, p. 206. Ibn Durayd, *al-Ishtiqaq*, p. 484; Ibn al-Kalbi, *Maᶜadd wa al-Yaman*, II, p. 470.
146. Caskel and Strenziok, *Gamharat*, I, p. 176.
147. Caskel and Strenziok, *Gamharat*, I, p. 210.
148. Baladhuri, *Ansab*, IVb, pp. 119–20.
149. Wilkinson, *Ibadism*, pp. 42–3.
150. Caskel and Strenziok, *Gamharat*, I, p. 327; Ibn al-Kalbi, *Maᶜadd wa al-Yaman*, II, p. 699.
151. Caskel and Strenziok, *Gamharat*, II, p. 485.
152. Caskel and Strenziok, *Gamharat*, II, pp. 87–8.
153. Wilkinson, *Ibadism*, p. 140.
154. Hawting, *First Dynasty*, pp. 54–5. However, he also notes ᶜUbayd Allah's attempt to seek Azd support against the Tamim.
155. Tabari, *History*, XXXIX, p. 96.
156. Ibn Hazm, *Jamhara*, p. 370. Another once gives him the al-ᶜAtaki nisba, but elsewhere calls him al-Maᶜni. Mubarrad, *Kamil*, I, pp. 140, 229, 284.
157. Ibn Hazm, *Jamhara*, pp. 371, 381.
158. Wilkinson, *Ibadism*, p. 104.
159. Rotter, p. 73, though he over-estimates the similarities between Wahb b. Jarir and al-Madᵓini.
160. Ibn al-Nadim, *Fihrist*, p. 85. See also Mubarrad, *Kamil*, I, pp. 140–3.
161. In addition to sources mentioned in the text, see Zubaydi, *Tabaqat*, pp. 175–8; Dhahabi, *Tadhkira al-Huffaz*, I, pp. 371–2; Ibn al-Anbari, *Nuzha*, pp. 68–74; Yaqut, *Udabaᵓ*, V, pp. 509–14.
162. Ignaz Goldziher, *Muslim Studies*, I, pp. 181–7; H. A. R. Gibb, 'The Social Significance of the Shuubiya', pp. 67–8.
163. A. A. Duri, *The Rise of Historical Writing Among the Arabs*, pp. 57, 148; Charles Pellat, *Milieu*, p. 143.
164. Scott Savran, *Arabs and Iranians*, p. 37.

165. Lughawi, *Maratib*, pp. 60–1; Ibn Qutayba, *al-Maᶜarif*, p. 543. On Ibn Shabba, see Ibn al-Nadim, *Fihrist*, pp. 179–80; Baghdadi, *Taʾrikh*, XI, pp. 208–10; Yaqut, *ᶜUdabaʾ* IV, pp. 465–9.
166. Wilferd Madelung, 'Abu Ubayda Ma'mar b. al-Muthanna as a Historian', p. 55.
167. Ibn Saᶜd, *Tabaqat*, VII, p. 132; Samᶜani, *al-Ansab*, I, p. 295.
168. This was part of the Mirbad. See al-Afghani, *al-Aswaq*, pp. 408–9; A. T. Naji and S. Y. Ali, 'The Suqs of Basra: Commerical Organization and Activity in a Medieval Islamic City', pp. 303–4.
169. Tabari, *Taʾrīkh*, II, pp. 437–9; Tabari, *History*, XX, pp. 12–13; Abu ᶜUbayda, *Naqaʾid*, pp. 722–3; al-Baladhuri, *Ansab*, IV/a, pp. 402.
170. Some claimed the B. Najiya were related to the Quraysh, as in Caskel and Strenziok, *Gamharat*, II, 4–5.
171. Tabari, *Taʾrīkh*, II, pp. 439–41; Tabari, *History*, XX, pp. 14–7; Abu ᶜUbayda, *Naqaʾid*, pp. 724–6; Baladhuri, *Ansab*, IV/a, pp. 402–3.
172. Tabari, *Taʾrīkh*, II, pp. 445–7; Tabari, *History*, XX, pp. 21–2; Abu ᶜUbayda, *Naqaʾid*, pp. 726–7; Baladhuri, *Ansab*, IV/a, p. 403.
173. Tabari, *Taʾrīkh*, II, pp. 446–7; Tabari, *History*, XX, pp. 21–2; Baladhuri, *Ansab*, IV/a, p. 405.
174. Tabari, *History*, XX, p. 25 n. 118. See Crone, *Slaves*, p. 120 for more on this leader and his family background. The rivalry with Malik goes back at least as far as the Battle of the Camel, when Shaqiq b. Thawr commanded the Bakr b. Waʾil on behalf of ᶜAli, while Malik b. Mismaᶜ head a group loyal to ᶜAʾisha. See Madelung, *Succession*, p. 168.
175. Tabari, *Taʾrīkh*, II, p. 449; Tabari, *History*, XX, p. 26. The leadership situation was actually much more complex, and the text traces it back to balances in pre-Islamic Arabia that were transferred to Basra.
176. Tabari, *Taʾrīkh*, II, pp. 447–9; Tabari, *History*, XX, pp. 24–7; Abu ᶜUbayda, *Naqaʾid*, pp. 727–9; Baladhuri, *Ansab*, IV/a, p. 406.
177. Tabari, *Taʾrīkh*, II, pp. 450–2; Tabari, *History*, XX, pp. 28–9; Baladhuri, *Ansab* IV/a, pp. 407–8; Abu ᶜUbayda, *Naqaʾid*, pp. 730.
178. Samᶜani, *al-Ansab*, IV, p. 145.
179. Tabari, *Taʾrīkh*, II, pp. 452–6; Tabari, *History*, XX, pp. 30–4; Baladhuri, *Ansab*, IV/a, pp. 408–9, 413; Abu ᶜUbayda, *Naqaʾid*, pp. 731–7. Abu ᶜUbayda's report is arranged with the 'Order of Battle' topos described by Noth/Conrad, pp. 111–14.
180. Baladhuri, *Ansab*, IV/a, pp. 413–14; Abu ᶜUbayda, *Naqaʾid*, pp. 737–8. Several smaller tribes are listed in such a way that they could either be *alfaf* to the B. Saᶜid or a separate unit of the army.
181. Baladhuri, *Ansab*, IV/a, pp. 414–15; Abu ᶜUbayda, *Naqaʾid*, pp. 738–40.
182. Baladhuri, *Ansab*, IV/a, p. 417.
183. Baladhuri, *Ansab*, IV/a, p. 411.
184. Baladhuri, *Ansab*, IV/a, p. 413.

185. For an argument along these lines with respect to other traditions from Abu ᶜUbayda, see Madelung, 'Abu Ubayda', pp. 51–2.
186. Ibn Qutayba, *al-Maᶜarif*, p. 502; Dhahabi, *Tadhkira al-Huffaz*, I, pp. 336–7.
187. al-Khatib al-Baghdadi, *Taʾrikh*, IV, pp. 224–5; Samᶜani, *al-Ansab*, V, p. 422.
188. Ibn Hajar, *Tahdhib*, II, pp. 69–73; Dhahabi, *Tadhkira al-Huffaz*, I, pp. 199–200; Fuat Sezgin, *Geschichte*, I, pp. 310–11. Sezgin has him with the *nisba* 'al-Jahdami'.
189. Al-Baladhuri, *Ansab*, IV/a, pp. 418–20.
190. Tabari, *History*, XX, p. 17 n. 76.
191. Tabari, *Taʾrīkh*, II, pp. 441–2; Tabari, *History*, XX, pp. 17–18; Baladhuri, *Ansab*, IV/a, pp. 420–2.
192. Tabari, *Taʾrīkh*, II, pp. 442–3; Tabari, *History*, XX, pp. 18–19; Baladhuri, *Ansab*, IV/a, p. 421.
193. Baladhuri, *Ansab*, IV/a, pp. 421–2.
194. Tabari, *Taʾrīkh*, II, pp. 444–5; Tabari, *History*, XX, pp. 20–1; Baladhuri, *Ansab*, IV/a, pp. 422–3; Wilfred Madelung, ''Abd Allah b. al-Zubayr and the Mahdi', p. 301.
195. Baladhuri, *Ansab*, IV/a, pp. 418, 423.
196. Baladhuri, *Ansab*, IV/a, pp. 424–6.
197. Baladhuri, *Ansab*, IV/a, p. 424.
198. al-Baladhuri, *Ansab*, IV/a, p. 426.
199. Tabari, *Taʾrīkh*, II, pp. 682–3.
200. Baladhuri, *Ansab*, IVb, p. 120.
201. Ibn ᶜAsakir, *Taʾrikh*, LXI, pp. 92–3
202. Ibn Hajar, *Tahdhib*, II, pp. 69–72
203. Tabari, *Taʾrīkh*, II, pp. 464–5; Tabari, *History*, XX, pp. 44–5; Baladhuri, *Ansab*, IV/a, pp. 405–6.
204. Tabari, *Taʾrīkh*, II, pp. 465; Tabari, *History*, XX, p. 45; Baladhuri, *Ansab* IV/a, pp. 406–7.
205. Baladhuri, *Ansab*, IV/a, p. 416.
206. Baladhuri, *Ansab*, IV/a, pp. 416–17.
207. Baladhuri, *Ansab* VII/1, Beirut, pp. 100–42.
208. Baladhuri, *Ansab* VII/1, Beirut, p. 117.
209. Baladhuri, *Ansab* VII/1, Beirut, p. 119.
210. Tabari, *Taʾrīkh*, II, pp. 682–3.
211. Baladhuri, *Ansab* V, pp. 244–5.
212. Tabari, *History*, XXI, p. 47 n. 192.
213. Tabari, *Taʾrīkh*, II, pp. 460–1; Tabari, *History*, XX, pp. 39–40; Baladhuri, *Ansab*, 4/1, pp. 396–7. Tabari's account is clearly the same source, but somewhat trimmed and given without citation.
214. Tabari, *Taʾrīkh*, II, 461–4; Tabari, *History*, XX, pp. 40–3; Baladhuri, *Ansab*, 4/1, pp. 397–400.
215. Wellhausen also accepts al-Madaʾini's view, *Arab Kingdom*, pp. 410–1. An

additional point, highlighted by Gernot Rotter, is that the majority of the Kharijites in Basra were in fact from Tamim. In this case, the substitution may have been suggested by the overlap between the two groups. Rotter, *Der Umayyaden und der Zweite Bürgerkrieg (680–692)*, pp. 74–5.

216. Blankinship, *Jihad State*, p. 26.
217. Lecker, 'Tribes', p. 175. Morony calls the Tamim 'The real founders of Basra in terms of numbers', *Iraq*, p. 247. This discussion of Tamim preponderance, however, actually goes back to Pellat, who based it solely on the numbers of each tribe found in Ibn Saᶜd's *Tabaqat*.
218. Hinds, *Early Islamic Family*, p. 25; ᶜAwtabi, *al-Ansab*, II, p. 631.
219. Morony, *Iraq*, p. 256.
220. D. T. Potts, 'Contributions to the Agrarian History of Eastern Arabia I. Implements and Cultivation Techniques', pp. 161–3.
221. ᶜAbd al-Ameer ᶜAbd Dixon, *The Umayyad Caliphate 65–86/684–705 (A Political Study)*, pp. 129–31. At this battle, the Azd were led by Khalid b. Malik. Ziyad b. ᶜAmr al-ᶜAtaki was a supporter of the Marwanids at that time, as was a man named ᶜAbd Allah b. Fadala al-Zahrani. Abu Ubayda, *Naqaʾid*, pp. 749, 1091–2. Additions and Corrections for that work suggests an omitted 'ibn Malik' or reading it as 'ibn ᶜAbd Allah, ᶜAbd al-Malik's emissary to Basra, III, p. 630.
222. Dixon, *Umayyad*, p. 132.
223. Dixon, *Umayyad*, p. 132.
224. Tabari, *Taʾrīkh*, I, 3414–18; Tabari, *History*, XVII, pp. 166–70
225. William Lancaster and Fidelity Lancaster, 'Tribal Formations', p. 146.
226. See Lancaster and Lancaster, 'Tribal Formations', p. 157 for a discussion of Bedouin practice.
227. Patricia Crone, *Slaves*, pp. 29–33.
228. Lancaster and Lancaster, 'Tribal Formations', pp. 155–6.
229. Tabari, *Taʾrīkh*, II, pp. 682–3; Baladhuri, *Ansab*, V, pp. 243–5.
230. Jabali, *Companions*, p. 125.
231. Bariqi, *Diwan*, p. 79.
232. Wakiᶜ, *Akhbar al-Qudat*, II, p. 184, IbnᶜAsakir, *Taʾrikh*, XLIX, p. 97.
233. Wakiᶜ, *Akhbar al-Qudat*, II, pp. 186–7; Ibn Saᶜd, *Tabaqat*, VI, pp. 379–80; Samᶜani, *al-Ansab*, I, p. 265.
234. Ibn Saᶜd, *Tabaqat*, VI, p. 427.
235. Heather Keaney, *Medieval Islamic Historiography: Remembering Rebellion*, pp. 35–8, 64–9, 93–7, 121–7.
236. For a late attempt at systematising them, see Ibn ᶜAsakir, *Taʾrikh*, XI, pp. 303–16.
237. Tabari, *Taʾrīkh*, I, pp. 2845–6; Baladhuri, *Ansab*, IV/1, p. 519; Caskel and Strenziok, *Gamharat*, I, p. 218; Isfahani, al-*Aghani*, V, pp. 142–4; al-Yaᶜqubi, *Taʾrikh*, II, p. 165; al-ᶜAwtabi, *al-Ansab*, II, p. 683.
238. Baladhuri, *Ansab*, IV/1, pp. 521–2; Isfahani, *al-Aghani*, V, pp. 129–30; Masᶜudi, *Muruj*, II, p. 370; Ibn Aᶜtham al-Kufi, *Kitab al-Futuh*, II, pp. 168.

239. Baladhuri, *Ansab*, IV/1, pp. 528–9.
240. Keaney, p. 37.
241. Tabari, *Taʾrīkh*, I, pp. 2840–5; Tabari, *History*, XV, pp. 46–50.
242. Tabari, *Taʾrīkh*, I, p. 2921; Tabari, *History*, XV, p. 125.
243. Tabari, *Taʾrīkh*, I, pp. 3303–4; Tabari, *History*, XVII, pp. 50–1.
244. Tabari, *Taʾrīkh*, I, p. 3304; Ibn ᶜAsakir, *Taʾrikh*, XI, pp. 303–8.
245. Tabari, *Taʾrīkh*, I, p. 3201; al-Dinawari, *al-Akhbar*, p. 138.
246. Khalifa b. Khayyat, *Taʾrikh*, p. 118.
247. Tabari, *Taʾrīkh*, I, p. 3461; Tabari, *History*, XVII, p. 218.
248. Madelung, *Succession*, pp. 315–16.
249. Ibn Saᶜd, *Tabaqat*, VI, p. 380; ᶜAwtabi, *al-Ansab*, II, p. 681.
250. Tabari, *Taʾrīkh*, I, p. 3202; Tabari, *History* XVI, p. 142.
251. Bariqi, *Diwan*, pp. 80, 86–8.
252. Baladhuri, *Ansab*, VI, pp. 534–5. ᶜAbd al-Rahman was also known as '*ḍarṭa al-jamal*', or 'the camel's fart'. Baladhuri, *Ansab*, VI, p. 534.
253. Tabari, *Taʾrīkh*, II, pp. 50–1; Tabari, *History*, XVIII, pp. 55–6.
254. Tabari, *Taʾrīkh*, II, p. 62; Tabari, *History*, XVIII, p. 66.
255. Tabari, *Taʾrīkh*, II, pp. 57, 134; Tabari, *History*, XVIII, pp. 62, 143.
256. Tabari, *Taʾrīkh*, II, p. 118; Tabari, *History*, XVIII, p. 129.
257. Tabari, *Taʾrīkh*, II, p. 122; Tabari, *History*, XVIII, p. 132.
258. Tabari, *Taʾrīkh*, II, pp. 124–6; Tabari, *History*, XVIII, pp. 134–5; Baladhuri, *Ansab*, IVa, p. 218.
259. Tabari, *Taʾrīkh*, II, pp. 373–4; Tabari, *History*, XIX, pp. 167–8.
260. Ibn Aᶜtham al-Kufi, *Kitab al-Futuh*, V, pp. 229–35.
261. Timothy Power's observations of the influence of existing Yemeni agendas in the caliphate's Red Sea policy could perhaps be evaluated for whether his evidence, too, might fit this paradigm. Power, *Red Sea*, pp. 90–6.
262. For a discussion of 'periphery' in the context of empire, see Karen Barkey, *Empire of Difference: The Ottomans in Comparative Perspective*, pp. 9–15.
263. Tabari, *Taʾrīkh*, II, p. 73; Tabari, *History*, XVIII, p. 78.
264. Shelagh Weir, *A Tribal Order: Politics and Law in the Mountains of Yemen*, pp. 273–4.
265. Weir, *Tribal Order*, p. 275.

3

The Muhallabids: War, Politics and Memory

During the Marwanid period, the political fortunes of the Azd in the central Islamic lands closely followed those of the Muhallabid family, named after the general al-Muhallab b. Abi Sufra and led to its greatest influence by his son Yazid, who became governor of Iraq and the eastern caliphate under the caliph Sulayman b. ᶜAbd al-Malik. Although they subsequently fell into relative obscurity, they resurfaced during the Abbasid Revolution, and several rose to prominence under the Abbasids. In addition to the light their careers shed upon the political significance of al-Azd identity during the Marwanid period, as the great heroes of al-Azd's early Islamic history, the events of the lives of the first Muhallabids can also be studied as what Pierre Nora has termed '*lieux de mèmoire*' or 'sites of memory'. This term refers to elements of the past that, because they are no longer part of the inherent memory of a community, are deliberately commemorated in some fashion as part of that community's self-definition.[1]

This process of deliberate commemoration built on that from the days of the early Muhallabids themselves. Al-Muhallab was a generous patron of poets, particularly those who served in his army.[2] From numerous references in al-Isfahani's *Kitab al-Aghani*, we see that his descendants continued this tradition; in fact, al-Isfahani himself was the protégé of the Buyid vizier Abu Muhammad al-Hasan b. Muhammad al-Muhallabi.[3] Al-Muhallab's associates included Kaᶜb al-Ashqari, considered one of the most accomplished poets of his day.[4] Yazid's companions included the poet Thabit Qutna, who was either a client or foster brother of the B. Asad b. al-Harith b. ᶜAtik. His name came from the eyepatch he wore following an injury in a battle against the Turks. Thabit was also reportedly a governor under Yazid for a time.[5] During the second quarter of the eighth century, accounts of the family circulated particularly among the Azd, and judging by the pattern of preservation in later sources, the tribe was concerned with promoting their reputations as heroes and thus a repository of al-Azd's collective historic *sharaf*. With the rise of more named works by traditionists in the early Abbasid period, we find the Muhallabids swiftly represented in the works of Abu Mikhnaf al-Azdi. His titles include the 'Book of Yazid b. al-Muhallab and His Killing' and the 'Book of the Tale of the Azraqites'. The latter likely dealt substantially with al-Muhallab, as was posited above for Jarir b. Hazm's similar work.[6] In contrast, by the late ninth and early tenth centuries, the pattern of the narratives suggests that the main unit of interest had become the Muhallabid family specifically or the Arabs as a whole rather than al-Azd in particular.

Rise to Prominence

Al-Muhallab was almost certainly of Persian descent, part of a world found in much of the history of the Persian Gulf in which people of different ethnicities moved easily around its shores.[7] Al-Isfahani includes an impressive list of authorities who reported that Abu Sufra, his father, was non-Arab (*ᶜajam*, probably Persian): Abu ᶜUbayda, al-Haytham b. ᶜAdi, Ibn Mazruᶜ, Ibn al-Kalbi and multiple poets. He summarises them as saying that Abu Sufra was a non-Arab Omani who had a *walā* bond with al-Azd, and that they attached him to their lineage once al-Muhallab achieved greatness; as with Umm Ghaylan in Chapter 1, use of the *walā*/*mawlā* is probably anachronistic.[8] Al-Farazdaq said the Muhallabids' ancestors were Zoroastrians from Kharg, but makes them sailors instead of weavers.[9] According to al-Haytham b. ᶜAdi, Abu Sufra was part of the delegation from Oman to the caliph ᶜUmar, where he and one of the sons of al-Julanda admitted that he was not an Arab. His *kunya* came from his dyeing his beard with saffron for the occasion.[10] According to Abu ᶜUbayda, Abu Sufra was a Persian Zoroastrian (*majūs*) from Kharg named Biskhareh b. Bahbudhan, who went to Oman and became a weaver. Later he became a horse groom for ᶜUthman b. Abi al-ᶜAs al-Thaqafi, whom he accompanied to Basra.[11] This tradition is lent credence by frequent associations between the Muhallabids and horses. For example, Jarir b. Hazm reports that at the time of the fall of Yazid b. al-Muhallab, the family had many fine horses in Basra descended from stock which one of al-Muhallab's grandsons said Abi Sufra had originally brought from Oman.[12] Al-Muhallab, whose name actually means 'docked', was also considered the first Muslim to dock the tails of his horses, after being inspired by Turks in al-Qiqan, which today is the region around the western portion of the border between Pakistan and Afghanistan.[13] Abu ᶜUbayda also quoted a poem which traces Abu Sufra's *kunya* to his circumcision at ᶜUthman b. Abi al-ᶜAs's hands, a tradition also passed on by al-Isfahani.[14]

Multiple sources also seek to provide Abu Sufra with prominent

Islamic credentials. Pseudo-al-Waqidi makes him the first Omani to affirm adherence to Islam at the time of the *ridda*, even before the sons of al-Julanda, and also reports him as accompanying ᶜAmr b. al-ᶜAs to fight the *ridda* movement.[15] In contrast, an Ibn ᶜAsakir account sourced to Ibn Saᶜd says Abu Sufra was from the Azd of Daba, and as a youth was one of the prisoners sent to Medina after the *ridda* there, going to Basra after being freed by ᶜUmar.[16] Ps.-al-ᶜAwtabi claims that Abu Sufra was a *sharīf* of his people, the commander of the ᶜImran during the invasion of Fars, and perhaps the one who killed the Persian commander Shahrak.[17] He later campaigned in Sistan with the commander ᶜAbd al-Rahman b. Samura al-Qurashi before arriving in Basra three days after the Battle of the Camel. In this account, after Abu Sufra told ᶜAli b. Abi Talib that he would have seen that the Azd of Basra supported him rather than ᶜAʾisha, ᶜAli appointed him head of al-Azd in Basra, as well as three towns in Khuzistan.[18] According to ps.-al-ᶜAwtabi, Abu Sufra died during the governorship of Ibn al-ᶜAbbas, who said his funeral prayers.[19] Some of al-Baladhuri's sources say that Abu Sufra accompanied Ibn al-ᶜAbbas to join ᶜAli in Kufa, but died on the way.[20]

Al-Muhallab was reportedly born in the year of Muhammad's conquest of Mecca.[21] Ps.-al-ᶜAwtabi preserves several stories of him drawing the attention of early Islamic leaders. In one, the Companion ᶜArfaja b. Harthama recognised al-Muhallab's fine qualities when the latter was just a boy.[22] In Sistan, Ibn Samura tried to send him back because of his youth, but relented because of the fine quality of his horse. Al-Muhallab impressed Ibn Samura further when he wounded one of the lords of Kabul but did not brag about it.[23] Most significantly, when Abu Sufra arrived in Basra after the Battle of the Camel, ᶜAli asked for one of his sons for whom to tie a banner so that the family could acquire nobility. Abu Sufra's eldest son al-Nakhf refused on account of ᶜAli's forces having killed so many al-Azd, and so he instead presented al-Muhallab, his 27-year-old youngest son. ᶜAli anointed al-Muhallab and sent him to proclaim a guarantee of security to those who had fled Basra. This was when al-Azd began to look upon al-Muhallab with both awe and affection.[24] Coming after his material on Abu Sufra, this account continues ps.-al-ᶜAwtabi's portrayal of the Muhallabids as particularly close to ᶜAli. Andrew Marsham interprets this material as calling attention to parallels between the Muhallabids and Alids as two Iraq-based families massacred by the Umayyads.[25] Ps.-al-ᶜAwtabi eventually makes the comparison explicit:

> In having Al al-Muhallab killed in cold blood in his presence, Yazid b. ᶜAbd al-Malik emulated what Yazid b. Muᶜawiya – may God curse them both! – did,

> [this being] in order to show the Syrians that he had killed the family of the noblest Arabs of his time, just as Yazid b. Mu^cawiya – may God curse him! – killed the family of the Prophet of God. The Arabs coined a proverb about these two families and said, 'Banu Harb sacrificed religion at Karbala^ɔ and Banu Marwan sacrificed manly honour on the battle-day of al-^cAqr at Babil.'[26]

A plausible historical context for this comparison is the period of the Abbasid Revolution. The Muhallabids were prominent in anti-Umayyad activism during that time, both alongside the Ja^cfarid ^cAbd Allah b. Mu^cawiya and the Abbasid organisation, when lower Iraq was the centre of a movement to install an Alid caliph.[27]

Al-Muhallab rose to prominence on the caliphate's eastern frontier, first in Sistan and later in Khurasan, a region in which non-Arabian *mawali* frequently rose to prominence. According to the anonymous *Tarikh-i Sistan*, he was part of a force under Ibn Samura escorting a merchant caravan across the Dasht-i Lut from Kirman when they were robbed. Al-Muhallab succeeded in winning back their goods, after which Ibn Samura assigned him a command. He then participated in a raid against the Kabul-Shah, allegedly impressing that ruler so much that he sought peace with the Muslims. In another engagement with the Kabul-Shah, in an account credited by al-Baladhuri to Abu Mikhnaf, he slew an elephant, earning another promotion and the charge to campaign in South Asia. Al-Muhallab is said to have raided as far as Qandabil, the modern Gandava in the dry region west of the Indus River in central Pakistan.[28] There is, however, chronological confusion. According to ps.-al-^cAwtabi, al-Muhallab was in Sistan alongside his father before the First Civil War, whereas afterward he went with al-Hakam b. ^cAmr al-Ghifari to Khurasan.[29] Al-Baladhuri, on the other hand, has him in Sistan during Mu^cawiya's reign.[30]

^cUmar b. Shabba, citing al-Mada^ɔini, claims that the commander al-Hakam b. ^cAmr put al-Muhallab b. Abi Sufra in charge of the rearguard during a retreat from al-Ashall in one of the eastern campaigns early in Mu^cawiya's reign. ^cUmar also reports that al-Hakam placed al-Muhallab in charge of the entire war, and that the latter saved the army by capturing some of the other side's leaders and threatening to kill them unless they found a way out of a pass in which they were trapped. The men suggested setting fires as a decoy so the enemies would concentrate their efforts along a single road while al-Muhallab's forces took another. The Muslims did, and escaped with lots of booty.[31] The second story is probably embellished, and Hatim b. Qabisa, ^cUmar's source for it, was the son of Qabisa b. al-Muhallab, a Hatim whose own sons would lead the Muhallabids under the early Abbasids.[32] It also seems that al-Muhallab lost an eye in Khurasan, either during the siege of Samarqand or al-Taliqan.[33] Again,

after providing a heroic version of his command of al-Hakam b. ᶜAmr's rear, ps.-al-ᶜAwtabi links his successes to the blessings of ᶜAli b. Abi Talib and Saᶜd b. Abi Waqqas.[34] According to a Persian local history, al-Muhallab also raided Balkh along with Quthum b. ᶜAbbas.[35]

There is also an account connecting al-Muhallab with Khurasan governor Salm b. Ziyad, son of Muᶜawiya's viceroy Ziyad b. Abihi. When the Khurasanians began to oppose Salm b. Ziyad after the fall of the Sufyanids, Salm left and put al-Muhallab b. Abi Sufra over Khurasan. When Sulayman b. Marthad of Bakr b. Waᵓil complained that this favoured al-Yaman, Salm set him and one Aws b. Thaᶜlaba of Bakr b. Waᵓil over parts of Khurasan. Later, when Salm encountered ᶜAbd Allah b. Khazim al-Tamimi, the Mudari insisted on being given a letter of appointment over Khurasan and 100,000 dirhams, after which he set off for Merv. Upon hearing of this, al-Muhallab left, leaving behind a man of the Tamim as his deputy The deputy was soon defeated by Ibn Khazim.[36] This, however, is simply the most stylised of several accounts in which Ibn Khazim seizes control of Khurasan after it had been divided, and the only one which mentions al-Muhallab.[37] The source is al-Madaᵓini citing Abu Hafs al-Azdi from his paternal uncle, and it probably combines al-Madaᵓini's interest with tribal factionalism in Khurasan with an Azdi promotion of al-Muhallab's role in famous events.

During this period, al-Muhallab had a *mawlā* of Juzjani origin named ᶜAtaᵓ al-Khurasani, who became known as a hadith scholar and religious warrior who was active in Syria.[38] One tradition also alleges al-Muhallab was a gardener. Al-Madaᵓini reports that Qutayba b. Muslim, who would come to power after the Muhallabids, turned Yazid b. al-Muhallab's Merv garden into pasture for camels. He explained the action by saying that Yazid's father was a gardener, whereas Qutayba's was a camel driver.[39] Al-Dinawari claims al-Muhallab was the head of al-Azd in Basra before Masᶜud b. ᶜAmr, and as we saw last chapter, he appears in Wahb b. Jarir's account of the Fitna of Masᶜud b. ᶜAmr as a superior candidate for leadership to Ziyad b. ᶜAmr.[40] Neither account seems reliable, however, and al-Dinawari is probably simply trying to fit al-Muhallab into the important early notables of the garrison towns. The fact so little information about al-Muhallab exists before the Second Civil War leaves us to suspect that he played little if any role in events in the garrison towns during the Sufyanid period.

The Azraqite War

Al-Muhallab's reputation as a general was made during his campaign against the Azraqite Kharijites during the 680s and 690s.[41] Nafi^c b. al-Azraq emerged as a Kharijite leader during the Second Fitna, and set up an independent power center in al-Ahwaz. Although Ibn al-Azraq himself died in battle soon after, the Azraqites continued to maintain their independence in southern Iran under a successor, Qatari b. Fujaʾa, who in some accounts also fought with ᶜAbd al-Rahman b. Samura's army in Sistan during the caliphate of Muᶜawiya.[42] This Azraqite polity was firmly enough established under Qatari that it minted the earliest known Kharijite coins.[43] In combating it, al-Muhallab himself was able to set up his own independent administration in Fars, and we have coinage in the Sasanian style bearing his name.[44] Minting during this period closely matched the areas where campaigning armies were based, and new coinage was probably the primary means of paying and supplying troops.[45] Al-Muhallab's ultimate victory set him up for an appointment as governor of Khurasan and made the Muhallabids major figures in the politics of the caliphate for the next two decades.

The war against the Azraqites also had significance for al-Azd as a tribe. In ps.-al-ᶜAwtabi's work, the section on the Salima b. Malik b. Fahm begins with an account of how six subgroups of that division were *ᶜirāʾif* in al-Muhallab's army during that period.[46] Given that Salima was associated with the Iranian coast, these six tribes may have been recruited from the Arabs of southern Iran, and the Muhallabid period may have been when at least some of the Salima were added into the Malik b. Fahm, or even al-Azd as a whole. In the narratives of the campaign, it is the al-Azd sources of the late 700s and early 800s, regardless of whether they are from Basra or Kufa, which are particularly interested in passing on a heroic account. At the same time, several sources by those claiming al-Azd descent a century later show different agendas, indicating that for them al-Azd identity was no longer as significant. In what follows, we will both analyse the specifics of individual narratives for what we can learn about their authors' interests while also noting the major themes related to the course of al-Muhallab's career.

Al-Muhallab's accepting command of the Basran forces and defeating the Azraqites at Silla wa-Sillabra usually form a unit in the extant narratives. Al-Tabari's version, found in the year 65 (685), relies heavily on Ibn al-Kalbi's transmission of Abu Mikhnaf. For the beginning of al-Muhallab's command, Abu Mikhnaf cites Abu al-Mukhariq al-Rasibi, a Kufan traditionist who participated in the revolt of Ibn al-Ashᶜath.[47] In this version, al-Muhallab was passing through Basra on his way to Khurasan with his investiture over that province from ᶜAbd Allah b. al-Zubayr, when al-Ahnaf b. Qays declared that only al-Muhallab could save them. The Basran notables asked al-Muhallab to lead the battle against the Kharijites, but al-Muhallab insisted that he had to take charge of Khurasan as Ibn al-Zubayr had commanded. The governor Qubaᶜ and other Basrans then decided to forge a letter from Ibn al-Zubayr asking al-Muhallab to take on the Kharijites instead. When al-Muhallab read the letter, he insisted that if he were to take up the struggle, the Basrans had to give him whatever territory he won, as well as supply his army from the treasury and let him choose his own force. The Basrans agreed, and a contract was drawn up, though when Malik b. Mismaᶜ and some of the Bakr b. Waʾil refused to sign, other notables had to convince al-Muhallab that their stance did not matter. Abu Mikhnaf's report then specifies commanders al-Muhallab placed over the fifths of Bakr b. Waʾil and Tamim, presumably because of al-Ahnaf's age and Malik's refusal to cooperate.[48]

Abu Mikhnaf then describes al-Muhallab's forces pushing the Azraqites away from the bridges around Basra to a height in Ahwaz called Silla wa-Sillabra.[49] Al-Muhallab's camp there was defended by a trench, a technique that would be commented upon later. He was joined by the army of Haritha b. Badr al-Ghudani, which had been fighting the Azraqites before al-Muhallab's arrival. Here Abu Mikhnaf's source changes to Yusuf b. Yazid b. Bakr al-Azdi, who took his information from ᶜAbd Allah b. ᶜAwf b. al-Ahmar al-Azdi, himself referencing an anonymous member of the Azraqite army.[50] On what is presented as the next morning, the Azraqites, better equipped than the Basrans as a result of looting the countryside, sent the latter into a panicked flight back to Basra. Al-Muhallab, however, rallied to him several thousand fighters from Oman and his own people, presumably a reference to al-Azd, and they succeeded in routing the Azraqites, who with the death of their leader Ibn Mahuz fled to Isfahan and Kirman. Al-Muhallab then wrote to Qubaᶜ of his victory. Qubaᶜ's reply praising him as 'brother of al-Azd' earned his amusement and a contemptuous reference to Meccans as Bedouin (*aᶜrāb*).[51]

Abu al-Mukhariq often reads as a proponent of southern Iraq's garrison towns, and here his information sets up a Basran victory, with the story of the forged letter writing Ibn al-Zubayr out of command decisions in favor of the town's notables, the army organised into Basra's fifths, and the arrival of Haritha b. Badr's army. Abu Mikhnaf negates this, however, when he switches to Yusuf b. Yazid's report of the Basrans fleeing, leaving victory to be won by the overlapping categories of Azdis and Omanis. Al-Muhallab's contemptuous reaction to being called 'brother of al-Azd' is intriguing. Parallel passages specify that he was contemptuous of Qubaᶜ not using his name.[52] Al-Muhallab is described as wearing over his helmet a *qalansuwa*, a conical hat associated with Persian nobility.[53] In a tradition al-Baladhuri attributes to al-Haytham b. ᶜAdi, al-Muhallab responds to being called 'Mazuni' by alleging that al-Hajjaj's own Thaqif tribe was descended from Thamud, a group specifically mentioned in the Qur'an as punished by God.[54]

A strikingly different account is found in al-Mubarrad's *Kamil*; Al-Baladhuri's *Ansab al-Ashraf* has material which is very close to this, but shortened.[55] Here, Haritha b. Badr al-Ghudani drowned before al-Muhallab came on the scene. Amidst the Azraqite threat, the Basrans debated whom to put in command, with parties favouring Ziyad b. ᶜAmr al-ᶜAtaki and Malik b. Mismaᶜ al-Jahdari, Al-Ahnaf advocated for al-Muhallab. There follows the negotiation with al-Muhallab, which was carried out by Qubaᶜ in al-Baladhuri and al-Ahnaf in al-Mubarrad. As in Abu Mikhnaf's account, two of al-Muhallab's conditions were choosing his own force and governing the lands he conquered; these his interlocutor agreed to. Rather than his being paid from the treasury, however, his third condition was the right to collect the revenue of the territories. To this, Qubaᶜ/al-Ahnaf declared the revenue the property of the Muslims, and so it could be used only to provide stipends for the army, which al-Muhallab accepted.

Issues of revenue are a recurring theme in al-Mubarrad's account. After the general recruited an army from Basra's fifths, he found there was little money in the treasury, so he called the merchants and persuaded them that if his army restored security, their businesses would benefit; the result is that they agreed to help provision his force. He is also portrayed as collecting the land tax from areas he passed through, most notably for forty days after securing the bridge over the Euphrates. This tax collection is linked to paying his troops, as in the conditions of his appointment. One of al-Muhallab's speeches to his men also focuses on the booty they could gain from victory, and it is stated that people flocked to join his army to join in the profit. (Another speech mentions people whom the Kharijites had killed, including ᶜAli b. Abi Talib.) Al-Mubarrad also includes al-Muhallab's use of spies and defensive measures, an important theme discussed below.

Al-Muhallab's command in this version did not rely on the structure of the Basran fifths, and there are also a number of named fighters from the Tamim. Several times al-Muhallab placed his son al-Mughira in charge, and his brother al-Muᶜarik b. Abi Sufra was named governor of the strategic Nahr Tira district.[56] However, al-Muᶜarik was defeated, crucified, and the region then governed by an Azraqite commander named either Waqid or Faʾid, said to be a *mawlā* of the Al Abu Sufra captured in pre-Islamic times. This also brings up al-Muhallab's fallibility in al-Mubarrad. The general is forced to flee from an engagement at Sulaf, and there is poetry from an unnamed Tamimi denouncing him as a 'one-eyed liar', though the Azd are reported as saying the withdrawal was strategic.[57]

Al-Muhallab was planning to spend the summer at Silla wa-Sillibra when the Azraqites attacked, beginning a battle that lasted three days. This is one of the occasions where al-Mughira b. al-Muhallab plays an important role, this time as leader of a group of Omanis. There is also a report that a portion of the army fled back to Basra based on a rumour that al-Muhallab had been wounded. However, the glory is spread around, including to a person from Kinda, further presenting al-Muhallab's army as heterogeneous. Al-Muhallab wrote to Qubaᶜ of his victory and received separate replies from Qubaᶜ and the people of Basra. Al-Ahnaf proclaimed the city as 'Basra of al-Muhallab,' indicating the general's newfound glory in the city. Al-Muhallab also sent Ibn Mahuz's head to Qubaᶜ, but the messenger was intercepted and killed by the deceased leader's relatives, who buried the head.

Al-Mubarrad was active in Basra and Baghdad from perhaps the 830s until his death in 900, and a specialist in Arabic lore, including grammar and Arab elements of *adab*. He was of al-Azd descent, specifically from the B. Thumala of the Azd Sarat.[58] Given this, it is noteworthy that in contrast to the Azd sources previously studied, he does not seem to promote the tribe; indeed, he includes far more material hostile to al-Muhallab than any other source. It is probable that in Baghdad of the late ninth century, identity focused on the Arabs collectively rather than any particular tribe, as seems still to have mattered in the garrison towns of the 700s. One of al-Mubarrad's main interests in the text is poetry, seen by his day as a cornerstone of the Arab heritage. Al-Azd identity may also have been negligible for his younger contemporary Ibn Aᶜtham al-Kufi, whom Ilkka Lindstedt has identified as an Ahmad b. ᶜAtham al-Kufi al-Azdi who spent time in Jurjan in the early 900s.[59] That geographical region would explain why he appears as a source for passages in many manuscripts of al-Balᶜami.[60] However, prior to the Muhallabids, important events of al-Azd history play little or no role in his work, and here the focus is on the greatness of the family itself rather than al-Azd as a whole.

In Ibn Aᶜtham al-Kufi's account of the events leading up to Silla wa-Sillabra, Qubaᶜ called upon the Basran notables for someone to command the war against the Azraqites, and they replied that al-Muhallab was the only possible choice. Qubaᶜ replied that al-Muhallab was in Khurasan, but the people proposed forging a letter from Ibn al-Zubayr recalling him to Basra. Quba^c then wrote a letter that was surprisingly different from the one in Abu Mikhnaf given the similarity of context; an example is that where Abu Mikhnaf's letter mentions the Azraqite threat to Basra, Ibn A^ctham al-Kufi mentions them leaving it and occupying al-Ahwaz. Al-Muhallab then came to Basra and fought the Azraqites.[61]

After taking command, al-Muhallab gave all the command positions to his sons, including two named Zayd and Harun who are not found in the genealogies, though the latter is certainly Habib b. al-Muhallab, who was also called al-Harun.[62] He then gave an opening speech directed at his sons, indicating that this will be their first battle and calling them to courage and justice, noting that either martyrdom or victory will be theirs. The Azraqites listened to this speech and realised they were doomed. Al-Muhallab defeated them in an early engagement, after which the two sides met again at Silla wa-Sillabra. This version of the battle also mentions the false rumor of al-Muhallab's death, which resulted in the flight of much of his army, though he stood with his sons and some companions and won the victory. News of al-Muhallab's alleged death was carried to Basra by one Sa^cd b. Sa^cid al-Azdi, who had composed a poem about it, and the news was mourned in the mosque when a *ghulām* of the Tamim reported that the rumour was false and that Silla wa-Sillabra was a victory. Al-Muhallab then wrote to Basra of his victory. Ibn A^ctham al-Kufi also has an account of al-Muhallab sending heads of the Azraqite leaders, which were intercepted and buried.[63] In a detailed study, Conrad concludes that Ibn A^ctham al-Kufi constructed his text largely by linking didactic monographs together.[64] His material on the Azraqites is quite plausibly a Muhallabid family history, and there were plenty of Muhallabid descendants in Jurjan who could have produced or passed on such a text for Ibn A^ctham al-Kufi to transmit.[65]

Al-Muhallab remained governor of Fars and general against the Azraqites until Mus^cab b. al-Zubayr became governor of Basra, though only Ibn A^ctham al-Kufi situates accounts during this period. His series of battles seems mainly to serve as context for speeches and poetry, as well as highlighting the role of Habib b. al-Muhallab. At their end, al-Muhallab was besieging the Azraqites in Sabur.[66] Citing Yusuf b. Yazid and found in al-Tabari, Abu Mikhnaf has Mus^cab b. al-Zubayr recruit al-Muhallab for the final campaign against al-Mukhtar in Kufa. Ibn A^ctham al-Kufi and al-Baladhuri have similar accounts.[67] These accounts are all so similar, however, that it is far from certain that al-Muhallab was not simply inserted into the campaign by Abu Mikhnaf or some of his sources. We do know that Mus^cab appointed al-Muhallab as governor in Mosul, ostensibly to serve as a barrier between Mus^cab and ^cAbd al-Malik.[68] While al-Muhallab was in the north, the Azraqites returned to al-Ahwaz, leading either Musᶜab or his brother Hamza to bring back al-Muhallab. This is when Abu Mikhnaf places the fighting at Sulaf, which he says lasted for eight months. Other sources describe al-Muhallab fighting elsewhere.[69] Ibn Aᶜtham al-Kufi has Musᶜab remove al-Muhallab from command against the Azraqites before the campaign against al-Mukhtar and without appointing him governor of Mosul, but brought him back after realising that only al-Muhallab could defeat them, another example of his focus on al-Muhallab's greatness.[70]

When ᶜAbd al-Malik conquered lower Iraq, he appointed Khalid b. ᶜAbd Allah over Basra. We have accounts in al-Baladhuri (from al-Madaᵓini) and al-Mubarrad which are distinct, but can be briefly discussed together for our purposes. Khalid put his brother ᶜAbd al-ᶜAziz in charge of the war against the Azraqites and summoned al-Muhallab to Basra to assist in the defence of that city and take up the governorship of al-Ahwaz. There was fighting around Basra in which Khalid regretted not following all the advice of al-Muhallab, who led the eventual defeat of the Azraqite army. Al-Baladhuri indicates that Khalid may have only put ᶜAbd al-ᶜAziz in charge of the war at this point, in which case the effect is that Khalid inherited a threat to Basra and made his appointments only once that threat was removed; this threat would have come to the region on al-Muhallab's watch as commander. The two sources then describe the defeat of ᶜAbd al-ᶜAziz.[71] Abu Mikhnaf's account, on the other hand, begins with the defeat of ᶜAbd al-ᶜAziz, and then has Khalid seek al-Muhallab's assistance at ᶜAbd al-Malik's command. The implication is that Basra was threatened because al-Muhallab was relieved.[72]

Here we also have material from Wahb b. Jarir via his father, who as noted last chapter produced a book on the Azraqites. For earlier events, we have extant only a brief version of al-Muhallab's arrival with his investiture over Khurasan and the Basrans recruiting him to fight the Azraqites by means of the forged letter.[73] A brief bit from Wahb b. Jarir on the final campaign against al-Mukhtar does not involve al-Muhallab, further indication that this is solely from Yusuf b. Yazid/Abu Mikhnaf.[74] At this chronological juncture, however, Wahb has an account describing al-Muhallab seeking to find ᶜAbd al-ᶜAziz after his defeat, in which Jarir b. Hazm's paternal uncle Saᶜb b. Zayd plays a key role. Once ᶜAbd al-ᶜAziz was located, al-Muhallab accompanied him to Khalid.[75] Ibn Aᶜtham al-Kufi had a similar account, and presented al-Muhallab as leading victories both before and after ᶜAbd al-ᶜAziz's defeat, as if drawing on multiple traditions to give al-Muhallab as many victories as possible.[76]

In the wake of ᶜAbd al-ᶜAziz's defeat, ᶜAbd al-Malik replaced Khalid as governor with the caliph's own brother, Bishr b. Marwan, and ordered him to put al-Muhallab in command of the war against the Azraqites. There is broad similarity among the accounts of al-Baladhuri, al-Mubarrad, and Abu Mikhnaf in al-Tabari. Bishr resented having al-Muhallab forced on him, and in al-Baladhuri dismissed him as a 'Zubayri'. Bishr tried to persuade ᶜAbd al-Malik to let him appoint another, but the caliph insisted. Finally, when he selected ᶜAbd al-Rahman b. Mikhnaf to command a Kufan army as part of al-Muhallab's force, the governor instructed Ibn Mikhnaf to undermine al-Muhallab, a command to betray a fellow Azdi which Ibn Mikhnaf found offensive. A few days later, however, Bishr died, leading to mass desertions.[77] Bishr's resistance to accepting a general appointed by ᶜAbd al-Malik could relate to the governor's interest in setting himself up as an autonomous viceroy with interests in eventually succeeding to the caliphate.[78]

These well-attested mass desertions provide context for the subsequent appointment over the garrison towns of al-Hajjaj b. Yusuf, who upon arriving in both Basra and Kufa gave stern addresses and launched a crackdown aimed in part at pushing the deserters back to the Azraqite front. With his army newly formed, al-Muhallab pushed the Azraqites from Ramhurmuz to Sabur.[79] Ibn Aᶜtham al-Kufi's account has as key difference from these in that Bishr b. Marwan was persuaded to remove al-Muhallab by his advisors, but repented when the Azraqites subsequently entered al-Ahwaz. He then reappointed al-Muhallab, who drove the Azraqites to Sabur before Bishr's death, the desertions, and the coming of al-Hajjaj with his crackdown. His account does not mention Ibn Mikhnaf, which al-Mubarrad and al-Baladhuri may simply have had from Abu Mikhnaf.[80]

Al-Muhallab would remain in command for the remaining two or three years of the war against the Azraqites. Information on the course of the war during this period is found in Ibn Aᶜtham al-Kufi, al-Mubarrad, and a long poem of Kaᶜb al-Ashqari which seems to begin with the threat to Basra during the time of Khalid b. ᶜAbd Allah.[81] One episode worth noting for the way it connects to broader themes about al-Muhallab's career is the death of Ibn Mikhnaf at Kazarun in Sabur. The story, which al-Tabari has from Abu Mikhnaf and which is also found in al-Mubarrad and al-Baladhuri, is that Ibn Mikhnaf's Kufans had refused to dig a trench around their encampment as al-Muhallab's forces had done, saying 'Our trench is our swords'. The Azraqites then chose to attack Ibn Mikhnaf's camp instead, and the general was killed in the ambush.[82]

Al-Muhallab's use of trenches was distinctive among generals of the caliphate during his era. An indicative report from al-Madaʾini has al-Hajjaj criticise him for staying in his trenches rather than forthrightly attacking the enemy. In his reply, al-Muhallab mentions Muhammad's own use of trenches under divine command at Medina.[83] S. M. Yusuf has argued that al-Muhallab saw the need for and implemented a war of attrition against the Azraqites, whereas most other commanders sent against them sought victory via frequent direct engagements. In addition to trenches, al-Muhallab's strategy involved consolidating control over the countryside once taken.[84] This is the context into which Yusuf puts conflicts over revenue. These form a critical thread in accounts of al-Muhallab's relations with al-Hajjaj, with the governor frequently accusing his general of stalling the war to enrich himself.[85] In one account, after al-Muhallab had driven the Azraqites from Fars to Kirman, al-Hajjaj sent his own subordinates to administer it, but was ordered by ᶜAbd al-Malik to leave the area's tax collection in the hands of al-Muhallab. Abu Mikhnaf even quotes an anonymous al-Azd poet as complaining that the war was really about collecting taxes.[86] Al-Mubarrad claims that al-Mughira b. al-Muhallab and his fellow administrator al-Ruqad b. Ziyad al-ᶜAtaki did not, however, pass on their taxes to the troops.[87]

The most significant revenue conflict came when al-Hajjaj appointed ᶜAttab b. Warqaᵓ al-Riyahi, an experienced governor of Isfahan, as Ibn Mikhnaf's replacement over the Kufan contingent fighting the Azraqites. According to al-Mubarrad and al-Baladhuri, the latter citing al-Madaᵓini, after al-Hajjaj recalled ᶜAttab for another war, al-Muhallab refused to provision the Kufans as he did the Basrans; the implication is that previously ᶜAttab and Ibn Mikhnaf had done this. This led to conflict, but rather than simply being between the Basrans and Kufans, the al-Azd of Kufa supported al-Muhallab while the Tamim of Basra opposed him. Only after al-Mughira b. al-Muhallab intervened with his father did he relent.[88] On the other hand, Abu Mikhnaf's version in al-Tabari paints al-Muhallab more sympathetically, asserting that ᶜAttab was insubordinate towards him as commander, which caused a personal conflict when the former asked al-Muhallab to provision his troops. Al-Hajjaj removed him after this.[89] One notes there could be a potential version of these events from a pro-Kufan perspective, but the Kufan Abu Mikhnaf presents a pro-al-Azd narrative instead.

The Azraqites were finally driven out of Kirman when they became divided amongst themselves. Al-Mubarrad and al-Baladhuri present al-Muhallab as fomenting this division by the use of strategems. They have, for example, an account in which al-Muhallab sent the Azraqite blacksmith 1,000 dirhams with a note thanking him for his arrowheads, causing the Azraqite leader Qatari to have him executed as a traitor. However, another prominent Azraqite objected to this on the grounds the evidence was unsound. The dissenter ultimately left the camp with his followers. As the Azraqites gradually fractured, al-Muhallab defeated the groups individually, though Qatari fled to the north with his own followers, ultimately being defeated by other commanders sent by al-Hajjaj.[90] In Abu Mikhnaf and Ibn A^c^tham al-Kufi, al-Muhallab did not instigate the Azraqite divisions, which came from a tribal dispute in the former and from unspecified causes in the latter. The result is the same, however.[91]

The overall pattern of events dealt with above suggests that al-Muhallab represented an independent power centre which the caliphs and their governors in Basra found difficult to control, and who may not even have been worth controlling as long as he stood against the Azraqite threat. Wilkinson is undoubtedly correct that his concern with a contract, whether literal or not, represents the general's desire to gain the material benefits he would otherwise acquire in Khurasan.[92] Again, the focus on his revenue collection is striking, and can only partially be explained by a centralising state trying to gain control of provincial tax collection. Although his soldiers definitely benefited, the signs of conflict over wealth in the sources focus on al-Muhallab and his close associates and family members more than the army as a whole. In Abu Mikhnaf's defensively pro-al-Muhallab account, when al-Hajjaj forced the general to pay 1,000,000 dirhams from his governorship of al-Ahwaz under Khalid b. ^c^Abd Allah, he had to borrow and sell his wife's jewellery because he had no money, implying that he had spent his revenue rather than enriching himself.[93]

Al-Muhallab's loyalties were clearly flexible. A commonly told tale tells of how news of Mus^c^ab b. al-Zubayr's death reached the Azraqites one day before al-Muhallab's forces, leading the former to get the latter to voice their loyalty to Mus^c^ab and hostility to ^c^Abd al-Malik. When al-Muhallab's forces then learned of Mus^c^ab's death and swore loyalty to ^c^Abd al-Malik, the Azraqites accused them of hypocrisy.[94] He may also have been enabled by his ability to recruit Omani and southern Iranian manpower from the Malik b. Fahm tribes which formed a significant share of his armies, whereas other commanders appointed to fight the Kharijites may have relied on Basra's forces. Much poetry associated with the war promotes the role of al-Azd within it. For example, Ka^c^b al-Ashqari's poem mentioned above emphasises the war as an al-Azd victory.[95] An early ninth-century poem by Di^c^bil b. ^c^Ali al-Khuza^c^i, in which al-Azd are almost merged into al-Muhallab as the salvation of Basra, shows the further durability of the connection, though since Di^c^bil was much more of a pro-al-Yaman poet than a pro-al-Azd one, he should perhaps be seen as an intermediate stage in the merging of al-Azd into broader identities among the elite of Baghdad and the garrison towns.[96]

The accounts of Abu Mikhnaf and Wahb b. Jarir show that al-Muhallab's war against the Azraqites became the subject of a cycle of stories of particular interest to al-Azd, with the latter traditionist particularly relying on family sources. As mentioned in the last chapter, al-Muhallab's heroism was probably the major theme of Jarir b. Hazm's book on the campaign. Yet another version is found in ps.-al-ᶜAwtabi. This version is shorter and has no chronology, not really differentiating among the different battles. It does, however, stand out for the emphasis on al-Muhallab's sons. According to ps.-al-ᶜAwtabi, each had a day in which he took charge of the fighting independently, and al-Muhallab trusted their advice. There is, for example, a story of Mudrik b. al-Muhallab being driven back, but then charging to drive the Azraqites away as they settled in.[97] After the victory, Kaᶜb al-Ashqari listed to al-Hajjaj the virtues of eight of his sons, as well as the superiority of al-Muhallab to all of them.[98] Ps.-al-ᶜAwtabi even traces the Kharijite presence in North Africa to refugees fleeing al-Muhallab, adding today they are more numerous there than any other region.[99] Although ps.-al-ᶜAwtabi's work is organised as a genealogy, his al-Muhallab material clearly focuses on the family itself, with tribes gaining their own *sharaf* through association with him in their own sections of the text.

Governor of Khurasan and First Ouster

After his defeat of the Azraqites, al-Muhallab's career was at a high point, and al-Hajjaj appointed him governor of Khurasan. This was also probably when al-Hajjaj granted al-Muhallab's wife Khayra bt. Damra al-Qushayriya the estate of ᶜAbbasan in Basra.[100] Al-Muhallab's tenure in Khurasan lasted for three years until his death.[101] Militarily, he campaigned only around Kish, and enjoyed little success. He appointed his son Yazid as his successor, but al-Hajjaj soon manoeuvred the Muhallabids out of power. Al-Hajjaj imprisoned several of them and drove others into hiding in his attempts to mulct them. Under Yazid's leadership, however, they were soon able to find sanctuary with Sulayman b. ᶜAbd al-Malik, thus setting the stage for a return to power when he acceded to the caliphate.

Most historians explain al-Muhallab's appointment in terms of the tribal balance in Khurasan.[102] A more likely explanation, however, is that al-Hajjaj appointed al-Muhallab because his victory over the Azraqites and accumulated wealth from administering the territories he captured from them made him a figure who needed a significant boon lest he challenge al-Hajjaj himself. The broader political pattern in the eastern caliphate saw the Marwanids assert greater central control, which led to the sidelining or co-option of those who had previously enjoyed autonomy. Al-Muhallab's military command, including the terms by which he governed Fars, made him a crucial military notable, one who could not easily be eliminated. In addition, through his Oman ties, he drew for support on a population centre not truly controlled by the caliphate. Al-Muhallab was thus the gateway for the state to deploy those resources to further its own interests.

Accounts indicate that al-Hajjaj actually initially planned to appoint al-Muhallab over Sistan instead of or in addition to Khurasan. Abu Mikhnaf claims the original appointment was for both, but al-Muhallab recommended the eventual Sistan governor, ᶜUbayd Allah b. Abi Bakra, because he knew the region better, thus making al-Muhallab appear humble and as someone with the best interests of the caliphate at heart. Al-Madaᵓini, on the other hand, has a somewhat more mixed account from al-Mufaddal b. Muhammad al-Dabbi, a Kufan scholar of poetry and historical traditions who moved to Baghdad under Harun al-Rashid.[103] In this version, al-Muhallab was originally over Sistan and ᶜUbayd Allah over Khurasan, but al-Muhallab simply disliked Sistan, and so worked through intermediaries to persuade al-Hajjaj that he had really gotten it backwards. Al-Madaᵓini further reports that al-Muhallab was required by al-Hajjaj to pay one million dirhams from his days as governor of al-Ahwaz. Al-Muhallab, however, had no money, so he persuaded his son al-Mughira, who had been governor of Istakhr in Fars, to pay half of it. He then borrowed 300,000 from a friend and his wife sold jewellery for the other 200,000. After paying al-Hajjaj, he sent Habib ahead of him to Khurasan; al-Hajjaj gave Habib 10,000 dirhams and a spunky grey mule.[104] As we will see below, al-Madaᵓini treats al-Muhallab as the skilled patriarch of a powerful family whose work is undone by less worthy offspring.

During al-Muhallab's governorship, Ibn al-Ashᶜath rebelled with the Peacock Army. Al-Madaᵓini says that when Ibn al-Ashᶜath wrote to seek al-Muhallab's support for this revolt, al-Muhallab forwarded the letter on to the governor in Iraq.[105] In Abu Mikhnaf's account, al-Muhallab wrote to Ibn al-Ashᶜath warning him off his course, while also suggesting to al-Hajjaj that he wait to fight them until they reached Iraq. Al-Hajjaj ignored al-Muhallab's advice, believing he was only seeking to protect his cousin.[106] Citing Wahb b. Jarir, al-Baladhuri says that al-Muhallab had contempt for Ibn al-Ashᶜath's offer because of the latter's youth.[107] C. E. Bosworth suggests Ibn al-Ashᶜath was appealing to al-Muhallab as another former supporter of the Zubayrids.[108] According to the *Tarikh-i Sistan*, on al-Hajjaj's orders, al-Muhallab sent his son al-Mufaddal to Sistan as part of the final campaign which defeated the rebel.[109] In Abu Mikhnaf's account, Yazid b. al-Muhallab moved against the defeated army of Ibn al-Ashᶜath after they killed al-Ruqad b. Ziyad al-ᶜAtaki in Herat and Yazid became concerned they were encroaching on his territory.[110] Abu Mikhnaf's versions clearly show al-Muhallab displaying wisdom in his advice and loyalty to his superiors.

An example of how the Muhallabids became a point of reference on which later figures could hang their own status claims is one story of the origins of the poet Bashshar b. Burd. According to al-Isfahani, the poet's father, Burd b. Yarjukh, was among al-Muhallab's prisoners from a campaign in Tukharistan. Burd became the slave (*qinna*) of Khayra al-Qushayriyya, mentioned above, and lived with her on her namesake estate near Basra. Khayra married him off to an ᶜUqayli woman, with whom he sired Bashshar. Alternative accounts are that Burd married a woman of al-Azd who had an ᶜUqayli mother or that he was a *mawlā* of Umm al-Zabaʾ al-ᶜUqayliya al-Sadusiya.[111] The undisputed fact, however, is that Bashshar's father lived among the B. ᶜUqayl, and the Tukharistan link through al-Muhallab could easily be designed to enable his claim to descent from Sasanian nobility while also establishing a relationship of clientship with an important early Islamic family.[112] It was Rawh b. Hatim al-Muhallabi who introduced Bashshar to the court of the caliph al-Mahdi, though the poet later turned on both Rawh and his brother Yazid.[113]

The key to understanding al-Madaʾini's account of al-Muhallab is found in the general's death scene, which again comes from al-Mufaddal b. Muhammad al-Dabbi, as does most of what follows.[114] In it, as al-Muhallab was travelling from Kish to Merv, he fell ill at Zaghul. He then called Habib and his other sons together, and analogised them to a bundle of arrows that were strong together but could be broken separately. He then said:

> My testamentary command to you is pious fear of God and (respect for) the bond of kinship. The bond of kinship prolongs the allotted span, multiplies wealth, and increases numbers. I forbid you the forsaking of relations, for that occasions (hell)fire and brings about abasement and destitution. Love one another, relate to one another in a friendly fashion, be united and not at variance, and do good for one another; in this way your affairs will be as one. When the sons of a single mother fall out with one another, what hope is there for the sons of co-wives?! Incumbent upon you are the obedience and (respect for) the collective body.[115]

Al-Muhallab continued with advice on personal conduct, such as the virtue of generosity. He then named Yazid as his successor as head of the family, and placed Habib in charge of the army until they reached Yazid. Al-Mufaddal b. al-Muhallab expressed his support for the choice of Yazid, and then al-Muhallab passed away. Habib said his funeral prayers, and al-Hajjaj later confirmed Yazid's ascension.[116] Al-Mughira b. al-Muhallab had earlier died in Merv, where he had been his father's deputy during the campaign against Kish.[117] Al-Tabari describes this account as a *waṣiyya*, a *topos* of deathbed exhortations to heirs common in Arabic and Persian literature.[118] In this case, the virtues highlighted stand out through comparison with the parallel in Ibn Aᶜtham al-Kufi which has a version of al-Muhallab's *waṣiyya* which omits the arrow story, and generally has more about piety and less about kinship ties.[119] Ps.-al-ᶜAwtabi simply has al-Muhallab die in Merv after commenting briefly about dying in his bed after so many wars. He does not mention Kish, and is generally vague or simply wrong about matters in Khurasan. He says, for example, that al-Muhallab was governor for five years instead of three.[120] Ps.-al-ᶜAwtabi also has ᶜAbd al-Malik rather than al-Hajjaj appoint al-Muhallab as governor, and that the latter 'conquered most of its frontiers'.[121]

Al-Muhallab's advice to his sons becomes for al-Mada'ini the core of a morality play in which the virtues of a heroic forebear are not passed on to his progeny, leading to their destruction. First, however, al-Tabari relates from al-Mada'ini Yazid's encounter with the defeated army of Ibn al-Ashᶜath, noted above in an account which emphasises the themes of factionalism. After the death of al-Ruqad in Herat, Yazid sent a message demanding his forces move out of the territory to avoid a fight, offering to supply them for the journey. He was told that they were just resting before moving on, but when he learned that they had begun collecting taxes he sent his brother al-Mufaddal with an army against them. Yazid then placed his maternal uncle Judayᶜ b. Yazid in charge of Merv and after stopping at his father's tomb, went to Herat himself, where he offered to ᶜAbd al-Rahman b. ᶜAbbas al-Hashimi, the rebels' commander, to keep what he had taken and take more, but insisted he did not wish to fight. Al-Hashimi, however, insisted on fighting, and tried to undermine Yazid's authority with his army. When Yazid learned of this, he decided to engage, placing his brother al-Mufaddal in command of the actual battle, which his forces won, though he decided not to pursue the fleeing enemy.[122]

Sabra b. Nakhf b. Abi Sufra was one of Yazid's followers, and in charge of taking the prisoners of that battle to al-Hajjaj.[123] According to Abu ᶜUbayda, Yazid decided not to send ᶜAbd al-Rahman b. Talha of Khuzaᶜa because Habib reminded him of a favour his father had done for al-Muhallab. Abu ᶜUbayda implies this favouritism towards a fellow Yamani contributed to al-Hajjaj's later decision to dismiss Yazid. In this context, the fact Habib matter-of-factly told Yazid he should get used to the idea of being dismissed before reminding him of Ibn Talha's claims on a favour renders the act more noble.[124] Ibn al-Kalbi and al-Madaᵓini also both mention Yazid protecting this man.[125] Al-Tabari's addition of these supports for al-Madaᵓini's narrative shows his own emphasis on tribal factionalism as a theme, whereas al-Baladhuri uses al-Madaᵓini's material to emphasise character flaws, a pattern also noted by Steven Judd for a later period.[126]

In al-Baladhuri's recension of al-Madaᵓini, Yazid's haughty behavior leads al-Hajjaj to turn against him. In addition, this haughtiness is implied as the reason why al-Mufaddal b. al-Muhallab wrote to his brother ᶜAbd al-Malik against Yazid.[127] Al-Mufaddal and ᶜAbd al-Malik were both sons of an Indian woman named Bahla. Al-Tabari's al-Madaᵓini quotes an anonymous poet who accused the sons of Bahla of betraying their half-brother and thus falling, as al-Muhallab had predicted they would.[128] Al-Baladhuri also quotes al-Madaᵓini as saying that al-Hajjaj appointed Habib b. al-Muhallab over Kirman about a year into Yazid's governorship of Khurasan.[129] Yazid also appointed his brother Mudrik over Sistan.[130] One notes here that even though al-Tabari and al-Baladhuri are bringing out their own emphases, the underlying structure of al-Madaᵓini's work is discernable through the device of the *waṣiyya* foreshadowing material from both accounts.

Another story from al-Tabari/al-Madaᵓini/al-Dabbi has al-Muhallab tell his sons to beware of Musa b. ᶜAbd Allah b. Khazim, saying that as long as he lives they will govern Khurasan, but if he were killed they would be replaced by someone from Qays. Al-Muhallab himself never campaigned against Musa, nor did Yazid.[131] There were, however, two brothers from al-Muhallab's retinue who had joined him. When al-Muhallab left Kish after the death of al-Mughira, he placed a Khuzaᶜa *mawlā* named Hurayth b. Qutba in charge of collecting the tribute, and gave instructions to delay releasing the hostages from Kish until Hurayth reached Balkh. Hurayth, however, agreed to release them right away if the ruler of Kish paid promptly, which he did. Later, Hurayth encountered Turkish bandits who had previously waylaid Yazid, forcing the latter's party to ransom themselves. Hurayth refused to pay and defeated them, but accepted a ransom from them which he then returned. However, he had replied to the demand for ransom with, 'Do you imagine that Yazid's mother gave birth to me?' This caused al-Muhallab to grow indignant at this slight to the *mawlā*'s own kinsman.[132] Al-Muhallab, who was waiting for him at Balkh, expressed his anger in terms of his failure to retain the hostages, and had him stripped and given thirty lashes. Hurayth vowed to kill him for this insult, and one day ordered two *ghulāms* to attack al-Muhallab, which they failed to do. Hurayth then feigned illness. Al-Muhallab, learning of this trickery and Hurayth's design against him, sent his brother Thabit b. Qutba to bring him so the two could be reconciled. Hurayth, however, did not trust al-Muhallab, and so together the two and their private army (*shākiriyya*) and some Arab followers set off to join Musa b. ᶜAbd Allah.[133]

When Yazid became governor, he took Thabit and Hurayth's women and property and killed some of their relatives. Hearing of this, Thabit went to Tarkhun of Samarqand and complained about Yazid. Together with other Central Asian rulers, Tarkhun went with Thabit to Musa b. ᶜAbd Allah, who had also gathered the defeated forces of ᶜAbd al-Rahman b. al-ᶜAbbas, Ibn al-Ashᶜath, and Khurasan's Tamimis who had fought his father. His total forces numbered 8,000. The Central Asians offered to make him governor of Khurasan if he defeated Yazid, but his associates told him not to trust Thabit and Hurayth, given that they had betrayed the Muhallabids. Musa listened to these associates, and suggested instead taking Transoxania from Yazid's governors there, which they did, gaining vast riches. [134]

Shaban suggests that Thabit and Hurayth were Sogdian traders involved in financing the Muslim conquests from Khurasan.[135] Thabit was mentioned as popular among the 'non-Arabs' (*ᶜajam*).[136] De la Vaissière and Agha, however, both read their political connections and conduct as indicative of aristocratic origin. On the question of ethnicity, those two scholars, while acknowledging that the evidence is insufficient to draw firm conclusions, approach from opposite directions. De la Vaissiere points out correctly that all known members of the family had Arab names, but is incorrect that their family did not move across the Oxus. As Agha points out, al-ᶜAla b. Hurayth was actually the leader of the Abbasid movement in Transoxania, perhaps drawing upon dynastic loyalties to mobilise support.[137]

Al-Hajjaj's ouster of Yazid from Khurasan happened about the same time as a campaign against Oman, and as expected given the significance of that country for the Muhallabids, the two moves were clearly linked. An explicit example of this linkage from the sources is found in al-Baladhuri's al-Madaʾini and in ps.-al-ᶜAwtabi. According to them, al-Hajjaj asked Yazid to send him one of his trusted retainers, and Yazid sent al-Khiyar b. Sabra al-Mujashiᶜi. Al-Hajjaj asked this man about Yazid, and was told that if he confirmed Yazid in his place Yazid would be loyal, but if he thought to remove him then he must imprison him. Al-Hajjaj then appointed al-Khiyar governor of Oman with the charge of countering Muhallabid interests in that country.[138] This followed what appear to be several invasions ordered by al-Hajjaj, particularly after the defeat of Ibn al-Ash^c^ath. These invasions succeeded in driving out the ruling pair of brothers Sa^c^id and Sulayman b. ^c^Abbad, heirs of the family of al-Julanda, though the exact chronology involving their ouster and that of the Muhallabids is uncertain.[139]

There are, of course, more literary accounts of the events leading to Yazid's deposition. In al-Tabari/al-Mada^o^ini/al-Dabbi, al-Hajjaj was driven to be fearful of Yazid by an old man at a monastery who said that a man named Yazid would one day govern his territory. Al-Hajjaj determined that it must be Yazid b. al-Muhallab, and decided to move against him, consulting with the caliph ^c^Abd al-Malik to appoint Qutayba b. Muslim over Khurasan in his place. When word reached Yazid that he was about to be dismissed, he predicted that al-Hajjaj would appoint one of his brothers first before looking to one of the Qays, singling out Qutayba as a worthy candidate. Al-Hajjaj in fact summoned Yazid and asked him to appoint al-Mufaddal as his deputy. Yazid decided to go, saying that his family had been obedient and prone to avoid conflict, but when he dawdled, al-Hajjaj wrote to al-Mufaddal, who began nagging Yazid about his departure. Yazid told al-Mufaddal he would not be confirmed in Khurasan, but al-Mufaddal accused him of jealousy.[140] Al-Mada^o^ini also has another account involving Yazid's moral character, this one from Kulayb b. Khalaf al-^c^Ammi, in which he claims that al-Hajjaj ordered Yazid to campaign in Khwarazm, which Yazid refused on the grounds it had 'little plunder and fierce dogs'. Al-Hajjaj then summoned him, but Yazid said he preferred to campaign in Khwarazm, which he then did, defying al-Hajjaj. He was victorious, but he made the return to Khurasan during winter, and his men took the prisoners' clothes for warmth, leaving them to die of the cold.[141] Al-Hajjaj again summoned Yazid, who had people spreading plants before him everywhere he went as he made his way to Iraq.[142] According to al-Baladhuri's variant, Yazid heard of the death of the caliph ^c^Abd al-Malik in Istakhr, and proclaimed that this would bring the destruction of his family.[143]

Ibn A^c^tham al-Kufi presents Yazid as turning against the Arab armies in Khurasan, which alienated them and led al-Hajjaj to decide on his removal, though that author also includes al-Hajjaj wanting to bring the Muhallabids to heel as a rival power.[144] This may seem to go against Ibn A^c^tham al-Kufi's positive presentation of the Muhallabids, but he overcomes it by, during his story of Yazid's later arrest under the caliph ᶜUmar II, stitching in an account asserting that the Khurasan Arabs probably deserved it. Accounts from other al-Azd sources portray the potential of the Muhallabids to rival al-Hajjaj as the reason for the latter's move against them. Ibn al-Kalbi's account, drawn from Abu Mikhnaf and Abu al-Mukhariq al-Rasibi, says that after the defeat of Ibn al-Ashᶜath, al-Hajjaj saw the Muhallabids and their followers as the only ones who could compete with him, and began plotting against Yazid. Yazid, however, put off his summons pleading the importance of campaigning against the enemy, certainly laudable from Abu Mikhnaf's standpoint.[145] Ps.-al-ᶜAwtabi writes that the caliph ᶜAbd al-Malik refused to let al-Hajjaj remove Yazid b. al-Muhallab from the governorship because he knew the motive was jealousy, but that when al-Walid became caliph, al-Hajjaj persuaded him that Yazid b. al-Muhallab was a danger.[146]

Much as he explained al-Muhallab's appointment in terms of tribal balances, Gibb suggests that al-Hajjaj's motive in removing Yazid was to unify the province's tribal population by eventually handing power over to someone from a neutral tribe without giving Yazid the chance to unify the Azd in opposition.[147] This is peculiar, as there is no evidence of al-Azd disunity in Khurasan. In any event, according to al-Tabari/al-Madaᵓini/al-Dabbi, al-Mufaddal b. al-Muhallab was in charge of Khurasan for nine months, during which he conquered Badghis, Akharun and Shuman. He was famous for not having a treasury and simply distributing booty and other wealth among the people.[148] In violation of his father's advice, he also decided to move against Musa b. ᶜAbd Allah, sending a force under the command of one of Thabit's cousins named ᶜUthman b. Masᶜud whom Yazid had imprisoned. This ᶜUthman had wanted to avenge Thabit and Hurayth. Al-Mufaddal also commanded his brother Mudrik in Balkh to join him, which Mudrik did reluctantly. The force was also joined by two Central Asian rulers. Musa was killed, and his nephew Nadr b. Sulayman would only hand Tirmidh over to Mudrik, who gave him a safe-conduct and then passed the city to ᶜUthman.[149] Ps.-al-ᶜAwtabi completely omits al-Mufaddal's independent governorship under al-Hajjaj, probably because of his poor information about Khurasan.[150]

According to al-Tabari, in 86 (705), al-Hajjaj imprisoned Yazid and removed Habib b. al-Muhallab from Kirman and ᶜAbd al-Malik b. al-Muhallab from his *shurṭa*.[151] In al-Baladhuri's version, Habib, ᶜAbd al-Malik and al-Mufaddal were imprisoned along with Yazid, as was Abu ᶜUyayna.[152] Then, according to Ibn al-Kalbi's rendition of Abu Mikhnaf's account from Abu al-Mukhariq al-Rasibi, al-Hajjaj went to Rustaqubadh to oversee a war against the Kurds, taking with him Yazid, al-Mufaddal and ᶜAbd al-Malik. He imprisoned them in his camp under Syrian guard, and tortured them for money. Yazid showed great strength under pressure, but al-Hajjaj soon learned Yazid had an arrowhead lodged in his leg, and used that to elicit screaming. His sister Hind bt. al-Muhallab, one of al-Hajjaj's wives, heard this and began wailing, which led al-Hajjaj to divorce her. He then stopped the torture so as to get the money, which the prisoners began collecting while working out a plan of escape.[153] The brothers found a way to send word to Marwan b. al-Muhallab, who was in Basra where Habib was also being tortured. They asked him to prepare some horses by acting as if he were going to sell them, but keeping the price high so no one would buy them. Yazid then ordered food and drink for the guards, who distracted themselves with it while Yazid and al-Mufaddal slipped out, with Yazid disguised as an elderly cook. They had had boats prepared in southern Iraq's marshland, where they had to wait for ᶜAbd al-Malik, whom Yazid refused to abandon. Upon learning of their escape, al-Hajjaj assumed they were making for Khurasan to start a rebellion, and sent out an alert in that direction.[154] Al-Baladhuri, whose similar report suggests he once again has Abu Mikhnaf as part of a collective isnad, adds that Yazid b. al-Muhallab sought help from the *ᶜurafaᵓ* of al-Azd in Basra and that Habib hid among the Rasib.[155]

Meanwhile, Yazid and company came to a place called Mawquᶜ near Basra where they got the horses from Marwan, and set out with a guide named ᶜAbd al-Jabbar b. Yazid b. al-Rabᶜa al-Kalbi toward Syria, as al-Hajjaj learned two days later.[156] Yazid finally reached the Palestine home of Wuhayb b. ᶜAbd al-Rahman al-Azdi, who was on good terms with Sulayman b. ᶜAbd al-Malik. While Yazid stashed some of his family and possessions with Sufyan b. Sulayman al-Azdi, Wuhayb went to Sulayman to inform him that they had arrived and were seeking refuge. Sulayman promised to take them in.[157] Ibn al-Kalbi, citing al-Hasan b. Aban al-ᶜUlaymi, claims that Yazid once tried to make ᶜAbd al-Jabbar go back and look for his turban, and even whipped him for refusing, but relented when ᶜAbd al-Jabbar recited his genealogy.[158] This fits the pattern of non-al-Azd sources portraying Yazid as haughty. According to al-Baladhuri, their Palestine contact was Rajaᵓ b. Haywa al-Kindi, while ps.-al-ᶜAwtabi names him as ᶜUthman b. al-Mihsan al-Azdi and Ibn Aᶜtham al-Kufi as Zahra b. ᶜAbd al-Rahman.[159]

The next section of al-Tabari's narrative may return to Ibn al-Kalbi's narrative from Abu Mikhnaf, though it runs parallel to the account of the mid-ninth-century al-Zubayr b. Bakkar from the *adīb* Muhammad b. Sallam al-Jumahi (d. 846).[160] In it, Sulayman wrote to his brother the caliph al-Walid, offering to pay the remaining three million dirhams of the allegedly embezzled six million, indicating he had given safe conduct to

Yazid. Al-Walid, however, insisted that Yazid be sent to him in chains. In al-Tabari, but not Ibn Bakkar, Yazid intervened, saying he would rather go to al-Walid than become the cause of discord. Sulayman sent Yazid and his own son Ayyub to al-Walid, telling Ayyub to bind them both with chains upon entering the caliph's presence. Ayyub bore a note from Sulayman piously asking al-Walid to respect the security he has offered, and al-Walid relented, writing to al-Hajjaj to relent also. Al-Hajjaj then stopped pursuing Habib, as well as Abu ᶜUyayna b. al-Muhallab, who owed al-Hajjaj 100,000 dirhams.[161] Yazid and Sulayman became close companions, even when al-Walid objected. According to this account Yazid stayed with him nine months, until al-Hajjaj died, though al-Tabari's timeline does not work as provided.[162] Most likely, Sulayman was forming an alliance with the Muhallabids as a counterweight to al-Walid's desire to remove him from the succession in favour of his son ᶜAbd al-ᶜAziz b. al-Walid.[163] Ps.-al-ᶜAwtabi has the striking report that Sulayman paid off the funds al-Hajjaj claimed the Muhallabids had embezzled by taking it from the al-Yaman of Syria.[164]

The accounts of al-Muhallab's governorship in Khurasan and the family's subsequent fall draw out the differences between Azdi and other sources seen in accounts of al-Muhallab's rise and war against the Azraqites. For Abu Mikhnaf, the Muhallabids were collectively noble. In the material from al-Madaʾini, however, al-Muhallab's sons fail to match his wisdom and standards of temperament and conduct, leading to the fall of the family at the hands of al-Hajjaj. The account, in other words, is a form of didactic literature as marked out by al-Muhallab's testament, with the fate of the family serving as a warning. As far as the historical events are concerned, the fall of the Muhallabids stands as the case where al-Hajjaj removed the last major rivals to his and the Marwanids' consolidation of power in the east. The slow process of extending effective central control that began with missions to the Julandas and the Azd of Tawwaj reached its culmination under al-Hajjaj, when the entire eastern caliphate came to be ruled by governors owing their position to him. Yazid himself would make the transition to a new style of politics, in which one's rise to power depended on connections with the centre, in this case the caliph Sulayman.

Yazid's Second Governorship and Revolt

In 715, Sulayman, having become caliph, placed Yazid b. al-Muhallab over Iraq, and a year later he became governor of Khurasan.[165] Sulayman's reign marked the height of the Muhallabids' influence, as Yazid became to the new caliph most of what al-Hajjaj b. Yusuf was to ᶜAbd al-Malik. A difference was that Yazid was checked by an experienced Persian-speaking scribe named Salih b. ᶜAbd al-Rahman, who supervised the finances, while Yazid's remit was war and prayer.[166] Pro-Yazid sources explain this lesser role by attributing it to his own will. According to Ibn al-Kalbi citing Abu Mikhnaf, Yazid wanted someone else in charge of agricultural taxes so that he would not have to extort from the people in the manner of al-Hajjaj, and so he recommended Salih b. ᶜAbd al-Rahman.[167] In Ibn Aᶜtham al-Kufi, Yazid's desire not to be like al-Hajjaj led him to forego the governorship of Iraq entirely in favor of Salih, and he proceeded straight to Khurasan, though that source's account of the rebellion of Qutayba b. Muslim has Yazid as governor in Iraq, a case in which the author has not quite smoothed over the seams between his sources.[168] Reports also describe conflict between Yazid and Salih over spending, In the account of al-Madaᵓini citing ᶜAbbad b. Ayyub, Salih was extremely tight with money. Yazid had one thousand tables prepared to feed his men, but Salih seized them, so Yazid said he would assume their cost. He also acquired many goods and sent the bills to Salih, which the financial administrator would not accept. When Yazid, frustrated, talked with him, Salih claimed that while the men had been paid their stipends, the administration could not pay for the food. Salih finally agreed to pay the bills just that once.[169]

Yazid's brothers also had important posts throughout the eastern caliphate, showing the power of the Muhallabids as a family. According to al-Baladhuri, Yazid placed Marwan over Basra, Mudrik over Sistan, Habib over Sind, and commissioned Ziyad with killing al-Khiyar b. Sabra before assuming control of Oman.[170] ᶜAbd al-Malik b. al-Muhallab served as a torturer for Salih b. ᶜAbd al-Rahman against al-Hajjaj's family.[171] In al-Baladhuri's version, his victims included al-Hajjaj's niece who was the wife of Yazid b. ᶜAbd al-Malik and mother of al-Walid b. Yazid b. ᶜAbd al-Malik, both of them future caliphs.[172] This detail accounts for Yazid b. al-Muhallab's fear of the son of ᶜAbd al-Malik who shared his name, and provides context for the conflict between the two and Yazid's rebellion.

Many sources, including al-Madaᵓini and Abu Mikhnaf, claim Sulayman considered appointing ᶜAbd al-Malik b. al-Muhallab over Khurasan.[173] Yazid, during the time when he was vexed with Salih, learned of this, and summoned ᶜAbd Allah b. al-Ahtam, who volunteered to go to the caliph and procure the appointment for Yazid instead. He was successful, and Yazid sent his son Mukhallad ahead to the province, placing deputies in the garrison towns and his brother Marwan over his personal affairs in Basra. Mukhallad sent ᶜAmr b. ᶜAbd Allah b. Sinan al-ᶜAtaki ahead of him to Merv, and the latter forced Waki^c b. Abi Sud to come out to meet Mukhallad, who imprisoned him and his followers and tortured them all.[174] Abu ^cUbayda reports that Yazid felt threatened by Waki^c b. Abi Sud, who had given Sulayman the head of Qutayba b. Muslim, and so bribed ^cAbd Allah b. al-Ahtam to denounce him. Sulayman ordered Yazid to move against Waki^c if the Qays in Iraq could prove claims that Qutayba had remained loyal. Yazid, however, sent Mukhallad against Waki^c, while at the same time refusing to pay ^cAbd Allah b. al-Ahtam what he had promised for his services.[175] Al-Mada^oini also claims based on testimony from Kulayb b. Khalaf that ^cAbd Allah b. al-Ahtam forged letters to Qutayba persuading him to revolt lest a 'Mazuni' take his place.[176] Like Yazid , ^cAbd Allah b. al-Ahtam was given sanctuary by Sulayman, in his case after failed scheming against Qutayba b. Muslim.[177]

Ps.-al-^cAwtabi emphasises Yazid b. al-Muhallab's closeness to the caliph Sulayman and developments in Oman. On the former topic, he conveys the impression that Yazid spent Sulayman's reign at the caliph's side, only briefly leaving to conquer Jurjan. (A failed Tabaristan campaign is unmentioned.) According to ps.-al-^cAwtabi, Yazid appointed his son Mukhallad as governor in Khurasan at the tender age of twelve years, much younger than he is in other sources. In ps.-al-^cAwtabi, Mukhallad was responsible for the conquest of Daylam, southwest of the Caspian Sea. Sulayman relied heavily upon Yazid, and the latter even sat upon the caliph's throne (*sarīr*) when the caliph was not present, sitting at his right hand at other times.[178] In this material, ps.-al-^cAwtabi shows again his flaws as a reporter of chronology, for Yazid's period of proximity to Sulayman was before he became caliph; afterward, he spent the reign in the east. Regarding Oman, ps.-al-^cAwtabi reports that Sulayman initially intended to appoint Salih b. ^cAbd al-Rahman its governor, but then changed his mind. Yazid then appointed his brother Ziyad b. al-Muhallab, who upon arrival in Oman began torturing al-Khiyar b. Sabra. Yazid then sent his *ghulām* Muratti^c to kill him. In a letter to Ziyad, Yazid writes, 'I have sent you not as a tax-collector, but as an avenger.' Yazid also appointed al-Minhal b. Abi ^cUyayna b. al-Muhallab over Qeshm, where his responsibilities included sending to Basra soldiers whom Ziyad recruited in Oman.[179] In other words, Yazid immediately drew upon Oman as a source of manpower, as he would again during his rebellion against the caliph Yazid II a few years later.

Yazid campaigned south of the Caspian Sea. His favoured companions included Jahm b. Zahr al-Ju^cfi and his brother Jamal, prominent figures among the Kufans in the region. This demonstrates how he had broader influence than his father's Basra-centred retinue; he also had

Syrian troops. Yazid also appreciated Muhammad b. Abd al-Rahman b. Abi Sufra al-Ju^{c}fi, but objected to his drunkenness.[180] Yazid would make Jahm his governor of Jurjan, and after the Muhallabid's death, Jahm was killed during the course of seeking allegedly embezzled funds.[181] Jamal was arrested in Kufa when Yazid b. al-Muhallab first rebelled and died in prison in Damascus.[182] According to al-Mada$^{\circ}$ini, in a letter to Sulayman bragging about his conquests, Yazid mentioned a figure of millions of dirhams as his booty, despite the warning of his scribe that a successor to Sulayman might demand the money.[183] Al-Baladhuri has similar information, adding that this letter arrived in Damascus only after Sulayman died, and so actually reached ^{c}Umar b. ^{c}Abd al-^{c}Aziz.[184] According to Ibn A^{c}tham al-Kufi, after his campaign, Yazid began oppressing the people of Khurasan and unjustly seizing its wealth, which caused some of its people to write to Sulayman accusing him of overpowering them instead of campaigning against enemies.[185]

In 717, the new caliph ^{c}Umar II dismissed Yazid and ^{c}Adi b. Artat al-Fazari, the new Basran governor, sent Musa b. al-Wajih al-Himyari after the Muhallabid.[186] As one of ^{c}Umar's own governors over Khurasan would be from the Ghamid, this clearly did not represent an attack on al-Azd, but was rather an attempt to removal a powerful figure whose loyalty to himself was less sure than it had been to Sulayman.[187] In terms of the narratives' didactic strategies, the non-al-Azd sources from the ninth century focus on ^{c}Umar's hostility to the governor, which given the idealisation of that caliph suggests they saw Yazid as in the wrong.[188] Al-Mada$^{\circ}$ini reports that ^{c}Umar b. ^{c}Abd al-^{c}Aziz disapproved of Yazid's assigning a concubine a stipend equal to that of 1,000 soldiers.[189] Abu ^{c}Ubayda reports that ^{c}Umar had long been opposed to Yazid, and tried to trick Sulayman into turning against him. Yazid was thus certain that the new caliph meant to relieve him, and when summoned, appointed Mukhallad as his deputy and came straight away with a group of Khurasani notables, as well as the imprisoned Waki^{c} b. Abi Sud and a man known as '*ṣadīq* Iblis' named ^{c}Abd Allah b. Hilal al-Hajri. ^{c}Adi b. Artat met Yazid at Wasit as the Azd gathered to Yazid and proclaimed him Amir. The two entered the Dar al-Imara together, where Salih b. ^{c}Abd al-Rahman was waiting to shackle the Muhallabid, whom he sent to ^{c}Umar. Yazid's keeper during the trip to ^{c}Umar was Musa b. al-Wajih, whom Yazid had forced to divorce his wife, a sister of Yazid's own wife Umm Fadl bt. Ghaylan b. Kharasha al-Dabbi. Because of this, Musa reviled the Muhallabids' *mawālī* origins during the journey.[190] According to al-Mada$^{\circ}$ini, al-Jarrah b. ^{c}Abd Allah al-Hakami put Mukhallad b. Yazid in chains in Khurasan and sent him via the *barīd* to ^{c}Umar II.[191]

According to Abu Mikhnaf, Yazid was captured near Basra and sent to ᶜUmar. Some sources report an al-Azd rescue attempt at the Aban Canal. ᶜUmar was seeking the wealth Yazid gained from his recent conquests, wealth which Yazid claimed he had exaggerated so as to boost Sulayman's reputation. ᶜUmar did not believe him, and kept him imprisoned. Mukhallad b. Yazid, who in this account was not imprisoned, went from Khurasan to the caliph spreading wealth and offered to pay part of what Yazid owed, but ᶜUmar refused to settle for less than the whole amount despite liking Yazid's son. Mukhallad died shortly afterward. ᶜUmar considered sending Yazid to the Red Sea prison island of Dahlak, but was dissuaded by the fact that the Azd were already disturbed by the situation and would probably attempt another rescue.[192] Here Abu Mikhnaf's different handling of Mukhallad allows him to show the revered ᶜUmar II showing approval of a member of the family.

In Ibn Aᶜtham al-Kufi's account, upon learning of Sulayman's death, Yazid initially sought to support Ayyub b. Sulayman before learning that he had died, too. When ᶜUmar II wrote to demand his wealth, he left for Iraq with some of the leaders of Khurasan, and upon reaching Rayy sent much of the wealth he had taken from Khurasan ahead of him to Basra. Musa b. al-Wajih met him just outside Basra and escorted him to ᶜAdi b. Artat in Wasit. ᶜAdi sought the wealth of Yazid's conquests, which the Muhallabid insisted he spent on the troops. ᶜAdi did not believe him, and prepared to send him on to the caliph as a prisoner. Before this happened, however, the Khurasan dignitaries testified to his tyranny, and Yazid offered a defence, after which ᶜAdi proclaimed him a leader (*ᶜamīd*) of the people of Iraq with both he and his father having accomplishments. Thereafter, Ibn Aᶜtham al-Kufi follows something like Abu Mikhnaf's account of Yazid and his son's encounters with ᶜUmar, including an account that when Mukhallad died, ᶜUmar II said his funeral prayers.[193] Ibn Asakir has some similarly favourable accounts of Mukhallad's mission to the caliph which are traced back to Muhallabid sources, including Wahb b. Jarir and Khalid b. Khidash (d. 838).[194] The latter was a Basran *mawlā* of the Muhallabids who relocated to Baghdad and whose students included Ahmad b. Ibrahim al-Dawraqi, who appeared in Chapter 2 transmitting material from Wahb b. Jarir.[195]

Intriguingly, ps.-al-ᶜAwtabi seems to participate in the general tendency of the sources to portray ᶜUmar II's administration positively. According to this source, ᶜAdi b. Artat appointed his own governors over Oman, while Ziyad b. al-Muhallab took shelter among the al-Yaman. ᶜAdi's governors behaved unjustly, so ᶜUmar II appointed ᶜUmar b. ᶜAbd Allah al-Ansari, who ruled through the country's tribal leaders, putting them in charge of collecting their own taxes. He otherwise governed in ways ps.-al-ᶜAwtabi approves of until the death of ᶜUmar b. ᶜAbd al-ᶜAziz, when he left the country again in the hands of Ziyad b. al-Muhallab.[196] It is quite likely, of course, that Ziyad simply took over amidst the rebellion of Yazid b. al-Muhallab, which began almost immediately upon ᶜUmar II's death.

According to Abu Mikhnaf, while in prison, Yazid feared the accession of Yazid II (b. ᶜAbd al-Malik) because he was in-law to al-Hajjaj's family, whom he had tortured when he first became governor under Sulayman as noted earlier. He therefore arranged for his *mawālī* to get some camels, and together with a retinue that included his wife ᶜAtika bt. al-Furat b. Muᶜawiya al-Amiriyya of the B. al-Bakka, escaped from prison and evaded capture by some pursuing Qaysis.[197] In al-Baladhuri, Yazid got out of prison by bribing his guards during the illness of ᶜUmar II and escaped on camels provided by his brothers.[198] Al-Waqidi claims, however, that Yazid remained in prison until after ᶜUmar II's death.[199] Al-Haytham b. ᶜAdi has Yazid imprisoned in the citadel of Aleppo until he heard of ᶜUmar II's illness, at which time he bribed both his guards and the governor of Aleppo to escape. Once on his way, Yazid wrote to ᶜUmar to say that he escaped mainly for fear of his life anticipating the succession of Yazid b. ᶜAbd al-Malik.[200]

The fullest account of the rebellion of Yazid b. al-Muhallab is found in al-Baladhuri's *Ansab al-Ashraf.* According to al-Baladhuri, upon his accession, nothing mattered to Yazid II except the hunt for Yazid b. al-Muhallab, though his sources offer many names for whom the caliph put in charge of the search. He also wrote to the governors in Basra and Kufa to command them to seek for Yazid, with ᶜAdi b. Artat in Basra ordered to also arrest the Muhallabids in that city. These orders ᶜAdi carried out in consultation with Wakiᶜ b. Abi Sud, who advised him to also destroy the Muhallabids' homes but died shortly thereafter.[201] Wahb b. Jarir indicates that while Habib, Marwan, al-Mufaddal and ᶜAbd al-Malik were in prison, Muhammad b. al-Muhallab was in the al-Huddan quarter of Basra, while the remainder of their brothers sheltered with other al-Azd, who kept ᶜAdi from them.[202]

In his account of Yazid's uprising, al-Baladhuri's information from Wahb b. Jarir is cited through Rawh b. ᶜAbd al-Muʾmin. This Rawh b. ᶜAbd al-Muʾmin also transmitted from an al-Azd source, ᶜAli b. Nasr al-Jahdami, who seems to have drawn upon generic al-Azd tribal tradition. According to this ᶜAli b. Nasr, ᶜAdi sent al-Hasan b. Abi al-Hasan to arrest the Muhallabids. Al-Hasan's party first sought to call the Muhallabids to loyalty to their governor, but ᶜAbd al-Malik

b. al-Muhallab declared that al-Hasan's group had already decided to support the authorities in the Muhallabids' destruction. Al-Hasan then called ᶜAbd al-Malik a liar, at which point ᶜAbd al-Malik became angry and moved to draw his sword, speaking harsh words to al-Hasan. After further discussion, al-Hasan declared that ᶜAdi had granted the Muhallabids sanctuary from the vengeance they feared from the family of al-Hajjaj. Al-Mufaddal b. al-Muhallab trusted this, and he and ᶜAbd al-Malik accompanied al-Hasan to ᶜAdi, where they were imprisoned along with Habib, Marwan, Mudrik and Abu ᶜUyayna.[203] In the wake of these arrests, ᶜAdi b. Artat announced the death of ᶜUmar b. ᶜAbd al-Aziz. He then distributed stipends to the people, but had to borrow the money rather than taking it from the treasury. Finally he prepared Basra for war against Yazid b. al-Muhallab, massing its troops and digging a trench to defend the city.[204]

Al-Baladhuri has a combined account from al-Madaʾini and Abu ᶜUbayda in which Yazid b. al-Muhallab sent his brother Muhammad and cousin al-Muhallab b. al-ᶜAlaʾ b. Abi Sufra to battle ᶜAdi's forces around the city. The two armies met at a bridge, which the Muhallabid forces succeeded in capturing. Yazid then placed Bukayr al-Farahidi in charge of this bridge, while ᶜAdi began arranging his forces inside Basra between the Mirbad and the Dar al-Imara.[205] ᶜAdi ordered the destruction of the market. Yazid's forces engaged ᶜAdi's in the *mirbad*, gradually pressing into the city. The next day, fighting took place around the mosque of the Ansar, in the course of which ᶜAdi himself was captured. Abu ᶜUyayna and ᶜAbd al-Malik b. al-Muhallab then granted ᶜAdi their protection.[206]

Citing Bishr b. ᶜIsa, al-Madaʾini says that on the night Yazid b. al-Muhallab entered Basra, he passed by al-Azd guards whose commanding officer was actually from Tamim. When the guards called out for their identity, Yazid's party replied 'Al-Amir Abu Khalid', using Yazid's *kunya*, at which the guards enthusiastically allowed them entry despite the fact they were wanted by the governor. Yazid made his way to the home of the Muhallabids, where he was greeted by al-Minhal b. Abi Uyayna and Hind bt. al-Muhallab. Meanwhile, the Tamim guard commander went to ᶜAdi and offered to capture Yazid for him, but ᶜAdi declined and scattered the armed Azd, presumably fearing that if united they would rally behind the rebel. Yazid b. al-Muhallab then wrote to Yazid II asking for a safe-conduct, sending the letter with Humayd b. ᶜAbd al-Malik b. al-Muhallab, his own son Khalid, and al-Muthanna b. ᶜAbd al-Malik b. Rabaᶜa, though some say the messengers other than Humayd were named Yazid b. Judayᶜ and al-Muthanna b. ᶜAbd Allah.[207]

Meanwhile, still according to al-Madaᵓini, al-Qasim b. ᶜAbd al-Rahman b. al-Hilali, whose mother was Fatima bt. Abi Sufra, asked ᶜAdi b. Artat on Yazid's behalf to release his brothers from prison. When he refused, Yazid wrote to al-Azd and Rabiᶜ, and the Azd came quickly and Rabiᶜ slowly. Yazid then addressed them, and commissioned their aid in freeing his kinsmen, ordered the *ᶜurafāᵓ* to assign stipends to the people, and sought and received aid from the market and the *qurrāᵓ*, as well. The stage was thus set for a battle in which the Rabiᶜa and al-Yaman were with Yazid, while the Mudar sided with ᶜAdi, Basra's standard factional opposition.[208]

Several prominent Azdis remained in Umayyad service during the revolt. Sabra b. Nakhf b. Abi Sufra, a close associate of ᶜAdi, was warned by Yazid b. al-Muhallab that he could not guarantee his safety, and Sabra went inside his home. One al-Bakhtari b. Mughraᵓ b. al-Mughira b. Abi Sufra openly opposed the rebel and fled to Yazid II in Syria, who imprisoned him for his trouble.[209] ᶜAdi b. Artat put al-Mughira b. Ziyad al-ᶜAtaki in charge of the al-Azd fifth when he was preparing for battle against the Muhallabids.[210] His brother al-Hawari b. Ziyad fled when Yazid b. al-Muhallab took Basra, and sided against the family in the final battle at al-ᶜAqr.[211] Sabra b. ᶜAbd al-Rahman b. Mikhnaf also commanded a Kufan contingent in that battle.[212] When Mudrik b. al-Muhallab advanced towards Khurasan after Yazid's capture of Basra, ᶜAbd al-Rahman b. Nuᶜaym al-Azdi rallied the Tamim against him, but they were intercepted by al-Azd who joined Mudrik in the desert of Raᵓs al-Mafaza.[213] Meanwhile, Humayd b. ᶜAbd al-Malik had obtained from Yazid II a safe conduct for Yazid b. al-Muhallab and his household, and was returning to Basra with it accompanied by men loyal to the caliph. However, when they learned of Yazid's seizure of Basra, they delivered him to ᶜAbd al-Rahman b. Sulaym al-Kalbi, Yazid II's governor in Khurasan. ᶜAbd al-Rahman reaffirmed his loyalty to Yazid II and sent him Humayd as a prisoner.[214]

Al-Tabari's account of Yazid b. al-Muhallab's revolt comes from Abu Mikhnaf. In it, Yazid's primary motive was self-defence, and in the beginning he wanted only a safe-conduct from the new caliph. Instead, however, Yazid II wrote to his governors in Kufa and Basra as described by al-Baladhuri. ᶜAdi b. Artat in Basra arrested three of Yazid's brothers: al-Mufaddal, Habib and Marwan. ᶜAbd al-Malik b. al-Muhallab suggested putting his son Humayd in prison in his place while he went out and persuaded Yazid to head for Fars where he would simply seek the safe conduct; however, the governor, ᶜAdi b. Artat, refused the offer. Muhammad b. al-Muhallab assembled some of the men, youths and clients from his household and went out to join Yazid. Yazid offered to leave the city alone if he released his brothers, but the Basran governor refused. Yazid also began distributing generous stipends to his troops, who were joined by ᶜImran b. ᶜAmir b. Mismaᶜ, who was angry because ᶜAdi had placed a different branch of the family in command of Bakr b. Waʾil for the battle. Yazid also drew support from Rabiᶜa, part of Tamim, Qays, some Syrians and many soldiers who joined as individuals, while many units simply let him pass. He captured Basra and imprisoned ᶜAdi, saying he did so only because of ᶜAdi's actions against the Muhallabids.[215] Yazid then sent to the Kufans with a promise to increase their stipends.[216]

Yazid also appointed his brother Marwan as governor over Basra before departing for Wasit, although Habib suggested he go to Fars and wait for reinforcements from the Azd of Mosul. Habib's long speech on this occasion probably reflects the rivalries of the early Abbasid period.[217] Some of al-Baladhuri's sources claim that after he took Basra, the people gave an oath of allegiance to Yazid b. al-Muhallab on the book of God and the *sunna* of his messenger, and that Yazid proceeded to appoint ᶜUthman b. Abi al-Hakam al-Hinaʾi of al-Azd over his *shurṭa*, Muhammad b. al-Muhallab over Fars, Hilal b. ᶜIyad b. Hinaʾi over al-Ahwaz, Ziyad b. al-Muhallab over Oman, al-Minhal b. Abi ᶜUyayna over Jazira Ibn Kawan (Qeshm), one of the ᶜAbd al-Qays over Baḥrayn, Mudrik b. al-Muhallab over Khurasan, and Wadaᶜ b. Humayd al-Yahmadi over Qandabil.[218] This last appointee would betray them in their last stand, and so perhaps unsurprisingly we have a tradition in which Habib advises his brother against it.[219]

After the conquest of Basra, Yazid began forming alliances with other Umayyad opponents. Yazid was joined by some Kharijites led by al-Samaydaᶜ al-Kindi, whom he made governor of al-Ubulla.[220] They and a group of Murji'ites defected from him at al-ᶜAqr, however, saying that the Syrians had accepted their doctrines.[221] According to al-Baladhuri, Yazid wrote to Ziyad in Oman and asked him to commission 3,000 men under the command of Mishmas b. ᶜAmr al-Azdi al-Jadidi and send them to Basra.[222] An account from al-Haytham b. ᶜAdi mentioning 3,000 Ibadis with Yazid at al-ᶜAqr under the command of Jaᶜfar b. Sulayman al-Azdi probably reflects a similar historical memory of Yazid's support from Oman.[223] Some accounts try to make Yazid into an early proponent of the Abbasids. On Eid al-Fitr during his time in Basra, he allegedly went out and called people to favour the B. Hashim over the B. Marwan, and on another occasion reportedly pledged allegiance to al-Mufaddal b. ᶜAbd al-Rahman b. al-ᶜAbbas.[224] With these accounts, proponents of the Muhallabids sought to gain legitimacy during a period of secure Abbasid rule.

Abu Mikhnaf and Ibn Aᶜtham al-Kufi report Yazid b. al-Muhallab as saying that fighting against the Syrians was more meritorious that fighting against the Turks and Daylamites.[225] Ursula Sezgin was unable to identify Abu Mikhnaf's source, but he seems to have been concerned with accounts of al-Hasan al-Basri.[226] According to some sources, al-Hasan al-Basri was a vocal opponent of Yazid's revolt.[227] This reflects the position of Sunni sources which hold that he was a political quietist. Suleiman Mourad, however, has examined conflicting evidence for his possible role in the revolt of Ibn al-Ashᶜath and concluded that he most likely was involved in that uprising.[228] Wakiᶜ reports that Yazid b. al-Muhallab may have appointed Hasan al-Basri as qadi when he left Basra to fight at al-ᶜAqr, but that al-Hasan remained in his house. He also says, however, that authorities rejected the authenticity of this report.[229]

Yazid II sent his brother Maslama against Yazid b. al-Muhallab, who decided to go out and meet him, and put his son Muᶜawiya b. Yazid in charge of Wasit before marching to and setting up his defences at al-ᶜAqr. The Kufans and Medinese he placed under the control of ᶜAbd Allah b. Sufyan b. Yazid b. al-Mughaffal al-Azdi. Over all of the groups which joined him he placed his brother al-Mufaddal. Habib served as his other primary lieutenant. In the ensuing battle, many of Yazid's troops fled, and he was killed along with his brothers Habib and Muhammad and several of his sons. According to al-Baladhuri, both he and Muhammad sat on sedan chairs during the battle, with Yazid being carried from place to place supervising the fighting, while Maslama commanded from a hill.[230] According to Abu Mikhnaf, al-Mufaddal b. al-Muhallab kept fighting the Syrians after Yazid's death, not knowing that the battle had been lost, and trying to rally the troops. Finally, he learned what had happened from some fighters of Rabiᶜa, and fell back to Wasit.[231] Al-Madaʾini has the story, also found in ps.-al-ᶜAwtabi, that ᶜAbd al-Malik told al-Mufaddal that Yazid himself had fallen back to Wasit. When the latter found out the truth, he resolved not to speak to ᶜAbd al-Malik, a vow he kept.[232]

Ps.-al-ᶜAwtabi says very little about the rebellion, completely omitting the events in Basra and Yazid's quest for a security guarantee while proceeding directly to the battle at al-ᶜAqr. His portrayal of the two sides is striking, however. The Muhallabid supporters are characterised as '*qabāʾil al-ᶜarab*', ('tribes of the Arabs') while the caliph musters '*al-yamāniya min ahl al-shām*' ('al-Yaman from Greater Syria') against them. The southern tribal affiliations of the latter are repeatedly emphasised, leading up to Yazid saying, 'God curse Maslama, with my people does he fight me and not his!'[233] The overall effect is to position Yazid as a defender of Arab values concerning solidarity against a force which subverts them. Ps.-al-ᶜAwtabi also says that after Habib was killed, Yazid entered the battle in the grip of a severe illness while reciting poetry that their defeat was the result of fate and not cowardice.[234] These are clearly ps.-al-ᶜAwtabi's attempt to explain the one Muhallabid defeat he cannot simply ignore. Yazid even has an achievement in death, for Maslama orders a turban be placed on his severed head to aid in recognition, and according to ps.-al-ᶜAwtabi this was the only severed head ever so dignified.[235]

Yazid b. al-Muhallab was crucified at the Jisr Babal next to a wineskin and either a hog or a fish.[236] According to Ibn ᶜAtham al-Kufi, the crucifixion took place upside down on the mast of a boat.[237] Even when applied post mortem, crucifixion was a significant punishment in Umayyad times, exposing bodily decomposition in an era when Muslim ritual practice was coming to emphasise privacy and corporeal dignity. As Sean Anthony says, 'From the Umayyad view, the power behind the act of crucifixion lies in its signaling of the ultimate exclusion of the crucified from the Muslim *umma* by the caliphs' power to debase the somatic self.'[238] For this reason, accounts sympathetic to those crucified often downplay or mitigate the potential significance of the indignities suffered.[239]

When word of the defeat reached Wasit, Muᶜawiya b. Yazid killed thirty-two prisoners including ᶜAdi b. Artat, but spared Rabiᶜa b. Ziyad b. al-Rabiᶜa b. Anas b. al-Rayyan, whom he called a noble shaykh from his people. He then went to Basra, and with the arrival there of al-Mufaddal b. al-Muhallab, the entire clan was gathered in one place. Although Muᶜawiya wanted the leadership, they made al-Mufaddal their chief. They then fled by ship as far as Kirman, where they took to land. There or in Fars, al-Mufaddal was killed by forces loyal to the caliph. The rest fled to Qandabil in Sind, where Yazid had appointed Wadaᶜ b. Humayd al-Azdi in order to provide a place for the Muhallabids to flee if they were defeated. Wadaᶜ betrayed them, however, and in a final charge all the Muhallabids were killed except Abu ᶜUyayna b. al-Muhallab and ᶜUthman b. al-Mufaddal b. al-Muhallab, both of whom fled to the Turks. This section of Abu Mikhnaf's text is confused, however, as al-Mufaddal remained alive in it after dying in Iran, and pieces of text are clearly missing.[240] Al-Mubarrad reports that Muᶜawiya killed two sons of Mismaᶜ b. Malik b. Mismaᶜ.[241] Ibn ᶜAsakir also has an account in which al-Mufaddal and some of his brothers were killed in Sistan, though he also reports their deaths in Sind.[242] Ps.-al-ᶜAwtabi's account of the flight has the Muhallabids stop in Oman, where Ziyad b. al-Muhallab offered shelter and the idea of fleeing to al-Shihr. Although they declined this offer and went on to Sind, al-Muhallab's daughters Hind, Fatima and Nafisa came later and did stay in Oman with Ziyad until receiving their safe-conducts from Maslama [243] Thabit Qutna recited an elegy to al-Mufaddal b. al-Muhallab before his sister Hind.[244]

In al-Mada'ini's account, al-Mufaddal definitely remained alive and in charge of the Muhallabids at Qandabil, where he and ᶜAmr b. Qabisa b. al-Muhallab carried their banner. Mudrik sought a duel, found one with Salm b. al-Ahwaz at-Tamimi, and was killed therein. Hilal b. al-Ahwaz at-Tamimi, the Umayyad commander, offered a safe-conduct to everyone except Muᶜawiya b. Yazid, because of his killing of ᶜAdi b. Artat. He was killed by a Tamimi from the army of Syria. In addition to ᶜUthman b. al-Mufaddal and Abu ᶜUyayna b. al-Muhallab, ᶜUmar b. Yazid b. al-Muhallab also escaped, though al-Mada'ini does not tell us how or to where. Hilal did protect the Muhallabid women, and allowed them to bury the dead.[245] Ibn Aᶜtham al-Kufi says that some Muhallabid supporters escaped to India before finding refuge with a Turkish khan, and also says that Hilal sent the Muhallabid women and children to Maslama along with the heads of the slain.[246]

Wahb b. Jarir claims based on the testimony of his father and Muhammad b. Abi ᶜUyayna that Maslama ordered the Muhallabid dwellings to be destroyed and sent Mudrik b. Dabb to pursue them. When he came to Kirman, he found Mudrik b. al-Muhallab coming from Khurasan having been joined by some of the defeated Kufans, and they battled. This encounter is also reported by Abu Mikhnaf and others.[247] An additional report claims that Hind bt. al-Muhallab received a safe conduct from Yazid II for Abu ᶜUyayna b. al-Muhallab, who subsequently came to Iraq. ᶜUthman and ᶜUmar, meanwhile, remained with the Rutbil of Sijistan until Asad b. ᶜAbd Allah al-Qasri came to govern Khurasan in the 720s, when they went there under his protection.[248]

Abu Ubayda briefly recounts the deaths of the Muhallabids in Qandabil, including among the named dead Ziyad, Marwan, al-Minhal b. Abi ᶜUyayna, and ᶜAmr and al-Mughira, both sons of Qabisa b. al-Muhallab.[249] Ps.-al-ᶜAwtabi's list is al-Mufaddal, Mudrik, Ziyad, Marwan, and ᶜUmar among al-Muhallab's sons, along with two grandsons.[250] Ps.-al-ᶜAwtabi also presents Maslama b. ᶜAbd al-Malik positively, and particularly as praising members of the Muhallabid family. At Qandabil, when the Muhallabids were abandoned by all except their immediate family and retainers, Maslama ordered those who do not fight to be spared, and later advised Yazid II to spare the prisoners.[251] Maslama also unsuccessfully proposed marriage to Hind bt. Al-Muhallab when she arrived in Syria after the massacre of Muhallabid prisoners, and praised her courage when she declined.[252] When he heard a Syrian mock Yazid with the derogatory term 'Mazuni', Maslama rebuked the man saying that Yazid came close to becoming caliph.[253]

Amabe sees Yazid's revolt as an attempt to stop Syrian troops from being re-introduced into Iraq.[254] After the Muhallabids' defeat, Yazid II appointed the Syrian Sufyan b. ᶜUmayr al-Azdi as governor in Basra.[255] Some poetry on Yazid's death seems to pit 'Iraq' against 'Qudaᶜa,' which would be a reference to Syria.[256] Certainly there is in the historical tradition and in poetry a frequent depiction of the Muhallabids as distinctively Iraqi heroes, while Maslama b. ᶜAbd al-Malik was Syrian.[257] Regionalism may have been an issue for some of Yazid's supporters, but as Yazid himself had brought Syrians to Khurasan, it was probably not for the Muhallabids themselves. Yazid's motive in rebelling was almost certainly because of the factional rivalry that had developed between al-Hajjaj's family and his own, with the ascension of a caliph who was on the other side.

Hawting locates the major significance of Yazid's career in its role in the intensification of a factional division between 'northern' and 'southern' Arabs. Only tentative statements can be made concerning this matter on the basis of studying al-Azd alone, as crucial developments clearly happened in Syria and Egypt. However, over time the Muhallabids came to rely on al-Azd and related tribes as their primary base of support, and the defeat of their rebellion led to the ouster of their al-Yaman allies and their replacement by Qaysis.[258] There is also a striking development in Thabit Qutna's poetry, which is the earliest to have substantial elements of the ᶜAmr Muzayqiyaᵓ genealogical framework, using him as the forefather of the Azd, Ansar and Ghassan.[259] The occurrence of ᶜAmr Muzayqiyaᵓ as an al-Azd forefather in poetry, however, has a striking resonance with the development of the narrative discussed in the first chapter and Retsö's argument that Yamanis began claiming to be the foremost of the Arabs at about the same time.[260] A case can be made that while al-Yaman identity probably existed earlier, this was the period in which a new patch was added to the genealogy and a story explaining their distribution. At the same time, the al-Azd genealogy remained unsettled. Thabit Qutna identifies some al-Azd who protected Mudrik b. al-Muhallab as 'Dawsar', which is subdivided into Shanuᶜa and ᶜImran b. Hazm.[261] Under the Lakhmids, the *dawsar* were elite cavalry troops recruited from Tanukh, and one wonders here if Thabit is playing off the similarity between the term and the tribal name Daws.[262] 'ᶜImran b. Hazm' may be the ᶜImran elsewhere represented as a son of ᶜAmr Muzayqiya and the grandfather of the Muhallabids' own ᶜAtik.

Whatever their significance in the development of 'Yamani Arabs', the significance of the Muhallabids for al-Azd *sharaf* is seen in the fact that the defeat at Qandabil was used against the tribe in poetry.[263] As noted previously, the recruitment into Muhallabid armies, especially in the eastern caliphate, was based heavily on tribal ties, with the Azd of Oman continually tapped as a source of manpower. Arabic sources portray Umayyad-era Oman as functionally independent under the al-Julanda family from the reign of Muᶜawiya until al-Hajjaj mounted his expedition to conquer it in the early 700s. During al-Hajjaj's time, two brothers named Sulayman and Saᶜid dominated the region, collecting non-Islamic taxes from coastal populations on expeditions carried out by boat.[264] In addition to the Salima from the Azraqite War, several other Malik b. Fahm groups are are defined in terms of *ᶜirāʾif.* Twelve were from the ᶜAmr b. Malik b. Fahm, four were from the Shababa b. Malik, the Hinaʾa boasted eight.[265] This access to Omani manpower was a crucial factor in the Muhallabids' ability to act autonomously of the caliphs and their governors.

However, there is no evidence of a significant break, as opposed to evolution, in terms of how tribal leaders related to their followers. Michael Bonner sees continuity between the role of generosity in Bedouin leadership and the reputation for generosity of both Yazid b. al-Muhallab and his brother al-Mufaddal. The private armies of the Marwanid period are in some ways an updated version of the pre-Islamic tribal leader who attracted followers by guaranteeing access to wealth.[266] The preservation of tribal accounts focusing on particular leaders also fits pre-Islamic patterns. What did change between the Muhallabids and pre-Islamic al-Azd leaders is the scale of operations and the strategies of the leaders themselves. In particular, the emergence of the caliphate curtailing the independence of powerful tribal magnates meant, as it did in Basra, that connections to the rulers became an important means of acquiring status and distributing benefits to followers. In this way, tribal leaders also became the links incorporating Arab followers into the state apparatus, particularly those who were recruited from the loosely ruled Oman.

Later Muhallabids

The fall of Yazid b. al-Muhallab was accompanied by a decimation of male Muhallabids. In addition, an enmity arose between the Muhallabids and the Umayyads which would last until the Abbasid takeover, which Muhallabids would support. One sign of this enmity is that the caliph Hisham dismissed a governor for marrying al-Fadila bt. Yazid b. al-Muhallab.[267] Part of the opposition may have been support for the growing Ibadi movement, particularly by the women of the Muhallabid family who must have become most prominent within it following the decimation of the men.[268] When a new generation of Muhallabids surfaced at the time of the Abbasid takeover, their area of prominence remained Basra.

Sulayman b. Habib b. al-Muhallab, who in the 740s was governor of al-Ahwaz, was one such politically active figure of the new generation. Although literary sources are muddled regarding the beginning of his governorship, coinage indicates that by the end of it he was a loyalist of ᶜAbd Allah b. Muᶜawiya, whose territories became a general refuge for those opposed to the Umayyads.[269] There is also dispute within the sources over whether Sulayman was deposed by the Abbasids or the Umayyads, with the most common tradition being that he sent his cousin Dawud b. Hatim al-Muhallabi against an invading Umayyad army, a campaign in which Dawud was killed. Thereafter Sulayman fled to Ibn Muᶜawiya in Fars.[270] In al-Madaᵓini's version, this is when he pledged loyalty to Ibn Muᶜawiya, who was advised by ᶜAbd al-Rahman b. Yazid b. al-Muhallab not to trust him and to make him come in person. Sulayman came, and Ibn Muᶜawiya accepted his sincerity.[271] After Ibn Muᶜawiya's defeat, Sulayman fled to Oman, where he attempted to rally support, but was instead driven away and went into hiding in Basra.[272] He was executed by either the caliph al-Saffah or al-Mansur.[273] His failure to rally support in Oman occurred in the context of a brief period of Abbasid control over the province through a governor from the B. Hinaᵓa.[274]

We have more material dealing with Yazid b. al-Muhallab's grandson Sufyan b. Muᶜawiya. According to al-Tabari's version of al-Madaᶜini, in 132 (750), an Abbasid commander appointed Sufyan to govern Basra, and he went there to depose the Umayyad governor Salm b. Qutayba with the support of al-Yaman and Rabiᶜa. Sufyan fled, however, when his son was killed in an encounter with Tamim horsemen from Salm's army. Al-Madaᵓini's account continues with an attack on al-Azd in Basra, resulting in the plundering of their quarter. Sufyan later did become the governor during the caliphate of al-Saffah.[275] Al-Baladhuri provides a more detailed account in which Sufyan sought and received appointment over Basra from Abu Salama (not the commander from al-Tabari's version), then confronted Salm. Salm rallied the Tamim by invoking the memory of ᶜAdi b. ᶜArtat, and Sufyan then hesitated given Salm's reputation as a fighter to be reckoned with, one vouched for by his previously mentioned uncle, ᶜAbd al-Rahman b. Yazid. Abu Salama, however, grew impatient and appointed a grandson of Habib b. al-Muhallab in his place, which spurred Sufyan into the battle where his son was killed.[276]

In ps.-al-ᶜAwtabi's account, after the battle in which Sufyan lost his son, he began attempting to burn down the city, but the people of Basra instead were able to sue for peace pending Abu Salama's revelation of the new caliph. Because of Sufyan's pro-Abbasid efforts, al-Saffah, once caliph, appointed him governor of Basra and asked him what he wanted from the new dynasty. Sufyan requested the confiscated estates of his grandfather, and al-Saffah granted this. The future al-Mansur, however, objected that the caliph had given him too much when the dynasty needed wealth, and with al-Saffah's backing went to Sufyan and persuaded him to agree to accept only half of Yazid's old property.[277] The estate called Muhallaban, once the property of al-Mughira b. al-Muhallab, was still with Sufyan's descendants in al-Baladhuri's time.[278]

In the early 760s, Dafif b. Rashid, a *mawlā* of the B. Yazid b. Hatim of Al Muhallab, went to Sufyan during his governorship asking for troops to fight Ibrahim b. ᶜAbd Allah, the brother of the Shi'ite rebel Muhammad the Pure Soul, but Sufyan sent him away. This is one of several reports which describe Sufyan's refusal to deal with the matter, and even allege that he was in league with the Alid claimant.[279] However, another set of sources claims that Ibrahim imprisoned Sufyan.[280] There are also at least two later reports involving these branches of the Muhallabids. Muhammad b. ᶜAbbad b. Habib al-Muhallabi was a Basran governor in the time of al-Maᵓmun noted for his generosity.[281] Under 196 (812), al-Tabari reports that the Abbasid general Tahir b. al-Husayn killed Muhammad b. Yazid al-Muhallabi, a descendant of Yazid b. Hatim who was governor of al-Ahwaz.[282] Khalid b. Yazid b. Hatim of the Muhallabids was governor of Jurjan under al-Mansur.[283]

These accounts highlight the influence in early Abbasid times of scions of both Yazid b. al-Muhallab and Habib b. al-Muhallab, branches of the family also prominent in genealogical literature.[284] This is important because a clear strain within the Muhallabid historical tradition discussed previously in this chapter favoured Habib at Yazid's expense, which undoubtedly reflects the perspective of Habib's descendants. Despite this historiographic rivalry, the two branches still maintained marriage links.[285] The descendants of Abu ᶜUyayna b. al-Muhallab were also important in passing on Muhallabid accounts. Abu ᶜUyayna had a grandson with the same name whose son Muhammad was a poet who served as governor of Rayy under al-Mansur before he was imprisoned and mulcted.[286] Muhammad's sons, ᶜAbd Allah and yet another Abu ᶜUyayna, were also poets, the latter a general litterateur known as al-Minhal and, confusingly, Ibn Abi ᶜUyayna.[287] He accompanied Khalid b. Yazid b. Hatim al-Muhallabi to his governorship in Jurjan, though the two had a falling out leading to a famous satire. While in Jurjan, however, Ibn Abi ᶜUyayna and two friends also produced poetry praising the Azd Sarat in Jurjan, showing the continual relevance of Azd identity.[288]

Another important Muhallabid was actually descended from al-Muhallab's brother Qabisa. Al-Tabari reports that in 142 (759), ᶜUmar b. Hafs b. ᶜUthman b. Qabisa b. Abi Sufra, known as Hazarmard, was sent to suppress a revolt in and govern Sind and al-Hind.[289] While there, he may have conspired in the escape of Muhammad the Pure Soul's son ᶜAbd Allah. However, these reports come from the Abbasid branch most prominent in Basra, which had a rivalry with the Muhallabids over the governorship of that city.[290] ᶜUmar's daughter Fatima was married to one of Basra's Abbasids, though she is more famous for Ibn Abi ᶜUyayna's love poetry dedicated to her.[291] ᶜUmar was later transferred to Ifriqiya, becoming the first of eight consecutive Muhallabid governors of that province.[292] The most famous descendants of al-Muhallab, and the ones who ruled Ifriqiya after Hazarmard, were the descendants of Qabisa b. al-Muhallab, of whom a few have already been mentioned. Near the start of al-Mansur's reign, Dawud's brother Yazid fought a revolt near Mosul and was defeated. He later spent most of the 760s as governor of Egypt before following Hazarmard in Ifriqiya and leading the war against the Ibadis of North Africa, whom he defeated. Al-Tabari reports Yazid died in 170 (787), and he was succeeded as governor by his brother Rawh.[293]

Rawh b. Hatim had been an Abbasid commander in the battle for Wasit, and later against an *iṣpahbadh* in Tabaristan.[294] At the start of al-Mahdi's reign, he became governor of Sind.[295] Later that year al-Mahdi made him governor of Kufa and appointed over the *shurṭa* of that city Khalid b. Yazid b. Hatim, the former governor of Jurjan whom Ibn Abi ᶜUyayna al-Muhallabi had satirised. The caliph hoped Rawh would move against his unwanted heir ᶜIsa b. Musa., but they could not find an adequate reason.[296] A few years later, Rawh became governor of Basra, where his son Dawud was sent to him for re-education after an arrest for heresy.[297] Two years later he was again in charge of Kufa when ᶜIsa b. Musa died, and Rawh earned the enmity of al-Mahdi for not praying first over his body.[298] He died in 174 (790) in Ifriqiya.[299]

Conclusion

The narratives of Abu Mikhnaf in particular show the persistence of tribal identity into the late eighth century through their promotion of an idealised version of the Muhallabids and the Azd with whom they were linked. In discussing the oral traditions of the Al Rasheed, Madawi al-Rasheed writes:

> The rise and fall of the amirs signify the rise and fall of the tribes as a whole. The narratives do not unfold an 'elitist' history. On the contrary, they are full of references to the Shammar, their relations with their amirs, their support for or disagreement with them, the joy of the supporters over the victory of the amirs or the discontent of the dissenters. The amirs tell us about both the amirs and their tribesmen and this seems to be an important feature of the oral tradition.[300]

This is similar to what we see with many of the accounts discussed above. The family of al-Muhallab became a key repository of al-Azd 'segmentary *sharaf*' into the Abbasid period, a 'site of memory' on which al-Azd traditionists perceived tribal honour to be at stake. In contrast, al-Madaʾini was willing to present al-Muhallab positively, but primarily by way of contrast with his sons' quarrelling and haughtiness. By the days of al-Mubarrad, events concerning al-Muhallab had become part of a more generalised Arab heritage focused on language and poetry, while for Ibn Aᶜtham al-Kufi, the family could easily be detached from the tribal identity, in which he took little interest despite sharing it. Still, these developments were not even across the Islamic world, as ps.-al-ᶜAwtabi still focused on the tribes of Oman to which the Muhallabids were inevitably connected.

Although the family was not initially of al-Azd origins, their rise to prominence saw them become closely tied to the Azd ᶜUman. Their recruitment of that tribe into their armies provided them with a base of manpower independent of the garrison towns, and their prominence made them major assets to Azdis, who in exchange came to count them as authentically Arab genealogically, with their tribe granted a prominent place just a few generations removed from ᶜAmr Muzayqiyaʾ. The Muhallabids also became crucial links between al-Azd and the caliphate. While the Marwanids placed Basra under closer administrative supervision, the loyalties of the tribal individuals to a household which acted within the framework of the state provided one means which also incorporated them into that state's mechanisms of action.

This tie between the Muhallabids and al-Azd persisted despite the fact that many other tribes were represented in Muhallabid armies. However, the fact that status within the caliphate, not only as a governor or general, but also as the hero to a significant body of tribesmen, depended on ties with the caliph ultimately gave rise to factionalism as centralisation reduced the number of hands wielding independent power. Because of these factors, al-Hajjaj's assault on the Muhallabids and later Yazid II's massacre of them also broke the ties of al-Azd with Quraysh and Thaqif which had existed since the first decades of the Islamic state. In its place, perhaps because of the close proximity of the revolt of Ibn al-Ashᶜath al-Kindi, the Azd would identify fully with 'al-Yaman', a grouping which also provided them with a new origin story connecting them with the Ansar and ancient kings.

Notes

1. Pierre Nora, 'Between Memory and History: Les Lieux de Mémoire', p. 12.
2. S. Yusuf, 'Al-Muhallab and the Poets', pp. 197–9.
3. Hilary Kilpatrick, *Making the Great Book of Songs: Compilation and the Author's Craft in Abû l-Faraj al-Isbahani's Kitab al-aghani*, p. 18.
4. Isfahani, *al-Aghani*, XIV, pp. 283–301.
5. Isfahani, *al-Aghani*, XIV, p. 263; Ibn Qutayba, *al-Shi*ᶜ*r*, p. 419.
6. Ibn al-Nadim, *Fihrist*, p. 149.
7. J. C. Wilkinson also concluded this in 'The Early Development of the Ibadi Movement in Basra,' p. 141.
8. Isfahani, *al-Aghani*, XX, p. 75.
9. Isfahani, *al-Aghani*, XXII, p. 345; Hell, 'Lieder', 1905, pp. 597–9.
10. Isfahani, *al-Aghani*, XX, p. 76; Ibn Qutayba, *al-Ma*ᶜ*arif*, p. 399.
11. Ibn Rusteh, *Kitab al-A*ᶜ*laq al-Nafisa*, pp. 205–6; Yaqut, *Buldan*, II, p. 385. On the association of weaving with non-Arab descent, see Chapter 1, n. 62.
12. Hinds, *Early Islamic Family*, p. 25; ᶜAwtabi, *al-Ansab*, II, p. 631.
13. Adam Silverstein, *Postal Systems in the Pre-Modern Islamic World*, p. 69, n. 87.
14. Baladhuri, *Ansab*, VII, Damascus, p. 236; Isfahani, *al-Aghani*, XX, pp. 76–7
15. Waqidi, *al-Ridda*, pp. 55–6.
16. Ibn ᶜAsakir, *Ta*ᵓ*rikh*, LXI, pp. 283–4.
17. Hinds, *Early Islamic Family*, pp. 12–14; ᶜAwtabi, *al-Ansab*, II, pp. 625–6.
18. Hinds, *Early Islamic Family*, pp. 20–1, 23; ᶜAwtabi, *al-Ansab*, II, pp. 629–30. In Baladhuri, Abu Sufra makes his declaration to Ziyad b. Abihi. Baladhuri, *Ansab*, II, p. 379. The towns were Nahr Tira, Manadhir and al-Kubra.
19. Hinds, *Early Islamic Family*, p. 25; ᶜAwtabi, *al-Ansab*, II, p. 630.
20. Baladhuri, *Ansab*, II, p. 377.
21. Ibn ᶜAsakir, *Ta*ᵓ*rikh*, LXI, p. 304.
22. Hinds, *Early Islamic Family*, p. 12; ᶜAwtabi, *al-Ansab*, II, p. 625; Ibn ᶜAsakir, *Ta*ᵓ*rikh*, LXI, p. 288.
23. Hinds, *Early Islamic Family*, pp. 23–4; ᶜAwtabi, *al-Ansab*, II, p. 630.
24. Hinds, *Early Islamic Family*, pp. 21–3; ᶜAwtabi, *al-Ansab*, II, pp. 629–30.
25. Andrew Marsham, *Rituals of Islamic Monarchy: Accession and Succession in the First Muslim Empire*, p. 73.
26. Hinds, *Early Islamic Family*, p. 78; ᶜAwtabi, *al-Ansab*, II, p. 658. I have used Hinds' translation.
27. Agha's highly plausible reconstruction is that Abu Salama in Basra was

pursuing the public agenda of the revolutionary organisation, and Abu Muslim's promotion of Abbasid interests was an internal coup. Saleh Said Agha, *The Revolution with Toppled the Umayyads: Neither Arab nor ᶜAbbasid*, pp. 117–35.

28. *Tarikh-i Sistan*, Bahar, pp. 85–8; *Tarikh-i Sistan*, Gold, pp. 68–71; Ibn ᶜAsakir, *Taʾrikh*, LXI, p. 289. For the identity of this Kabul-Shah, see Khodadad Rezakhani, *ReOrienting the Sasanians: East Iran in Late Antiquity*, p. 167. On the sources for the *Tarikh-i Sistan*, see C. E. Bosworth, 'Sistan and Its Local Histories', pp. 35–7; Julie Scott Meisami, *Persian Historiography to the End of the Twelfth Century*, pp. 108–9.
29. Hinds, *Early Islamic Family*, pp. 23, 27.
30. Baladhuri, *Futuh*, pp. 396, 432.
31. Tabari, *Taʾrīkh*, II, pp. 109–10; Tabari, *History*, XVIII, p. 120.
32. Hatim himself had it from an ᶜAbd al-Rahman b. Subh via Ghalib b. Sulayman. I have been unable to identify either.
33. Baladhuri, *Futuh*, p. 411; Ibn Habib, *al-Muhabbar*, pp. 261, 302; Al-Thaᶜalibi, *The Book of Curious and Entertaining Information*, p. 94.
34. Hinds, *Early Islamic Family*, pp. 27–9; ᶜAwtabi, *al-Ansab*, II, pp. 631–2.
35. Al-Waᶜiz al-Balkhi, *Fazaʾil Balkh*, p. 30.
36. Tabari, *Taʾrīkh*, II, pp. 489–90; Tabari, *History*, XX, pp. 71–2.
37. Tabari, *Taʾrīkh*, II, pp. 490–6; Tabari, *History*, XX, pp. 72–9; Baladhuri, *Futuh*, p. 414.
38. Al-Waᶜiz al-Balkhi, *Fazaʾil Balkh*, pp. 82–5; Ibn ᶜAsakir, *Taʾrikh*, XL, pp. 416–38.
39. Thaᶜalibi, *Curious*, p. 102.
40. Dinawari, *al-Akhbar*, pp. 259–60.
41. For accounts of this war apart from those discussed below, see Dinawari, *al-Akhbar*, pp. 247–57; Yaᶜqubi, *Taʾrikh*, II, pp. 264–5, 272.
42. Baladhuri, *Futuh*, p. 396; Ibn Khayyat, *Taʾrikh*, p. 125.
43. Adam Gaiser, 'What Do We Learn about the Early Kharijites and Ibadiyya from Their Coins?', pp. 174–6.
44. Stuart D. Sears, 'A Monetary History of Iraq and Iran, ca CE 500–750', pp. 390–1.
45. Sears, 'Monetary', pp. 387–8; Kennedy, *Armies*, pp. 69–70; Hugh Kennedy, 'Military pay', pp. 165–8.
46. ᶜAwtabi, *al-Ansab*, II, p. 744.
47. Ursula Sezgin, *Abu Mihnaf: ein Beitrag zur Historiographie der umaiyadischen Zeit*, p. 189.
48. Tabari, *Taʾrīkh*, II, pp. 583–4; Tabari, *History*, XX, pp. 166–8; Balᶜami, *Tarikh*, pp. 741–2 is mostly an abbreviated version, but does provide a reason for al-Muhallab's presence in Basra in that his wealth (*khān va mān*) was there.
49. Yaqut, *Buldan*, III, p. 262 says the height was used as a lookout post.
50. U. Sezgin, *Abu Mihnaf*, p. 226.

51. Tabari, *Taʾrīkh*, II, pp. 585–90; Tabari, *History*, XX, pp. 169–74.
52. Mubarrad, *Kamil*, III, p. 315; Baladhuri, *Ansab*, VI, p. 269.
53. Mubarrad, *Kamil*, III, p. 322; Savran, *Arabs and Iranians*, pp. 163–4.
54. Baladhuri, *Ansab*, VI, p. 532. On the purported descent of Thaqif from Thamud, see Webb, *Imagining the Arabs*, pp. 216–20.
55. The material analysed below is from Mubarrad, *Kamil*, III, pp. 310–33; Baladhuri, *Ansab*, VI, pp. 264–70.
56. Nahr Tira was a canal believed to have been dug by Ardashir or even before. Yaqut, *Buldan*, V, pp. 368–9.
57. For Sulaf see Yaqut, *Buldan*, III, p. 324.
58. R. Sellheim, 'al-Mubarrad', *EI2*, VII, pp. 279–82; Zubaydi, *Tabaqat*, pp. 101–10; Ibn al-Anbari, *Nuzha*, pp. 148–57; Yaqut, *Udabaʾ*, IV, pp. 479–86.
59. Ilkka Lindstedt, 'Sources for the Biography of the Historian Ibn A^{c}tham al-Kufi', pp. 299–309.
60. Peacock, *Mediaeval Islamic Historiography*, pp. 94–7; Borrut, *Entre*, p. 93.
61. Ibn A^{c}tham al-Kufi, *Kitab al-Futuh*, V, pp. 10–15.
62. Mubarrad, *Kamil*, I, pp. 311–12; Ibn A^{c}tham al-Kufi, *Kitab al-Futuh*, VI, p. 34.
63. Ibn A^{c}tham al-Kufi, *Kitab al-Futuh*, VI, pp. 15–24.
64. Lawrence I. Conrad, 'Ibn A^{c}tham and His History,' pp. 97–8.
65. Sahmi, *Taʾrīkh Jurjan*, passim.
66. Ibn A^{c}tham al-Kufi, *Kitab al-Futuh*, VI, pp. 28–38. Baladhuri briefly mentions different engagements, *Ansab*, VI, p. 271. For the city and region of Sabur, see Le Strange, *Lands of the Eastern Caliphate: Mesopotamia, Persia, and Central Asia from the Moslem conquest to the time of Timur*, pp. 262–8.
67. Tabari, *History*, XXI, pp. 86–100; Tabari, *Taʾrīkh*, II, pp. 719–33; Ibn A^{c}tham al-Kufi, *Kitab al-Futuh*, VI, pp. 184–93; Baladhuri, *Ansab*, V, pp. 251–4, 258–60; Baladhuri, *Ansab*, VI, pp. 81–4, 90–2, 271. See also Dinawari, *al-Akhbar*, pp. 278–9.
68. Baladhuri, *Ansab*, V, pp. 332; Baladhuri, *Ansab*, VI, pp. 185–6; Tabari, *History*, XXI, p. 123; Tabari, *Taʾrīkh*, II, p. 723; Mubarrad, *Kamil*, III, p. 334.
69. Tabari, *History*, XXI, pp. 133–4; Tabari, *Taʾrīkh*, II, p. 765; Mubarrad, *Kamil*, III, pp. 347–8; Baladhuri, *Ansab*, VI, pp. 273–4, 280.
70. Ibn A^{c}tham al-Kufi, *Kitab al-Futuh*, VI, pp. 41–7.
71. Baladhuri, *Ansab*, VI, pp. 518–21; Mubarrad, *Kamil*, III, pp. 349–55.
72. Tabari, *Taʾrīkh*, II, pp. 822–8; Tabari, *History*, XXI, p. 200–5.
73. Baladhuri, *Ansab*, V, p. 252; Baladhuri, *Ansab*, VI, p. 82.
74. Baladhuri, *Ansab*, VI, p. 86.
75. Baladhuri, *Ansab*, VI, pp. 524–5; Mubarrad, *Kamil*, III, pp. 353–4.
76. Ibn A^{c}tham al-Kufi, *Kitab al-Futuh*, VI, pp. 298–313.

77. Tabari, *Taʾrīkh*, II, pp. 855–9; Tabari, *History*, XXII, pp. 3–7; Mubarrad, *Kamil*, III, pp. 362–6; Baladhuri, *Ansab*, VI, pp. 527–30.
78. Joshua Mabra, *Princely Authority in the Early Marwanid State: The Life of [c]Abd al-Aziz ibn Marwan*, pp.167–87.
79. Tabari, *Taʾrīkh*, II, pp. 863–75; Tabari, *History*, XXII, pp. 13–25; Baladhuri, *Ansab*, VI, pp. 530–1; Mubarrad, *Kamil*, III, pp. 366–89; Bal[c]ami, *Tarikh*, p. 785; Mas[c]udi, *Muruj*, III, pp. 154–7.
80. Ibn A[c]tham al-Kufi, *Kitab al-Futuh*, VI, pp. 313–22, VII, pp. 11–15. On Abu Mikhnaf as a source for *Ansab al-Ashraf*, see U. Sezgin, *Abu Mihnaf*, pp. 50–2.
81. Tabari, *Taʾrīkh*, II, pp. 1008–17; Tabari, *History*, pp. 155–61; Ibn A[c]tham al-Kufi, *Kitab al-Futuh*, VII, pp. 23–46; Isfahani, *al-Aghani*, XIV, p. 284.
82. Tabari, *Taʾrīkh*, II, pp. 875–7; Tabari, *History*, XXII, pp. 25–7; Mubarrad, *Kamil*, III, pp. 369, 372; Baladhuri, *Ansab*, VI, pp. 531–4.
83. Baladhuri, *Ansab*, VI, p. 535.
84. Yusuf, 'Al-Muhallab-B.-Abi-Sufra: His Strategy and Qualities of Generalship', pp. 3–9.
85. For sample accounts, see Tabari, *Taʾrīkh*, II, pp. 1004–6; Tabari, *History*, XXII, pp. 151–2; Mubarrad, Kamil, III, pp. 370, 373–4, 377–8.
86. Tabari, *Taʾrīkh*, II, pp. 1003–4; Tabari, *History*, XXII, pp. 150–1.
87. Mubarrad, *Kamil*, III, p. 390.
88. Mubarrad, *Kamil*, III, pp. 380–1; Baladhuri, *Ansab*, VI, p. 536.
89. Tabari, *Taʾrīkh*, II, pp. 877–8; Tabari, *History*, XXII, pp. 27–8.
90. Mubarrad, *Kamil*, III, pp. 382–94; Baladhuri, *Ansab*, VI, pp. 537–8, 543–4, 546–9.
91. Tabari, *Taʾrīkh*, II, pp. 1006–7; Tabari, *History*, XXII, pp. 153–4; Ibn A[c]tham al-Kufi, *Kitab al-Futuh*, VII, pp. 55–71.
92. Wilkinson, *Ibadism*, p. 109.
93. Tabari, *Taʾrīkh*, II, pp. 1034–5; Tabari, *History*, XXII, pp. 179–80.
94. Tabari, *Taʾrīkh*, II, pp. 821–2; Tabari, *History*, XXI, pp. 198–9; Mubarrad, *Kamil*, III, p. 349; Baladhuri, *Ansab*, VI, p. 280.
95. Tabari, *Taʾrīkh*, II, pp. 1016–7; Tabari, *History*, XXII, p. 160.
96. Hinds, *Early Islamic Family*, pp. 45–7; [c]Awtabi, *al-Ansab*, II, pp. 640–2. Hinds doubts its authenticity, but examples of similar work by that early Abbasid poet could be Leon Zolondek, *Di[c]bil b. [c]Ali: The Life and Writings of an Early [c]Abbasid Poet*, pp. 97, 100, 108, 123. On Di[c]bil's Yaman orientation, see Peter Webb, 'Yemeni Identity in Abbasid Iraq: From the Sublime to the Ridiculous'.
97. Hinds, *Early Islamic Family*, pp. 34–6; [c]Awtabi, *al-Ansab*, II, pp. 635–6.
98. Hinds, *Early Islamic Family*, pp. 40–1; [c]Awtabi, *al-Ansab*, II, pp. 638–9; See also Baladhuri, *Ansab*, VI. Bal[c]ami links this with al-Hajjaj's emissary to report on the course of the war. Bal[c]ami, *Tarikh*, p. 786.
99. Hinds, *Early Islamic Family*, p. 40; [c]Awtabi, *al-Ansab*, II, p. 638.

100. Baladhuri, *Futuh*, p. 369. Khayra also held estates named Khayratan and Muhallaban. Ibid. p. 360.
101. Al-Tabari says that in the year 81, al-Muhallab was in charge of war in Khurasan, but his son al-Mughira over the *kharaj*. Tabari, *Ta'rīkh*, II, p. 1063; Tabari, *History*, XXIII, p. 13.
102. H. A. R. Gibb, *The Arab Conquests in Central Asia* (New York: AMS Press, 1970 reprint), p. 25; Clifford Edmund Bosworth, *Sistan under the Arabs: From the Islamic Conquest to the Rise of the Saffarids (30–250/651–864)* (Rome: IsMEO, 1968), p. 48.; M. A. Shaban, *The Abbasid Revolution*, p. 54.
103. Lughawi, *Maratib*, p. 92; Ibn Qutayba, *al-Ma^carif*, p. 545; Sam^cani, *al-Ansab*, III, pp. 591–2; Ibn al-Anbari, *Nuzha*, pp. 35–7.
104. Tabari, *Ta'rīkh*, II, pp. 1033–5; Tabari, *History*, XXII, pp. 178–80. For yet another alternate account, see Ibn ^cAsakir, *Ta'rikh*, LXI, p. 294.
105. Tabari, *Ta'rīkh*, II, p. 1042; Tabari, *History*, XXII, p. 190.
106. Tabari, *Ta'rīkh*, II, pp. 1058–60; Tabari, *History*, XXIII, pp. 9–10; Ibn A^ctham al-Kufi, *Kitab al-Futuh*, VII, pp. 118–19.
107. Baladhuri, *Ansab*, VI, p. 433.
108. Bosworth, *Sistan under the Arabs*, p. 60.
109. *Tarikh-i Sistan*, Bahar, p. 116; *Tarikh-i Sistan*, Gold, p. 93.
110. Though the text here calls him al-Ruqad b. ^cUbayd. Tabari, *Ta'rīkh*, II, pp. 1106–9; Tabari, *History*, XXIII, pp. 53–6.
111. Isfahani, *al-Aghani*, III, p. 136; Ibn Qutayba, *al-Shi^cr*, p. 511.
112. See Isfahani, *al-Aghani*, III, pp. 135, 138, where he claims descent from ancient Persian nobility.
113. Isfahani, *al-Aghani*, III, pp. 162, 213–18.
114. Lughawi, *Maratib*, p. 92; Ibn Qutayba, *al-Ma^carif*, p. 545; Sam^cani, *al-Ansab*, III, pp. 591–2; Yaqut, *Udaba'*, V, pp. 515–17.
115. Tabari, *Ta'rīkh*, II, pp. 1082–3; Tabari, *History*, XXIII, p. 31.
116. Tabari, *Ta'rīkh*, II, p. 1083; Tabari, *History*, XXIII, p. 32. Sam^cani, who lived in Merv in the twelfth century, mentions al-Muhallab's tomb in Zaghul, *al-Ansab*, III, p. 134.
117. See the elegy composed by Ziyad al-A^cjam, which refers to al-Mufaddal's tomb in Merv: Isfahani, *al-Aghani*, p. 382; Ibn Qutayba, *Shi^cr*, p. 280.
118. Crone, *God's Rule: Government and Islam*, pp. 149, 151.
119. Ibn A^ctham al-Kufi, *Kitab al-Futuh*, VII, pp. 119–20.
120. Hinds, *Early Islamic Family*, pp. 49–50; ^cAwtabi, *al-Ansab*, II, p. 643. Baladhuri quotes Mada'ini as reporting that Zaghul was a village of Merv al-Rudh. Baladhuri, *Ansab*, Damascus, VII, p. 222; Baladhuri, *Futuh*, p. 417.
121. Hinds, *Early Islamic Family*, p. 44, ^cAwtabi, *al-Ansab*, II, p. 640.
122. Tabari, *Ta'rīkh*, II, pp. 1106–9; Tabari, *History*, XXIII, pp. 53–6.
123. Tabari, *Ta'rīkh*, II, p. 1110; Tabari, *History*, XXIII, p. 56.
124. Tabari, *Ta'rīkh*, II, pp. 1119–22; Tabari, *History*, XXIII, pp. 63–7.

125. Tabari, *Ta'rīkh*, II, pp. 1110; Tabari, *History*, XXIII, pp. 56–7.
126. Steven Judd, 'Character Development in al-Tabari's and al-Baladhuri's Narratives of Late Umayyad History', pp. 210–25.
127. Baladhuri, *Ansab*, Damascus, VII, p. 222.
128. Tabari, *Ta'rīkh*, II, pp. 1141–2; Tabari, *History*, XXIII, p. 86.
129. Baladhuri, *Ansab*, Damascus, VII, p. 222.
130. Baladhuri, *Futuh*, p. 400.
131. Tabari, *Ta'rīkh*, II, pp. 1151–2; Tabari, *History*, XXIII, p. 96.
132. Remember that Khuza^c^a was sometimes considered a part of al-Azd.
133. Tabari, *Ta'rīkh*, II, pp. 1080–2; Tabari, *History*, XXIII, pp. 29–31
134. Tabari, *Ta'rīkh*, II, pp. 1152–3; Tabari, *History*, XXIII, pp. 96–7.
135. Shaban, *Abbasid Revolution*, p. 59.
136. Tabari, *Ta'rīkh*, II, p. 1152; Tabari, *History*, XXIII, p. 96.
137. Etienne de la Vaissière, *Sogdian Traders: A History*, pp. 275–6; Agha, *Revolution*, pp. 149–51.
138. Baladhuri, *Ansab*, Damascus, VII, pp. 222–3; Hinds, *Early Islamic Family*, pp. 56–9; ^c^Awtabi, *al-Ansab*, II, pp. 646–7.
139. Al-Rawas, *Oman*, pp. 62–5; Wilkinson, *Ibadism*, p. 118; Dixon, *Umayyad*, p.150.
140. Tabari, *Ta'rīkh*, II, pp. 1138–41; Tabari, *History*, XXIII, pp. 83–6; Bal^c^ami, *Tarikh*, pp. 812–14; Ibn ^c^Asakir, *Ta'rikh*, LX, pp. 95–6.
141. Bal^c^ami says this Khwarizm expedition was led by al-Mufaddal during Yazid's governorship, p. 814.
142. Tabari, *Ta'rīkh*, II, pp. 1142–3; Tabari, *History*, XXIII, p. 87; Baladhuri, *Futuh*, p. 417.
143. Baladhuri, *Ansab*, Damascus, VII, pp. 223–4.
144. Ibn A^c^tham al-Kufi, *Kitab al-Futuh*, VII, pp. 197–9.
145. Tabari, *Ta'rīkh*, II, pp. 1143–4; Tabari, *History*, XXIII, p. 88.
146. Hinds, *Early Islamic Family*, pp. 53–4; ^c^Awtabi, *al-Ansab*, II, pp. 644–5.
147. Gibb, *Arab Conquests*, p. 27.
148. Tabari, *Ta'rīkh*, II, pp. 1144–5; Tabari, *History*, XXIII, pp. 88–9.
149. Tabari, *Ta'rīkh*, II, pp. 1161–4; Tabari, *History*, XXIII, pp. 105–8; Baladhuri, *Futuh*, p. 419.
150. If ps.-al-^c^Awtabi's concern were to eliminate hints of rivalry among the sons of al-Muhallab, it would have been too easy to do so and still keep al-Mufaddal's victories.
151. Tabari, *Ta'rīkh*, II, p. 1182; Tabari, *History*, XXIII, p. 129.
152. Baladhuri, *Ansab*, Damascus, VII, p. 224. Ps.-al-^c^Awtabi names Mudrik, Ziyad, ^c^Abd al-Malik and Abu ^c^Uyayna. *Ansab*, p. 648; Hinds, *Early Islamic Family*, p. 60.
153. Tabari, *Ta'rīkh*, II, pp. 1208–9; Tabari, *History*, XXIII, pp. 156–7; Bal^c^ami, *Tarikh*, p. 850; Ibn A^c^tham al-Kufi, *Kitab al-Futuh*, VII, pp. 208–9.
154. Tabari, *Ta'rīkh*, II, pp. 1209–11; Tabari, *History*, XXIII, pp. 157–8;

Ibn Aʿtham al-Kufi, *Kitab al-Futuh*, VII, pp. 210–11; Balʿami, *Tarikh*, pp. 850–1 has al-Mufaddal be the one most insistent on waiting for ʿAbd al-Malik.

155. Baladhuri, *Ansab*, Damascus, VII, pp. 225–6.
156. On this point, see also the account derived from Abu Hanifa Dinawari in Ibn ʿAsakir, *Taʾrikh*, XXXIV, pp. 37–8.
157. Tabari, *Taʾrīkh*, II, pp. 1211–2; Tabari, *History*, XXIII, pp. 158–9; Balʿami, *Tarikh*, pp. 851–2; Ibn Habib, *al-Muhabbar*, p. 191.
158. Tabari, *Taʾrīkh*, II, pp. 1212–3; Tabari, *History*, XXIII, p. 160.
159. Baladhuri, *Ansab*, Damascus, VII, p. 227; Hinds, *Early Islamic Family*, p. 62; ʿAwtabi, *al-Ansab*, II, p. 649; Ibn Aʿtham al-Kufi, *Kitab al-Futuh*, VII, pp. 211–12. Ibn ʿAsakir has a substantial biography of Rajaʾ b. Haywa, but does not mention this affair, *Taʾrikh*, XVIII, pp. 96–116.
160. For Muhammad b. Salam, see Yaqut, *Udabaʾ*, V, pp. 345–6. For Ibn Bakkar, F. Sezgin, *Geschichte*, I, pp. 317–18.
161. Tabari, *Taʾrīkh*, II, pp. 1213–15; Tabari, *History*, XXIII, pp. 160–2; Ibn Bakkar, *al-Akhbar al-Muwaffaqiyat*, pp. 497–500; Baladhuri, *Ansab*, Damascus, VII, pp. 227–30; Balʿami, *Tarikh*, pp. 852–4; Ibn Aʿtham al-Kufi, *Kitab al-Futuh*, VII, pp. 213–14.
162. Tabari, *Taʾrīkh*, II, pp. 1215–17; Tabari, *History*, XXIII, pp. 162–3; Balʿami, *Tarikh*, p. 854; Reinhard Eisener, *Zwischen Faktum und Fiktion: Eine Studie zum Umayyadenkalifen Sulaiman b. ʿAbdalmalik und seinem Bild in den Quellen*, p. 28.
163. Eisener, *Faktum und Fiktion*, pp. 29–31.
164. Hinds, *Early Islamic Family*, p. 62; ʿAwtabi, *al-Ansab*, II, p. 649.
165. For an examination of chronological issues in Yazid's career under Sulayman, see Eisener, *Faktum und Fiktion*, pp. 101–4.
166. According to Ibn ʿAsakir, Salih b. ʿAbd al-Rahman, the son of a prisoner captured in Sistan under the caliph ʿUthman, began serving in the administration of Basra under Ziyad b. Abihi and was the first to keep the diwan in Arabic instead of Persian, *Taʾrikh*, XXIII, p. 344.
167. Tabari, *Taʾrīkh*, II, pp. 1306–7; Tabari, *History*, XXIV, p. 31; Baladhuri, *Ansab*, Damascus, VII, pp. 232.
168. Ibn Aʿtham al-Kufi, *Kitab al-Futuh*, VII, pp. 252–5.
169. Tabari, *Taʾrīkh*, II, pp. 1307–8; Tabari, *History*, XXIV, pp. 31–2; Ibn ʿAsakir, *Taʾrikh*, XXIII, p. 344.
170. Baladhuri, *Ansab*, Damascus, VII, pp. 233.
171. Tabari, *Taʾrīkh*, II, pp. 1282–3; Tabari, *History*, XXIV, pp. 1–2.
172. Baladhuri, *Ansab*, Damascus, VII, pp. 230–1.
173. Tabari, *Taʾrīkh*, II, p. 1308; Tabari, *History*, XXIV, p. 32.
174. Tabari, *Taʾrīkh*, II, pp. 1308–12; Tabari, *History*, XXIV, pp. 32–6; Balʿami, *Tarikh*, pp. 879–81.
175. Tabari, *Taʾrīkh*, II, p. 1311; Tabari, *History*, XXIV, p. 35.
176. Tabari, *Taʾrīkh*, II, p. 1312; Tabari, *History*, XXIV, p. 36.

177. Wellhausen, *Arab Kingdom*, p. 441.
178. Hinds, *Early Islamic Family*, pp. 64–6; ᶜAwtabi, *al-Ansab*, II, pp. 650–1.
179. Hinds, *Early Islamic Family*, pp. 63–4; ᶜAwtabi, *al-Ansab*, II, p. 650. The translation of Yazid's note to Ziyad is Hinds', though I have attempted to clarify the sense of his relationship with al-Minhal.
180. Tabari, *Taʾrīkh*, II, pp. 1313, 1318–19; Tabari, *History*, XXIV, pp. 37, 43–4.
181. Tabari, *Taʾrīkh*, II, pp. 1333, 1419–20; Tabari, *History*, XXIV, pp. 58, 150–1.
182. Tabari, *Taʾrīkh*, II, p. 1389; Tabari, *History*, XXIV, p. 120.
183. Tabari, *Taʾrīkh*, II, pp. 1334–5; Tabari, *History*, XXIV, pp. 59–60.
184. Baladhuri, *Ansab*, Damascus, VII, p. 234.
185. Ibn Aᶜtham al-Kufi, *Kitab al-Futuh*, VII, pp. 297–8.
186. Tabari, *Taʾrīkh*, II, p. 1346; Tabari, *History*, XXIV, p. 75.
187. Eisener, *Faktum und Fiktion*, pp. 113–14.
188. On the image of ᶜUmar II, see Borrut, *Entre*, pp. 283–320.
189. Tabari, *Taʾrīkh*, II, p. 1313; Tabari, *History*, XXIV, p. 37.
190. Baladhuri, *Ansab*, VII, Damascus, pp. 234–6.
191. Baladhuri, *Ansab*, VII, Damascus, p. 238; See also Ibn ᶜAsakir, *Taʾrikh*, LVII, p. 168.
192. Tabari, *Taʾrīkh*, II, pp. 1350–2; Tabari, *History*, XXIV, pp. 79–81.
193. Ibn Aᶜtham al-Kufi, *Kitab al-Futuh*, VII, pp. 306–7, 311–20.
194. Ibn ᶜAsakir, *Taʾrikh*, LVII, pp. 168–72.
195. Al-Khatib al-Baghdadi, *Taʾrikh*, VIII, pp. 301–4.
196. Hinds, *Early Islamic Family*, pp. 66–8; ᶜAwtabi, *al-Ansab*, II, pp. 651–2.
197. Tabari, *Taʾrīkh*, II, pp. 1359–61; Tabari, *History*, XXIV, pp. 89–91.
198. Baladhuri, *Ansab*, VII, Damascus, pp. 237–8.
199. Tabari, *Taʾrīkh*, II, p. 1361; Tabari, *History*, XXIV, p. 91.
200. Baladhuri, *Ansab*, VII, Damascus, p. 239.
201. Baladhuri, *Ansab*, VII, Damascus, p. 240.
202. Baladhuri, *Ansab*, VII, Damascus, p. 244.
203. Baladhuri, *Ansab*, VII, Damascus, pp. 244–5.
204. Baladhuri, *Ansab*, VII, Damascus, pp. 245–6.
205. Baladhuri, *Ansab*, VII, Damascus, p. 248.
206. Baladhuri, *Ansab*, VII, Damascus, pp. 249–52.
207. Baladhuri, *Ansab*, VII, Damascus, pp. 242–3; Ibn ᶜAsakir, *Taʾrikh*, XV, p. 284.
208. Baladhuri, *Ansab*, VII, Damascus, pp. 243–4.
209. Baladhuri, *Ansab*, VII, Damascus, p. 244.
210. Tabari, *Taʾrīkh*, II, p. 1381; Tabari, *History*, XXIV, p. 113; Baladhuri, *Ansab*, VII, Damascus, p. 246.
211. Tabari, *Taʾrīkh*, II, pp. 1387–8, 1406; Tabari, *History*, XXIV, p. 119, 138; Baladhuri, *Ansab*, VII, Damascus, p. 253. Baladhuri has him as the one who

informed Yazid II of Yazid b. al-Muhallab's seizure of Basra. Baladhuri, *Ansab*, VII, Damascus, pp. 260–1.

212. Tabari, *Ta'rīkh*, II, p. 1399; Tabari, *History*, XXIV, p. 131.
213. Tabari, *Ta'rīkh*, II, pp. 1390–1; Tabari, *History*, XXIV, pp. 121–3.
214. Tabari, *Ta'rīkh*, II, pp. 1382, 1387–9; Tabari, *History*, XXIV, pp. 114, 119–20; Baladhuri, *Ansab*, Damascus, VII, pp. 259–60.
215. Tabari, *Ta'rīkh*, II, pp. 1379–86; Tabari, *History*, XXIV, pp. 111–18. For ᶜImran b. ᶜAmir b. Mismaᶜ, a nephew of Malik b. Mismaᶜ from the fitna of Masᶜud b. ᶜAmr, see also Baladhuri, *Ansab*, VII, Damascus, p. 247. Ibn Aᶜtham al-Kufi reads like a shorter adaptation of Abu Mikhnaf, *Kitab al-Futuh*, VIII, pp. 1–8.
216. Tabari, *Ta'rīkh*, II, p. 1389; Tabari, *History*, XXIV, p. 120.
217. Tabari, *Ta'rīkh*, II, pp. 1393–4; Tabari, *History*, XXIV, pp. 124–6; Baladhuri, *Ansab*, Damascus, VII, p. 263.
218. Baladhuri, *Ansab*, Damascus, VII, pp. 255–6.
219. Baladhuri, *Ansab*, Damascus, VII, p. 256.
220. Tabari, *Ta'rīkh*, II, pp. 1386–7; Tabari, *History*, XXIV, p. 118.
221. Tabari, *Ta'rīkh*, II, pp. 1399–1400; Tabari, *History*, XXIV, p. 132.
222. Baladhuri, *Ansab*, Damascus, VII, p. 257.
223. Baladhuri, *Ansab*, Damascus, VII, p. 274.
224. Baladhuri, *Ansab*, VII, Damascus, pp. 310, 313.
225. Tabari, *Ta'rīkh*, II, p. 1391; Tabari, *History*, XXIV, p. 123; Ibn Aᶜtham al-Kufi, *Kitab al-Futuh*, VIII, pp. 8–9.
226. U. Sezgin, *Abu Mihnaf*, p. 210.
227. Tabari, *Ta'rīkh*, II, pp. 1391–3, 1400–1; Tabari, *History*, XXIV, pp. 123–4, 133; Wakiᶜ, *Akhbar al-Qudat*, I, p. 308. Ibn Aᶜtham al-Kufi, *Kitab al-Futuh*, VIII, pp. 9–10.
228. Suleiman Ali Mourad, *Early Islam between Myth and History: Al-Hasan al-Basri (D. 110H/728CE) and the Formation of His Legacy in Classical Islamic Scholarship*, pp. 33–40. Leder lists this as an example of anti-Muhallabid material transmitted by Haytham b. ᶜAdi, *Korpus*, p. 240.
229. Wakiᶜ, *Akhbar al-Qudat*, I, pp. 307–8, II, p. 14.
230. Tabari, *Ta'rīkh*, II, pp. 1395–1407; Tabari, *History*, XXIV, pp. 127–39; Baladhuri, *Ansab*, Damascus, VII, pp. 260–9; Ibn Aᶜtham al-Kufi, *Kitab al-Futuh*, VIII, pp. 11–20.
231. Baladhuri, *Ansab*, Damascus, VII, p. 273.
232. Baladhuri, *Ansab*, Damascus, VII, pp. 273–4; Hinds, *Early Islamic Family*, pp. 72–3; ᶜAwtabi, *al-Ansab*, II, pp. 654–5.
233. Hinds, *Early Islamic Family*, pp. 68–70; ᶜAwtabi, *al-Ansab*, II, pp. 652–3. This translation is my own and not Hinds', as al-Nass's text has 'to fight' rather than 'to kill' and is in the present tense. The difference, of course, is that in this version Yazid does not accept defeat and death prior to the battle, even if he does shortly thereafter following the death of Habib.

234. Hinds, *Early Islamic Family*, pp. 70–1; ʿAwtabi, *al-Ansab*, II, pp. 653–4.
235. Hinds, *Early Islamic Family*, pp. 71–2; ʿAwtabi, *al-Ansab*, II, p. 654.
236. Baladhuri, *Ansab*, Damascus, VII, pp. 278; Ibn Habib, *al-Muhabbar*, p. 482.
237. Ibn Aʿtham al-Kufi, *Kitab al-Futuh*, VIII, p. 22.
238. Sean Anthony, *Crucifixion and Death as Spectacle: Umayyad Crucifixion in its Late Antique Context*, p. 43.
239. Anthony, *Crucifixion*, pp. 44–9.
240. Tabari, *Taʾrīkh*, II, pp. 1409–13; Tabari, *History*, XXIV, pp. 141–5; Baladhuri, *Ansab*, Damascus, VII, pp. 269–70, 275.
241. Mubarrad, *Kamil*, I, p. 219.
242. Ibn ʿAsakir, *Taʾrikh*, LXI, pp. 97–8.
243. Hinds, *Early Islamic Family*, p. 81; ʿAwtabi, *al-Ansab*, II, pp. 659–60.
244. Isfahani, *al-Aghani*, XIV, pp. 275–6.
245. Baladhuri, *Ansab*, Damascus, VII, pp. 278–80.
246. Ibn Aʿtham al-Kufi, *Kitab al-Futuh*, VIII, pp. 24–5.
247. Baladhuri, *Ansab*, Damascus, VII, p. 281.
248. Baladhuri, *Ansab*, Damascus, VII, p. 284.
249. Baladhuri, *Ansab*, Damascus, VII, pp. 281–2.
250. Hinds, *Early Islamic Family*, p. 74; ʿAwtabi, *al-Ansab*, II, p. 655.
251. Hinds, *Early Islamic Family*, pp. 74–5; ʿAwtabi, *al-Ansab*, II, pp. 655–6.
252. Hinds, *Early Islamic Family*, pp. 77–8; ʿAwtabi, *al-Ansab*, II, p. 657.
253. Hinds, *Early Islamic Family*, pp. 79–80; ʿAwtabi, *al-Ansab*, II, p. 659.
254. Amabe, *Emergence*, p. 17.
255. Baladhuri, *Ansab*, Damascus, VII, p. 285.
256. Isfahani, *al-Aghani*, XIX, p. 29.
257. Borrut, *Entre*, pp. 260-4.
258. Hawting, *First Dynasty*, p. 76. His view of Marwanid military factionalism is that of Crone, *Slaves*, pp. 37–45. He also believes the Muhallabids promoted al-Azd interests seeking acceptance within the tribe to make up for their questionable pedigree, *First Dynasty*, pp. 55–6. See also Crone, *Slaves*, pp. 43–4.
259. Tabari, *Taʾrīkh*, II, p. 1416; Tabari, *History*, XXIV, p. 148.
260. Retsö, *Arabs*, p. 33.
261. Tabari, *Taʾrīkh*, II, p. 1391; Tabari, *History*, XXIV, p. 122.
262. Gustav Rothstein, *Die Dynastie der Laḫmiden in al-Ḥira: Ein Versuch zur arabisch-persischen Geschichte zur Zeit der Sasaniden*, pp. 134–6.
263. Isfahani, *al-Aghani*, XIX, p. 65; Hell, 'Al-Farazdaḳ's Lieder auf die Muhallabiten', 1906, p. 39.
264. Wilkinson, *Ibadism*, p. 89.
265. ʿAwtabi, *al-Ansab*, II, pp. 776, 791, 797.
266. Michael Bonner, *Aristocratic Violence and Holy War: Studies in the Jihad and the Arab-Byzantine Frontier*, pp. 4–6.
267. Tabari, *Taʾrīkh*, II, p. 1564; Tabari, *History*, XXV, p. 102.

268. Wilkinson, *Ibadism*, p. 188; Savage, *A Gateway to Hell, and Gateway to Paradise: The North African Response to the Arab Conquest*, pp. 32–7, 66.
269. Steven Clark Judd, 'The Third Fitna: Orthodoxy, Heresy and Coercion in Late Umayyad History', p. 277; Teresa Bernheimer, 'The Revolt of ᶜAbdallah b. Muᶜawiya, AH 127–130: A Reconsideration Through the Coinage', pp. 384–5.
270. Tabari, *Ta'rīkh*, II, pp. 1946–7, 1977–8; Tabari, *History*, XXVII, pp. 57–8, 86–7; Baladhuri, *Ansab*, II, pp. 74–5.
271. Tabari, *Ta'rīkh*, II, pp. 1978; Tabari, *History*, XXVII, pp. 87.
272. Baladhuri, *Ansab*, II, p. 75.
273. Ibn Habib, *al-Muhabbar*, p. 486; Ibn Hazm, *Jamhara*, p. 369; Baladhuri, *Ansab*, II, p. 75.
274. Wilkinson, *Ibadism*, p. 212; al-Rawas, *Oman*, pp. 112–13.
275. Tabari, *Ta'rīkh*, III, pp. 21–3; Tabari, *History*, XXVII, pp. 143–5.
276. Baladhuri, *Ansab*, III, pp. 184–6.
277. Hinds, *Early Islamic Family*, pp. 82–4; ᶜAwtabi, *al-Ansab*, II, pp. 660–1. Yet another account from the *Akhbar al-Dawla* involves both Sufyan and Rawh b. Hatim al-Muhallabi as co-commanders in Basra, which is anachronistic for the latter. *Akhbar al-Dawla*, pp. 355–6
278. Baladhuri, *Futuh*, p. 367.
279. Tabari, *Ta'rīkh*, III, pp. 296–8; Tabari, *History*, XXVIII, pp. 268–70; Isfahani, *Maqatil al-Talibiyin*, p. 320.
280. Tabari, *Ta'rīkh*, III, pp. 298–300; Tabari, *History*, XXVIII, pp. 270–2.
281. Tabari, *Ta'rīkh*, *History*, XXVIII, p. 89, n. 420.
282. Tabari, III, pp. 851–5; Tabari, *History*, XXXI, pp. 114–18.
283. *Tarikh Jurjan*, p. 12.
284. Ibn Hazm, *Jamhara*, pp. 368–9.
285. Isfahani, *al-Aghani*, XX, p. 91.
286. Isfahani, *al-Aghani*, XX, p. 79.
287. Ibn Hazm, *Jamhara*, p. 369; Isfahani, *al-Aghani*, p. 75.
288. Isfahani, *al-Aghani*, pp. 107–18.
289. Tabari, *Ta'rīkh*, III, p. 139; Tabari, *History*, XXVIII, p. 78.
290. Amikam Elad, *The Rebellion of Muḥammad al-Nafs al-Zakiyya in 145/762: Ṭalibis and Early ᶜAbbasis in Conflict*, pp. 142–4. Elad has also demonstrated that Muhammad's followers were not exclusively Shi'ite. Amikam Elad, 'The Rebellion of Muhammad b. Abd Allah b. al-Hasan (Known as an-Nafs az-Zakiya) in 142/762', pp. 185–6; Tabari, *Ta'rīkh*, III, pp. 359–63; Tabari, *History* XXIX, pp. 51–5.
291. Isfahani, *al-Aghani*, XX, pp. 79–95.
292. Tabari, *Ta'rīkh*, III, p. 363; Tabari, *History* XXIX, p. 55.
293. Tabari, *Ta'rīkh*, III, pp. 120, 142, 370–3, 569; Tabari, *History*, XXVIII, pp. 45–6, 83; Tabari, *History*, XXIX, pp. 63, 67–9; Tabari, *History*, XXX, p. 41.

294. Tabari, *Ta'rīkh*, III, pp. 64–5, 69, 139–40; Tabari, *History*, XXVII, pp. 187–8, 191; Tabari, *History*, XXVIII, pp. 78–80.
295. Tabari, *Ta'rīkh*, III, p. 461; Tabari, *History*, XXIX, p. 172.
296. Tabari, *Ta'rīkh*, III, p. 467; Tabari, *History*, XXIX, p. 178.
297. Tabari, *Ta'rīkh*, III, pp. 505, 517; Tabari, *History*, XXIX, pp. 222, 234–5.
298. Tabari, *Ta'rīkh*, III, p. 519; Tabari, *History*, XXIX, pp. 236–7.
299. Tabari, *Ta'rīkh*, III, p. 609; Tabari, *History*, XXX, p. 109.
300. al-Rasheed, *Politics in an Arabian Oasis: The Rashidis of Saudi Arabia*, p. 162.

4

Eastern Conquests and Factionalism

In pre-Islamic Arabia, the religious and military realms were two key ways in which leaders staked their claims to prominence and provided resources to the individuals with whom they shared an identity carrying mutual moral claims. With the rise of Islam, the state came rapidly to monopolise religious leadership, at least by setting the framework in which it was articulated, and somewhat more gradually to structure military leadership as well. In the early 700s, the eastern frontier became a critical arena for conquests. This chapter will explore two key questions. The first is what role, if any, al-Azd as a potential network or interest group played in this eastward expansion and its significance for the relationship of the tribe with the state. The second explores the nature of tribal society and identity, noting the development of military factionalism in Khurasan probably dating back to the early 700s and conflict between the Muhallabids and the Abu ᶜAqil family of al-Hajjaj, as described in the previous chapter.

Early Conquests of Khurasan and Sistan

During the first phase of Arab conquests east of Khurasan, frontiers moved little. From the 650s, there were seasonal raids across the Oxus River (Amu Darya) by armies based in Basra. These were often presented as conquests in later Arabic accounts. In 671, Ziyad b. Abihi transferred 50,000 fighters from lower Iraq to Merv; these became the first permanent force stationed in the region. After Ziyad's death in 673, his son ᶜUbayd Allah b. Ziyad began launching more sustained operations, and in 681, Salm b. Ziyad, another son, became the first commander to winter beyond the river before returning to the core of the caliphate following the death of Yazid I. Any gains were lost in the civil war.[1] However, the 650s and 660s were the period in which the Muslims established themselves in Sistan under ᶜAbd al-Rahman b. Samura, though not without some turmoil during the First Civil War.[2] Sistan, the valley of the Helmand River, is an oval lowland stretching between the mountains of eastern Iran and the Hindu Kush, with permanent water sources found mainly in large lakes in the west in what is now the far east of Iran.[3] Because of its desert climate, agriculture depends on irrigation from these permanent water sources.[4] Once conquered, it served as a base from which the Muslims attempted, mostly unsuccessfully, to advance to Sind. The intervening territory, however, was controlled by the rulers of Zabul, and an inability to defeat them led to Sistan's eclipse by Khurasan as the centre for eastern conquests.[5]

Following the ouster of ᶜAbd Allah b. Khazim and a brief interlude under an ineffective member of the Umayyad family named Umayya b. ᶜAbd Allah b. Khalid, the caliph ᶜAbd al-Malik added Khurasan to al-Hajjaj's governorship, and the latter sent al-Muhallab b. Abi Sufra to take charge. Al-Baladhuri credits al-Muhallab with the conquest of al-Khuttal and Khujanda and raids against Kish and Nasaf.[6] These are all probably exaggerations, however, as they paid tribute, but no permanent imperial presence seems to have been established. Al-Muhallab's three years as governor were largely taken up with the siege of the city of Kish. Known today as Shahr-i Sabz, Kish was located in a fertile valley along a land-locked river on the road between Samarqand and Tirmidh and on towards Balkh through the Iron Gates pass. In later centuries it exported agricultural products to Bukhara, a function it may also have served around 700.[7]

Al-Muhallab first took the Oxus River crossing at Zamm, converting Ghazwan al-Iskaf, 'lord of Zamm', to Islam. Both he and an Abu Muhammad al-Zammi are reported later as Muhallabid companions.[8] Al-Tabari's account of this campaign comes from al-Madaᵓini, who says al-Muhallab was assisted by the superbly heroic Abu al-Adham Ziyad b. ᶜAmr al-Zimmani. During the campaign, an attack on al-Khuttal was suggested to al-Muhallab by a cousin of its king. Al-Muhallab sent his son Yazid with him, but the ruler of al-Khuttal tricked his cousin into thinking the Muslims had betrayed him, and captured and killed the rebellious family member. Yazid's forces then surrounded the king's army and extracted payment before returning to al-Muhallab. Al-Muhallab sent his other son Habib to Rabinjan where he encountered the King of Bukhara; there follow several brief stories concerning Habib's campaign accompanied by his *ghulām* Jabala. Al-Muhallab also imprisoned some Mudaris whom he suspected of a plot, but released them after he withdrew following a truce in which the people of Kish agreed to pay tribute.[9] Al-Muhallab remained at Kish for two years, rejecting suggestions that he advance on al-Sughd. In al-Madaᵓini's version, his reason for staying is that his primary concern was the safe return to Merv of all his troops.[10] This unusual interest in saving lives may be partly to counter charges later laid against him of failing to fight aggressively enough. Several sources, including al-Madaʾini and Abu Mikhnaf, report that Qutayba b. Muslim disparaged al-Muhallab for not collecting tribute or fighting enemies.[11]

The brief tenure of al-Muhallab's sons before al-Hajjaj deposed the family also yielded little. According to al-Madaʾini, when Yazid became governor, he took a fortress in Badghis which had been held by Nizak, a Buddhist prince who would later try to start an anti-Arab uprising in Tukharistan. When Nizak left this fortress, Yazid blocked him from returning, extorting a ransom and control of the fortress. Judging from the poetry of Kaᶜb al-Ashqari, the fortress was in a mountainous area from which one could rule over the lowlands.[12] Yazid may also have raided the Khwarizmians.[13] After al-Mufaddal b. al-Muhallab succeeded Yazid, he was in charge of Khurasan for nine months, during which al-Madaʾini reports that he conquered Badghis, Akharun and Shuman.[14] His main move, however, was against Musa b. ᶜAbd Allah as noted in Chapter 3.

The greatest era of eastern conquests followed the first ouster of the Muhallabids, when al-Hajjaj appointed Qutayba b. Muslim al-Bahili over Khurasan and Muhammad b. al-Qasim al-Thaqafi as commander of an army that successfully conquered the Indus Valley. This campaign in Sind will be dealt with below. As for Qutayba b. Muslim, during the ten years from 705–715, he subjected the great Soghdian oasis cities of Paykand, Bukhara and Samarqand, as well as many other areas, including Kish and Nasaf, while sending emissaries to the Tang court in China.[15] At one point, Qutayba invaded the lands of the Khawarzm-Shah, who had invited him to defeat his rebellious brother Khurrazadh in exchange for tribute. This Qutayba did and left a governor alongside the Khawarizm-Shah, who was immediately killed in an uprising. After the conquest of Samarqand, Qutayba sent a force to reconquer the region, massacring significant numbers while maintaining the dynasty.[16]

Sind

Andre Wink emphasises commercial factors in the early Islamic conquests of the Indus Valley. He points to the importance of Kabul and Zabul in the caravan route connecting India with Khurasan.[17] There was also a southern route passing through the Kij valley, Makran and Sistan.[18] Sistan also had direct maritime trade at the time of the *Tarikh-i Sistan*.[19] Makran is a sparsely settled desert region extending northward from the Gulf of Oman. Water is scarce because of impermeable rocks, while the topography makes *qanāt* construction difficult. Rainfall leads mainly to flash floods, with moisture quickly returning to the sea.[20] Wink also states that 'the main motivation of the Arab conquest of Sind was the safeguarding of the trade in the Persian Gulf and the western Indian Ocean.'[21] The trade was threatened by people known as the Mids who engaged in piracy along the southern coast and as far as the Persian Gulf and Sri Lanka.[22]

Derryl MacLean also believes the security of the maritime trade routes was of critical importance to al-Hajjaj, and that the conquest of Sind was of a piece with Qutayba b. Muslim's campaigning in Central Asia.[23] Suchandra Ghosh says that 'the economic interest behind the Sind campaign was so obvious and so carefully calculated that is resembled rather a commercial venture than a military campaign', and notes that it was followed shortly afterwards by an invasion of Gujarat.[24] Regarding the pirates of Daybul simply as a convenient excuse, J. J. Bede places the initiative for the Arab conquest of Sind on the shoulders of al-Hajjaj and the need for new sources of wealth to maintain the Umayyad economic system. In addition to the wealth of the territory itself, he also notes the importance of maritime trade, referring to the tendency of governors of provinces along maritime trade routes to be portrayed as more likely to support South Asian conquests than the caliphs.[25] With a broader scope, he suggests that conquest of the rich plains of India was a natural result of an expansionist power's consolidation over the Iranian plateau and the Hindu Kush when no strong South Asian state can defend against them.[26] Wink, however, notes that, with the significant exception of the Indus delta, sedentary agriculture in Sind was limited by the deserts and dense forests, and played a much smaller economic role than pastoralism.[27]

It is Wink who highlights the Azd in particular as an important force driving the conquests of Sind in furtherance of commercial interests. He references the tradition that Ardashir settled Azdis along the Iranian coasts of the Persian Gulf and Gulf of Oman, claiming that they were seafaring merchants who 'dominated a Persian maritime trade diaspora which extended into western India'.[28] Al-Azd allegedly represented the major commercial group in both Oman and al-Ubulla and extended this diaspora into Sind, importing Indian goods while exporting Arabian horses.[29] He draws on the reports that Suhar and Daba were ruled by a Sasanian governor in alliance with al-Azd clients, and references Hinds' conclusion based on ps.-al-ᶜAwtabi's *al-Ansab* that the Azd ᶜUman played a crucial role in the conquests of Fars, Makran and Sind. These conquests, he says, allowed both commercial consolidation and the establishment of al-Azd political authority.[30] In what follows, however, we shall draw a somewhat different picture of the significance of commerce to the conquests and al-Azd political fortunes. In particular, we shall see that the final conquest of Sind by Muhammad b. al-Qasim was, if anything, undertaken as part of an expansion against the interests of many Omani Arabs, including al-Azd, already active in the region, but that Azdis did likely benefit from an increase in trade which followed.

Most of our information about the conquest of Sind is credited to al-Madaᵓini, with the earliest extant version being that of al-Baladhuri in *Futuh al-Buldan*.[31] According to his information, the conquests were begun by ᶜUthman b. Abi al-ᶜAs al-Thaqafi, who sent his brother al-Hakam to raid several South Asian ports, one of which was Daybul in Sind. That was it until the fall of Sistan and the campaigns of al-Muhallab described earlier. The 660s saw further raiding in the region of al-Qiqan and along the coast, as well as the establishment of a permanent Muslim presence in Makran. Most of the generals during this period were of Gulf extraction: ᶜAbd Allah b. Sawwar al-ᶜAbdi; Sinan b. Salama al-Hadhali; Hakim b. Jabala al-ᶜAbdi; Rashid b. ᶜAmr al-Jadidi; and al-Mundhir b. al-Jarud al-ᶜAbdi, interrupted only by Ziyad b. Abihi's son ᶜAbbad.[32]

Still according to al-Madaᶜini, during the viceroyship of al-Hajjaj b. Yusuf, the ruler of an island in the Indian Ocean sent a ship with some women who had been born to Muslim traders. This ship was captured by pirates off Daybul. Al-Hajjaj wrote to Dahir, ruler of the area, demanding the women be freed, but Dahir replied that he had no control over the pirates. Al-Hajjaj then began mounting expeditions to conquer Sind, leading to his kinsman Muhammad b. al-Qasim's successful campaign at the same time Qutayba b. Muslim was conquering Sogdiana.[33] At the time of his appointment, Muhammad b. al-Qasim was in Rayy with Jahm b. Zahr al-Juᶜfi, who joined him on the march from Makran to Daybul.[34] Daybul fell after a siege, and Muhammad spent three days killing its inhabitants before laying out districts for 4,000 Muslim settlers and building a mosque. He continued subduing cities, often without fighting, until he reached the Indus River, while Dahir prepared to fight him. Muhammad crossed the Indus near the land of a ruler named Rasil, after which his forces defeated and killed Dahir, whose wife burned herself alive to avoid capture. There followed a series of additional battles before Muhammad's final victory at Multan.[35] Shortly thereafter, however, he fell from power with al-Hajjaj's other lieutenants; al-Yaᶜqubi reports that Yazid b. al-Muhallab sent his brother Habib against him.[36] Habib b. al-Muhallab faced attacks from Indian leaders, including the son of Dahir, and took sanctuary in al-Rur, Dahir's old capital, though ᶜUmar b. ᶜAbd al-ᶜAziz supposedly prevailed upon these leaders to convert to Islam and take new Arab names.[37]

The picture in al-Baladhuri fits well the paradigm laid out in previous chapters according to which during the seventh century, the caliphate slowly exerted more control over movements of expansion led by local and regional Arab leaders, only firmly establishing its dominance after the Second Civil War under the caliph ᶜAbd al-Malik and his eastern viceroy al-Hajjaj. There is every reason to suspect that the array of generals involved in Makran acted largely independent of the caliphate, much as the al-Julanda family of Oman did during the same period. This picture is enhanced further on the basis of the *Chachnama*, a Persian history which purports to recount in detail the history of Dahir's dynasty and Muhammad b. al-Qasim's conquests. The text dates from the thirteenth century, but its source, ᶜAli al-Kufi, claims to have translated an earlier lost Arabic work for presentation to a vizier of Sultan Nasir al-Din Qabacha. Based on the isnads and the mention of works on conquests in India by al-Madaᵓini in Ibn al-Nadim's *Fihrist*, some modern historians have supposed it to be related to a lost work of al-Madaᵓini.[38]

Evaluations of the *Chachnama* as a historical source vary. In the judgment of its original English translator, Henry Miers Elliot, 'there is no reason to doubt that the work is a translation of a genuine Arab history, written not very long after the conquest.'[39] Gabrieli, however, sees it as a 'romantic and spurious' work comparable to others which appeared during the twelfth and thirteenth centuries.[40] Manan Ahmed Asif also sees it as a thirteeth-century text, composed in Uch by ᶜAli al-Kufi to speak to the concerns of that day. As evidence, he notes the frequent lack of isnads, and suggests that some were included solely to provide an illusion of older authority, a function also served by the claim of translation.[41] He also highlights the ways in which it serves as a work of political theory, with exchanges of letters communicating political advice.[42] Asif is correct to note the integrity of the *Chachnama* as a product of the thirteenth century, but that does not automatically mean it is worthless for the eighth and that ᶜAli al-Kufi invented all of its material out of whole cloth. A clear analogy is al-Balᶜami's Persian 'translation' of al-Tabari, which removed the *isnads*, consolidated accounts and added information from other sources to produce a new text relevant to his own concerns.[43] Several minor participants in the conquest of Sind mentioned in the *Chachnama* are known from other sources as hadith transmitters.[44] Friedman finds additional individuals mentioned in the *Chachnama* in other sources as later commanders and governors, part of his case that the *Chachnama* was at least partly dependent on earlier Arabic material.[45]

Elements of the *Chachnama*'s account of the Islamic conquest of Sind go well with a model in which al-Hajjaj extended the caliphate's control within an existing independent expansion. An early stage was his appointment of the Syrian Saʿid b. Islam al-Kilabi as governor in Makran. According to the *Chachnama*, en route he met Safhawi b. Lam al-Hammami, from a clan of the Malik b. Fahm, who resisted his leadership. Saʿid killed Safhawi and sent his head to al-Hajjaj.[46] Some time after this, Saʿid himself was killed by the trio of Kulayb b. Khalaf al-Mughanni, ʿAbd Allah b. ʿAbd al-ʿAziz al-ʿIlafi and Muhammad b. Muʿawiya al-ʿIlafi, who are portrayed as avenging Safhawi b. Lam as a fellow Omani from their area and kin. The three avengers then settled in Makran themselves.[47] In retaliation to this retaliation, al-Hajjaj ordered the death of Sulayman al-ʿIlafi and had his head sent to Saʿid's family.[48] Later, Mujaʿa b. Siʾr b. Yazid al-Tamimi went to Khurasan and conquered Qandabil, afterward sending men to find the al-ʿIlafis, who had fled to the court of Dahir in Sind.[49] The *Chachnama* also reports an earlier al-ʿIlafi presence in Sind, when Dahir recruited Muhammad b. al-Harith al-ʿIlafi of the B. Sama to lead 500 Arab followers and a contingent of royal soldiers against the invading King of Zabul.[50]

ʿIlaf was another name for Rabban b. Hulwan, the progenitor of the Jarm, which as noted previously was a tribe closely related to al-Azd in Oman.[51] In other words, the *Chachnama* does not, as sometimes claimed, encourage the theory that the Azd were a major driving force behind the conquests ordered by al-Hajjaj. On the contrary, they and their allies were already present along both coasts of the Gulf of Oman, and al-Hajjaj was moving to install his own allies, shunting them aside if needed. During the actual conquest of Sind, Muhammad b. al-Harith al-ʿIlafi continued to advise Dahir against Muhammad b. al-Qasim, though a shorter tradition exists according to which he refused to fight his fellow Muslims.[52] There are also various accounts of this al-ʿIlafi's fate.[53] The implication is that a contingent of al-Azd's Jarm allies actively opposed Muhammad b. al-Qasim, perhaps having previously become Dahir's mercenaries, but that accounts survived exonerating them. This contradiction also testifies to the existence of earlier material used by ʿAli al-Kufi in shaping his own work.

Among the dozens of fighters the *Chachnama* names from Muhammad b. al-Qasim's expedition, only a handful are of al-Azd. Nothing here would lead to a conclusion that the Azd were leading supporters of the venture. The most important al-Azd was Hudhayl b. Sulayman al-Azdi who became the governor of Kurij. Two Azdis with Omani *nisbas* were among a handful of Arabs sent to settle in Daybul and Nirun, presumably key figures in the new garrison towns.[54] These points highlight the fact that al-Azd was not a unitary faction with a common attitude toward conquests in Sind, and that Omanis continued to have influence in the region's trade after the conquest. In fact, the case that trade developed further with the conquests can draw support from archaeology. Based on the evidence of coin hoards, MacLean argues for a significant expansion of Sind's trade by the ninth century.[55] S. Q. Fatimi has argued convincingly that Daybul had two ports, a riverine port at Thatta and an oceanic one at Banbhore.[56] An inscription from the Daybul mosque claims it was built in the year 109 (727).[57] F. A. Khan, the excavator of the site, reported a temple and lingams associated with the cult of Shiva in the immediate pre-Islamic level. Chinese pottery was introduced during the Abbasid period, though he is not more specific on the time period. Perhaps indicative of the extent of Daybul's commercial activity before the conquests is the fact that almost no pre-Islamic coins were found, though there are some Islamic coins which predate the currency reform under ᶜAbd al-Malik which may, of course, have been deposited in the 700s.[58]

It is correct to say that Gulf tribes did play a unique role in Arab expansion in southern Iran and Sind during the seventh century. However, there is no evidence that al-Azd represented, to use Kennedy's phrase, a 'powerful lobby' calling for the invasion of Sind by the caliphate itself.[59] Asif notes that in the context of the Indian Ocean trade, there was an Arabian presence in Sind in pre-Islamic times which continued with the coming of Islam, and that from the perspective of the Umayyad caliphs it was a potential base for rebels.[60] Al-Hajjaj's sending Muhammad b. al-Qasim to conquer Sind followed conflict with al-Azd and Jarm on the Makran trade route and was primarily an attempt to consolidate the control of his own government and faction by tapping rich new sources of revenue. In fact, the entire sequence raises a different paradigm for expansion in this period, one in which governors and commanders sought to conquer territories with which their internal rivals for power had commercial connections. There is further evidence for this pattern in Yazid b. al-Muhallab's campaigns south of the Caspian Sea.

Yazid's Caspian Campaign

Yazid b. al-Muhallab's governorship under Sulayman was occupied with campaigning south of the Caspian Sea.[61] These countries, Tabaristan (modern Mazandaran) and Jurjan (Gorgan), lie across the high Elburz Mountains from the Iranian plateau. Part of their strategic significance for the caliphate lay in the vulnerability of the main Rayy-Khurasan road through the province of Qumis to attacks from the Elburz Mountains, in which the rulers of Tabaristan in particular were militarily at home.[62] According to Le Strange, the term '*ṭabar*' itself meant 'mountain', though Minorsky traces it to an ancient people called the Tapyres.[63] Topographically most of Tabaristan consists of Elburz foothills descending toward a narrow coastal plain along the southern shore of the Caspian Sea. The region is watered by multiple streams running down from the mountains.[64] In Jurjan, the Caspian Sea coast has often been sparsely populated, a semi-arid region of lagoons and sand spits. Settlement clusters in the Elburz foothills, where the Jurjan River provides some fertility, as do loess deposits along the hill slopes.[65] A longer river, the Atrak ('Turks'), flows along the region's northern border.[66] On the basis of literary sources, Fisher sees frequent variances in Jurjan's agricultural fertility, with the coming of the Turks eventually bringing about a significant agricultural decline.[67]

According to al-Baᶜlami, a source friendly to Qutayba b. Muslim, Qutayba wanted to conquer Jurjan so as to secure the road between Qumis and Khurasan, but al-Hajjaj forbid him based on the difficulties of campaigning in that country.[68] In context, this is likely later apologetics for the known gap in Qutayba's conquests. Al-Madaᵓini reports that Yazid b. al-Muhallab told the caliph Sulayman that Qutayba's conquests were nothing without Jurjan's strategic location connecting Fars with Khurasan, with control of the road between Qumis and Nishapur a particular problem.[69] According to Ibn al-Kalbi's report from Abu Mikhnaf, after his appointment to the governorship of Khurasan by Sulayman, Yazid spent a few months in Khurasan before deputising Mukhallad over the province and setting out on a campaign. He first laid siege to Dehistan with an army of 100,000 plus *mawālī*, slave soldiers and irregular volunteers. Eventually the city surrendered, and Yazid gave a safe conduct to the Turkish Sul and his household before seizing the city's treasures and massacring 14,000 of its inhabitants.[70]

After Dehistan in Abu Mikhnaf's account, Yazid b. al-Muhallab advanced on Jurjan, which upon his arrival increased a tribute it had been paying to the Kufans. Yazid left Asad b. ᶜAbd Allah from al-Azd as its governor.[71] Yazid's next stop was Tabaristan, where the *iṣpahbadh* tried to get by with just increasing tribute. Yazid, however, hoped to conquer the area. In one engagement, Abu ᶜUyayna b. al-Muhallab led an army of Kufans and Basrans into the Elburz Mountains where they encountered a Daylamite army which had arrived as reinforcements. The Muslims initially prevailed, but got caught in a mountain pass with enemy archers and stone-throwers on the high ground and were forced to retreat. At the same time, the *iṣpahbadh* instigated an uprising in Jurjan, and the Muslims were driven from that city and had to wait for Yazid to reinforce them. Yazid finally agreed to terms with the *iṣpahbadh* in Tabaristan for a tribute several times higher than had initially been offered. Abu Mikhnaf is at pains to note that Yazid only failed to subdue the city because of the revolt in Jurjan.[72]

Continuing the pattern from Chapter 3, al-Mada'ini has a less laudatory account of the Caspian campaign.[73] Quoting three sources from the B. ᶜAmm, he reports that the Jurjanis had long violated a tribute agreement from an earlier conquest, and that the agreement with Yazid was on the same terms as the original. Al-Mada'ini also draws a longer, more detailed account from two of his ᶜAmmi sources, an account for which he also cites Abu Hafs al-Azdi, Sulayman b. Kathir al-Khuzaᶜi and others.[74] According to it, Fayruz b. Qul, the ruler of Jurjan, was frequently raided by Sul the Turk from Dehistan and al-Buhayra, an island in the Caspian. When Fayruz had a falling out with a cousin called 'the Marzuban', Fayruz went to Yazid while Sul took Jurjan. Fayruz suggested and Yazid implemented a strategy whereby they asked the *iṣpahbadh* of Tabaristan to keep Sul in Jurjan and not go to al-Buhayra, knowing that the *iṣpahbadh* would betray them to Sul. This worked, and after Sul had left for al-Buhayra, Yazid deputised Mukhallad over Khurasan, Muᶜawiya b. Yazid over Kish, Samarqand, Nasaf, and Bukhara, and Hatim b. Qabisa b. al-Muhallab over Tukharistan. Accompanied by Fayruz, he then marched on Jurjan with 30,000 men and entered it unopposed as the Marzuban fled.[75]

It is after this, in al-Mada'ini's rendering, that Yazid marched on al-Buhayra to fight Sul. After several months, the Turks became ill because of bad water. Here al-Mada'ini says that Sul asked for safe passage only for himself and his household. Yazid then had 14,000 killed at al-Buhayra.[76] He then left ᶜAbd Allah b. al-Muᶜammar al-Yashkuri in charge of Dehistan and al-Buhayra and invaded Tabaristan. Al-Mada'ini next provides a version of the battle in the mountain pass. The *iṣpahbadh* then wrote to the Marzuban in al-Bayasan to attack the Muslims, which they did, slaying ᶜAbd Allah b. al-Muᶜammar, with the B. al-ᶜAmm in particular taking heavy losses, a detail which probably owes is existence to al-Mada'ini's ᶜAmmi sources. Yazid then turned to one Hayyan al-Nabati, who intervened to broker a peace agreement similar to that described by Abu Mikhnaf. Yazid then returned to Jurjan, where he spent several months besieging a fortress called al-Wajah where the Marzuban had taken refuge.[77] The siege ended when a man hunting discovered a way into the Jurjani fortress of al-Wajah. With this, Yazid was able to conquer the valley, crucifying many of the soldiers and, according to Abu Mikhnaf, allowing his troops blood revenge on the rest. He then built the city of Jurjan.[78] Another account says that after the conquest of Jurjan,

Yazid wrote to one of his brothers to ensure the reputation of his conquests over the Tamim general Qutayba b. Muslim's, which al-Farazdaq had trumpeted.[79]

Parvaneh Pourshariati calls attention to the claims of Ibn Isfandiyar, author of *Tarikh-i Tabaristan*, that the *ispahbadh* Farrukhan was an ally to Qutayba b. Muslim.[80] An alliance with the Umayyad state may have been formed some time earlier, when according to Ibn Isfandiyar, Farrukhan assisted the army of the caliphate in defeating the Azraqites.[81] The silk trade could have provided a common interest. Silk was the most lucrative bulk commodity traded in Central Asia. The Chinese used it as currency, and when the Chinese state expanded into Central Asia, millions of rolls of silk followed as salaries for soldiers and officials. Sogdian traders in particular acquired this silk in exchange for other products and traded it westward with a high profit margin: in the early eighth century, silk sold at Samarqand for double what it cost at Dunhuang.[82] Literary sources list silk as an important product of the Caspian provinces.[83] Richard Bulliet's study of names from biographical dictionaries shows that in Jurjan, 10 of the 38 names related to cotton, wool or silk were for the last of those. In the other three Iranian cities he checked, Isfahan, Nishapur and Qavin, of the 162 names, only 11 involved silk.[84] Although religious scholars condemned it as unacceptable luxury, silk continued to symbolise wealth in the eastern Islamic world.[85]

The trade of Tabaristan and Jurjan was oriented northward rather than eastward, and their goods were traded into Russia both by sea and overland caravan routes. The Gorgan Wall, which extended eastward from the Caspian Sea's southeast corner for over 120 miles, may have been involved in trade regulation during the sixth and early seventh centuries, when it was occupied. Near its western end, the site of Gomish Tappeh is probably to be associated with a port founded by the Sasanian ruler Kavad I near what was then the mouth of the Jurjan River. The archaeological evidence links it with trade in silver and textiles into the Volga River basin and northward.[86] This offers support for information in Ibn Isfandiyar that Tabaristan's major trading partners were the Bulgars and 'Saqasayn', both of which point to the Volga River, as well as the account of Ibn ᶜAtham al-Kufi that the people of Jurjan mingled with 'Turks' who in an earlier century threatened them from the lands of Khwarazm.[87] Archaeological evidence from Russia also suggests that Sasanian trade passed through Khwarazmian hands, indicating an overland route across the steppe between the Caspian and Aral seas during the seventh and eighth centuries, perhaps replacing the seaborne trade with the abandonment of the wall amidst Sasanian military collapse.[88] The Khwarazmian and Sogdian commercial spheres only merged more fully during the eighth century, in the wake of the Muslim conquests of the region, as seen from the development during the mid-eighth century of coins with inscriptions in both languages, to which Arabic was added as a third language by 800.[89]

The conquest of Jurjan was thus the conquest of a major silk-producing region which was part of a Khwarazmian commercial zone. Qutayba b. Muslim had campaigned in the Khwarazmian lands, but at the invitation of its king, with numismatic support for the Arabic account that he was helping suppress a rebellion.[90] He also entrusted the important Oxus river crossing to a Khwarazmian commander during his revolt against Sulayman.[91] Unfortunately the accounts of the caliphate and Khwarazmians are scanty compared to many other areas in Central Asia, probably due to the lack of a local historical tradition informing the surviving historiography. There is, however, sufficient evidence to suggest that the faction of Qutayba b. Muslim and al-Hajjaj had good relations with the Khwarzmian commercial sphere and campaigned in the Sogdian one to gain influence there. At the same time, Yazid's conquest of Jurjan was, perhaps a deliberate targeting of a region where a rival faction had connections, but at the very least a result of that rival's previous lack of interest in conquering it due to those connections.

Azd of Khurasan

Qutayba's successes led the Sogdian princes to seek help from the Tang Dynasty, and it was probably with Chinese encouragement that Suluk (Chinese Sü-Lü), chief of the Turgesh confederation of Turks, formed an alliance with the Sogdians which was to blunt the Arab advance. In 724, his forces won a clear victory in the Ferghana Valley in a battle known to Arabic sources as the 'Day of Thirst'. In the wake of their defeat, the Arabs faced uprisings across Transoxania, and their control was reduced to just Samarqand and the smaller fortified town of Dabusiya. In 731 Suluk besieged Samarqand, and a relief column under Khurasan's governor Junayd al-Murri was stalled in the mountain passes between Kish and the city. Samarqand's troops had to save their saviours, taking heavy casualties in the Battle of the Defile. Samarqand itself was saved, but only temporarily. Amidst these defeats, al-Harith b. Surayj al-Tamimi rebelled against the Umayyads with an agenda which has been read as a precursor of that of the Abbasids.[92] He formed an alliance with Suluk, but in 737 Suluk was killed by Turgesh rivals following an unsuccessful attempt to take Balkh.[93]

During the Umayyad and early Abbasid periods, 'Khurasan' referred not only to the province which extended to the Oxus and Murghab Rivers and included the areas of Merv, Nishapur and Quhistan, but also to the southern region of Sistan and the areas of conquest beyond the Oxus.[94] The region's society has been studied primarily by scholars of the Abbasid Revolution seeking to understand the social milieu which gave rise to that movement. Pourshariati sums up the state of the field as follows:

> As is evident, there is a high degree of consensus about a number of major issues in the works discussed above. To begin with there is agreement that very little change was imposed on the social structure of the Sasanid society in Khurasan. It is agreed that after the invasion a series of 'protectorates' were established based on treaties that stipulated the payment of a tribute to the Arabs. The native rulers continued in power and were responsible for the assessment and collection of these tributes. As the Umayyad rule did not change the status quo for these, they, in fact, collaborated with the Arabs during this period. Second, there is agreement that once there was a substantial migration of the Arabs, assimilation occurred, and that the interests of the various strata of the Iranian and Arab population of Khurasan converged. Finally, and most importantly, there is agreement that the majority of the Arabs settled in the oasis of Marv.[95]

Arab settlement in Khurasan was a matter of state policy, not migrating tribes, and first occurred in 671 on the initiative of Ziyad b. Abihi.[96] One reason for this migration may have been to remove Arabian migrant populations from the central lands of the caliphate. Scholars have looked to the usually consistent claims in the sources that the province had around 50,000 fighters as the basis for general Arab population estimates, though their conclusions have varied. Wellhausen suggested an upper limit of 200,000, though he left out the Kufans.[97] Scholars seeking to correct this oversight raised that maximum to 250,000.[98] Agha, however, argues that there was no evidence supporting the idea of four dependents for every fighter, and drawing on the demographic concept of the dependency ratio, concludes that the population was between 115,000 and 175,000.[99] All these figures, however, represent only a small part of the overall population of the region.

Arabs in Khurasan did not found new cities, but rather occupied villages and outlying districts of Sasanian ones.[100] Merv was selected as the primary base of operations because of its location near the Turkish frontier.[101] Pourshariati, in examining the spread of Arab settlement, concludes that as the basis for armies of conquest, it was confined to a zone she calls 'Outer Khurasan', beyond a series of mountains which divided that from 'Inner Khurasan'.[102] Agha calls the pattern of that settlement a 'military archipelago', and claimed that when not assembled for a campaign, the local units were 'little more than contingents of police forces'.[103] He also says that the different settlement areas had mixed tribal populations, and that regarding attempts to geographically map tribal areas, 'The data in the sources are sketchy, scattered, confused, and overlapping.'[104]

Wellhausen attributed the first organised al-Azd settlement in Khurasan to al-Muhallab's governorship while noting some individuals may have been there previously.[105] It seems likely, however, that al-Muhallab was not alone during his sojourn in Khurasan during the Sufyanid period. As noted in Chapter 2, Ziyad b. Abi Sufyan appointed Nafiᵓa b. Khalid al-Tahi of al-Azd over part of the region.[106] According to one source, during ᶜAbd Allah b. Khazim's war against the Bakr b. Waᵓil at Herat, the Turks besieged a largely al-Azd garrison at Qasr Asfad. The Azd within sent for other Azdis in the area, but the reinforcements were defeated. Ibn Khazim then sent Zuhayr b. Hayyan to them with a group of Tamim, who defeated the Turks. Kaᶜb al-Ashqari and Thabit Qutna both had poems praising Tamim for this battle.[107] Wellhausen believed this account belonged to a later time.[108] However, the account was clearly passed on to glorify Ibn Khazim and the Tamim; thus, the periodisation is not incidental. Al-Madaᵓini claims that during Qutayba b. Muslim's revolt, there were in Khurasan 9000 from the Ahl al-ᶜAliya, 10,000 from Tamim, 10,000 al-Azd, 4,000 ᶜAbd al-Qays, and 7000 Bakr b. Waᵓil. There were also 7,000 Kufans and 7,000 *mawālī*, with each unit having its own commander. These numbers explain why even though the Azd were the first to rebel, the Tamimi Wakiᶜ b. Abi Sud was placed in charge.[109] Regarding a later period, another narrative from al-Madaᵓini placed by al-Tabari in 126 (744) has ᶜIsma b. ᶜAbd Allah al-Asadi say that the Rabiᶜa equalled the Qays and the Tamim equaled the Azd, with only the Kinana left out.[110]

In the west, al-Azd primarily inhabited Jurjan and Abiward in the Nishapur quarter. Like all other tribes, they were represented in Merv, though only the Tamim and Rabiᶜa are known in Merv al-Rudh. Within the Balkh quarter, al-Azd are found in Balkh itself, Baruqan and Khulm. Al-Muqaddisi listed Khulm in the Balkh district as a village of al-Azd, though Agha's data also show Qays, Tamim and Rabiᶜa. Agha found no record of al-Azd in Herat, Quhistan or Transoxania.[111] Few elites in the Nishapur area used al-Azd nisbas in the eleventh century, a development Bulliet suggests might have occurred if Azdis originally settled in cities in support of the Muhallabids, a pattern which could have led to a faster rate of absorption into the local Persian population.[112] Pourshariati, however, has questioned whether there was ever a significant Arab presence in Nishapur during the Umayyad period, pointing out that the Companions of the Prophet mentioned as connected with that city were almost all simply passing through, that Nishapur had only one mosque, as opposed to the forty in Jurjan, and that this single mosque drew only seventy worshippers.[113] In Jurjan, one of the mosques was originally called the al-Azd Mosque, though by the early eleventh century it had instead become known as the Abu al-Khattab Mosque.[114] Amabe's chart of al-Azd military leaders in the early Abbasid period shows that all of them were based in Abiward except for a man named ᶜAbdawayh in Herat and Abu ᶜAwn ᶜAbd al-Malik in Jurjan. In this they closely resemble the ᶜAkk and Kinana.[115] There were also definitely al-Azd in Balkh and Merv al-Rudh. Pourshariati's theory of different settlement models in an Inner and Outer Khurasan thus definitely holds up based on what we can glean about al-Azd.

The Azd played a central role in a significant conflict which al-Tabari presents as crucial context for the Abbasid takeover, an interpretation many modern historians have followed. Briefly, Judayᶜ b. ᶜAli al-Kirmani of Maᶜn, who had been governor in the later years of the caliph Hisham's reign, led an al-Azd revolt against the governor, Nasr b. Sayyar al-Kinani. The motives for this revolt are reported as a dispute over the level of stipends and a desire to avenge the destruction of the Muhallabids a quarter-century before. Nasr imprisoned Judayᶜ, but he escaped and joined forces with al-Harith b. Surayj against the governor. Following this, al-Harith and Judayᶜ had a falling out attributed to the rivalry between Qays and al-Yaman generally and al-Azd and Tamim specifically. Al-Harith was killed in the ensuing conflict, but then Judayᶜ was assassinated by al-Harith's son, perhaps with Nasr's involvement. Abu Muslim, leader of Khurasan's Abbasid movement, then joined ᶜAli b. Judayᶜ's quest for revenge. Together the two drove Nasr out of Merv, but then Abu Muslim defeated ᶜAli and assumed power.[116]

Historians should be cautious about al-Tabari's overall presentation, for as Steven Judd has demonstrated, al-Tabari deliberately emphasised the impact of tribal feuding in his presentation of late Umayyad politics as a way of warning about the dangers of factional disputes during his own day.[117] In Chapter 3, we saw something similar in his use of al-Madaʾini's narrative of the Muhallabids, emphasising how dissension among the sons of al-Muhallab led to the family's fall before al-Hajjaj. Judd contrasts al-Tabari's handling of the late Umayyads with that of al-Baladhuri, who instead emphasised religious factors in the collapse of their rule. However, al-Tabari achieved such effects by what he chose to include or omit, and so it is likely that something like the factional fighting described did occur.

The accounts in al-Tabari and ps.-al-ᶜAwtabi provide useful resources for a prosopographical overview of al-Azd in Khurasan during the Marwanid period. In terms of genealogical identity, Khurasan's al-Azd show few clear patterns, though there are a few interesting families. There is a strong dominance of Azd ᶜUman and Azd Shanuᵓa, which makes sense given the settlement patterns noted in Chapter 2 and the fact that Khurasan's Arab population came largely from southern Iraq. Seldom does any tribal identity beyond 'al-Azd' appear to matter on questions of leadership or loyalty, though the sources do portray some antagonistic solidarity between northerners and southerners.

One of the most prominent groups was the Jadhima b. Malik b. Fahm. The head of al-Azd during the revolt against Qutayba b. Muslim was ᶜAbd Allah b. Hawdhan al-Jahdami, who had refused leadership of the revolt when the Azd offered it.[118] He was killed at the Battle of the Defile in 731, as was a possible son, Muhammad b. ᶜAbd Allah al-Jahdami.[119] Al-Mughira b. Shuᶜba al-Jahdami was also a tribal leader in the days of Judayᶜ b. al-Kirmani.[120] Ps.-al-ᶜAwtabi calls attention to the power of the B. Hinaᵓa, with Sahm b. Maᶜdan al-Hinaᵓi being succeeded as head of the Azd in Khurasan by an al-Hakm b. Nuᶜayb al-Hinaᵓi, indicating that the office was not passed strictly from father to son.[121] The B. Maᶜn also seem to have made an impact on the region. The most significant were Judayᶜ al-Kirmani and his son ᶜAli. Although of Maᶜn descent, Judayᶜ was called 'al-Kirmani' because he had been born there.[122] Descendants of Masᶜud b. ᶜAmr, whose death sparked the conflict in Basra analysed in Chapter 2, also appear frequently. ᶜAbd Allah b. Bistam b. Masᶜud b. ᶜAmr gave a guarantee for good behaviour on the part of the poet Thabit Qutna, who had spoken out on an issue involving Sogdian Muslims.[123] Judayᶜ actually had a deputy named Masᶜud b. ᶜAmr al-Kirmani.[124]

ᶜAbd Allah b. Bistam was also one of the commanders at the Battle of the Defile, in which his brother Zunaym was killed.[125] At the same time, ᶜAbd Allah b. Hawdhan al-Jahdami, noted above as a leader of al-Azd, commanded the light cavalry and al-Fudayl b. Hannad al-Harithi commanded the armoured cavalry. Both Ibn Hawdhan and Ibn Hannad were killed, as was al-Azd flagbearer Hamza b. Mujjaᶜa b. ᶜAbd al-Rahman al-ᶜAtaki.[126] Other al-Azd killed in this engagement all had Omani nisbas: Yazid b. al-Mufaddal al-Huddani, Muhammad b. ᶜAbd Allah al-Jahdami, Zunaym b. Bistam al-Maᶜni, and Jusham b. Qurt al-Hilali of the B. al-Harith.[127] Azd ᶜUman tribes regularly appear elsewhere, from both the Malik b. Fahm and other branches. Among the Malik b. Fahm, Muhammad b. al-Muthanna, listed by ps.-al-ᶜAwtabi as a head of al-Azd, was from the Farahid.[128] He was initially a follower of the rebel al-Harith b. Surayj, but soon defected to the Azd of the governor ᶜAsim b. Abd Allah al-Hilali's army along with 2,000 men.[129] Later, Nasr b. Sayyar sent the same Muhammad b. al-Muthanna along with a Tamim cavalry contingent during a campaign in Farghana, during which he captured the son of a *dihqān*.[130] ᶜAbd Allah b. ᶜAmir appointed one of the B. al-Harith b. Kaᶜb over Zaranj.[131] In 728, al-Haytham b. al-Munakhkhal al-Jurmuzi of al-Azd was killed at the Battle of Ashras.[132] His son Yazid died seven years later at Tirmidh during the revolt of al-Harith b. Surayj.[133] Abu al-ᶜAwjaᵓ al-ᶜAtaki and his companions were among those prisoners whom the Turks killed at the Battle of Kamarja.[134] At one point, al-Azd chose a Yazid al-Nahwi to guarantee Judayᶜ al-Kirmani's safety in prison.[135]

There were also Azd Shanuᵓa in the province. One of the al-Azd leaders in Balkh, Yazid b. al-Mufaddal al-Huddani, was sent to negotiate with Nasr b. Sayyar.[136] Following the imprisonment of Judayᶜ al-Kirmani, ᶜAbd al-Malik b. Harmala al-Yahmadi discussed the situation with al-Mughira b. Shuᶜba al-Jahdami and other shaykhs of Yahmad at a place called Nawsh. The shaykhs of Yahmad counselled caution and waiting for Judayᶜ himself to take action, but al-Azd as a group is presented as demanding action, and ultimately burned the house of one of Nasr's concubines.[137] From the west Arabian branches of the Azd Shanuᵓa, ᶜAbd al-Rahman b. Nuᶜaym al-Ghamidi was governor of Khurasan for eighteen months under the caliph ᶜUmar II.[138] This al-Ghamidi later gave from his twenty waterskins on the Day of Thirst in 724, after which the governor Asad b. ᶜAbd Allah al-Qasri named him commander of the army.[139] During al-Junayd b. ᶜAbd al-Rahman al-Murri's governorship, the same ᶜAbd al-Rahman b. Nuᶜaym commanded a contingent of Kufan reinforcements.[140] He also commanded a Kufan and Syrian force which went to Merv seeking al-Harith b. Surayj.[141]

Groups which are not part of al-Azd in Ibn al-Kalbi's genealogical system do become attached to them in Khurasan. Asad b. ᶜAbd Allah al-Qasri had ᶜAbd al-Rahman b. Nuᶜaym al-Ghamidi beaten in an attempt to show he was not favouring the al-Yaman. Either a man from his own house or Abu Numayla Salih b. al-Abbar, a *mawlā* of ᶜAbs, covered him with his cloak to spare his modesty.[142] Another al-Azd leader in Khurasan at this time was Abu al-Dahhak al-Rawahi whom al-Madaᵓ'ini says was among the B. Rawaha of the B. ᶜAbs yet counted among al-Azd.[143] A battle among Muslims at Baruqan near Balkh is the occasion for a discussion of whether the B. Bahil are descended from Taghlib or al-Azd. The affair of Baruqan began when Muslim b. Saᶜid al-Kilabi, governor of Khurasan, went on an expedition across the Oxus, and some of the Bakr b. Waᵓil were slow in joining him. He sent a predominately Tamim expedition after them under Nasr b. Sayyar, but ᶜAmr b. Muslim al-Bahili, brother of Qutayba b. Muslim, prevented them from entering Balkh. Nasr then went to Baruqan, where he was joined by the army of the Hepthalite state of Saghaniyan, which included many Mudari Arabs. The forces of Bakr b. Waᵓil and al-Azd gathered under al-Bakhtari b. Dirham of Bakr b. Waᵓil. Soon the people of Balkh split, with the Mudar going to join Nasr and al-Azd and Rabiᶜa rallying behind ᶜAmr b. Muslim, accusing Muslim b. Saᶜid of planning a revolt. At that point, the Taghlib claimed to ᶜAmr b. Muslim that the B. Bahil were descended from them. The Bakr b. Waᵓil rejected this, however, fearing the Taghlib would gain too much in numbers. Al-Azd, and specifically the Maᶜn, was the alternative Bahil genealogy. A source named Sharik b. Abi Qayla al-Maᶜni said that ᶜAmr b. Muslim al-Bahili used to say that if he were not from the B. Maᶜn then he was not an Arab. Some sources claim that the Bakr decided not to fight under ᶜAmr against the Mudar because he did not believe they had a blood relationship.[144]

We also have occasional glimpses of the politics of leading families. Salih b. al-Qaᶜqaᶜ al-Azdi commanded 500 Syrians under Asad during a campaign against al-Harith b. Surayj.[145] Yaᶜqub b. al-Qaᶜqaᶜ was a qadi in Khurasan when his sister al-Janub bt. al-Qaᶜqaᶜ b. al-Aᶜlam, noted as daughter of the head of al-Azd, was the wife of al-Hasan b. Abi al-ᶜAmarrata al-Kindi.[146] Their father, al-Qaᶜqaᶜ b. al-Aᶜlam, is probably the al-Qaᶜqaᶜ al-Azdi who served as a governor in Khurasan under Yazid b. al-Muhallab.[147] If so, a family which established its reputation with a military figure tied to al-Azd's most prominent general had in a later generation begun continuing that prestige partly through religious learning. Continuing connections to Basra are seen in that Yaᶜqub transmitted from al-Hasan al-Basri and was a cousin of al-Qasim b. al-Fadl al-Huddani, a traditionist mentioned in Chapter 2.[148] Also, while a single marriage is a thin reed on which to hang a theory, the account suggests intermarriage between tribal elites in Khurasan as an important glue holding al-Yaman together.

There is also evidence that al-Azd in Khurasan became increasingly tied to the non-Arab population within which they were enmeshed. When Khalid b. ᶜAbd Allah al-Qasri was removed as governor of the east, ᶜAbd al-Rahman b. Subh of al-Azd was governor of Balkh; his nisba of al-Kharaqi came from his home oasis in Merv.[149] This al-Kharaqi was also one of the commanders at the Battle of the Defile.[150] In al-Madaᵓini's account, he was also one of the commanders in Khurasan when Junayd b. ᶜAbd al-Rahman went to Samarqand, and was known for his military wisdom.[151] Abu Fatima al-Azdi and Bishr b. Zunbur al-Azdi openly supported the rights of Sogdian Muslims not to pay *jizya*.[152] 'Zunbur' is not an Arab name, though 'Bishr' certainly indicates arabisation, perhaps linked to conversion to Islam. When Nasr b. Sayyar was paying stipends after Juday^c al-Kirmani's escape from prison, a *mawlā* of al-Azd named Abu al-Shayatin spoke on the matter, though his opinion is unknown, as is the source of the narrative.[153]

Our examination suggests that in Khurasan, Crone's view of the tribes as primarily military factions holds up rather well.[154] Probably because of the size of the Arab presence in the region, the settlement in a zone primarily geared toward conquest, and the importance of the military stipends, military imperatives dominated tribal development. In fact, Juday^c al-Kirmani's revolt against Nasr b. Sayyar has all the features of a rebellion by an ousted governor as opposed to a more classic tribal feud. Where Crone errs, however, is in ignoring the kinship links between members of the military and others, such as the qadi Ya^cqub b. al-Qa^cqa^c al-Azdi mentioned above. At the same time, it is clear that the fifths served consistently as both military units and as the primary actors in intra-Arab politics and that their most important leaders were the centrally appointed commanders. They also carried consistent identity material. When Qutayba was trying to rouse the troops to rebellion in al-Mada^ɔini's account, he calls out each of the Basran fifths specifically, with his last being the accusation to al-Azd that 'You have taken ships' cables in exchange for the reins of fleet stallions.'[155] A few decades later, Juday^c's followers would be derided as sailors.[156]

Conclusion

This chapter has established, first of all, that the pattern of autonomous tribal expansion in the Gulf discussed in Chapter 2 regarding the founding of the garrison towns also holds up for the Iranian coast of the Gulf. It also refutes the idea that the Azd were pushing for the area's conquest by state authorities by noting that Azdis and close allies from Oman were already active in the region, and in fact came into conflict with the authorities sent by the state. This raises the possibility that at least some conquests may have been motivated by factionalism within the caliphate, something which is also suggested by the local Persian history on Yazid b. al-Muhallab's campaigns south of the Caspian Sea. It may also be that the extant sources disguise Muhallabid alliances and interests in Central Asia which account for al-Muhallab's lack of campaigning in the region, though this is truly speculation.

Beyond that, however, we can see that al-Azd in Khurasan was a clearly distinct yet internally allied identity grouping, probably based on the military organisation of the province's settlement. This differed from the classical genealogical scheme later articulated in Iraq, and there were individuals and possibly even whole groups who became attached to al-Azd only in Khurasan. This in part confirms earlier scholarship on the Arabs of this region, though the lack of patterns in the al-Azd *nisbas* suggests no particular sub-group had a prevalence. As described previously by Crone, what we have in Khurasan is largely military factionalism on a tribal base, though in the family of al-Qaᶜqaᶜ al-Azdi we see a preview of developments which we will explore further in the next chapter: a shift from military background to religious learning as a claim to prominence under the caliphate and a route to government office.

Notes

1. Hugh Kennedy, *Conquests*, pp. 236–8; H. A. R. Gibb, *The Arab Conquests in Central Asia* (New York: AMS Press, 1970), pp. 15–22; Robert Hoyland, *God's Path*, pp. 120–1.
2. Hoyland, *God's Path*, pp. 121–2; C. E. Bosworth, *Sistan under the Arabs*, pp. 17–19.
3. W. B. Fisher, 'Physical Geography', p. 77.
4. Peter Christensen, *The Decline of Iranshahr: Irrigation and Environments in the History of the Middle East 500 BC to AD 1500*, p. 223.
5. Bosworth, *Sistan under the Arabs*, pp. 19–20, 33. For Zabul's rulers, see Rezakhani, *ReOrienting*, pp. 164–75.
6. Baladhuri, *Futuh*, p. 417. Ibn Aᶜtham al-Kufi has a much more extensive list, *Kitab al-Futuh*, VII, p. 78.
7. Le Strange, *Lands*, p. 469.
8. Tabari, *Taʾrīkh*, II, p. 1078; Tabari, *History*, XXIII, p. 27.
9. Tabari, *Taʾrīkh*, II, pp. 1040–2; Tabari, *History*, XXII, pp. 188–90.
10. Tabari, *Taʾrīkh*, II, p. 1041; Tabari, *History*, XXII, p. 189.
11. Tabari, *Taʾrīkh*, II, p. 1287; Tabari, *History*, XXIV, p. 9.
12. Tabari, *Taʾrīkh*, II, pp. 1129–31; Tabari, *History*, XXIII, pp. 74–6. See also Balᶜami, *Tarikh*, p. 812; Hoyland, *God's Path*, p. 151. On the issues identifying the Nizak Tarkhan rulers of this area, see Rezakhani, *ReOrienting*, pp. 143–4, 158–9. Al-Madaʾini's source is al-Mufaddal b. al-Muhallab al-Dabbi.
13. Baladhuri, *Futuh*, p. 417.
14. Tabari, *Taʾrīkh*, II, p. 1144; Tabari, *History*, XXIII, pp. 88–9; Baladhuri, *Futuh*, p. 417; Balᶜami, *Tarikh*, p. 814.
15. Kennedy, *Conquests*, pp. 255–72; Gibb, *Central Asia*, pp. 29–53; Hoyland, *God's Path*, pp. 148–51.
16. Gibb, *Central Asia*, pp. 42–3.

17. Andre Wink, *Al-Hind: The Making of the Indo-Islamic World*, pp. 127–8, 171.
18. Wink, *Al-Hind*, p. 171.
19. *Tarikh-i Sistan*, Gold, p. 10; *Tarikh-i Sistan*, Bahar, pp. 12–13.
20. Fisher, 'Geography', p. 85.
21. Wink, *Al-Hind*, p. 164.
22. Wink, *Al-Hind*, pp. 51, 164.
23. Derryl N. MacLean, *Religion and Society in Arab Sind*, p. 67.
24. Suchandra Ghosh, 'The Western Coast of India and the Gulf: Maritime Trade during the 3rd to 7th Century AD', p. 370.
25. J. J. Bede, 'The Arabs in Sind, 712–1026 AD', pp. 55–6.
26. Bede, 'Arabs', pp. 57–9.
27. Wink, *Al-Hind*, pp. 169–70.
28. Wink, *Al-Hind*, p. 48.
29. Wink, *Al-Hind*, p. 52.
30. Wink, *Al-Hind*, pp. 52–3.
31. Manan Ahmed, 'The Many Histories of Muhammad b. Qasim: Narrating the Muslim Conquest of Sindh', pp. 64–5. See also the brief version in Ya^cqubi, *Ta^ɔrikh*, II, pp. 288–9.
32. Baladhuri, *Futuh*, pp. 431–5; M. Ahmed, 'Muhammad b. Qasim', pp. 66–8.
33. Baladhuri, *Futuh*, pp. 435–6; M. Ahmed, 'Muhammad b. Qasim', pp. 68–70.
34. Baladhuri, *Futuh*, pp. 436; M. Ahmed, 'Muhammad b. Qasim', p. 72.
35. Baladhuri, *Futuh*, pp. 436–40; M. Ahmed, 'Muhammad b. Qasim', pp. 73–5 For a careful analysis of this tradition highlighting points of relevance to Baladhuri's ninth-century Baghdad milieu, see Manan Ahmed Asif, *A Book of Conquest: The Chachnama and Muslim Origins in South Asia*, pp. 34–44.
36. Ya^cqubi, *Ta^ɔrikh*, II, p. 296.
37. Baladhuri, *Futuh*, pp. 440–1.
38. See, for example, Yohanon Friedman, 'The Origins and Significance of the Chach Nama', p. 27; Valeria Fiorani Piacentini, 'History and Historiography: The Court Genre in Arabic and the *Fatḥnamah-i Sind*', pp. 94–5.
39. Henry Miers Elliot and John Dowson, *The History of India, As Told by Its Own Historians*, p. 135.
40. Francesco Gabrieli, 'Muḥammad ibn Qasim ath-Thaqafi and the Arab Conquest of Sind', pp. 281–2.
41. Manan Ahmed, 'The Long Thirteenth Century of the Chacnama', pp. 469–71.
42. Asif, *Book*, pp. 78–102.
43. Meisami, *Persian Historiography*, pp. 23–37.
44. MacLean, pp. 99–100.
45. Friedman, p. 28.
46. Kufi, *Fathnamah-i Sind*, p. 85; Kufi, *The Chachnamah: An Ancient History of Sind*, pp. 66–7.

47. Kufi, *Fathnamah-i Sind*, pp. 85–6; Kufi, *Chachnamah*, pp. 67–8.
48. Kufi, *Fathnamah-i Sind*, p. 87; Kufi, *Chachnamah*, p. 68.
49. Kufi, *Fathnamah-i Sind*, p. 88; Kufi, *Chachnamah*, p. 69.
50. Kufi, *Fathnamah-i Sind*, pp. 70–2; Kufi, *Chachnamah*, pp. 55–7. For the identification of Zabul as the text's 'Ramal', see B. D. Mirchandani, 'Chach-Nama: References to Persia, Zabul, Kashmir and Kanauj', pp. 376–7, 380.
51. Caskel and Strenziok, *Gamharat*, I, p. 327; Ibn al-Kalbi, *Ma^{c}add wa al-Yaman*, p. 693.
52. Kufi, *Chachnamah*, pp. 127–36
53. Kufi, *Chachnamah*, pp. 128, 160, 178.
54. Kufi, *Chachnama*, pp. 172–3; Kufi, *Fathnamah-i Sind*, p. 218; J. J. Bede, 'Arabs', pp. 135–8. The English translation of the *Chachnama* used here has 'Dahlaleh' for 'Daybul'. Nirun is near modern Hyderabad.
55. MacLean, *Religion and Society in Arab Sind*, p. 69.
56. S. Qudratullah Fatimi, 'The Twin Ports of Daybul: A Study in the Early Maritime History of Sind', pp. 103–4.
57. F. A. Khan, *Banbhore: A Preliminary Report on the Recent Archaeological Excavations at Banbhore*, p. 16
58. F. A. Khan, *Banbhore*, pp. 25–8, 35, 42; Wink, *Al-Hind*, p. 174.
59. Kennedy, *Conquests*, p. 298.
60. Asif, *Book*, pp. 25, 37.
61. The account of Ibn A^{c}tham al-Kufi includes elements of both Abu Mikhnaf and al-Madaʾini discussed below, but is also noteworthy for the descriptions of the historical background to Jurjan, including its wall, *Kitab al-Futuh*, VII, pp. 286–96.
62. Le Strange, *Lands*, pp. 364–8.
63. Le Strange, *Lands*, p. 369; V. Minorsky, 'Mazandaran', EI 2.
64. Fisher, 'Geography', p. 51.
65. Fisher, 'Geography', p. 52.
66. Le Strange, *Lands*, p. 377.
67. Fisher, 'Geography', p. 53.
68. Bal^{c}ami, *Tarikh*, p. 888; Ibn A^{c}tham al-Kufi, *Kiṭab al-Futuh*, VI, p. 287.
69. Tabari, *Taʾrīkh*, II, p. 1327; Tabari, *History*, XXIV, p. 52. See also Tabari, *Taʾrīkh*, II, p. 1322; Tabari, *History*, XXIV, p. 47; Baladhuri, *Futuh*, p. 336.
70. Tabari, *Taʾrīkh*, II, pp. 1317–20; Tabari, *History*, XXIV, pp. 42–5; Baladhuri, *Futuh*, pp. 335–6.
71. Tabari, *Taʾrīkh*, II, p. 1320; Tabari, *History*, XXIV, p. 45; Baladhuri, *Futuh*, p. 336.
72. Tabari, *Taʾrīkh*, II, pp. 1320–2; Tabari, *History*, XXIV, pp. 45–6; Baladhuri, *Futuh*, p. 338.
73. The transmission of this material was studied in Rotter, 'Zur Überlieferung einiger historischer Werke Madaʾini's in Tabari's Annalen', pp. 119–22.
74. For Sulayman b. Kathir al-Khuza^{c}i, see Sam^{c}ani, *al-Ansab*, III, p. 387.

75. Tabari, *Ta'rīkh*, II, pp. 1322–4; Tabari, *History*, XXIV, pp. 46–9; Baladhuri, *Futuh*, p. 336. This account is also the closest to one found in Isfahani, in which Sul was the brother of Fayruz and converted to Islam at Yazid's hands. He became a *mawlā* and accompanied Yazid until the latter's death. Sul's son Muhammad later became an Abbasid da'i, and the poet Ibrahim b. al-'Abbas was Muhammad b. Sul's grandson. Isfahani, *al-Aghani*, X, p. 43.
76. Tabari, *Ta'rīkh*, II, pp. 1324–5; Tabari, *History*, XXIV, pp. 49–50; Baladhuri, *Futuh*, p. 336.
77. Tabari, *Ta'rīkh*, II, pp. 1327–9; Tabari, *History*, XXIV, pp. 52–4; Baladhuri, *Futuh*, pp. 336–7.
78. Tabari, *Ta'rīkh*, II, pp. 1330–4; Tabari, *History*, XXIV, pp. 55–8; Baladhuri, *Futuh*, p. 337.
79. Isfahani, *al-Aghani*, XXI, p. 310; Ibn Sallam al-Jumahi, *Tabaqat*, p. 338.
80. Pourshariati, *Decline and Fall*, pp. 310–11.
81. Ibn Isfandiyar, *Tarikh-i Tabaristan*, p. 161.
82. De la Vaissière, *Sogdian*, pp. 176–8.
83. Ibn Isfandiyar, *Tarikh*, p. 81.
84. Richard Bulliet, *Cotton, Climate, and Camels in Early Islamic Iran: A Moment in World History*, p. 44.
85. Bulliet, *Cotton*, pp. 51.
86. Eberhard Sauer et al., *Persia's Imperial Power in Late Antiquity: The Great Wall of Gorgan and Frontier Landscapes of Sasanian Iran*, pp. 601–2. For a long-term examination of the connections between the Khazars and Jurjan, see Farda Asadov, 'Jurjan in the External Relations and the History of the Khazar Khaqanate (7th–10th Centuries)', pp. 23–38.
87. Ibn Isfandiyar, *Tarikh*, pp. 80–1; Ibn A'tham al-Kufi, *Kitab al-Futuh* VI, p. 286. See also Ibn Khurdadhbeh, p. 124. Abu al-Hasan Muhammad al-Yazdadi was the author of an Arabic work used by Ibn Isfandiyar as a source both here and elsewhere. See Mimi Hanaoka, *Authority and Identity in Medieval Islamic Historiography: Persian Histories from the Peripheries*, p. 44.
88. Sauer et al., *Imperial Power*, pp. 602–5. More detailed information on finds between the Volga and Ural Mountains is in de la Vaissière, *Sogdian*, pp. 249–52. There are a small number of Sogdian dishes, but that of course does not mean Sogdians were present. Hopper notes similarities in ceramic form between Jurjan and Dehistan may also have extended to Khwarazm. Kristen Hopper, 'Connectivity on a Sasanian Frontier: Route Systems in the Gorgan Plain of North-East Iran', p. 140.
89. De la Vaissière, *Sogdian*, p. 257.
90. E. E. Nerazik and P. G. Bulgakov, 'Khwarizm', *History of Civilizations of Central Asia, Volume III: The Crossroads of Civilizations: AD 250–750*, pp. 229–30.
91. Kennedy, *Conquests*, p. 273.

92. Moshe Sharon, *Revolt: The Social and Military Aspects of the ʿAbbasid Revolution*, pp. 27–34; Wellhausen, *Arab Kingdom*, pp. 464–72.
93. Kennedy, *Conquests*, pp. 276–90; Hoyland, *God's Path*, pp. 181–5; Gibb, *Central Asia*, pp. 59–85.
94. Andre Wink, *Al-Hind*, pp. 109–10.
95. Parvaneh Pourshariati, 'Iranian Tradition in Tus and the Arab Presence in Khurasan', pp. 83–4.
96. Agha, *Revolution*, p. 178.
97. Wellhausen, *Arab Kingdom*, p. 427, n. 3.
98. Saleh Said Agha, 'The Arab Population in Ḫurasan during the Umayyad Period: Some Demographic Computations', p. 217.
99. Agha, 'Arab Population', pp. 217–24.
100. Ira Lapidus, 'Arab Settlement and Economic Development of Iran and Iraq in the Age of the Umayyad and Early Abbasid Caliphs', p. 201.
101. Wheatley, p. 186.
102. Pourshariati, 'Iranian Tradition', pp. 8–10.
103. Agha, *Revolution*, p. 185.
104. Agha, *Revolution*, p. 186.
105. Julius Wellhausen, *Arab Kingdom*, p. 427.
106. Baladhuri, *Futuh*, p. 409.
107. Tabari, *Taʾrīkh*, II, pp. 493–4; Tabari, *History*, XX, pp. 76–7.
108. Julius Wellhausen, *Arab Kingdom*, p. 418, n. 1.
109. Tabari, *Taʾrīkh*, II, pp. 1289–11; Tabari, *History*, XXIV, pp. 12–14.
110. Tabari, *Taʾrīkh*, II, p. 1849; Tabari, *History*, XXVI, p. 213.
111. Agha, *Revolution*, p. 189; Muqaddisi, p. 246.
112. Richard Bulliet, *The Patricians of Nishapur: A Study in Medieval Islamic Social History*, p. 17.
113. Pourshariati, 'Iranian Tradition', pp. 172, 176–7.
114. Sahmi, *Taʾrīkh Jurjan*, p. 56.
115. Amabe, *Emergence*, pp. 56–60.
116. Sharon, *Revolt*, pp. 23–48; Wellhausen, *Arab Kingdom*, pp. 482–91, 528–39; Hawting, *First Dynasty*, pp. 107–9; Orthmann, pp. 473–5; Eva Orthmann, 'Yaman und Rabiʿa'.
117. Steven Judd, 'Character Development', pp. 222–4; Steven C. Judd, 'Medieval Explanations for the Fall of the Umayyads', pp. 92–4.
118. Tabari, *Taʾrīkh*, II, pp. 1290–1; Tabari, *History*, XXIV, pp. 13.
119. Tabari, *Taʾrīkh*, II, p. 1536; Tabari, *History*, XXV, pp. 74–5.
120. Tabari, *Taʾrīkh*, II, p. 1860; Tabari, *History*, XXVI, p. 227.
121. ʿAwtabi, *al-Ansab*, II, p. 776.
122. Tabari, *Taʾrīkh*, II, p. 1858; Tabari, *History*, XXVI, p. 224.
123. Tabari, *Taʾrīkh*, II, p. 1512; Tabari, *History*, XXV, p. 50.
124. Tabari, *Taʾrīkh*, II, p. 1606; Tabari, *History*, XXV, p. 142.
125. Tabari, *Taʾrīkh*, II, p. 1532; Tabari, *History*, XXV, p. 71
126. Tabari, *Taʾrīkh*, II, pp. 1534–6; Tabari, *History*, XXV, pp. 73–5

127. Tabari, *Ta'rīkh*, II, pp. 1536–7; Tabari, *History*, XXV, p. 75.
128. ᶜAwtabi, *al-Ansab*, II, p. 782; Tabari, *Ta'rīkh*, pp. 1569–70; Tabari, *History*, XXV, pp. 107–8.
129. Tabari, *Ta'rīkh*, II, pp. 1569–70; Tabari, *History*, XXV, pp. 107–8.
130. Tabari, *Ta'rīkh*, II, p. 1695; Tabari, *History*, XXVI, p. 32.
131. Baladhuri, *Futuh*, p. 394.
132. Tabari, *History*, XXV, p. 53, n. 240.
133. Tabari, *Ta'rīkh*, II, p. 1585; Tabari, *History*, XXV, p. 121.
134. Tabari, *Ta'rīkh*, II, p. 1520; Tabari, *History*, XXV, p. 58.
135. Tabari, *Ta'rīkh*, II, p. 1850; Tabari, *History*, XXVI, p. 227.
136. Tabari, *Ta'rīkh*, II, p. 1474; Tabari, *History*, XXV, p. 11.
137. Tabari, *Ta'rīkh*, II, pp. 1860–1; Tabari, *History*, XXVI, p. 228.
138. Tabari, *Ta'rīkh*, II, p. 1418; Tabari, *History*, XXIV, p. 150.
139. Tabari, *Ta'rīkh*, II, pp. 1480, 1484–5; Tabari, *History*, XXV, pp. 16, 21–2.
140. Tabari, *Ta'rīkh*, II, pp. 1545, 1552; Tabari, *History*, XXV, pp. 82, 89.
141. Tabari, *Ta'rīkh*, II, p. 1582; Tabari, *History*, XXV, p. 119.
142. Tabari, *Ta'rīkh*, II, pp. 1498–9; Tabari, *History* XXV, p. 36.
143. Tabari, *Ta'rīkh*, II, p. 1478; Tabari, *History*, XXV, p. 14.
144. Tabari, *Ta'rīkh*, II, pp. 1472–4; Tabari, *History*, XXV, pp. 9–11.
145. Tabari, *Ta'rīkh*, II, pp. 1589–91; Tabari, *History*, XXV, pp. 126–8.
146. Tabari, *Ta'rīkh*, II, p. 1485; Tabari, *History*, XXV, p. 22.
147. Tabari, *Ta'rīkh*, II, pp. 1419–20; Tabari, *History*, XXIV, pp. 150–1.
148. Ibn Hajar, *Tahdhib*, XI, p. 393.
149. Tabari, *Ta'rīkh*, II, p. 1497; Tabari, *History*, XXV, p. 35.
150. Tabari, *Ta'rīkh*, II, p. 1532; Tabari, *History*, XXV, p. 71.
151. Tabari, *Ta'rīkh*, II, p. 1544; Tabari, *History*, XXV, p. 81.
152. Tabari, *Ta'rīkh*, II, pp. 1508–9; Tabari, *History*, XXV, p. 47.
153. Tabari, *Ta'rīkh*, II, p. 1856; Tabari, *History*, XXVI, p. 221.
154. Crone, *Slaves*, pp. 42–5.
155. Tabari, *History*, XXIV, p. 10; Tabari, *Ta'rīkh*, II, pp. 1287–8.
156. Tabari, *Ta'rīkh*, II, p. 1971; Tabari, *History*, XXVII, p. 81.

5

The Azd of Mosul

Mosul was both the most important cultural and economic centre of the region between the northern stretches of the Tigris and Euphrates, known as al-Jazira, and the main entrepôt through which that region's goods were shipped to Baghdad.[1] As Chase Robinson says:

> Like the Alpine ranges of Italy, the region's topography obscures local diversity; the Jazira is rather like the Mediterranean, an ocean of steppe, punctuated by archipelagos of river valleys and hills, and settled only unevenly on its shores. Communication and travel, except towards the south, were difficult; news (often bad) did travel, and the elite of one city only occasionally responded to problems suffered by another.[2]

Based on environmental conditions and what little information is available in the literary sources, scholars have generally assumed that the patterns of livestock husbandry in early Islamic times were much the same as in later centuries, with camel herding dominating in the desert, sheep and goats in the steppe, and cattle, donkeys and horses in the more fertile areas, particularly along the Tigris in the immediate vicinity of Mosul.[3] The importance of Arab pastoralists in this region is seen in its division into tribally named administrative units: Diyar Rabiᶜa; Diyar Bakr; and Diyar Mudar.[4] Before the Islamic conquest, ongoing pastoralist migrations into the area intensified during the fifth century, when the rise of the Kinda was one factor pushing the B. Taghlib northward.[5] During the Abbasid period, the tribes provided the reserve of military power for urban notables who wished to assert control within Mosul.[6]

Mosul itself was in the Diyar Rabiᶜa along the west bank of the Tigris across from ancient Ninevah. Significantly to the northwest was Nasibin, along the upper stretches of the Hirmas River. The Hirmas, in turn, flowed through the Wadi Tharthar to enter the Tigris at Tikrit south of Mosul as a rare western tributary.[7] According to Yaqut, the Wadi Tharthar was a large valley in the desert between Sinjar and Tikrit featuring bogs and salty springs. It was home to many of the B. Taghlib, and passed by many villages and the agricultural area surrounding the city of al-Satrun.[8] Sinjar was a city located by a prominent height amidst a fertile plain just east of the Tharthar river channel. This peak gained new notoriety in the twenty-first century for its role in the Yazidi genocide. The main road northwest from Mosul split at a city called Balad, with one branch heading to Nasibin and another to Sinjar.[9]

Between Mosul and Tikrit were two eastern tributaries of the Tigris both of which were called Zab, with the city of Irbil on the plain between them near the borders of Azerbaijan. Near where the Upper Zab met the Tigris was al-Haditha, a city refounded by Marwan II on a height overlooking the plains.[10] Two mountains featuring in this chapter lay east of the Tigris. One, al-Salaq, lay at the edge of Mosul's and Shahr Zur's administrative regions, which actually indicates the Lower Zab. Yaqut associated this peak with al-Hasan b. al-Sabah b. ᶜAbbaḍ al-Hamdani, which is certainly a mistake for al-Hasan b. Salih b. ᶜUbada, who will appear below.[11] Al-Baladhuri associated it with al-Hurr b. Salih b. ᶜUbada al-Hamdani, and Robinson sees it as a reservoir of Hamdan's tribal military manpower.[12] It also had a community of Persian Christians.[13] Robinson also convincingly sees as a Hamdan stronghold the mountain of Hibtun, near the Upper Zab and al-Haditha.[14]

Al-Azd Settlement in al-Jazira

The most important source for the history of eighth- and ninth-century Mosul is the tenth-century *Taʾrikh al-Mawsil* of Abu Zakariyya Yazid b. Muhammad al-Azdi.[15] His sources probably included one or two lists of governors and qadis, as well as reports from local authorities. The latter become especially prominent in his accounts of the late Marwanid period, when Robinson detects the emergence of a true local historical tradition.[16] The tenth-century geographer Ibn Hawqal, a native of Nasibin, is also useful.[17] The al-Azd presence in Mosul goes back to ᶜArfaja b. Harthama al-Bariqi, who became governor of the city under ᶜUmar b. al-Khattab and brought a garrison that included Azdis. Ibn al-Kalbi credits him with planning and founding a *miṣr*; he is also sometimes credited with building the first congregational mosque.[18] According to other sources, he also saw to the settlement and fortification of al-Haditha, which had been the provincial capital under the Sasanians.[19] The B. Harathima were his descendants.[20] Here, of course, we should be wary of the topoi concerning central planning of garrison towns under ᶜUmar b. al-Khattab, though there is again testimony to the central role of the Bariq in the early caliphate and links between early Mosul and Kufa.

There are several additional reports of al-Azd groups coming to the area. According to al-Ya^cqubi, descendants of Hawala b. al-Hinw b. al-Azd settled Mosul. Some of that group had, in pre-Islamic times, allegedly joined Malik b. Fahm in Oman, from whence they spread out into eastern Arabia.[21] Although al-Yaᶜqubi does not say where the Hawala came from before arriving in Mosul, their connection to Malik b. Fahm suggests a sojourn in Basra. When al-Mansur appointed Yazid b. Hatim al-Muhallabi as governor of Azerbaijan, he brought al-Yaman supporters from Basra. The first was al-Rawwad b. al-Muthanna al-Azdi, who settled from Tabriz to Badhdh. He was followed by Murra b. ᶜAli al-Taʾi in Nariz and ᶜAbd Allah b. Jaᶜfar al-Hamdani in Miyanij.[22] According to Armenian sources, during the late eighth century, Uthmanid Azd, presumably Azd Shanuʾa, settled along the eastern shore of Lake Van much further northwest and fought the Arcrunis, the Armenian lords of Albaq.[23]

Taʾrikh al-Mawsil traces the descent of the most famous al-Azd clans in Mosul to one Jabir b. Jabala, the leader of a group of B. Salima and follower of the Kharijite leader Abu Hamza.[24] Al-Azdi gives Jabir b. Jabala's full name as Jabir b. Jabala b. ᶜUbayd b. Labid b. Mahasin b. Salima b. Malik b. Fahm.[25] In the last years of the Umayyad Caliphate, Abu Hamza was stirring his revolt against that dynasty in the Hijaz when ᶜAbd Allah b. Yahya came and persuaded him to come to Hadramawt, where Abu Hamza acknowledged him as caliph.[26] Al-Azdi claims that Jabir was Abu Hamza's *ibn amm*, and that the two of them were from the sons of Mahasin b. Salima in Basra, where that clan was prominent and had lent its name to a famous mosque.[27] Abu Hamza does seem to have relied on al-Azd merchant networks in Basra and Oman to provide revenue for his movement.[28] Al-Azdi lists a great number of tribes as rebelling with Jabir b. Jabala and Abu Hamza. These include, from the subgroups of Nasr b. Zahran, the Yahmad, the B. al-Harith, B. Ghitrif, B. Tamthan, B. Maᶜwala, B. Mukhallad, and unnamed others as well as the descendants of the sons of Malik b. Fahm, the B. Salima, B. Maᶜn, and others. In addition, he mentions two groups from the sons of Jabir b. Jabala. The B. ᶜImran b. Nufayl b. Jabir, and B. Razin b. Jabir al-Mawsilin.[29]

According to al-Azdi, after the Battle of Wadi Qurra in which Abu Hamza was defeated, Jabir b. Jabala fled to Basra, where he received a letter from his kinsman Abu al-Ashhal al-Hakam b. ᶜAtaʾ al-Salimi describing his people's prosperity in Mosul. Jabir then set off with thirty companions and, after a brief battle with the companions of the Kharijite leader Buhlul b. Bishr, arrived in that city.[30] This account serves as an introduction to an account of major Omani al-Azd groups in the region, but some Yahmad at least arrived before Jabir, as one Ibn Talid served as commander of the *shurṭa* around 700. This Ibn Talid was reportedly responsible for the paving of the city's streets, part of a larger campaign of development in and around Mosul during the Marwanid period.[31] One piece of evidence that al-Azd pastoralists were involved in these movements is found in the caliph Hisham's purchase of a large piece of land from a group called the Burayda al-Azd. He began investing in cultivation, and turned it into some of the best land available.[32] During the early 700s, the city was undergoing a social transformation as, in Robinson's words, 'An elite of tribesmen/soldiers yielded to an elite of landholders and office holders . . . the two principal factors being the growing value of the land and the city's increased administrative differentiation as it was integrated into an imperial system.'[33]

Most of our information about the distribution of al-Azd groups in the region comes from al-Azdi and presumably dates to the tenth century. Several groups of B. Salima are associated with Jabir b. Jabala's migration to the city. The most prestigious of these was the B. ᶜImran b. Nufayl b. Jabir, who boasted both the respected religious scholar Abu Masᶜud al-Muᶜafa b. ᶜImran and his brother, a governor named Sulayman.[34] Nufayl b. Jabir had a house in the al-Sikka al-Kabira.[35] There also lived with the B. Salima near the al-Sikka al-Kabira a group called the B. al-Hashshash, described as descendants of ᶜAbd b. Salima and including a man named ᶜAmr b. Jaru b. Nusayr b. Zaᵓida b. ᶜUmar b. al-Hashshash b. Dhuhl b. ᶜAqiba b. Ghazal b. Saᶜd b. Jabir b. ᶜAdi b. ᶜAbd b. Salima, as well as Abu al-Hashshash b. Jaᶜfar b. Warqan.[36] Jammaᶜ b. Ahmad b. Aslam b. Zayd al-Salimi was in charge of the Sikka Jammaᶜ. His *mawālī* included the B. Abu Sardah in the Sikka Jammaᶜ. Likewise the B. Hadhili were the *mawālī* of the shadowy Zayd b. ᶜImran.[37] All of these groups were clustered on the city's west side.[38]

Al-Azdi also uses this section to mention a number of other tribes besides the B. Salima. The first of these is the B. Maᶜn, which like the B. Salima come from the Malik b. Fahm. In Mosul, they lived near the Bab Sinjar and had their own mosque. Their clans included the B. Tharthar, perhaps from either the valley of the Tharthar River or Tall Khawsa, a village on one of the Zabs.[39] During the Abbasid period the northern Wadi Tharthar produced dates even though today it is too far north, which certainly does not contradict a Maᶜn presence given Andrew Watson's argument that migrants were probably responsible for most crop dissemination in the early Islamic centuries, especially when the newly introduced crops would have required extra skill to cultivate.[40] Another clan in Mosul was the B. Rawwad, some of whom later moved to Azerbaijan and conquered a district there.[41]

The Farahid of Malik b. Fahm were also in Mosul, and had come from Oman. Among the Farahid was Biyan b. Khalid b. Akhi Duwala b. al-Mubarak, with Duwala being someone appointed over the horses by Khalid b. ᶜImran. The Biyan lived in the quarter of the B. ᶜImran in a house later occupied by Muhammad b. al-Fadl b. Zayd b. ᶜImran.[42] The ᶜAmr b. Malik are an odd case, as according to al-Azdi they died out, leaving only a remnant of their *mawālī*. One of these *mawālī* was al-ᶜAbbas b. Sulaym b. Jamil b. Salim b. Rashid b. Jabala b. ᶜUbayd b. al-Sulaymi, a scholar who died in 223 (838). One wonders if this usage of *mawālī* shows a survival of the collective bonds of pre-Islamic Arabia rather than the individual ones of the early caliphate. There was also a man named Hiddan who was an assassin in Mosul before going to Tarsus, and a poet called Muhammad b. al-Hasan b. Kamil who lived on the estate of Dur al-Tamthiniyin.[43]

Al-Azdi also lists as descendants of ᶜAdi b. ᶜAmr b. Malik the B. Thawban, whom he calls the 'people of Basata'. Their full lineage is Thawban b. al-ᶜAlaʾi b. ᶜUmar b. Mihzam b. Thawban b. al-Harith b. ᶜUbada b. al-Harith b. ᶜAfiya b. Hudayr b. Hadir b. Asad b. ᶜAdi b. Malik b. ᶜAmr b. Malik b. Fahm. According to a portion of al-Azdi's unnamed sources, Thawban b. al-Harith b. ᶜUbada arrived in Mosul from Basra and settled the villages of Tharthar, Safta, Bahwatha and al-ᶜAruba in the region of al-Daybur. Abu Khattab Malik b. al-Harith, presumably his brother, lived with him. The people of Bajarbaq, a village between al-Balqaʾ and Nasibin, ruled over Basata at that time.[44] Noting their identification by their village, Orthmann suggests they were losing their tribal identity, though it may also have been that they developed an al-Azd identity only after others of the tribe arrived in the area, and that Thawban's uncertain genealogy is evidence of that.[45]

Al-Muqaddisi reported that the Harithis, presumably the descendants of al-Harith b. Malik b. Fahm, were the most numerous tribal group within Mosul.[46] Al-Azdi's scheme discusses three distinct branches, which corroborates al-Muqaddisi's reckoning assuming the largest groups were the most likely to divide into smaller segments. These included the al-ᶜAqa b. al-Harith b. Malik b. Fahm, owners of a village on the shores of the Zab called Baᶜaqqa. Muhammad b. Shaddad al-ᶜAwfi al-Basri, a scholar, was among their number, as was a poet named ᶜAdi b. Wadaᶜa al-ᶜAwfi. This tribe was related to the al-Qaradis, who were the Qurdus b. al-Harith b. Malik, as well as the al-Jaramiz, who were the Jurmuz b. al-Harith b. Malik.[47] The former included Hisham b. Hassan al-Qurdusi of Basra and al-Muᶜalli b. Ziyad. We have an extant poem connecting them to the Muhallabids.[48] Ibn Hajar says Hisham b. Hassan was a *mawlā* who died in 148 (765) and lived among the al-Qaradis in Basra and that al-Muᶜalli b. Ziyad was an ascetic there.[49] Each of these three groups had Basran connections, which probably indicates that kinship played a role in various members' decisions to settle in the north, probably under the Muhallabids. Finally, there is mention of the al-Ashaqir, which included al-Muhallab's poet Kaᶜb al-Ashqari, some of whose poetry is included. The Hummam of Oman were also in Mosul and Basra, but al-Azdi did not know whether any were left. There was a poetic connection with them, as well, and they had an estate called al-Hamima. Dayr Taymuna was their property.[50]

Mosul's al-Azd in the Abbasid Period

At the time of the Abbasid takeover there was a massacre of Mosul's shaykhly families recorded in detail by al-Azdi and studied by Robinson. Al-Azdi gives several accounts of the events leading up to it centring around the theme that the urban elite remained sympathetic to the Umayyads. According to one, the Abbasids tried to appoint Muhammad b. Sul to the governorship, but the people rejected him saying they did not want a *mawlā* of Khathᶜam to govern them. At the same time, two unnamed Muhallabids had come to power in Armenia, who together made their way to Mosul, where one was asked by the people to assume their governorship. Both parties wrote to al-Saffah pleading their case. The caliph ordered Ibn Sul to take up his governorship while commanding al-Muhallabi to step aside. He proceeded to have the Muhallabid claimant drowned. This may be a reference to ᶜAbd al-Rahman b. Yazid b. al-Muhallab, who according to al-Azdi was killed after the massacre on the orders of Sulayman al-Aswad despite having a safe conduct. Also relevant is the death of Sulayman b. Habib al-Muhallabi in al-Ahwaz at the hands of al-Mansur. The Mosul uprising clearly involved the entire Arab urban elite, who were massacred at the Manqusha palace by trickery and collaboration between Ibn Sul and Yahya b. Muhammad. The list of victims includes Shurayh b. Shurayh b. ᶜUmar b. Salama al-Khawlani, holder of his family's riches in Mosul, as well as Wathaq b. al-Shahhaj al-Azdi, al-ᶜUrahim b. al-Mukhtar al-Azdi and many others. The massacre was, in fact, so great that the markets took three years to recover.[51]

Robinson entertains the notion of tribal feelings as a factor in the conflict, either with a rivalry between Azd and Khathᶜam or the distaste of Arabs for succumbing to *mawālī* rule.[52] The latter explanation is more likely, for not only did the resistance have broad support among the Mosul elite, but also conflicts between Arabs and *mawālī* became a central theme in recollections of early Abbasid history. However, there were deeper issues in play than simple aristocratic pride. Robinson notes that seeing the Mosul elite as Umayyad loyalists is problematic given its history of Kharijite sympathies.[53] He portrays the conflict as arising from a desire for more direct rule on the part of both Marwan II and the first Abbasids which clashed with the interests of a local elite that had become accustomed to controlling its own revenue under caliphal patronage during the reign of Hisham.[54]

One might expect that this massacre did not serve to conciliate the surviving members of the elite to Abbasid rule. However, the ruling dynasty quickly began to repair the damage by giving generously to the shaykhly families through which they would rule the city. With regard to the Azd, al-Saffah gave two estates on the outskirts of Mosul to ᶜAbd Allah b. Muhammad b. ᶜAli b. Waᵓil al-Shahhaji al-Azdi al-Mawsili, ostensibly because the B. Waᵓil had aided in the hunt for Marwan II some years before, playing a noteworthy role in Egypt. Other traditions claim that Samak b. al-Shahhaj and several others of that clan were among the first to join with ᶜAbd Allah b. ᶜAli in that expedition.[55] Al-Mansur made him a similar grant of a former date and palm grove of Hisham b. Marwan.[56]

Many notices in al-Azdi testify to the Azd's continuing prominence in Mosul and its environs. Under 146 (763), al-Harith b. Jarud al-ᶜAtaki was in charge of Mosul's judiciary when al-Mansur made him responsible for the agricultural tax, as well, replacing one of the B. Hamdan. His dwelling was at the gate to the main congregational mosque below al-Minara, he had a son named Abu al-Harith and died in 153 (770).[57] In 148 (765), al-Saqr b. Najda b. al-Hakm al-Azdi al-Mawsili succeeded Harb b. ᶜAbd Allah as head of the fortifications of Mosul. He fought a religious rebel named al-Hasan b. Mujalid b. Yahya b. Malik b. al-Ajdaᶜ al-Wadaᶜa al-Hamdani al-Mawsili, who fled to Sind. While there he tried to get support from the people of Oman, but this was not forthcoming, and he returned to the fight. Al-Saqr, a man named al-Hasan b. Salih b. ᶜUbada al-Hamdani and another anonymous figure accompanied him. Al-Saqr also had Kalbites in his army, and ultimately lost.[58] In 153 (770), al-Saqr was still over the fortifications, while Mosul's governor, Yazid b. Usayd b. Zafir al-Sulami, was an opponent of the Yaman.[59] In 178 (794), the qadi Ismaᶜil b. Ziyad decided in favour of ᶜAsar b. Waᵓil b. al-Shahhaj in the matter of the estate of the B. Waᵓil before Harun ar-Rashid came to Mosul.[60]

In 177 (793), al-Attaf b. Sufyan al-Azdi, from the Mosuli horsemen, rebelled against Harun al-Rashid and gathered many from among the freebooters and urban notables from several different tribes. He also prevented the governors of Harun al-Rashid from collecting taxes and taking from the city's wealth. In retaliation, Harun al-Rashid came to Mosul and demolished its walls.[61] A few years later, there was a general amnesty announced at the hajj that did not apply to al-Attaf and his main supporters.[62] Robinson sees in this revolt the last gasp of the pattern of Mosuli politics which gave rise to the massacre under Yahya b. Muhammad, as al-Attaf was a wealthy landowner from the old tribal elite, and his supporters included prominent descendants of massacre survivors.[63] In the aftermath of this conflict, which involved increased taxation to make up the shortfall of the revolt years, many tribes fled Mosul for Azerbaijan, including the B. al-Harith b. Ka^{c}b.[64]

In the closing years of the eighth century, tribal politics came to the forefront in Mosul and the Jazira. One early development was a conflict between the Hamdan and Taghlib in 171 (787). It began when Rawh b. Hatim al-Hamdani was appointed to collect taxes from the B. Taghlib, but was militarily defeated in the attempt. His father Hatim b. Salih b. ^{c}Ubada al-Hamdani then sent a Hamdani force which killed many of the Taghlib in what seems to have been a tribal war of revenge.[65] In 183 (799), the governor of Mosul was Ahmad b. Yazid al-Sulami. He decided to move against al-Yaman because they were more numerous than the Nizar, as the northerns are usually called in al-Azdi's work. The governor got their leaders out of the city to al-Haditha with him, then went in the direction of al-Baqi^{c}a and sought to incite the Mudar group of the northerners to his side. The southerner al-Mu^{c}afa b. Shurayh al-Khawlani learned of this, and with his companions set out and prevented the governor from entering Mosul. In one account, Ahmad was supported by ^{c}Amir b. Nu^{c}aym al-Tamimi and al-Muthanna b. ^{c}Abd al-Rahman al-Dhuhli. A man named either Salman or Sulayman b. al-Hakam, however, tipped off some companions of his from the ^{c}Anaza, who said that the Yamanis had been their neighbours and in-laws. One of that tribe then warned them, while about 120 men then dribbled out of the governor's military camp into Mosul. At the command of Anas b. ^{c}Amr al-Talidi, a member of the most prominent group within the B. Yahmad, he was punished and imprisoned on the mountain Hibtun. Ahmad then went to al-Salaq where he killed and burned. Hatim b. Salih al-Hamdani saw this and sent Abu Thawr al-Hamdani to remonstrate with the governor, which was unsuccessful. Hatim then gathered an army to himself and encircled Ahmad, who was wounded while losing the battle which ensued.[66]

By the next year, Yazid b. Mazid al-Shaybani had become governor of Mosul following the defeat of Ahmad b. Yazid. Hatim al-Hamdani and the

Yaman met the new governor in battle at Shahr Zur, a large Kurdish town (*kura*) between Irbil and Hamadhan.[67] Yazid won, driving the Yamanis back toward al-Salaq, which they prevented him from accessing. After a lengthy stalemate, when Yazid began running low on provisions, Hatim began supplying him, bringing an end to the conflict. The sultan, however, sent another army against Hatim, which Yazid refused to join. Hatim was even joined by Yazid's former followers. Yazid himself went to plead Hatim's case to Harun al-Rashid, which resulted in everyone being reconciled.[68] In 192 (808), the governor of Mosul was Khalid b. Yazid b. Hatim of the Muhallabids.[69]

In 193 (809), al-Hasan b. Salih al-Hamdani, Hatim's brother, was killed by the tribes of ᶜAnaza and Shayban in the village of Hazza on a tax-gathering expediton. His son ᶜAli b. al-Hasan, a religious ascetic, set out to avenge him with a handful of Sufis on mules, but Anas b. ᶜAmr al-Talidi armed them. It was, however, his nephew al-Husayn b. Zubayr b. Salih al-Hamdani, who with reinforcements led by Tamim b. Iyas al-Tamathani and recruited from other Yamani tribes defeated the ᶜAnaza and Shayban, with ᶜAli b, al-Hasan assuming his father's prominence in Mosul's politics.[70] With the collapse in central authority occasioned by the war between al-ᶜAmin and al-Maʾmun, ᶜAli then emerged as the city's main power-broker, with al-Azdi making clear that the Hamdan dominated even when a centrally appointed governor held nominal office.[71]

In 198 (814), there was a significant conflict in which 'al-Azd and al-Yaman' served as the designation of one party despite Hamdan's ascent. At that time, Hashim b. Ahmad b. al-Hasan al-Hamdani, a nephew of ᶜAli b. al-Ḥasan, was in charge of Bedouin matters around Mosul. The conflict began when one ᶜUthman b. Nuᶜaym al-Burjumi al-Mawsili left the region with an unknown grievance against its people and went to Diyar Mudar. There, he complained that the Azd and Yaman fell short of their obligations. After recruiting an army of about 20,000 people, he marched on Mosul. The governor responded with various expeditions, including some with Nizaris, and the people tried to negotiate with ᶜUthman, who, however, refused their entreaties. In the ensuing conflict in which ᶜAli b. al-Hasan led a united al-Yaman, about 6,000 Nizaris were killed. The year following these events, war broke out between the B. Thaᶜlaba and the B. Usama. The former were sometimes traced to the al-Azd in late sources, and were probably from the B. Ghassan. The B. Usama were from the ᶜAdnan.[72]

Four years later, a war broke out between the B. al-Hasan and the al-Azd in which ᶜAli b. al-Hasan al-Hamdani was killed with much of his household. Al-Azdi provides several accounts of the conflict's origins. In one, the conflict began when ᶜAli and his brother Muhammad revolted, perhaps fearing losing their position with al-Ma'mun's decision to move his seat to Baghdad from Merv. The two brothers were driven out with a number of al-Azd and al-Yaman followers, and they went to Jabal al-Tanin. While looking out over Ninevah and al-Marj, one said to the other, 'What a perfect two villages for one person!' One of the al-Azd then said, 'What will we do?' One of the Hamdan brothers then replied, 'You will go to Oman.' News of this incident spread.[73]

According to a separate account, one ᶜAwn b. Jabala was sitting with one Ibn Masrur dismissively discussing the doings of the B. al-Hasan. Word of this reached the brothers, and Ahmad b. Rawh b. Salih al-Hamdani, the head of the *shurṭa*, arrived in order to arrest Ibn Masrur and ᶜAwn and take them to ᶜAli b. al-Hasan by force. They did not get far before their companions gathered and freed them, and the clamour of that reached ᶜAli b. al-Hasan who came himself to the courts of the B. al-Shahhaj, where the two escaped prisoners had presumably sought shelter. There was fighting between them, and ᶜAli took ᶜAwn to his home where the latter quarreled with Muhammad. Muhammad struck ᶜAwn with a pole, to which ᶜAwn replied 'Woe unto you if you fight me!'[74]

These events ostensibly led to the war in which the B. al-Shahhaj and al-Azd fought against the B. al-Hasan and al-Yaman, a war which tottered back and forth until many of the Azd poured forth from Mosul led by al-Sayyid b. Anas al-Yahmadi along with the B. Talid.[75] ᶜAli wrote to a Kharijite named Mahdi b. ᶜAlwan al-Shari for help, and his allies entered Mosul from the west side while the Azd were leaving from the east. Mahdi then led prayer in the city. Abu Harb and al-Muᶜafa al-Khawlani dissociated themselves from this conflict. Abu Harb fortified himself and his family in an old citadel atop a high mountain, though his al-Azd sympathies damaged his relationship with ᶜAli and Muhammad. Eventually the B. al-Hasan fled to al-Haditha, with al-Sayyid and al-Azd in hot pursuit. There, al-Azd won a great battle and returned to Mosul. The heads of ᶜAli and Ahmad were placed in the dwellings of the B. ᶜImran.[76] The B. al-Hasan emigrated from Mosul, and the pro-Azd Abu Yazid al-Khurasani became governor. Al-Azdi includes three elegies of ᶜAli b. al-Hasan, including one by his brother Muhammad and another by his nephew Muhammad b. Ahmad.[77]

It is striking that, during this conflict, al-Azd was not counted as part of al-Yaman. In addition to al-Azdi's narrative, we have the poet Mukhallad b. al-Bakkar's elegies for ᶜAli b. al-Hasan and, a few years later, that for al-Sayyid b. Anas. The former's people are mentioned as Al Qahtan, and the latter as al-Azd.[78] There is something similar in al-Azdi's account of the battle involving ᶜUthman b. Nuᶜaym, where the author says ᶜUthman complained of 'al-Azd and al-Yaman'.[79] Robinson saw this as meaning that Hamdan, through its power, had come to be synonymous with al-Yaman in the region.[80] Before these events the Hamdan had dominated the city's politics for perhaps a decade. However, the two were not exactly synonymous any more than the B. al-Shahhaj were synonymous with the Azd. The wording identifies only the leading clan of a given tribal grouping in a specific military encounter.

This evolution of the tribal system is not dependent solely on Hamdan's power, but on that of al-Azd. Under the caliph Harun al-Rashid, several Hamdanis did become important tax farmers in al-Jazira, such as at al-Salaq and with the Taghlib.[81] However, when ᶜAli b. al-Hasan sought to avenge his father's death, he depended on al-Azd support, especially from the B. Talid. In fact, even as the Hamdan came to exercise influence within Mosul, the Azd continued to enjoy the wealth from the estates such as those granted to them by al-Mansur. These estates and the wealth they produced were the most important sources of power in al-Jazira, as they allowed the estate owners to exercise patronage, spreading around their wealth and in turn enjoying the loyalty of the tribesmen who could serve as military levies.

As noted above, the B. al-Shahhaj had gained land under the early Abbasids. In the tenth century, Ibn Hawqal still listed them among Mosul's historically important land-owning families, along with two other Azd groups, the B. Fahd and B. ᶜImran. At the time Ibn Hawqal was writing, however, the Hamdanid dynasty, a Taghlib clan completely unrelated to the B. Hamdan of the eighth and ninth centuries, broke their power by breaking up their estates.[82] We see a parallel to this in al-Azdi, when in 200 (816), ᶜAli b. al-Hasan was riding to the village of Barsatiq with Saᶜid b. Muᶜawiya al-Shahhaji. They saw fields to either side of the road, which Saᶜid claimed were the best of fields just as they had the best Amir. Saᶜid b. Muᶜawiya ended up having to sell the property to the governor.[83]

The rise of the Hamdan to political dominance during the early 800s obscures the fact that they were, compared to the Azd, a new power. The Azd had the old money, and the Hamdan were beginning to use their position to obtain some of it, as well as cut into their privilege in other ways. This led the Azd to gather their forces and oust, not the Hamdan, but the B. al-Hasan, and replace ᶜAli with a governor sympathetic to their interests. The anthropology concerning Bedouin indicates that often previously autonomous weaker groups cluster together under a common uniting ancestor or layer of identity, a development which, given the performative nature of tribal genealogical nomenclature, could effectively move levels down a linear genealogical representation in ways that excluded groups which would previously have been considered part of it.[84] Although anthropological information cannot be applied carelessly to incidents found in the sources, these developments involving the relationship of the al-Azd and al-Yaman identities seem to fit this model perfectly. One implication of this, of course, is that the Hamdan could command the loyalty of a number of less powerful al-Yaman groups, suggesting that tribal labels retained their importance within al-Azd patronage in this period.

Orthmann argues that the tribal conflicts in early Abbasid Mosul fit a pattern of conflict between cities and their hinterland which she also finds in Damascus. Her evidence for Mosul however, is not convincing. For example, in the conflict following the death of al-Hasan b. Salih, she sees urban Yamanis combating the rural Bedouin. The Hamdan, however, were not urban, but tied to a manpower reserve in the mountains east of the Tigris in what is today the Iraqi province of Hamdaniya. One of Orthmann's key assumptions seems to be that the notables exercising power from the cities depended on supporters who were entirely urban, which is true sometimes, but not always. She also argues that there is no clear evidence of cooperation between rural and urban clusters of the same tribe.[85] However, there is also no clear evidence of conflict between the two, and Orthmann ignores the ties between the city and the mountains to the east. Ibn al-Bakkar's elegy of al-Sayyid b. Anas also links him to the Azd of rural districts.[86] Orthmann's analysis may be influenced by her definition of tribes as functional economic and political communities. If we focus on tribe as identity, however, then we also note the significance of the fact that al-Azdi chose to represent the Azd of the surrounding agricultural areas as related to those resident in Mosul itself.

The next major developments in the history of the northern Azd involved the mountainous regions north of the city, especially Azerbaijan. As described by Kennedy, this province was only sparsely settled by Arabs, and during the Umayyad period the indigenous inhabitants retained independence in exchange for tribute. During the early Abbasid period, however, Arab settlement in the area increased. ᶜAli b. Sadaqa al-Azdi was typical of those who came seeking mineral wealth in the mountains.[87] ᶜAli was a *mawlā* of the Kharijite leader Abu Hamza and had become governor of Mosul near the end of the reign of Harun al-Rashid.[88] After he died, his place was inherited by his son Zurayq.[89] Zurayq was the brother-in-law of al-Sayyid b. Anas who in 203 (819) was a Mosul officeholder.[90] Al-Sayyid went to the court of al-Maʾmun, where he found Muhammad b. al-Hasan giving his side of the recent conflict between al-Azd and

Hamdan. Al-Sayyid gave the caliph goods from Armenia and Azerbaijan, including gold, lead, iron, mercury and arsenic, saying it came from the hands of Zurayq b. Sadaqa.[91]

This period saw the rise of a rebel movement led by Babak, a movement which may have represented the interests of the indigenous inhabitants against the influx of Arab newcomers.[92] In 205 (820), Zurayq b. ᶜAli b. Sadaqa agreed to go to war against Babak on behalf of al-Maᵓmun in exchange for an appointment as governor over Armenia and Azerbaijan. He then recruited an army of 50,000 from the tribes and workers of Mosul and led them against Babak. His army included Hamdanis, indicating that tribal enmity could be put aside given the promise of plunder and a common enemy. He won a battle, but decided to sit on his gains. Al-Maᵓmun requested the presence of al-Sayyid to explain his behaviour, and placed him in charge of the war.[93] The next year, al-Sayyid and Zurayq fought a battle on the shores of the Zab in which Zurayq had twice as many men and won. The sons of ᶜImran b. Khalid, Zayd and Sulayman, mentioned in the account of Jabir b. Jabbala as among the brothers of al-Muᶜafa b. ᶜImran, were with Zurayq, who granted them boons.[94] Kennedy suggests that Zurayq and Babak may have reached an understanding, as after Babak's defeat of the expedition, there was no further conflict between them.[95] Under the year 207 (822), al-Azdi records a poem about the still-governing al-Sayyid b. Anas al-Yahmadi.[96]

In 208 (823), there was a battle between Zurayq and al-Sayyid at Ba Jabbara. Al-Sayyid fought him with javelins and other weapons. Ahmad b. ᶜUmar al-ᶜAdawi showed up with 4,000 horses and camped near Dayr al-ᶜAla. He proclaimed himself their neighbour, and said that he had not left this unchanged and had come to make peace between them and deal fairly between them. He wanted to use a boat, but Zurayq refused, so al-Sayyid left Mosul and went to the shore of the river where Zurayq came to him and they made peace.[97] Two years later, al-Sayyid imprisoned Sulayman b. ᶜImran and his brother Zayd b. ᶜImran and blocked their door, though they were fed through a peephole. These two wrote to Zurayq b. ᶜAli and asked his help against al-Sayyid, who was married to al-Babunaj bt. ᶜAli b. Sadaqa and had already taken possession of the estates of the B. Sadaqa as far as the borders of Azerbaijan. There followed a war between Zurayq and al-Sayyid in which Yahya b. al-Qasim al-ᶜAbdi intervened.[98] Amidst this war, al-Sayyid killed Hatim b. Salih at al-Salaq, and the general Tahir b. al-Husayn threatened to kill him. Al-Sayyid expressed regret for Hatim's death, but said it was God's will.[99] In 211 (826), al-Sayyid b. Anas died campaigning against Zurayq b. ᶜAli with 4,000 men to Zurayq's 40,000. The latter put his son Abu al-Suᶜalik in charge of the war against al-Sayyid. When al-Ma'mun learned of al-Sayyid's death, he appointed the Khurasani general Muhammad b. Humayd at-Tusi over the war against Zurayq, who received al-Sayyid's head and whose domains yielded 100,000 dirhams a year.[100]

In 212 (827), Muhammad b. Humayd al-Tusi took charge of the war against Zurayq and Babak, and al-Ma'mun made him governor of Mosul. He arrived with the military leaders of Khurasan, and men from Talid gathered to him. After getting provisions, he met Zurayq camping on the east bank of the Zab, while Muhammad himself was on the west. Zurayq went to visit one of several shaykhs who was influential in a place called Muska. Zurayq addressed this shaykh, who was named al-Duhhak al-Kindi, as 'sister's son'.[101] Muhammad b. Humayd was joined by Muhammad b. al-Sayyid b. Anas and the tribes of Talid, Tamthan, Hamdan, Tayy, and al-Harith b. Ka^cb. During the ensuing battle, al-Habab b. Bakr al-Talidi defected to Zurayq. Muhammad b. al-Sayyid informed Muhammad b. Humayd of this, and because he did not want his kinsmen annihilated, sought forces to pursue him himself. Ibn Humayd refused, however, and Ibn al-Sayyid left angrily and called to his people. The tribes of Talid, Tamthan, Ma^cn and the al-Harith b. Ka^cb rallied to him, and they defeated Zurayq's forces.[102] Zurayq retreated and received a safe conduct in exchange for allowing himself to be sent to al-Ma'mun.[103]

The affair of Zurayq b. ^cAli shows both the importance and limitations of tribal identities in this region in the early ninth century. Amabe notes that the Arab notables of Azerbaijan functioned as independent lords in the lands they acquired, especially during periods of weak government such as the civil war between the caliphs al-Amin and al-Ma'mun.[104] The B. Sadaqa were clearly independent rulers in their areas of Azerbaijan, and had a number of estates in the region between Azerbaijan and Mosul. They were also linked by marriage to one important al-Azd clan in the city and tapped by another for assistance. Al-Sayyid used Zurayq's wealth in order to appease al-Ma'mun, who later held al-Sayyid responsible for Zurayq's failure to prosecute the war. Even without centralised leadership, the Azd existed as a palpable force straddling the effective boundary of the Abbasid caliphate in the north, and the wealth gained from the mines enabled Zurayq to field a sizeable army. It is also striking that even though Zurayq had apparently thrown in his lot with someone regarded as a heretic, two brothers of the B. ^cImran, a family noted for its religious learning, appealed to him for help. These bonds were not, however, absolute, and individuals remained free. Although tribal ties represented an important set of assets and options, these could be trumped by others. Al-Sayyid agreed to turn against his brother-in-law on the orders of al-Ma'mun, as did many who later joined the army of Muhammad b. Humayd al-Tusi, presumably for the money involved. Even then, however, Muhammad b. al-Sayyid was concerned about battling a fellow Azdi even though that Azdi had gone over to the force which killed his father.

Sulayman b. ᶜImran and his brother Zayd were great-grandsons of Jabir b. Jabala through his son Nufayl, and their clan was the most prestigious amongt his descendants. The extensive account of this clan, to which the account of Jabir b. Jabala is primarily an introduction, allows us to examine an influential clan of al-Azd urban notables in Mosul during the ninth century. In addition to Sulayman, who at one point served as governor, they boasted his brother, the respected religious scholar Abu Masᶜud al-Muᶜafa b. ᶜImran and his brother. Nufayl was one of the three sons of Jabir in Mosul listed by al-Azdi, with ᶜAbd Allah and Wahb as the other two. The 'Razin' mentioned above in the list of tribes is not mentioned here, and may have been a means of absorbing local Christian notables into the city's new elite; the fact that the sons of al-ᶜAla b. Razin, their only listed branch, all have Christian names is interesting. There is also a Yazid b. Yazid b. Jabir al-Azdi, who died in first years of the Abbasid caliphate.[105]

As noted above, Nufayl, the ancestor to whom the B. ᶜImran b. Nufayl trace themselves, had a house in Mosul in the al-Sikka al-Kabira, where a lane was named for him in al-Azdi's day. Abu Masᶜud al-Muᶜafa b. ᶜImran b. Nufayl was his grandson, and died at the beginning of the ninth century.[106] He had four or five sons, two of whom were killed in his lifetime. One of al-Muᶜafa's sons was ᶜAbd al-Kabir, another scholar who went to places called Adhana and al-Massisa to work apart from the cares of the world. Al-Muᶜafa's oldest son was Abu ᶜImran Nufayl b. al-Muᶜafa, and al-Muᶜafa in his will left someone – most likely his other children – to this Nufayl's care.[107] Abd al-Kabir b. al-Muᶜafa b. ᶜImran al-Azdi died in the 830s.[108]

Khalid b. ᶜImran was also a governor of Mosul under al-Mutawakkil, and the two travelled there together. As Ali Habiba suggests in the footnotes to his edition of *Tarikh al-Mawsil*, al-Mutawakkil was also probably the caliph with whom Khalid traveled to Syria on a journey in which he visited Abd al-Kabir b. al-Muᶜafa.[109] Another member of the family was Abu Khalid Muhammad b. Zayd b. ᶜImran, known as a generous shaykh who ruled over a mountain north of Mosul called Dasin east of the Tigris and a city called Kalar in the mountains between Mosul and Rayy near Tabaristan.[110] Ishaq b. Muhammad al-Hurrani, the paternal uncle of one Yahya b. Razin, disputed his rights to these territories and approached him with 4,000 horses and men. Muhammad responded by relocating the

Hamidiyya at Dasin while himself going to Kalar to take up residence with the Ibn ᶜImran family,[111] where he was pursued by Ishaq until the latter camped in the Suq al-Ahad. Battle was joined when Muhammad was stirred by a poem. Muhammad died with Sulayman in the early 770s, though whether this was connected to the battle is unclear.[112] The identity of Yahya b. Razin is unknown, but it is tempting to see in him the otherwise unknown Yahya b. al-ᶜAla b. Razin. His name fits the previously noted pattern of Christian names in that clan.

Al-Azdi cites additional information about Sulayman b. ᶜImran, who was at one time Mosul's governor in charge of war and taxes. Once a man lodged a complaint to his agent asking about the purchase of an unspecified piece of land to which Sulayman had agreed. The man claimed the agent had stolen a stack of useful plants, which Sulayman made him return. There is also a brief poem glorifying him.[113] He was governor of the prayers and war in Mosul when he died.[114] Sulayman's son ᶜAbd Allah b. Sulayman b. ᶜImran was also in charge of Mosul's wars and taxes. Another son, Yahya b. Sulayman, reportedly led al-Yaman in Mosul during the 860s, though given the time frame one cannot help but suspect confusion of some sort in this identification. In any event, he seized power in the city, and with popular support attempted to resist the caliph's appointee al-Haytham b. ᶜAbd Allah al-ᶜAdawi's attempt to enter. He was, however, killed with all his companions. Ishaq b. Ayyub al-ᶜAdawi subsequently became governor supported by 30,000 Taghlibis, though they were resisted by the people of Mosul.[115] Dawud b. Sulayman was a third son of Sulayman b. ᶜImran, and described by al-Azdi as a humble lover of truth and blessedness, yet careless.[116]

After this account of the B. ᶜImran b. Nufayl, al-Azdi mentions a few of the B. Razin b. Jabir. The first of these is a poet named Muhammad b. Ayyub b. al-ᶜAlaᵓ b. Razin. Nothing else is known of him except a tone in the text which suggests one should know who Ayyub b. al-ᶜAlaᵓ was. Ismaᶜil b. al-ᶜAlaᵓ b. Razin is presented as another important patriarch, who had a son named Razin b. Ismaᶜil. The text says only that this Razin had offspring. Another son of al-ᶜAlaᵓ b. Razin was Harun b. al-ᶜAlaᵓ, listed as a freebooter with Khalid b. ᶜImran who later left that lifestyle to return to his home in Mosul. Finally, al-Azdi mentions two sons of one Musa b. Yahya b al-ᶜAlaᵓ b. Razin named Yahya and Bakr. Yahya b. Musa was a government employee with Sulayman b. ᶜImran and others who had no offspring, while Bakr b. Musa had offspring of the B. Razin.[117] If the Razinids were added to the B. Jabir b. Jabala after the latter's migration to Mosul, the connection between Yahya b. Musa and Sulayman may have provided the incentive.

Conclusion

This detailed account of the descendants of Jabir b. Jabala in the ninth century shows an important development of al-Azd as a tribal group. The Abbasid period saw the emergence of a common elite culture, and Islamic learning was among the most dependable entry points into this culture. Whereas for the Umayyad period we read of traditional tribal leaders such as Maᶜsud b. ᶜAmr in Basra and ᶜAbd al-Rahman b. Mikhnaf in Kufa, the most important figure to the B. ᶜImran was al-Muᶜafa b. ᶜImran, a religious scholar. Although there continued to be connections between these urban elites and their larger tribal units, we are clearly no longer in a Bedouin cultural world, despite the significance of Bedouin in the surrounding area. A century later, the B. Rawwad would assert their independence in Tabriz and still maintain their Arab roots despite the extent to which they had become Kurdicised.[118] Given the use of older material such as al-Azdi's account of the Malik b. Fahm migration to Oman, this use of tribal heritage represents another example of the appropriation of the pre-Islamic past, this time by individual families, alongside those noted by Toral-Niehoff.[119]

At the same time, the persistence of a living genealogical idiom is unmistakable. Unlike in Khurasan, tribal identities in al-Jazira continued to shift in a manner we would expect from Bedouin society, and important figures of the early Abbasid period would go on to become the eponyms of genealogical groupings in their own right. Although these new tribes would not exist without the state, it was certainly not a deliberate Abbasid policy to create them. Instead, the Abbasids provided wealth and position for individuals who proceeded to use it for their own purposes and those of their relations. Unlike the Umayyads, the Abbasids seldom practised indirect rule through tribal leaders. Those through whom they ruled, however, became sometimes tribal leaders, but always assets in areas where tribalism was still strong, and the culture associated with the Abbasid regime became a new means of prestige and hence leadership within the tribal system.

Notes

1. Paul Wheatley, *The Places Where Men Pray Together: Cities in Islamic Lands Seventh Through the Tenth Centuries* (Chicago: University of Chicago Press, 2001), pp. 104–5.
2. Chase Robinson, *Empire and Elites after the Muslim Conquest*, p. 34.
3. Wheatley, *Places*, p. 105.

4. Robinson, *Empire and Elites*, p. 61.
5. Wheatley, *Places*, p. 108.
6. Hugh Kennedy, 'Central Government and Provincial Elites in the Early 'Abbasid period', p. 27.
7. Le Strange, *Lands*, p. 87. Al-Sam^{c}ani knew an account that Tikrit was named for a sister of Bakr and Taghlib b. Waʾil, showing the Rabi^{c}a's significance even that far south. Sam^{c}ani, *al-Ansab*, I, p. 495.
8. Yaqut, *Buldan*, II, pp. 88–9.
9. Le Strange, *Lands*, pp. 98–9. On Balad, sometimes called Balad al-Ḥaṭab, see Sam^{c}ani, *al-Ansab*, I, 408.
10. Le Strange, *Lands*, pp. 90–2; Sam^{c}ani, *al-Ansab*, II, p. 223.
11. Yaqut, *Buldan*, III, p. 269.
12. Baladhuri, *Futuh*, p. 407; Robinson, 'The Early Islamic History of Mosul', p. 390.
13. Morony, *Iraq*, p. 204.
14. Robinson, 'Early Islamic', p. 390. For the location of Hibtun, see Idrisi, *Kitab Nuzha al-Mushtaq fī Ikhtiraq al-Afaq* II, p. 658.
15. F. Rosenthal, 'al-Azdi', EI, I, p. 813.
16. Robinson, *Empire and Elites*, pp. 129–30.
17. Miquel, A, 'Ibn Hawqal', EI, III, pp. 786–8.
18. Baladhuri, *Futuh*, pp. 464–5; Robinson, *Empire and Elites*, pp. 72–4; Sallam, *al-Mawsil*, pp. 30–1.
19. Baladhuri, *Futuh*, p. 200. Ibn al-Faqih, p. 129. Wheatley, *Places*, p. 105.
20. Azdi, *Taʾrikh*, p. 24
21. Ya^{c}qubi, *Taʾrikh*, I, pp. 204–5.
22. Ya^{c}qubi, *Taʾrikh*, II, p. 371; Baladhuri, *Futuh*, p. 463; Yaqut, *Buldan*, V, pp. 278, 324–5; Le Strange, *Lands*, p. 170.
23. Fukuzo Amabe, *Emergence*, p. 112.
24. Azdi, *Taʾrikh*, pp. 77–8.
25. Azdi, *Taʾrikh*, p. 77. Both this and the next citation actually have 'Salama' for 'Salima'. In his biography of the religious scholar al-Mu^{c}afa b. ^{c}Imran, al-Baghdadi provides the genealogy as Jabir b. Wahb b. Ubayd b. Labid b. Jabala b. Ghanm b. Daws b. Mujashi'a b. Salima b. Fahm. Al-Khatib al-Baghdadi, *Taʾrīkh*, XIII, p. 228.
26. Tabari, *Taʾrīkh*, II, pp. 1942–3; Tabari, *History*, XXVII, p. 53; Azdi, *Taʾrikh*, p. 77.
27. Azdi, *Taʾrikh*, p. 78. Here the text has the same name al-Tabari gives to Abu Hamza, with the 'yaa'.
28. Wilkinson, *Ibadism*, pp. 179–82.
29. Azdi, *Taʾrikh*, pp. 77–8.
30. Azdi, *Taʾrikh*, pp. 80–1. Buhlul b. Bishr was a Kharijite also known as 'Kuthara'.
31. Baladhuri, *Futuh*, p. 332.
32. Robinson, *Empire and Elites*, p. 84; Sallam, *al-Mawsil*, pp. 108–9.

33. Robinson, *Empire and Elites*, p. 88.
34. Azdi, *Taʾrikh*, pp. 81, 84.
35. Azdi, *Taʾrikh*, p. 81.
36. Azdi, *Taʾrikh*, p. 91.
37. Azdi, *Taʾrikh*, p. 91.
38. Robinson, *Empire and Elites*, pp. 75–6.
39. Azdi, *Taʾrikh*, p. 92; Yaqut, *Buldan*, I, p. 867.
40. Wheatley, *Places*, p. 105; Andrew Watson, *Agricultural Innovation in the Early Islamic World*, pp. 88–9.
41. Azdi, *Taʾrikh*, p. 92.
42. Azdi, *Taʾrikh*, pp. 92–3.
43. Azdi, *Taʾrikh*, p. 93.
44. Azdi, *Taʾrikh*, p. 94.
45. Orthmann, *Stamm und Macht*, p. 114.
46. Muqaddisi, p. 123.
47. See Caskel and Strenziok, *Gamharat*, I, p. 211 for all these groups.
48. Azdi, *Taʾrikh*, p. 94.
49. Ibn Hajar, *Tahdhib*, XI, pp. 34–7; X, p. 237. Al-Azdi gives the year of death as 154 (771), Azdi, *Taʾrikh*, p. 203.
50. Azdi, *Taʾrikh*, p. 95.
51. Robinson, *Empire and Elites*, pp.127–64; Azdi, *Taʾrikh*, pp. 145–55.
52. Robinson, *Empire and Elites*, p. 150.
53. Robinson, *Empire and Elites*, pp. 147–8.
54. Robinson, *Empire and Elites*, pp. 152–4.
55. Azdi, *Taʾrikh*, pp. 158; Robinson, *Empire and Elites*, pp. 154–5.
56. Azdi, *Taʾrikh*, pp. 171–2.
57. Azdi, *Taʾrikh*, pp. 199, 217.
58. Azdi, *Taʾrikh*, pp. 203–4; Robinson, *Empire and Elites*, 151.
59. Azdi, *Taʾrikh*, p. 217.
60. Azdi, *Taʾrikh*, p. 289.
61. Azdi, *Taʾrikh*, pp. 279–80. See pp. 284–7 for more details.
62. Azdi, *Taʾrikh*, p. 292.
63. Robinson, *Empire and Elites*, p. 162.
64. Robinson, 'Early Islamic', pp. 352–3.
65. Robinson, 'Early Islamic', pp. 254–5; Azdi, *Taʾrikh*, pp. 258, 279–80.
66. Azdi, *Taʾrikh*, pp. 296–7.
67. Yaqut, *Buldan*, III, p. 425; Le Strange, *Lands*, pp. 190–1.
68. Azdi, *Taʾrikh*, pp. 297–8.
69. Azdi, *Taʾrikh*, p. 310.
70. Azdi, *Taʾrikh*, pp. 313–16.
71. Azdi, *Taʾrikh*, p. 324; Robinson, 'Early Islamic', pp. 364–7; Paul G. Forand, 'The Governors of Mosul According to al-Azdi's *Taʾrikh al-Mawsil*', p. 100. Orthmann notes a parallel development in Damascus, Orthmann, *Stamm und Macht*, p. 110.

72. Azdi, *Taʾrikh*, pp. 332–8; Robinson, 'Early Islamic', pp. 368–9.
73. Azdi, *Taʾrikh*, pp. 343–4.
74. Azdi, *Taʾrikh*, pp. 344.
75. Al-Sayyid's full name was al-Sayyid b. Anas b. ᶜAmr b. Maᶜdan b. Jarir b. Saᶜd b. Khalid b. Thaᶜala b. ᶜAʾid b. Talid b. al-Yahmad. Azdi, *Taʾrikh*, pp. 363–4.
76. Azdi, *Taʾrikh*, pp. 344–6; Robinson, 'Early Islamic', p. 370.
77. Azdi, *Taʾrikh*, pp. 347–50.
78. Azdi, *Taʾrikh*, pp. 349, 375.
79. Azdi, *Taʾrikh*, p. 332.
80. Robinson, 'Early Islamic', p. 371.
81. Robinson, 'Early Islamic', pp. 362–3. Presumably because the B. Taghlib were Christian, they had only a small government role during the Umayyad and early Abbasid periods. All five of the known officials who collected their taxes were non-Taghlibis. This began to change only in the early ninth century.
82. Ibn Hawqal, *Kitab Surat al-Ard*, II, p. 216.
83. Azdi, *Taʾrikh*, pp. 339–40.
84. A form of coalescence is found in William Lancaster, *Rwala*, p. 27.
85. Orthmann, *Stamm und Macht*, pp. 108–13.
86. Azdi, *Taʾrikh*, p. 375.
87. Kennedy, *The Early Abbasid Caliphate: A Political History*, p. 170.
88. Amabe, *Emergence*, p. 109; Forand, 'Governors', p. 99.
89. This is the same as the Sadaqa b. ᶜAli b. Sadaqa b. Dinar described in Baladhuri, *Futuh*, p. 331 as '*mawlā* al-Azd.' See Crone, *The Nativist Prophets of Early Islamic Iran: Rural Revolt and Zoroastrianism*, p. 58.
90. Azdi, *Taʾrikh*, p. 352.
91. Azdi, *Taʾrikh*, p. 354. See rest of the page, in which al-Ma'mun appoints al-Sayyid over Baghdad.
92. Kennedy, *Early Abbasid*, p. 171; Crone, *Nativist Prophets*, pp. 46–76.
93. Azdi, *Taʾrikh*, pp. 356–8.
94. Azdi, *Taʾrikh*, pp. 359–60.
95. Kennedy, *Early Abbasid*, p. 172.
96. Azdi, *Taʾrikh*, p. 363.
97. Azdi, *Taʾrikh*, pp. 365–6.
98. Azdi, *Taʾrikh*, pp. 371–2.
99. Azdi, *Taʾrikh*, pp. 365.
100. Azdi, *Taʾrikh*, pp. 373–4; for elegies of al-Sayyid b. Anas, see pp. 375-8.
101. Azdi, *Taʾrikh*, pp. 378–9.
102. Azdi, *Taʾrikh*, pp. 379–80.
103. Azdi, *Taʾrikh*, p. 381.
104. Amabe, *Emergence*, pp. 110–11.
105. Azdi, *Taʾrikh*, p. 156.

106. See also Ibn Hajar, *Tahdhib*, X, pp. 199–200; Dhahabi, *Tadhkira al-Huffaz*, I, pp. 287–8; al-Khatib al-Baghdadi, *Taʾrikh*, XIII, pp. 227–31.
107. Azdi, *Taʾrikh*, p. 81, where there is also an account of al-Muʿafa's meeting with his brothers after this murder.
108. Azdi, *Taʾrikh*, p. 423.
109. Azdi, *Taʾrikh*, pp. 82–3.
110. For Dasin, see Yaqut, *Buldan*, II, p. 493. On Kalar, Yaqut, *Buldan*, IV, pp. 538–9; Le Strange, *Lands*, p. 373.
111. Habiba notes from Yaqut the existence of a village by this name east of Mosul. Azdi, *Taʾrikh*, p. 83, n. 4.
112. Azdi, *Taʾrikh*, pp. 83–4.
113. Azdi, *Taʾrikh*, pp. 84–5.
114. Azdi, *Taʾrikh*, p. 87. This tradition gives the year as 129 (747), but clearly this is incorrect.
115. Azdi, *Taʾrikh*, p. 88.
116. Azdi, *Taʾrikh*, pp. 89–90.
117. Azdi, *Taʾrikh*, p. 90.
118. Wilferd Madelung, 'The Minor Dynasties of Northern Iran', pp. 236–7. Paul A. Blaum, 'Life in a Rough Neighborhood: Byzantium, Islam, and the Rawwadid Kurds', p. 2.
119. Toral-Niehoff, 'Arab Origins', pp. 61–9.

Conclusion

During the middle of the ninth century, a son of the poet Di^c^bil b. ^c^Ali al-Khuza^c^i produced a book called *Wasaya al-Muluk wa Anba^ʾ^ al-Muluk min Walad Qahtan b. Hud* which became attributed to his father.[1] The book consists of anecdotes about supposed ancient South Arabian rulers who also pass down in the form of poetry political advice to their offspring. It includes material closely related to the 'Scattering of al-Azd' traditions discussed in Chapter 1, but with key differences, the most important of which is that the figures of the al-Azd genealogy are all now servants of the rulers of Himyar. Al-Gawth sends his son al-Azd to Ma^ʾ^rib, where he and his descendants rule the frontiers on behalf of rulers of Himyar to whom their loyalty is repeatedly stressed.[2] Al-Azd is thus folded into a vision of al-Yaman identity grounded in traditions of royal authority, a historical construction which, for the courtiers of Baghdad and Samarra, was a core part of how they envisioned themselves and their place in the world.

This book has focused on the shifting meanings of al-Azd identity for those who held it and the way it served to mediate the transition from the societies of the pre-Islamic Arabian Peninsula to the culture of the Abbasid caliphate. It has also sought to move beyond genealogical sources, seeing them as a literary representation of tribal identity's main idiom, an idiom which in practice was continually reconstructed over time. As Lecker states, 'Genealogies are not correct or incorrect; genealogical claims reflect the situation at a certain point in time, or attempts to transform it.'[3] We have used a model that begins from the standpoint that tribesmen are autonomous actors for whom a tribal label is an asset the reputation of which they defend even as they also frequently act independently of it. It is the meaning of this asset that changes over time in terms of how it is seen in relation to the other identities around it, the people whom the label includes, and the types of activity involved in using and protecting it.

On the eve of Islam, an idea of al-Azd probably existed, drawing on faint memories of the power of al-Azd rulers in the Wadi Bisha. This identity, however, seldom had practical significance, and understanding the tribal groups of pre-Islamic Arabia involved finding ways to get around the assumptions of the ninth-century codifiers of genealogical literature. Tribal identity was not fixed, but often incorporated new groups, such as the Daws, and could take names from places as well as ancestors. Tribal society was hierarchical, yet leadership was also contested and depended on a combination of military skill, religious prestige and mediation. As the early caliphate developed, it came to dominate the tribal leadership in the region around Mecca and Medina, but was reliant on local leadership further afield in Oman. The exact nature of loyalty to the state is often difficult to determine, however, given the fact that temporal priority in Islam came to be a status marker for elite families, tribes and regions. It does seem clear that the spread of at least theoretical political loyalty to Medina depended in part upon the spread of the influence of the al-Julanda family, a prominent Omani line willing to forward a level of revenue in exchange for legitimacy.

One of the major themes of this work has been to connect the significance of tribal labels to shifting configurations of state and society. The Arabian Peninsula was never a desert filled with Bedouin untouched by outside forces. The kings of ancient South Arabia, the Sasanians, the Romans, and the Ethiopians all influenced societies across the peninsula, whether through using them as auxiliaries, deputising groups to defend frontiers, or simply through their economic activity. The rise of the caliphate continued and intensified this involvement, with settlement in garrison towns as a stipendiary military force providing a novel new environment in which, for administrative reasons, the groups with which individuals concerned themselves became larger. At some point, in the garrison towns tribal identity came to be a function of residence, but even that had precedent in South Arabia, and perhaps elsewhere.

Another key factor in this work has been the nature of the prominent individuals who served as intermediaries between the tribe and the rest of the world. Initially the caliphate managed the tribes through the old *ashrāf* class, but again, the scale became bigger. Nonetheless, tribesmen defended their leaders as if defending the tribe itself. This is seen in the months of fighting which followed the killing of Mas[c]ud b. [c]Amr in Basra. As the caliphate replaced indirect rule through the *ashrāf* with more centralised administration by an appointed governor, the traditional tribal notability declined in importance in Iraq. The most prominent figures represented in our sources were now military generals, as represented by al-Muhallab b. Abi Sufra and his son Yazid. This family of non-Arab origin rose to prominence entirely based on their role in the conquests, yet played a critical role for the fortunes of al-Azd within the caliphate and became the most important repositories of tribal honour during the early 700s. The largely al-Azd region of Oman was an important source of their manpower, and many al-Azd sub-groups had their own military divisions tied to the Muhallabid armies. The Muhallabids themselves represented a transition, however, as influence in government and the military increasingly came to flow from the caliph. In Mosul, urban notables with tribal ties vied for government office and enjoyed the proceeds of agricultural estates. Nonetheless, when the state weakened, tribal pressure could make a difference in local balances of power which Baghdad was forced to recognise.

Identity is constituted in part through memory, and both the forms and content of al-Azd historical memory evolved over time. The early settlers in Iraq and Syria brought stories of groups such as Ghamid and Thumala, but seem not to have had a historical connection to anything larger until al-Azd became more important as an organisational unit under the early caliphate. Stories of tribes' pre-Islamic deeds were told in private tribal sessions into the Umayyad period, and as time passed, accounts of tribal lore from the early decades of Islam were added. As the eighth century passed, traditionists such as Abu Mikhnaf passed down this material in set works that could be recited and would eventually be written in permanent form. Where individual tribes lost their political significance, such as in ninth-century Baghdad, the exact tribe became less important than a broad faction such as al-Yaman or a more broadly conceived Arab identity incorporating all peoples claiming roots on the peninsula. This new material incorporated aspects of al-Azd history, whether the legendary accounts of the al-Azd migrations following the bursting of the Maʾrib dam or the deeds of the Muhallabids and their retinue of poets. At the same time, where tribal identity did still matter, as in Mosul, the history would be deployed on behalf of a new class of notables still taking pride in al-Azd identity. An example of this process is seen in the deployment of a story of Malik b. Fahm in Abu Zakariya al-Azdi's account of the descendants of Jabir b. Jabala in Mosul, the family of one of the city's prominent *ʿulamāʾ*. Whether in Baghdad or Mosul, however, such notables were creating the empire's common elite culture in ways which connected that culture to all who claimed al-Azd ancestry.

Al-Azd is only one of the many tribal groups prominent in the late seventh and eighth centuries, and as with any, its history is unique. More research is needed to truly understand what tribe might have meant for others of the diverse groups linked to the Arabian Peninsula in late antiquity. Given the Iraqi focus of so much of the study of Arab tribalism, work on Syria and Egypt, and for that matter North Africa, is particularly needed to see if patterns noted in Iraq hold there as well. In addition, more research is needed on the social, political and cultural contexts in which tribal narratives were passed down in the Abbasid period and later, as well as when and how such narratives came to inform the identities of the peoples of the Arabian Peninsula on whom they were ostensibly based. Finally, the economic dimensions of al-Azd and other groups requires a deeper understanding to form a better picture of the material life of individual tribespeople. Archaeological investigation and incidental mentions in poetry are possible avenues through which to approach this topic.

Notes

1. Webb, 'Yemeni Identity'.
2. Khuzaʾi, *Wasaya*, pp. 74–95.
3. Lecker, 'Tribes', p. 2.

Bibliography

Primary Sources

Abū ᶜUbayda Maᶜmar b. al-Muthannā, *Naqāʾid Jarīr wa al-Farazdaq*, 3 vols, ed. A. A. Bevan (Leiden: Brill, 1905-12).

al-Āmidī, Abū al-Qāsim al-Ḥasan b. Bishr [1354], *Al-Muʾtalif wa al-Mukhtalif*, ed. F. Krenkow (Cairo: Maktabāt al-Qudsī, 1935), pp. 9–198.

al-ᶜAwtabī, Salima b. Muslim, *al-Ansāb*, ed. Muḥammad Iḥsān al-Naṣṣ (Muscat: ᶜĀṣima al-Thaqāfa al-ᶜUmānīya, 2006).

al-Azdī, Abū Ismāᶜīl Muḥammad b. ᶜAbd Allāh, *Futūḥ al-Shām*, eds ᶜIṣām Muṣṭafā ᶜUqla and Yūsuf Aḥmad Banī Yāsīn (Irbid, Jordan: Muᶜssasat Ḥammāda, 2005).

al-Azdī, Abū Zakariyyāʾ [1387], *Taʾrīkh al-Mawṣil*, ed. ᶜAlī Ḥabība. (Cairo: al-Majlis al-ᶜAlā li-l-Shuʾūn al -Islāmiyya, 1967).

al-Azraqī, Abū al-Walīd [1416], *Taʾrīkh Makkah*, ed. Hishām b. ᶜAbd al-ᶜAzīz ᶜAṭā (Mecca: al-Maktaba al-tijāriyya, 1995).

al-Bakrī, Abū ᶜUbayd [1364, 1371], *Muᶜjam mā Staᶜjam*, ed. Muṣṭafa al-Saqqā (Cairo: Lajnat al-Taʾlīf wa al-Tarjama wa al-Nashr, 1945, 1951). Reprint: Beirut: ᶜAlam al-Kutub, n.d., 2 vols.

al-Balādhurī, Aḥmad b. Yaḥyā, *Futūḥ al-Buldān*, ed. M. J. De Goeje (Leiden: Brill, 1968).

al-Balādhurī, Aḥmad b. Yaḥyā, *Ansāb al-Ashrāf*, vol. 1, ed. Muḥammad Hamīd Allāh (Cairo: Dār al-Maᶜārif, 1959).

al-Balādhurī, Aḥmad b. Yaḥyā, *Ansāb al-Ashrāf*, vol. 2, ed. Wilferd Madelung (Wiesbaden: Klaus Schwarz Verlag, 2003).

al-Balādhurī, Aḥmad b. Yaḥyā, *Ansāb al-Ashrāf*, vol. 3, ed. ᶜAbd al-Azīz al-Dūrī (Wiesbaden: Franz Steiner Verlag, 1978).

al-Balādhurī, Aḥmad b. Yaḥyā, *Ansāb al-Ashrāf*, vol. 4a, ed. M. J. Kister (Jerusalem: Magnes Press, 1971).

al-Balādhurī, Aḥmad b. Yaḥyā, *Ansāb al-Ashrāf*, vol. 4b, ed. M. Schloessinger (Jerusalem: Magnes Press, 1938).

al-Balādhurī, Aḥmad b. Yaḥyā, *Ansāb al-Ashrāf*, vol. 5, ed. S. D. F. Goitein (Jerusalem: Magnes Press, 1936).

al-Balādhurī, Aḥmad b. Yaḥyā, *Ansāb al-Ashrāf*, vol. 6, ed. Maḥmūd al-Firdaws al-ᶜAẓm (Damascus: Dār al-Yaqaẓa al-ᶜArabiya, 1999).

al-Balādhurī, Aḥmad b. Yaḥyā, *Ansāb al-Ashrāf*, vol. 7, ed. Maḥmūd al-Firdaws al-ᶜAẓm (Damascus: Dār al-Yaqaẓa al-ᶜArabiya, 2000).

al-Balādhurī, Aḥmad b. Yaḥyā, *Ansāb al-Ashrāf*, vol. 7/1, ed. Ramzi Baalbaki (Beirut: Klaus Schwarz Verlag, 1997).

al-Balādhurī, Aḥmad b. Yaḥyā, *Ansāb al-Ashrāf*, vol. 7/2, ed. Wilferd Madelung (Beirut: Klaus Schwarz Verlag, 2003).

al-Balᶜamī, Abū ᶜAlī, *Tārīkh-i Balᶜamī*, ed. Muḥammad Taqī Bahār (Tehran: Zavvār, 1974).

al-Bāriqī, Suraqa b. Mirdās, *Dīwān*, ed. Ḥusayn Naṣṣār (Cairo: Maktaba al-Thaqāfa al-Dīnīya, 2001).

al-Ḍabbī, al-Mufaḍḍal b. Muḥammad, *The Mufaddaliyat: An Anthology of Ancient Arabian Odes According to the Recension*, 4 vols, ed. Charles James Lyall (Oxford: Clarendon Press, 1918–21).

al-Dīnawarī, Abū Ḥanīfa, *Kitāb al-Nabāt*, ed. Bernhard Lewin (Beirut: Klaus Schwarz Verlag, 2009).

al-Dīnawarī, Abū Ḥanīfa, *al-Akhbār al-Ṭiwāl*, ed. ᶜUmar Fārūq al-Ṭabbāᶜ (Beirut: Sharikat Dār al-Arqam ibn al-Arqam, 1995).

al-Dhahabī, Abū ᶜAbd Allāh Shams al-Dīn Muḥammad, *Kitāb Tadhkira al-Ḥuffāẓ*, 4 vols (Hyderabad: Dāʾirāt al-Maᶜārif al-ᶜUthmāniyya, 1958).

al-Hamdānī, al-Ḥasan b. Aḥmad, *Al-Iklīl (al-Juzʾ al-Thāmin)*, ed. Nabīh Amīn Fāris (Princeton: Princeton University Press, 1940).

al-Hamdānī, al-Ḥasan b. Aḥmad, *Ṣifa Jazīra al-ᶜArab*, ed. D. H. Müller as *al-Hamdānī's Geographie der Arabischen Halbinsel* (Leiden: Brill, 1968).

Anonymous, *Akhbār al-Dawla al-ᶜAbbāsīya*, ed. ᶜAbd al-Azīz al-Dūrī et al. (Beirut: Dār al-Ṭalīᶜa lil -Ṭibāᶜa wa-al-Nashr, 1971).

Ibn ᶜAbd al-Barr, Yūsuf b. ᶜAbd Allāh [1350], *al-Inbāh ᶜalā Qabāʾil al-Ruwāt* (Cairo: al-Qudsī, 1931).

Ibn ᶜAbd al-Barr, Yūsuf b. ᶜAbd Allāh, *al-Istīᶜāb fī Maᶜrifa al-Aṣḥāb*, 4 vols (Beirut: Dār al-Kutub al-ᶜIlmiya, 2010).

Ibn ᶜAbd Rabbih, Aḥmad b. Muḥammad, *al-ᶜIqd al-Farīd*, 7 vols, 2nd edn (Beirut: Dār Sādr, 2006).

Ibn al-Nadīm, Muḥammad b. Isḥāq, *Fihrist*, ed. Yūsuf ᶜAlī Ṭawīl, 3rd edn (Beirut: Dār al-Kutub al-ᶜIlmiyya, 2010).

Ibn al-Anbārī, Abū l-Barakāt, *Nuzha al-Alibbāʾ fī Ṭabaqāt al-Udabāʾ*, ed. Ibrāhīm al-Sāmarrāʾī (Baghdad: Maṭbaᶜat al-Maᶜārif, 1959).

Ibn ᶜAsākir, ᶜAlī b. al-Ḥasan *Taʾrīkh Madīnāt Dimashq*, ed.ᶜUmar b. Gharāma al-ᶜAmrawī and ᶜAlī Shīrī, 80 vols (Beirut: Dār al-Fikr, 1995).

Ibn Aᶜtham al-Kūfī, Abū Muḥammad Aḥmad, *Kitāb al-Futūḥ*, 8 vols (Hyderabad: Maṭbaᶜa Majlis Dāʾira al-Maᶜarif al-ᶜUthmāniyya, 1967–75).

Ibn Bakkār, al-Zubayr, *Al-Akhbār al-Muwaffaqiyyāt*, ed. Sāmī Makkī al-ᶜAnī (Baghdad: Maṭbaᶜa al-ᶜAnī, 1972).

Ibn Durayd [1378], *al-Ishtiqāq*, ed. ᶜAbd al-Salām Hārūn (Cairo: al-Khānjī, 1958).

Ibn Ḥabīb, Muḥammad, *Kitāb al-Muḥabbar*, ed. Ilse Lichtenstadter (Cairo: Maṭbaᶜa Jamᶜīyat Dāʾirat al-Maᶜārif al-ᶜUthmānīya, 1942).

Ibn Ḥabīb, Muḥammad, *Kitāb al-Munammaq fī Akhbār Quraysh*, ed. Khūrshīd Aḥmad Fāriq (Hyderabad: Osmania Oriental Publications Bureau, 1964).

Ibn Ḥajar, al-ᶜAsqalānī, Aḥmad b. ᶜAlī, *Tahdhīb al-Tahdhīb*, 12 vols (Hyderabad: Maṭbaᶜa Majlis Dāʾira al-Maᶜarif al-ᶜUthmāniyya, 1907–9). Reprinted Beirut: Dār Ṣādr, 1968.

Ibn Ḥawqal, Abū al-Qāsim, *Kitāb Ṣūrat al-Arḍ*, ed. J. H. Kramers (Leiden: Brill, 1938–9). Reprinted 2014.

Ibn Ḥazm, Abū Muḥammad ᶜAlī b. Aḥmad, *Jamhara Ansāb al-ᶜArab*, ed. ᶜAbd al-Munᶜim Khalīl Ibrāhīm (Beirut: Dār al-Kutub al-ᶜIlmiya, 2009).

Ibn Hishām, ᶜAbd al-Malik, *Kitāb al-Tījān fī Mulūk Ḥimyar* (Sana'a: Markaz al-Darāsāt wa al-Abḥāth al-Yamaniyya, 1980).

Ibn Hishām, ᶜAbd al-Malik, *The Life of Muḥammad*, trans. A. Guillaume (Oxford: Oxford University Press, 1955).

Ibn Hishām, ᶜAbd al-Malikm, *Sīra al-Nabawiya* (Beirut: Dār al-Fikr, 1992).

Ibn Iṣfandiyar, Muḥammad b. Ḥasan, *Tārīkh-i Ṭabaristān*, ed. Ḥasan Iqbāl (Tehran: n.p., 1941).

Ibn al-Kalbī, Ḥishām b. Muḥammad, *Kitāb al-Aṣnam*, ed.Aḥmad Zākī (Cairo: al-Dār al-Qawmiya l-il -Ṭibāᶜa al-Nashr, 1965).

Ibn al-Kalbī, Ḥishām b. Muḥammad, *Jamhara al-Nasab*, ed. Nājī Ḥasan (Beirut: Ālam al-Kutub, 1986).

Ibn al-Kalbī, Ḥishām b. Muḥammad, *Nasab Maᶜadd wa al-Yaman al-Kabīr*, 2 vols, ed. Nājī Ḥasan (Beirut: Ālam al-Kutub, 1988).

Ibn Khaldūn, ᶜAbd al-Raḥmān b. Muḥammad, *The Muqaddimah: An Introduction to History*, 3 vols, 2nd edn, trans. Franz Rosenthal (Princeton: Princeton University Press, 1967).

Ibn Khayyāṭ, Khalīfa, *Kitāb al-Ṭabaqāt*, ed. Akram Ḍiyāʾ al-ᶜUmarī (Baghdād: Maṭbaᶜa al-ᶜĀnī, 1967).

Ibn Khayyāṭ, Khalīfa, *Taʾrīkh* (Beirut: Dār al-Kutub al-ᶜIlmiiyya, 1995).

Ibn Manẓūr, *Lisān al-ᶜArab*, 10 vols, ed. ᶜAbd al-Munᶜim Khalīl Ibrāhīm (Beirut: Dār al-Kutub al-ᶜIlmiyya, 2005).

Ibn Qutayba, ᶜAbd Allāh b. Muslim, *Faḍl al-ᶜArab wa-al-Tanbīh ᶜalā ᶜUlūmihā*, ed. Walīd Muḥammad Khāliṣ (Abu Dhabi: al-Majmaᶜ al-Thaqāfī, 1998).

Ibn Qutayba, ᶜAbd Allāh b. Muslim, *al-Maᶜārif*, ed. Tharwat ᶜUkāsha (Cairo: Dār al -Maᶜārif, 1969).

Ibn Qutayba, ᶜAbd Allāh b. Muslim, *Al-Shiᶜr wa al-Shuᶜarāʾ* (Beirut: Dār al-Thaqāfa, 1969).

Ibn Qutayba, ᶜAbd Allāh b. Muslim, *ᶜUyūn al-Akhbār*, 4 vols (Cairo: al-Muʾassasa al-Miṣryya al-ᶜĀmma li'l-Taᶜlīf wa'l-Tarjama wa'l-Nashr, 1964).

Ibn Rusteh, Aḥmad b. ᶜUmar, *Kitāb al-Aᶜlāq al-Nafīsa*, ed. M. J. de Goeje (Leiden: Brill, 1892). Reprinted in 2014.

Ibn Saᶜd, Muḥammad, *al-Ṭabaqāt al-Kubrā*, ed. Riyādh ᶜAbdallāh ᶜAbd al-Hādī, 8 vols (Beirut: Dār Iḥyāᵓ al-Turāth al-ᶜArabī, 1996).

Ibn Shabba, ᶜUmar, *Kitāb Taᵓrīkh al-Madīna al-Munawwara*, 2 vols, ed. ᶜAlī Muḥammad Jandal and Yāsīn Saᶜd al-Dīn Bayān (Beirut: Dār al-Kutub al-ᶜIlmiya, 1996).

Ibn Sulayman, Muqātil, *Tafsīr*, 5 vols, ed. ᶜAbd Allah Maḥmūd Shiḥāta (Cairo: al-Ḥayaᵓ al-Miṣriyya al-Āmma lil-Kitāb, 1979–89).

al-Idrīsī, Abū ᶜAbd Allāh Muḥammad b. Muḥammad, *Kitāb Nuzha al-Mushtāq fī Ikhtirāq al-Āfāq*, 2 vols (Cairo: Maktabah al-Thaqāfah al-Dīnīyah, 1990).

al-Iṣfahānī, Abū al-Faraj [1345, 1394], *Kitāb al-Aghānī*, 24 vols (Cairo: Dār al-Kutub, 1927, 1974).

al-Iṣfahānī, Abū al-Faraj, *Maqātil al-Ṭālibīyīn*, ed. Aḥmad Ṣaqr (Beirut: Dār al-Maᶜrifa, 1978).

Jamme, Albert, *Sabaean Inscriptions from Maḥram Bilqīs (Mārib)* (Baltimore: The Johns Hopkins University Press, 1962).

Jamme, Albert, *The al-ᶜUqlah Texts (*Washington, DC: Catholic University of America Press, 1963).

al-Jumaḥī, Muḥammad b. Sallām [1394], *Ṭabaqāt Fuḥūl al-Shuᶜarāᵓ*, 2 vols, ed. Maḥmūd Muḥammad Shākir (Cairo: Maṭbaᶜat al-Madanī, 1974).

al-Khaṭīb al-Baghdādī, *Taᵓrīkh Baghdād*, ed. Muṣṭafā ᶜAbd al-Qādir ᶜAṭā, 14 vols (Beirut: Dār al-Kutub al-ᶜIlmiyya, 2004).

al-Kūfi, ᶜAlī b. Ḥāmid, *The Chachnamah: An Ancient History of Sind*, ed. and trans. Mirza Kalichbeg Fredunbeg (Delhi: Idarah-i Adabiyat-i Delli, 1900).

al-Kūfi, ᶜAlī b. Ḥāmid, *Fathnamah-i Sind*, ed. U. M. Daudpota (Hyderabad: Majlis Maktutat-e Farsia, 1939).

al-Lughawī, Abū al-Ṭayyib [1423], *Kitāb al-Marātib al-Naḥwīyīn*, ed. Muḥammad Zaynahum Muḥammad ᶜAzab (Cairo: Dār al-Āfāq al-ᶜArabiya, 2003).

al-Marzubānī, Abū ᶜUbayd Allāh Muḥammad b. ᶜImrān [1354], *Muᶜjām al-Shuᶜarāᵓ*, ed. F. Krenkow (Cairo: Maktabāt al-Qudsī, 1935).

al-Masᶜūdī, ᶜAlī b. al-Ḥusayn, *Murūj al-Dhahab*, 4 vols, ed. Mufīd Muḥammad Qumīḥa (Beirut: Dār al-Kutub al-ᶜIlmiya, 2012).

al-Mubarrad, Muḥammad b. Yazīd, *Al-Faḍl*, ed. ᶜAbd al-ᶜAzīz al-Maymanī (Cairo: Dār al-Kutub al-Miṣriyya, 1956).

al-Mubarrad, Muḥammad b. Yazīd, *Al-Kāmil*, 4 vols, ed. Muḥammad Dālī (Beirut: Muᵓassasa al-Risāla, 1986).

al-Mubarrad, Muḥammad b. Yazīd [1429], *Nasab ᶜAdnān wa-Qaḥṭān* (Damascus: Dār al-ᶜArabiyya, 2008).

al-Sahmī, Ḥamza b. Yūsuf, *Taᵓrīkh Jurjān*, ed. Yaḥyā Marād (Beirut: Dār al-Kutub al-ᶜIlmiyya, 2004).

al-Samᶜānī, ᶜAbd al-Karīm b. Muḥammad, *Al-Ansāb*, 6 vols, ed. Muḥammad ᶜAbd al-Qādir ᶜAṭā (Beirut: Dār al-Kutub al-ᶜIlmiyya, 1998).

al-Sijistānī, Abū Ḥātim, *Kitāb al-Muᶜammarīn*, ed. Mustafā ᶜAbd al-Qādir ᶜAṭā (Beirut: Muᶜassasa al -Maᶜārif, 1997).

al-Ṭabarī, Abū Jaᶜfar Muḥammad b. Jarīr, *Taʾrīkh al-Rusul wa al-Mulūk*, 15 vols, ed. M. J. De Goeje et al. (Leiden: Brill, 1879–1901).

al-Ṭabarī, Abū Jaᶜfar Muḥammad b. Jarīr, *The History of al-Ṭabarī*, 40 vols, ed. Ehsan Yarshater et al. (Albany, NY: SUNY Press, 1985–2007).

Anonymous, *Tārīkh-i Sīstān*, ed. Muḥammad Taqī Bahār (Tehran: Zavvār, 1935).

Anonymous, *Tārīkh-i Sīstān*, trans. Milton Gold (Rome: Istituto italiano per il Medio ed Estremo Oriente, 1976).

al-Thaᶜālibī, Abū Mansūr ᶜAbd al-Malik, *The Book of Curious and Entertaining Information*, trans. C. E. Bosworth (Edinburgh: Edinburgh University Press, 1968).

Wāᶜiẓ al-Balkhī, Abū Bakr ᶜAbd Allāh b. ᶜUmar [1350], *Faẓāʾil Balkh*, ed. ᶜAbd al-Hayy Ḥabībī (Tehran: Intishārāt-i Bunyād-i Farhang-i Īrān, 1971).

Wakīᶜ [1366–9], *Akhbār al-Qudat*, 3 vols, ed. ᶜA.-ᶜA. M. al-Maraghī (Cairo: Maṭbaᶜa al-Istiqāma, 1947–50).

al-Wāqidī, Muḥammad b. ᶜUmar, *Kitāb al-Maghāzī*, ed. Marsden Jones (London: Oxford University Press, 1966).

al-Wāqidī, Muḥammad b. ᶜUmar [1410], *Kitāb al-Ridda*, ed. Yaḥyā al-Jabūrī (Beirut: Dār al-Gharb al-Islāmī, 1990).

al-Wāqidī, Muḥammad b. ᶜUmar, *The Life of Muḥammad*, ed. Rizwi Faizer, trans. Rizwi Faizer, Amal Ismail and AbdulKader Tayob (London and New York: Routledge, 2011).

al-Yaᶜqūbī, Aḥmad b. Abī Yaᶜqūb, *Kitāb al-Buldān*, ed. M. J. de Goeje (Leiden: Brill, 1892). Reprinted in 2014.

al-Yaᶜqūbī, Aḥmad b. Abī Yaᶜqūb, *Taʾrīkh*, 2 vols (Beirut: Dār Ṣādr, n.d.)

Yāqūt, Abū ᶜAbd Allāh, *Muᶜjam al-Buldān*, 7 vols, ed. Farīd ᶜAbd al-ᶜAzīz al-Jundī (Beirut: Dār al -Kutub al-ᶜIlmiyya, n.d.)

Yāqūt, Abū ᶜAbd Allāh, *Muᶜjam al-Udabāʾ*, 6 vols (Beirut: Dār al-Kutub al-ᶜIlmiyya, 2012).

Zubaydī, Muḥammad b. al-Ḥasan, *Ṭabaqāt al-Naḥwīyīn wa al-Lughawīyīn* (Cairo: Dār al-Maᶜārif, 1973).

Secondary Sources

Abdullah, Thabit A. J., *Merchants, Mamluks, and Murder: The Political Economy of Trade in Eighteenth-Century Basra* (Albany, NY: SUNY Press, 2001).

al-Afghānī, Saᶜīd, *Aswāq al-ᶜArab fī al-Jahiliya wa al-Islām* [1379], 2nd ed. (Damascus: al-Maṭbaᶜa al-Hāshimiyya, 1960).

Agha, Saleh Said, 'The Arab Population in Ḫurāsān during the Umayyad Period: Some Demographic Computations', *Arabica* 46 (1999), pp. 211–29.

Agha, Saleh Said, *The Revolution which Toppled the Umayyads: Neither Arab nor Abbasid (*Leiden: Brill, 2003).

Agha, Saleh Said and Tarif Khalidi, 'Poetry and Identity in the Umayyad Age', *al-Abhath* 50–1 (2002–3), pp. 55–120.

Ahmed, Asad Q, *The Religious Elite of the Early Islamic Ḥijāz: Five Prosopographical Case Studies* (Oxford: Unit for Prosopographical Research, 2011).

Ahmed, Manan, 'The Many Histories of Muhammad b. Qasim: Narrating the Muslim Conquest of Sindh' (Ph.D. dissertation, University of Chicago, 2008).

Ahmed, Manan, 'The Long Thirteenth Century of the Chachnama', *The Indian Social and Economic History Review* 49 (2012), pp. 459–91.

ᶜAlī, Ṣāliḥ Aḥmad, *Khiṭaṭ al-Baṣra wa-Minṭaqihā: Dirāsa fī Aḥwālihā al-ᶜUmrānīya wa-Mālīya fī al -ᶜUhūd al-Islāmīya al-Ūla*, revised edition (Baghdad: al-Majmaᶜ al-ᶜIlmī al-ᶜIrāqī, 1986).

Alpass, Peter, *The Religious Life of Nabataea* (Leiden: Brill, 2013).

Alsayyad, Nezar, *Cities and Caliphs: On the Genesis of Arab Muslim Urbanism* (New York: Greenwood Press, 1991).

Amabe, Fukuzo, *The Emergence of the ᶜAbbāsid Autocracy: The ᶜAbbāsid Army, Khurāsān and Adharbayjān* (Kyoto: Kyoto University Press, 1995).

Amin, Kamaruddin, 'Nāṣiruddin al-Albanī on Muslim's Ṣaḥīḥ: A Critical Study of His Method', *Islamic Law and Society* 11 (2004), pp. 149–76.

Anthony, Sean, *Crucifixion and Death as Spectacle: Umayyad Crucifixion in its Late Antique Context* (New Haven: American Oriental Society, 2014).

Asadov, Farda, 'Jurjan in the External Relations and the History of the Khazar Khaqanate (7th–10th Centuries)', in István Zimonyi and Osman Karatay (eds), *Central Eurasia in the Middle Ages: Studies in Honor of Peter B. Golden* (Wiesbaden: Harrassowitz Verlag, 2016), pp. 23–38.

Asif, Manan Ahmed, *A Book of Conquest: The Chachnama and Muslim Origins in South Asia* (Cambridge, MA: Harvard University Press, 2016).

al-ᶜAskar, Abd Allah Ibrahim, 'Migrations of the Banu Hanifa to Other Islamic Regions During the Umayyad Period', in Fahd al-Semmari (ed.), *A History of the Arabian Peninsula*, trans. Salma K. Jayyusi (London: I. B. Tauris, 2010), pp. 1–40.

Assmann, Aleida, 'Canon and Archive', in Astrid Eriland Ansgar Nünning (eds), *A Companion to Cultural Memory Studies* (Berlin: De Gruyter, 2010), pp. 97–107.

Assmann, Jan, *Culture and Early Civilization: Writing, Remembrance, and Political Imagination* (Cambridge: Cambridge University Press, 2011).

al-Azmeh, Aziz, *Ibn Khaldūn: An Essay in Reinterpretation* (London: Frank Cass, 1982).

al-Azmeh, Aziz, *The Emergence of Islam in Late Antiquity: Allah and His People* (Cambridge: Cambridge University Press, 2014).

al-Azmeh, Aziz, *The Arabs and Islam in Late Antiquity: A Critique of Approaches to Arabic Sources* (Berlin: Gerlach Press, 2014).

Bāfaqīh, Muḥammad ᶜAbd al-Qādir, *L'Unification du Yemen Antique* (Paris: Librairie Orientaliste Paul Geuthner SA, 1990).

Barfield, Thomas, 'Tribe and State Relations: The Inner Asian Perspective', in

Philip S. Khoury and Joseph Kostiner (eds), *Tribes and State Formation in the Middle East* (Berkeley: University of California Press, 1990), pp. 153–82.

Barkey, Karen, *Empire of Difference: The Ottomans in Comparative Perspective* (Cambridge: Cambridge University Press, 2008).

Bashear, Suliman, *Arabs and Others in Early Islam* (Princeton: Darwin Press, 1997).

Bede, J. J., 'The Arabs in Sind, 712–1026 AD', (Ph.D. dissertation, University of Utah, 1973).

Beeston, A. F. L., *Warfare in Ancient South Arabia (2nd–3rd Centuries AD)* (London: Luzac and Co. Ltd, 1976).

Berkey, Jonathan, *The Formation of Islam: Religion and Society in the Near East, 600–1800* (Cambridge: Cambridge University Press, 2003).

Bernheimer, Teresa, 'The Revolt of ᶜAbdallāh b. Muᶜāwiya, AH 127–130: A Reconsideration Through the Coinage', *Bulletin of the School of Oriental and African Studies* 69 (2006): pp. 381–93.

Bin Seray, Hamad, 'The Arabian Gulf in Syriac Sources', *New Arabian Studies* 4 (1997), pp. 205–32.

Blankinship, Khalid Yahya, *The End of the Jihad State: The Reign of Hishām Ibn 'Abd al-Malik and the Collapse of the Umayyads* (Albany, NY: SUNY Press, 1994).

Blaum, Paul A., 'Life in a Rough Neighborhood: Byzantium, Islam, and the Rawwadid Kurds', *The International Journal of Kurdish Studies* 20 (2006), pp. 1–50.

Bonner, Michael, *Aristocratic Violence and Holy War: Studies in the Jihad and the Arab-Byzantine Frontier* (New Haven: American Oriental Society, 1996).

Bonner, Michael, '"Time Has Come Full Circle": Markets, Fairs and the Calendar in Arabia before Islam', in Asad Ahmed, Behnam Sadeghi, and Michael Bonner (eds), *The Islamic Scholarly Tradition: Studies in History, Law, and Thought in Honor of Professor Michael Allan Cook* (Leiden: Brill, 2011), pp. 13–48.

Bonner, Michael, 'Commerce and Migration in Arabia before Islam: A Brief History of a Long Literary Tradition', in B. Aghaei and M. R. Ghanoonparvar (eds), *Iranian Language and Culture* (Malibu and Costa Mesa: Mazda, 2012), pp. 65–89.

Borrut, Antoine, *Entre mémoire et pouvoir: L'espace syrien sous les derniers Omeyyades et les premiers Abbassides (v. 72–193/692–809)* (Leiden: Brill, 2011).

Bosworth, Clifford Edmund, *Sīstān Under the Arabs: From the Islamic Conquest to the Rise of the Saffarids (30–250/651–864)* (Rome: IsMEO, 1968).

Bosworth, C. E., 'Sistan and Its Local Histories', *Iranian Studies* 33 (2000), pp. 31–43.

Bukharin, M. D., 'Towards the Earliest History of Kinda', *Arabian Archaeology and Epigraphy* 20 (2009), pp. 64–80.

Bulliet, Richard, *The Patricians of Nishapur: A Study in Medieval Islamic Social History* (Cambridge, MA: Harvard University Press, 1972).

Bulliet, Richard, *Cotton, Climate, and Camels in Early Islamic Iran: A Moment in World History* (New York: Columbia University Press, 2009).

Burbank, Jane and Frederick Cooper, *Empires in World History: Power and the Politics of Difference* (Princeton and Oxford: Princeton University Press, 2010).

Carter, R. A., K. Challis, S. M. N. Priestman and H. Tofighian, 'The Bushehr Hinterland: Results of the First Season of the Iranian-British Archaeological Survey of Bushehr Province, November–December 2004', *Iran* 44 (2006), pp. 63–103.

Caskel, Werner, *Ğamharat an-Nasab. Das Genealogische Werk des Hišham ibn Muḥammad al-Kalbi*, tables by Gert Strenziok, 2 vols (Leiden: Brill, 1966).

Christensen, Peter, *The Decline of Iranshahr: Irrigation and Environments in the History of the Middle East 500 BC to AD 1500* (Copenhagen: Museum Tusculanum Press, 1993).

Cline, Eric and Mark Graham, *Ancient Empires: From Mesopotamia to the Rise of Islam* (Cambridge: Cambridge University Press, 2011).

Conrad, Lawrence I. 'Al-Azdī's History of the Arab Conquests in Bilād al-Shām: Some Historiographical Observations', in Muḥammad ᶜAdnān al-Bakhīt (ed.), *Proceedings of the Second Symposium on the History of Bilād al-Shām during the Early Islamic Period up to 40 AH/640 AD* I (Amman: Jordanian University, 1987), pp. 28–62.

Conrad, Lawrence I.,'The Conquest of Arwad: A Source-Critical Study in the Historiography of the Medieval Near East', in Lawrence I. Conrad and Averil Cameron (eds), *The Byzantine and Early Islamic Near East, I: Problems in the Literary Source Material* (Princeton: Darwin Press, 1992), pp. 317–401.

Conrad, Lawrence, 'Recovering Lost Texts: Some Methodological Issues', *Journal of the American Oriental Society 113* (1993), pp. 258–63.

Conrad, Lawrence I., 'Ibn Aᶜtham and His History', *Al-ᶜUsur al-Wusta* 23 (2015), pp. 87–125, http://islamichistorycommons.org/mem/al-usur-al-wusta-volume-23-2015 (accessed 16 September 2018).

Crone, Patricia, *Slaves on Horses: The Evolution of the Islamic Polity* (Cambridge: Cambridge University Press, 1980).

Crone, Patricia, 'The Tribe and the State', in John A. Hall (ed.), *States in History* (New York: Basil Blackwell, 1986), pp. 48–77.

Crone, Patricia, *Roman, Provincial and Islamic Law: The Origins of the Islamic Patronate* (Cambridge: Cambridge University Press, 1987).

Crone, Patricia, 'Were the Qays and Yemen of the Umayyad Period Political Parties?' *Der Islam* 71 (1994), pp. 1–57

Crone, Patricia, *Meccan Trade and the Rise of Islam* (Piscataway, NJ: Georgias Press, 2004). Originally published (Princeton: Princeton University Press, 1987).

Crone, Patricia, *God's Rule: Government and Islam* (New York: Columbia University Press, 2004).
Crone, Patricia, *The Nativist Prophets of Early Islamic Iran: Rural Revolt and Local Zoroastrianism* (Cambridge: Cambridge University Press, 2012).
Daniel, Elton, 'Manuscripts and Editions of Balᶜamī's Tarjamah-i Tārīkh-i Ṭabarī', *Journal of the Royal Asiatic Society* 2 (1990), pp. 163–89.
de Cardi, Beatrice, 'A Sasanian Outpost in Northern Oman', *Antiquity* 46 (1972), pp. 305–10.
de la Vaissière, Etienne, *Sogdian Traders: A History*, trans. James Ward (Leiden: Brill, 2005).
Dixon, ᶜAbd al-Ameer ᶜAbd, *The Umayyad Caliphate 65–86/684–705 (A Political* Study) (London: Luzac & Company, 1971).
Doe, D. B. and A. Jamme, 'New Sabaean Inscriptions from South Arabia', *Journal of the Royal Asiatic Society* (1968), pp. 2–28.
Donner, Fred, 'The Bakr b. Wā'il tribes and politics in northeastern Arabia on the eve of Islam', *Studia Islamica* 51 (1980), pp. 5–38.
Donner, Fred, *The Early Islamic Conquests* (Princeton: Princeton University Press, 1981).
Donner, Fred McGraw, 'Centralized Authority and Military Autonomy in the Early Islamic Conquests', in Averil Cameron (ed.), *The Byzantine and Early Islamic Near East III: States, Resources and Armies* (Princeton: Darwin Press, 1995), pp. 337–60.
Donner, Fred, *Narratives of Islamic Origins: The Beginnings of Islamic Historical Writing* (Princeton: Darwin Press, 1998).
Donner, Fred, *Muhammad and the Believers: At the Origins of Islam* (Cambridge and London: Belknap Press, 2010).
Drory, Rina, 'The Abbasid Construction of the Jahiliyya: Cultural Authority in the Making', *Studia Islamica* 83 (1996), pp. 33–49.
Duri, A. A., *The Rise of Historical Writing Among the Arabs*, trans. Lawrence I. Conrad (Princeton: Princeton University Press, 1983).
Eisener, Reinhard, *Zwischen Faktum und Fiktion: Eine Studie zum Umayyadenkalifen Sulaiman b. ᶜAbdalmalik und seinem Bild in den Quellen* (Wiesbaden: Otto Harrassowitz, 1987).
Elad, Amikam, 'The Rebellion of Muhammad b. Abd Allah b. al-Hasan (Known as an-Nafs az-Zakiya) in 142/762', in James E. Montgomery (ed.), *Abbasid Studies: Occasional Papers of the School of Abbasid Studies, Cambridge, 6–10 July 2002* (Leuven: Uitgeverij Peeters en Department Oosterse Studies, 2004).
Elad, Amikam, *The Rebellion of Muḥammad al-Nafs al-Zakiyya in 145/762: Ṭālibīs and Early ᶜAbbāsīs in Conflict* (Leiden: Brill 2016).
Elliot, Henry Miers and John Dowson, *The History of India as Told by Its Own Historians*, vol. 1, (London: Trübner and Co., 1867).
Fatimi, S. Qudratullah, 'The Twin Ports of Daybul: A Study in the Early Maritime History of Sind', in Hamida Khuhro (ed.), *Sind Through the Centuries* (Karachi: Oxford University Press, 1981), pp. 97–105.

Fentress, James and Chris Wickham, *Social Memory* (Oxford: Blackwell, 1992).

Finer, S. E., *The History of Government from the Earliest Times*, 3 vols (Oxford: Oxford University Press, 1997).

Fiorani Piacentini, Valeria, 'History and Historiography: The Court Genre in Arabic and the *Fatḥnāmah-i Sind'*, in Derek Kennet and Paul Luft (eds), *Current Research in Sasanian Archaeology, Art and History* (Oxford: Archaeopress, 2008), pp. 93–7.

Fisher, Greg, *Between Empires: Arabs, Romans, and Sasanians in Late Antiquity* (Oxford: Oxford University Press, 2011).

Fisher, W. B., 'Physical Geography', *Cambridge History of Iran*, vol. I, ed. W. B. Fisher (Cambridge: Cambridge University Press, 1978), pp. 1–110.

Forand, Paul G., 'The Governors of Mosul According to al-Azdī's *Taʾrīkh al-Mawṣil'*, Journal of the American Oriental Society 89 (1969), pp. 88–105.

Fowden, Garth, *Empire to Commonwealth: Consequences of Monotheism in Late Antiquity* (Princeton: Princeton University Press, 1993).

Franz, Kurt, 'Resources and Organizational Power: Some Thoughts on Nomadism in History', in Stefan Leder and Bernhard Streck (eds), *Shifts and Drifts in Nomad-Sedentary Relations* (Wiesbaden: Dr. Ludwig Reichert Verlag, 2005), pp. 55–77.

Friedman, Yohanon, 'The Origins and Significance of the Chach Nāma', in Yohanon Friedman (ed.), *Islam in Asia*, vol. 1 (Boulder, CO: Westview Press, 1984), pp. 23–37.

Gabrieli, Francesco, 'Muḥammad ibn Qāsim ath-Thaqāfī and the Arab Conquest of Sind', *East and West* 15 (1964–5), pp. 281–95.

Gaiser, Adam, 'What Do We Learn about the Early Khārijites and Ibāḍiyya from Their Coins?', *Journal of the American Oriental Society* 130 (2010), pp. 167 –87.

al-Ghāmidī, Khālid b. ʿAlī al-Marḍī, *Qabīla Ghāmid: Ansābhā wa-Tārīkhhā* (Cairo: Dār al-Muḥaddithīn, 2008).

Ghosh, Suchandra, 'The Western Coast of India and the Gulf: Maritime Trade during the 3rd to 7th Century AD', in Eric Olijdam and Richard H. Spoor (eds), *Intercultural Relations between South and Southwest Asia: Studies in Commemoration of E. C .L. During Caspers (1934–1996)* (Oxford: Archaeopress, 2008), pp. 367–71.

al-Ghunaym, ʿAbd Allāh Yūsuf, *al-Ashkāl Saṭḥ al-Arḍ fī Shibh al-Jazīra al-ʿArabīya fī al-Maṣādir al -ʿArabīya al-Qadīma* (Kuwait Ciy: Waḥdat al-Baḥth wa-al-Tarjama, 2005).

Gibb, H. A. R., *The Arab Conquests in Central Asia* (New York: AMS Press, 1970 reprint).

Goldziher, Ignac, *Muslim Studies*, vol. 1, ed. S. M. Stern, trans. C. R. Barber and S. M. Stern (London: Transaction Publishers, 2006).

Graf, David F. and Salem Tairan, 'Jurash, cité caravanière sur la route de l'encens', *L'Archéo Thema* 9 (2010), pp. 24–9.

Hanaoka, Mimi, *Authority and Identity in Medieval Islamic Historiography:*

Persian Histories from the Peripheries (Cambridge: Cambridge University Press, 2016).

Hawting, G. R., *The Idea of Idolatry and the Emergence of Islam: From Polemic to History* (Cambridge: Cambridge University Press, 1999).

Hawting, G. R., *The First Dynasty of Islam: The Umayyad Caliphate 661–750*, 2nd ed. (New York: Routledge, 2000).

al-Ḥarīrī, Muḥammad b. ᶜAlī b. Ḥusayn [1422], *Qabīla al-Azd min Fajr al-Islām ilā Qiyām al-Dawla al-Saᶜūdiya al-Awlā* (Abhā: Nādī Abhā al-Adabī, 2001).

Heath, Peter, 'Some Functions of Poetry in Premodern Historical and Psuedo-Historical Texts: Comparing *Ayyām al-ᶜArab*, al-Ṭabarī's *History*, and *Sīrat ᶜAntar*', in Ramzi Baalbaki, Saleh Said Agha and Tarif Khalidi (eds), *Poetry and History: The Value of Poetry in Reconstructing Arab History* (Beirut: American University of Beirut Press, 2011), pp. 39–59.

Heck, Gene, *The Precious Metals of Western Arabia and Their Role in Forging the Economic Dynamic of the Early Islamic State* (Riyadh: King Faisal Center for Research and Islamic Studies, 2003).

Hell, Joseph, 'Al-Farazdaḳ's Lieder auf die Muhallabiten', *Zeitschrift der Deutschen Morgenländischen Gesellschaft* 59 (1905), pp. 589–621.

Hell, Joseph, 'Al-Farazdaḳ's Lieder auf die Muhallabiten', *Zeitschrift der Deutschen Morgenländischen Gesellschaft* 60 (1906), pp. 1–48.

Hinds, Martin, 'The First Arab Conquests in Fars', *Iran 22* (1984), pp. 39–53.

Hopper, Kristen, 'Connectivity on a Sasanian Frontier: Route Systems in the Gorgan Plain of North-East Iran', in Eberhard W. Sauer (ed.), *Sasanian Persia: Between Rome and the Steps of Eurasia* (Edinburgh: Edinburgh University Press, 2017), pp. 126–50.

Hosein, Rasheed, 'Tribal Alliance Formations and Power Structures in the Jāhilīyah and Early Islamic Periods: Quraysh and Thaqīf (530–750 CE)' (Ph.D. dissertation, University of Chicago, 2010).

Hoyland, Robert, 'History, Fiction, and Authorship in the First Centuries of Islam', in Julia Bray (ed.), *Writing and Representation in Medieval Islam* (London: Routledge, 2006), pp. 16–46.

Hoyland, Robert, *Arabia and the Arabs: From the Bronze Age to the Coming of Islam* (Abingdon: Routledge, 2001).

Hoyland, Robert, *In God's Path: The Arab Conquests and the Creation of an Islamic Empire* (Oxford: Oxford University Press, 2015).

Hoyland, Robert G., 'Reflections on the Identity of the Arabian Conquerors of the Seventh-Century Middle East', *Al-ᶜUsur al-Wusta* 25 (2017), pp. 113–40, http://islamichistorycommons.org/mem/wp-content/uploads/sites/55/2017/11/UW-25-Hoyland.pdf (accessed 16 September 2018).

Jabali, Fu'ad, *The Companions of the Prophet: A Study of Geographical Distribution and Political Alignments* (Leiden: Brill, 2003).

Jones, Alan, *Early Arabic Poetry: Select Poems*, 2nd ed. (Reading: Ithaca Press, 2011).

Judd, Steven Clark, 'The Third Fitna: Orthodoxy, Heresy and Coercion in Late Umayyad History' (Ph.D. dissertation, University of Michigan, 1997).

Judd, Steven, 'Character Development in al-Tabari's and al-Baladhuri's Narratives of Late Umayyad History', in S. Gunther (ed.), *Insights into Arabic Literature and Islam: Ideas, Concepts and Methods of Portrayal* (Leiden: Brill, 2005), pp. 209–26.

Judd, Steven C., 'Medieval Explanations for the Fall of the Umayyads', in Antoine Borrut and Paul M. Cobb (eds), *Umayyad Legacies: Medieval Memories from Syria to Spain* (Leiden: Brill, 2010), pp. 89–104.

Keaney, Heather, *Medieval Islamic Historiography: Remembering Rebellion* (New York: Routledge, 2013).

Kennedy, Hugh, *The Early Abbasid Caliphate: A Political History* (London: Croon Helm, 1981).

Kennedy, Hugh, 'Central government and provincial elites in the early Abbasid caliphate', *Bulletin of the School of Oriental and African Studies* 44 (1981), pp. 26–38. Reprinted in *The Byzantine and Early Islamic Near East* (Burlington, VT: Ashgate, 2006), X.

Kennedy, Hugh, *Muhammad and the Age of the Caliphates* (London and New York: Longman, 1986).

Kennedy, Hugh, 'From Oral Tradition to Written Record in Arabic Genealogy', *Arabica* 44 (1997), pp. 531–44.

Kennedy, Hugh, *The Armies of the Caliphs: Military and Society in the Early Islamic State* (London: Routledge, 2001).

Kennedy, Hugh, 'Military pay and the economy of the early Islamic state', *Historical Research* 75 (2002), pp. 155–63. Reprinted in *The Byzantine and Early Islamic Near East* (Burlington, VT: Ashgate, 2006), XI.

Kennedy, Hugh, *The Great Arab Conquests: How the Spread of Islam Changed the World We Live In* (Philadelphia: Da Capo Press, 2007).

Kennet, Derek, 'Kush: A Sasanian and Islamic-Period Archaeological Tell in Ras al-Khaimah (U.A.E.)', *Arabian Archaeology and Epigraphy* 8 (1997), pp. 284–302.

Kennet, Derek, 'The Decline of Eastern Arabia in the Sasanian Period', *Arabian Archaeology and Epigraphy* 18 (2007), pp. 86–122.

Khalidi, Tarif, 'Tribal Settlement and Patterns of Land Tenure in Early Medieval Palestine', in Tarif Khalidi (ed.), *Land Tenure and Social Transformation in the Middle East*, ed. Tarif Khalidi (Beirut: American University of Beirut, 1984), pp. 181–8.

Khalidi, Tarif, *Arabic Historical Thought in the Classical Period* (Cambridge: Cambridge University Press, 1994).

Khan, F. A., *Banbhore: A Preliminary Report on the Recent Archaeological Excavations at Banbhore*, 2nd ed. (Karachi: Department of Archaeology and Museums, 1963).

Kilpatrick, Hilary, *Making the Great Book of Songs: Compilation and the*

Author's Craft in Abû l-Faraj al-Işbahânî's Kitâb al-aghânî (London and New York: RoutledgeCurzon, 2003).

Kister, M. J., 'Tamim in the Period of the Jahiliyya: A Study in Tribal Traditions' (Ph.D. dissertation, Hebrew University in Jerusalem, 1964).

Kister, M. J. and M. Plessner, 'Notes on Caskel's Ğamharat an-Nasab', *Oriens* 25/26 (1976), pp. 48–68.

Klein, Konstantin, 'The Silence of the Gods: Some Observations on the Destruction of Pagan Temples, Shrines, and Statues in the Late Antique East (from Constantine to Muḥammad)', in Kirill Dmitriev and Isabel Toral-Niehoff (eds), *Religious Culture in Late Antique Arabia: Selected Studies on the Late Antique Religious Mind* (Piscataway, NJ: Gorgias Press, 2017), pp. 11–87.

Lancaster, William and Fidelity Lancaster, 'Tribal formations in the Arabian Peninsula', *Arabian Archaeology and Epigraphy* 3 (1992), pp. 145–72.

Lancaster, William, *The Rwala Bedouin Today*, 2nd ed. (Prospect Heights, IL: Waveland, 1997).

Lancaster, William and Fidelity Lancaster, 'Concepts of Leadership in Bedouin Society', in John Haldon and Lawrence I. Conrad (eds), *The Byzantine and Early Islamic Near East VI: Elites Old and New in the Byzantine and Early Islamic Near East* (Princeton: Darwin Press, 2004), pp. 29–61.

Landau-Tasseron, Ella, 'Asad from Jahiliyya to Islam', *Jerusalem Studies in Arabic and Islam* 6 (1985), pp. 1–28.

Landau-Tasseron, Ella, 'On the Reconstruction of Lost Sources', *al-Qantara* 25 (2004), pp. 45–91.

Landau-Tasseron, Ella, 'Alliances Among the Arabs', *al-Qantara* 26 (2005), pp. 141–73

Landau-Tasseron, Ella, 'Status of Allies in Pre-Islamic and Early Islamic Arabian Society', *Islamic Law and Society* 13 (2006), pp. 6–32.

Lapidus, Ira, 'Arab Settlement and Economic Development of Iran and Iraq in the Age of the Umayyad and Early Abbasid Caliphs', in A. L. Udovitch, *The Islamic Middle East, 700–1900: Studies in Economic and Social History* (Princeton: Darwin Press, 1981) pp. 177–208.

Lassner, Jacob, *The Middle East Remembered: Forged Identities, Competing Narratives, Contested Spaces* (Ann Arbor: The University of Michigan Press, 2000).

Lecker, Michael, *The Banu Sulaym: A Contribution to the Study of Early Islam* (Jerusalem: Hebrew University of Jerusalem, 1989).

Lecker, Michael, 'Judaism among Kinda and the *Ridda* of Kinda', *Journal of the American Oriental Society* 115 (1995), pp. 635–50.

Lecker, Michael, 'Tribes in Pre- and Early Islamic Arabia', *People, Tribes and Society in Arabia Around the Time of Muhammad* (Burlington, VT: Ashgate, 2005), XI.

Lecker, Michael, 'Was Arabian Idol Worship Declining on the Eve of Islam?', in *People, Tribes and Society in Arabia Around the Time of Muḥammad* (Burlington, VT: Ashgate, 2005), III.

Leder, Stefan, *Das Korpus al-Haiṯam ibn ᶜAdī* (Frankfurt: Vittorio Klostermann, 1991).

Leder, Stefan, 'Nomadic and Sedentary Peoples – A Misleading Dichotomy? The Bedouin and Bedouinism in the Arab Past', in Stefan Leder and Bernhard Streck (eds), *Shifts and Drifts in Nomad-Sedentary Relations* (Wiesbaden: Dr. Ludwig Reichert Verlag, 2005), pp. 401–16.

Leube, Georg, *Kinda in der frühislamischen Geschichte: Eine prosopographische Studie auf Basis der frühen und klassischen arabisch-islamischen Geschichtsschreibung* (Würzburg: Ergon Verlag, 2017).

Le Strange, Guy, *Lands of the Eastern Caliphate: Mesopotamia, Persia, and Central Asia from the Moslem Conquest to the Time of the Timur* (New York: AMS Press, 1976).

Lindstedt, Ilkka, 'The Life and Deeds of ᶜAlī b. Muḥammad al-Madāʾinī', *Zeitschrift für Geschichte der Arabisch-Islamischen Wissenschaft* 20–21 (2012–14), pp. 235–70.

Lindstedt, Ilkka, 'Sources for the Biography of the Historian Ibn Aᶜtham al-Kūfī', in Jaakko Hämeen-Antilla, Petteri Koskikallio and Ilkka Lindstedt (eds), *Contacts and Interaction: Proceedings of the 27th Congress of the Union Européenne des Arabisants et Islamisants* (Leuven: Peeters, 2016), pp. 299–309.

Mabra, Joshua, *Princely Authority in the Early Marwānid State: The Life of ᶜAbd al-Azīz ibn Marwān* (Piscataway, NJ: Gorgias Press, 2017).

MacLean, Derryl N., *Religion and Society in Arab Sind* (Leiden: Brill, 1989).

Madelung, Wilferd, ''Abd Allah b. al-Zubayr and the Mahdi', *Journal of Near Eastern Studies* 40 (1981), pp. 291–305.

Madelung, Wilferd, 'Abu Ubayda Ma'mar b. al-Muthanna as a Historian', *Journal of Islamic Studies* 3:1 (1992), pp. 47–56.

Madelung, Wilferd, 'The Minor Dynasties of Northern Iran', in R. N. Frye (ed.), *The Cambridge History of Iran*, vol. IV (Cambridge: Cambridge University Press, 1995), pp. 198–249.

Madelung, Wilferd, *The Succession to Muhammad: A Study of the Early Caliphate* (Cambridge: Cambridge University Press, 1997).

Madelung, Wilferd, 'Rabi'a in the Jahiliyya and in Early Islam', *Jerusalem Studies in Arabic and Islam* 8 (2003), pp. 153–70.

Marsham, Andrew, *Rituals of Islamic Monarchy: Accession and Succession in the First Muslim Empire* (Edinburgh: Edinburgh University Press, 2009).

Massignon, Louis, 'Explication du Plan de Basra (Irak)', in Massignon, *Opera Minora III* (Beirut: Dar al-Maaref, 1963).

May, Timothy, *The Mongol Art of War* (Yardley, PA: Westholme, 2007).

McCorriston, Joy, *Pilgrimage and Household in the Ancient Near East* (Cambridge: Cambridge University Press, 2011).

Meeker, Michael, 'Meaning and Society in the Near East: Examples from the Black Sea Turks and the Levantine Arabs (I)', *International Journal of Middle East Studies* 7 (1976), pp. 243–70.

Meisami, Julie Scott, 'The Past in Service of the Present: Two Views of History in Medieval Persia', *Poetics Today* 14 (1993), pp. 247–75.
Meisami, Julie Scott, *Persian Historiography to the End of the Twelfth Century* (Edinburgh: Edinburgh University Press, 1999).
Mirchandani, B. D., 'Chach-Nāma: References to Persia, Zabul, Kashmir and Kanauj', *Journal of Indian History* 43 (1965), pp. 369–85.
Morgan, David, *The Mongols* (Cambridge: Blackwell, 1986).
Morony, Michael, *Iraq after the Muslim Conquest* (Princeton: Princeton University Press, 1984).
Mourad, Suleiman, 'On Early Islamic Historiography: Abū Ismāᶜīl al-Azdī and his Futūḥ al-Shām', *Journal of the American Oriental Society* 120 (2000), pp. 577–93.
Mourad, Suleiman Ali, *Early Islam between Myth and History: Al-Hasan al-Basri (D. 110H/728CE) and the Formation of His Legacy in Classical Islamic Scholarship* (Leiden: Brill, 2006).
Mouton, Michael and Jérémie Schiettecatte, *In the Desert Margins: The Settlement Process in Ancient South and East Arabia* (Rome: L'Erma di Bretschneider, 2014).
Muᶜabbir, Muḥammad Aḥmad, *Madīna Jurash: min al-Marākiz al-Ḥaḍārīya al-Qadīma* (Khamīs Mushayṭ, Saudi Arabia: Dār Jurash, 1988).
Müller, Walter, 'Eine Sabaische Gesandtschaft in Ktesiphon und Seleucia', *Neue Ephemeris für Semitische Epigraphik* 2 (1974), pp. 155–65.
Munt, Harry, *The Holy City of Medina: Sacred Space in Early Islamic Arabia* (Cambridge: Cambridge University Press, 2014).
Munt, Harry, with contributions from Touraj Daryaee, Omar Edaibat, Robert Hoyland, and Isabel Toral-Niehoff, 'Arabic and Persian Sources for Pre-Islamic Arabia', in Greg Fisher (ed.), *Arabs and Empires before Islam* (Oxford: Oxford University Press, 2015), pp. 434–500.
Munt, Harry, 'Oman and Late Sasanian Imperialism', *Arabian Archaeology and Epigraphy* 28 (2017), pp. 264–84.
Naji, A. T. and S. Y. Ali, 'The Suqs of Basra: Commerical Organization and Activity in a Medieval Islamic City', *Journal of the Economic and Social History of the Orient* 24 (1981), pp. 298–309.
Nerazik, E. E. and P. G. Bulgakov, 'Khwarizm', in B. A. Litvinsky, Zhang Guang-da and R. Shabani Samghabadi (eds), *History of Civilizations of Central Asia, Volume III: The Crossroads of Civilizations:* AD *250–750* (Paris: UNESCO Publishing, 1996), pp. 207–31.
Nora, Pierre, 'Between Memory and History: Les Lieux de Mémoire', trans. Marc Roudebush *Representations* 26 (1989), pp. 7–24.
Northedge, Alastair, 'Archaeology and New Urban Settlement in Early Islamic Syria and Iraq', in G. R. D. King and Averil Cameron, *The Byzantine and Early Islamic Near East II: Land Use and Settlement Patterns* (Princeton: Darwin Press, 1994), pp. 231–65.
Noth, Albrecht, *The Early Arabic Historical Tradition: A Source-Critical Study,*

2nd ed. in collaboration with Lawrence I. Conrad (Princeton: Darwin Press, 1994).

Olinder, Gunnar, *The Kings of Kinda of the Family of Ākil al-murār* (Lund: C. W. K. Gleerup: 1927).

Olinder, Gunnar, 'Āl al-Ǧaun of the Family of Ākil al-murār', *Le Monde Oriental* 25 (1931), pp. 208–29.

Orthmann, Eva, 'Als Yaman und Rabīᶜa ihre Stirnlocken abschnitten. Kritische Anmerkungen zu einem Ḥilf-Bund in Ḫurāsān aus der späten Umaiyadenzeit', *Halleschen Beiträge zur Orientwissenschaft* 25 (1998), pp. 152–71.

Orthmann, Eva, *Stamm und Macht: Die arabischen Stämme im 2. und 3. Jahrhundert der Hiğra* (Wiesbaden: Reichert, 2002).

Parsons, Timothy, *The Rule of Empires: Those Who Built Them, Those Who Endured Them, and Why They Always Fall* (Oxford: Oxford University Press, 2010).

Peacock, A. C. S., *Mediaeval Islamic Historiography and Political Legitimacy: Balᶜamī's Tārīkhnāma* (London and New York: Routledge, 2007).

Pellat, Charles, *Le Milieu Baṣrien et la Formation de Ǧāhiẓ* (Paris: Adrien-Maisonneuve, 1953).

Potts, D. T., *The Arabian Gulf in Antiquity*, 2 vols (Oxford: Clarendon Press, 1990).

Potts, D. T., 'Contributions to the Agrarian History of Eastern Arabia I. Implements and Cultivation Techniques', *Arabian Archaeology and Epigraphy* 5 (1994), pp. 158–68.

Pourshariati, Parvaneh, 'Iranian Tradition in Tus and the Arab Presence in Khurasan', (Ph.D. dissertation, Columbia University, 1995).

Pourshariati, Parvaneh, *Decline and Fall of the Sasanian Empire: The Sasanian-Parthian Confederacy and the Arab Conquest of Iran* (London and New York: I. B. Tauris, 2008).

Power, Timothy, *The Red Sea from Byzantium to the Caliphate:* AD *500–1000* (Cairo: American University in Cairo Press, 2012).

Puin, Gerd-Rüdiger, *Der Dīwān von ᶜUmar Ibn al-Ḫaṭṭāb: Ein Beitrag zur frühislamischen Verwaltungsgeschichte* (Bonn: Königsberg, 1970).

al-Rasheed, Madawi, *Politics in an Arabian Oasis: The Rashidis of Saudi Arabia* (London: I. B. Tauris, 1991).

al-Rawas, Isam, *Oman in Early Islamic History* (Reading: Ithaca Press, 2000).

Retsö, Jan, *The Arabs in Antiquity: Their History from the Assyrians to the Umayyads* (New York: Routledge, 2003).

Rezakhani, Khodadad, *ReOrienting the Sasanians: East Iran in Late Antiquity* (Edinburgh: Edinburgh University Press, 2017).

Rihan, Mohammad, *The Politics and Culture of an Umayyad Tribe: Conflict and Factionalism in the Early Islamic Period* (London and New York: I. B. Tauris, 2014).

Robertson Smith, W., *Kinship and Marriage in Early Arabia* (Cambridge: Cambridge University Press, 1885).

Robin, Christian, 'Du Nouveau sur les Yaz'anides', *Proceedings of the Seminar for Arabian Studies* 16 (1986), pp. 181–97.

Robin, Christian Julien, 'Matériaux pour une prosographie de l'Arabie antique: les noblesses sabéenne et ḥimyarite avant et après l'Islam', in Christian Julien Robin and Jérémie Schiettecatte (eds), *Les préludes de l'Islam: Ruptures et continuités dans les civilisations du Proche-Orient, de l'Afrique orientale, de l'Arabie et de l'Inde à la veille de l'Islam* (Paris: De Boccard, 2013).

Robin, Christian Julien, 'Ghassan en Arabie', in Denis Genequand and Christian Julien Robin (eds), *Les Jafnides. Des rois arabes au service de Byzance (VIe siècle de l'ère chrétienne)* (Paris: De Boccard, 2015).

Robin, Christian Julien and Iwona Gajda, 'L'Inscription du Wadi ᶜAbadan', *Raydān* 6 (1994), pp. 113–37.

Robinson, Chase, 'The Early Islamic History of Mosul' (Ph.D. dissertation, Harvard University, 1992).

Robinson, Chase, *Empire and Elites after the Muslim Conquest* (Cambridge: Cambridge University Press, 2000).

Robinson, Chase, 'The Conquest of Khūzistān: A Historiographical Reassessment', *Bulletin of the School of Oriental and African Studies* 67 (2004), pp. 14–39.

Robinson, Majied, 'Prosopographical Approaches to the Nasab Tradition: A Study of Marriage and Concubinage in the Tribe of Muhammad (500–750 CE)' (Ph.D. dissertation, University of Edinburgh, 2013).

Rothstein, Gustav, *Die Dynastie der Laḫmiden in al-Ḥira: Ein Versuch zur arabisch-persischen Geschichte zur Zeit der Sasaniden* (Berlin: Reuther and Reichard, 1899).

Rotter, Gernot, 'Zur Überlieferung einiger historischer Werke Madāᵓinī's in Ṭabarī's Annalen', *Oriens* 23–4 (1974), pp. 103–133.

Rotter, Gernot, *Der Umayyaden und der Zweite Bürgerkrieg (680–692)* (Wiesbaden: F. Steiner Verlag, 1982).

Sallām, Ḥūriya ᶜAbduh, *Iqlīm al-Mawṣil fī al-Aṣr al-Umawī: Dirāsa Ḥaḍārīya* (Cairo: Dār al-Ālam al -ᶜArabī, 2008).

Sauer, Eberhard, H. Omrani Rekavandi, T. J. Wilkinson and J. Nokandeh, *Persia's Imperial Power in Late Antiquity: The Great Wall of Gorgān and Frontier Landscapes of Sasanian Iran* (Oxford: Oxbow Books, 2013).

Savage, Elizabeth, *A Gateway to Hell, A Gateway to Paradise: The North African Response to the Arab Conquest* (Princeton: Darwin Press, 1997).

Savant, Sarah Bowen, *The New Muslims of Post-Conquest Iran: Tradition, Memory, and Conversion* (Cambridge: Cambridge University Press, 2013).

Savant, Sarah Bowen, 'Genealogy and Ethnogenesis in al-Masᶜudi's *Muruj al-dhahab'*, in Sarah Bowen Savant and Helena de Felipe (eds), *Genealogy and Knowledge in Muslim Societies: Understanding the Past* (Edinburgh: Edinburgh University Press, 2014) pp. 115–30.

Savant, Sarah Bowen, 'Naming Shᶜūbīs', in A. Korangy, W. M. Thackston, R. Mottahedeh and W. Granara (eds), *Essays in Islamic Philology, History, and Philosophy: A Festschrift in Celebration and Honor of Professor*

Ahmad Mahdavi Damghani's 90th Birthday (Berlin: DeGruyter, 2016), pp. 166–84.

Savran, Scott, *Arabs and Iranians in the Islamic Conquest Narrative: Memory and Identity Construction in Islamic Historiography, 750–1050* (New York: Routledge, 2018).

Scheiner, Jens J., 'Grundlegendes zu al-Azdīs Futūḥ aš-Šām', *Der Islam* 84 (2007), pp. 1–16.

Schiettecatte, Jérémie and Mounir Arbach, 'The Political Map of Arabia and the Middle East in the third century AD revealed by a Sabaean inscription', *Arabian Archaeology and Epigraphy* 27 (2016), pp. 176–96.

Schoeler, Gregor, *The Oral and the Written in Early Islam*, ed. James Montgomery, trans Uwe Vagelpohl (London and New York: Routledge, 2006).

Sears, Stuart D., 'A Monetary History of Iraq and Iran, ca CE 500–750' (Ph.D. dissertation, University of Chicago, 1997).

Sezgin, Fuat, *Geschichte des Arabischen Schrifttums*, 16 vols (Leiden: Brill, 1967–2015).

Sezgin, Ursula, *Abū Miḫnaf: ein Beitrag zur Historiographie der umaiyadischen Zeit* (Leiden: Brill 1971).

Shaban, M. A., *The Abbasid Revolution* (Cambridge: Cambridge University Press, 1970).

Shaban, M. A., *Islamic History AD 600–750 (AH 132): A New Interpretation* (Cambridge: Cambridge University Press, 1971).

Shahid, Irfan, *Byzantium and the Arabs in the Fifth Century* (Washington, DC: Dumbarton Oaks, 1989).

Sharon, Moshe, *Revolt: The Social and Military Aspects of the ᶜAbbāsid Revolution* (Jerusalem: The Max Schloessinger Memorial Fund, 1990).

Shoshan, Boaz, *The Arabic Historical Tradition and the Early Islamic Conquests* (London and New York: Routledge, 2016).

Shoufani, Elias, *Al-Riddah and the Muslim Conquest of Arabia* (Toronto: University of Toronto Press, 1973).

Shryock, Andrew, *Nationalism and the Genealogical Imagination: Oral History and Textual Authority in Tribal Jordan* (Berkeley: University of California Press, 1997).

Sijpesteijn, Petra M., *Shaping a Muslim State: The World of a Mid-Eighth-Century Egyptian Official* (Oxford: Oxford University Press, 2013).

Silverstein, Adam, *Postal Systems in the Pre-Modern Islamic World* (Cambridge: Cambridge University Press, 2007).

Smith, Sidney, 'Events in Arabia in the 6th Century AD', *Bulletin of the School of Oriental and African Studies* 16 (1954), pp. 425–68.

Sneath, David, *The Headless State: Aristocratic Orders, Kinship Society and Misrepresentations of Nomadic Inner Asia* (New York: Columbia University Press, 2007).

Springberg-Hinsen, Monika, *Die Zeit vor der Islam in arabischen*

Universalgeschichten des 9. bis 12. Jahrhunderts (Würzburg: Echter; Altenberge: Telos-Verlag, 1989).

Stetkevich, Suzanne Pinckney, 'Archetype and Attribution in Early Arabic Poetry: al-Shanfarā and the Lāmiyyat al-ᶜArab', *International Journal of Middle East Studies* 18 (1986), pp. 361–90.

Stone, Lawrence, 'Prosopography', in Felix Gilbert and Stephen R. Graubard (eds), *Historical Studies Today* (New York: W. W. Norton & Company, 1972), pp. 107–40.

Szombathy, Zoltan, *The Roots of Arabic Genealogy: A Study in Historical Anthropology* (Budapest: The Avicenna Institute of Middle East Studies, 2003).

Szombathy, Zoltan, 'Fieldwork and Preconceptions: The Role of the Bedouin as Informants in Mediaeval Muslims Scholarly Culture (Second–Third/Eighth–Ninth Centuries)', *Der Islam* 92 (2015), pp. 124–47.

Talmon, Rafael, *Arabic Grammar in Its Formative Age: Kitāb al-ᶜAyn and Its Attribution to Ḫalīl b. Aḥmad* (Leiden: Brill, 1997).

Tapper, Richard, 'Anthropologists, Historians, and Tribespeople on Tribe and State Formation in the Middle East', in Philip S. Khoury and Joseph Kostiner (eds), *Tribes and State Formation in the Middle East* (Berkeley: University of California Press, 1990), pp. 48–73.

Tapper, Richard, *Frontier Nomads of Iran: A Political and Social History of the Shahsevan* (Cambridge: Cambridge University Press, 1997).

Togan, İsenbike, 'The Use of Sociopolitical Terminology for Nomads: An Excursion into the Term *Buluo* in Tang China', in Reuven Amitai and Michal Biran (eds), *Nomads as Agents of Cultural Change: The Mongols and Their Eurasian Predecessors* (Honolulu: University of Hawai'i Press, 2015), pp. 88–117.

Toral-Niehoff, Isabel, *Al-Ḥīra: Eine Arabische Kulturmetropole Im Spätantiken Kontext* (Leiden: Brill, 2014).

Toral-Niehoff, Isabel, 'Talking about Arab Origins: The Transmission of the *ayyām al-ᶜarab* in al-Kūfa, al-Baṣra and Baghdād', in Jens Scheiner and Damien Janos (eds), *The Place to Go: Contexts of Learning in Baghdād, 750–1000* CE (Princeton: Darwin Press, 2014), pp. 47–75.

Toral-Niehoff, Isabel, 'Nebukadnezar, Maᶜadd und seine Verwandten. Ein arabischer Migrationsmythos im Kontext biblischer Legenden', in Almut-Barbara Renger and Isabel Toral-Niehoff (eds), *Genealogie und Migrationsmythen im antiken Mittelmeerraum und auf der Arabischen Halbinsel* (Berlin: Edition Topoi, 2014), pp. 201–30.

Ulrich, Brian, 'The Azd Migrations Reconsidered: Narratives of ᶜAmr Muzayqiya and Mālik b. Fahm in Historiographic Context', *Proceedings of the Seminar for Arabian Studies* 38 (2008), pp. 311–18.

Ulrich, Brian, 'Oman and Bahrain in Late Antiquity: The Sasanians' Arabian Periphery', *Proceedings of the Seminar for Arabian Studies* 41 (2011), pp. 377–86.

Urban, Elizabeth, 'The Early Islamic *Mawālī*: A Window onto Processes of

Identity Construction and Social Change' (Ph.D. Dissertation, University of Chicago, 2012).

Vansina, Jan, *Oral Tradition as History* (Madison: University of Wisconsin Press, 1985).

von Wissmann, Hermann, *Zur Geschichte und Landeskunde von Alt-Südarabien* (Vienna: Hermann Böhlaus Nachf., 1964).

Weir, Shelagh, *A Tribal Order: Politics and Law in the Mountains of Yemen* (Austin: University of Texas Press, 2007).

Watson, Andrew, *Agricultural Innovation in the Early Islamic World* (Cambridge: Cambridge University Press, 1983).

Webb, Peter, 'Al-Jāhiliyya: Uncertain Times of Uncertain Meanings', *Der Islam* 91 (2014), pp. 69–94.

Webb, Peter, *Imagining the Arabs: Arab Identity and the Rise of Islam* (Edinburgh: Edinburgh University Press, 2016).

Webb, Peter, 'Yemeni Identity in Abbasid Iraq: From the Sublime to the Ridiculous', in Walter Pohl (ed.), *Empires and Communities in the Post-Roman and Islamic World* (Oxford: Oxford University Press, forthcoming)

Wellhausen, Julius, *The Arab Kingdom and Its Fall*, trans. Margaret Graham Weir (Calcutta: University of Calcutta, 1927).

Wheatley, Paul, *The Places Where Men Pray Together: Cities in Islamic Lands Seventh Through the Tenth Centuries* (Chicago: University of Chicago Press, 2001).

Whitcomb, Donald, 'Bushire and the Angali Canal', *Mesopotamia* 22 (1987), pp. 311–36.

White, Hayden, *The Content of the Form: Narrative Discourse and Historical Representation* (Baltimore and London: The Johns Hopkins University Press, 1987).

Wickham, Chris, 'Tributary Empires: Late Rome and the Arab Caliphate', in Peter Fibiger Bang and C. A. Bayly (eds), *Tributary Empires in Global History* (Basingstoke and New York: Palgrave Macmillan, 2011), pp. 205–13.

Wilkinson, J. C., 'Arab-Persian Land Relationships in Late Sasānid Oman', *Proceedings of the Seminar for Arabian Studies* 3 (1973), pp. 40–51.

Wilkinson, J. C., 'The Julanda of Oman', *Journal of Oman Studies* 1 (1975) pp. 97–108.

Wilkinson, J. C., *Water and Tribal Settlement in South-East Arabia: A Study of the Aflāj of Oman* (Oxford: Clarendon Press, 1977).

Wilkinson, J. C., 'The Early Development of the Ibadi Movement in Basra', in G. H. A. Juynboll (ed.), *Studies on the First Centuries of Islamic Society* (Carbondale: Southern Illinois University Press, 1982), pp. 125–44.

Wilkinson, John C., *The Imamate Tradition of Oman* (Cambridge: Cambridge University Press, 1987).

Wilkinson, John C., *Ibâḍism: Origins and Early Development in Oman* (Oxford: Oxford University Press, 2010).

Wink, Andre, *al-Hind: The Making of the Indo-Islamic World*, vol. 1 (Leiden: Brill, 1990).
Wood, Philip, 'Al-Ḥīra and Its Histories', *Journal of the American Oriental Society* 136 (2016), pp. 785–99.
Yule, Paul, 'The Samad Period in the Sultanate of Oman', *Iraq* 61 (1999), pp. 121–46.
Yusuf, S., 'Al-Muhallab-B.-Abī-Ṣufra: His Strategy and Qualities of Generalship', *Islamic Culture* 17 (1943), pp. 1–14.
Yusuf, S., 'Al-Muhallab and the Poets', *Islamic Culture* 24 (1950), pp. 197–9.
Zolondek, Leon, *Diᶜbil b. ᶜAlī: The Life and Writings of an Early ᶜAbbāsid Poet* (Lexington, KY: University of Kentucky Press, 1961).

Index

ᶜAbadān, 28
Abān Canal, 143
ᶜAbbād b. Ayyūb, 140
ᶜAbbād b. Ḥuṣayn al-Ḥabaṭī, 85
ᶜAbbād b. Ziyād, 173
al-ᶜAbbās b. Sulaym al-Sulaymī, 198
Abbasid, 4, 8, 82, 87, 106n, 147, 154, 155, 180, 199, 204, 207, 208, 210
  period, 2, 10, 11, 13, 16–17, 21n, 24, 25, 33, 68, 72, 116, 119, 147, 154, 156, 160n, 176, 180, 183, 194, 197, 199, 205, 210, 215, 218
  rise to power, 116, 119, 135, 152–4, 158n, 181, 183, 191n, 199–200
  see also individual members of the dynasty
ᶜAbd al-ᶜAzīz b. ᶜAbd Allāh, 126–7
ᶜAbd al-ᶜAzīz b. al-Walīd, 139
ᶜAbd al-ᶜAzīz b. Muᶜāwiya, 201
ᶜAbd al-Ghāfir b. Masᶜūd al-Maᶜnī, 92
ᶜAbd al-Jabbār b. Yazīd b. al-Rabᶜa al-Kalbī, 138
ᶜAbd al-Kabīr b. al-Muᶜāfa, 208
ᶜAbd al-Muṭṭalib, 89
ᶜAbd al-Qays, 15, 33, 75–6, 80, 90, 94, 98, 147, 182
ᶜAbd al-Malik (caliph), 78, 126–9, 133, 136–7, 140, 170, 174, 176
ᶜAbd al-Malik b. ᶜAbd Allāh b. Āmir, 95
ᶜAbd al-Malik b. al-Muhallab, 134, 137–8, 140, 144–6, 148, 163n
ᶜAbd al-Malik b. Ḥarmala al-Yaḥmadī, 185
ᶜAbd al-Raḥmān b. ᶜAbbās al-Hāshimī, 133, 135
ᶜAbd al-Raḥmān b. Jawshan, 88
ᶜAbd al-Raḥmān b. Mikhnaf al-Azdī, 102, 103, 115n, 127–8, 210
ᶜAbd al-Raḥmān b. Nuᶜaym al-Ghāmidī, 146, 185
ᶜAbd al-Raḥmān b. Samura al-Qurashī, 118, 121, 169
ᶜAbd al-Raḥmān b. Subḥ al-Kharaqī, 186
ᶜAbd al-Raḥmān b. Sulaym al-Kalbī, 146
ᶜAbd al-Raḥmān b. Ṭalḥa, 133–4
ᶜAbd al-Raḥmān b. Yazīd al-Ḥuddānī, 83
ᶜAbd al-Raḥmān b. Yazīd b. al-Muhallab, 153, 199
ᶜAbd al-Raḥmān b. ᶜAwf al-Ghāmidī, 39
ᶜAbd al-ᶜUzzā b. Ṣuhal al-Ghāmidī, 38–9
ᶜAbd al-Wāhid b. Abī Awn al-Dawsī, 43
ᶜAbd Allāh b. ᶜAbd al-ᶜAzīz al-ᶜIlāfī, 175
ᶜAbd Allāh b. Abī Bakr al-Anṣārī, 47
ᶜAbd Allāh b. ᶜAfīf al-Azdī, 103
ᶜAbd Allāh b. al-ᶜAbbās, 82, 118
ᶜAbd Allāh b. al-Ahtam, 140–1
ᶜAbd Allāh b. al-Ḥārith *see* Babba
ᶜAbd Allāh b. al-Ḥārith b. Sakhbara al-Azdī, 46
ᶜAbd Allāh b. al-Muᶜammar al-Yashkurī, 178
ᶜAbd Allāh b. ᶜAlī, 200
ᶜAbd Allāh b. Āmir, 185
ᶜAbd Allāh b. ᶜAmr b. Zuhayr al-Kaᶜbī, 47
ᶜAbd Allāh b. ᶜAwf b. al-Aḥmar al-Azdī, 122
ᶜAbd Allāh b. Aws al-Ṭāḥī, 85
ᶜAbd Allāh b. Bisṭām al-Maᶜnī, 184
ᶜAbd Allāh b. Faḍāla al-Laythī, 84
ᶜAbd Allāh b. Faḍāla al-Zahrānī, 114n
ᶜAbd Allāh b. Ḥawdhān al-Jahḍamī, 184

Qabīṣa b. Abī Ṣufra, 155
Qabīṣa b. al-Muhallab, 155
Qādis, 84
al-Qādisiyya, 39, 74, 75, 100, 108n
Qaḍiyya, pilgrimage, 45
Qaḥṭān, 1, 32, 203
Qalhāt, 50, 52
Qandābil, 119, 147, 149–50, 151, 175
Qanūnā, 38, 42
al-Qaᶜqāᶜ b. al-Aᶜlam al-Azdī, 186, 188
Qaryat al-Faw, 26, 28
al-Qāsim b. ᶜAbd al-Raḥmān b. al-Hilālī, 146
al-Qāsim b. al-Faḍl al-Ḥuddānī, 78, 92–3, 186
Qaṣr Asfād, 182
Qaṭarī b. Fujāʾa, 121, 128–9
Qavīn, 179
Qaynuqāᶜ, 38
Qays, 1, 7, 40, 41, 70, 134, 136, 141, 144, 151
  in al-Jazīra, 201, 202
  in Baṣra, 82, 94, 96, 147
  in Khurasan, 182, 183
  modern historiography of, 3–5
  origins of, 3, 16, 33, 55
Qeshm, 141, 147
al-Qīqān, 117, 173
Qubāᶜ, 94, 97, 122–5
Qudāᶜa, 33–4, 37, 41, 84, 86, 151
Qudāma b. al-ᶜAjlan al-Azdī, 102
Quhistān, 181, 182
Qūmis, 176
Qurān, 33, 123
Qurayb b. Murra al-Azdī, 84–5
Quraysh, 5, 32, 87, 112n, 104, 156
  in pre-Islamic Arabia, 38, 40, 43, 45–6, 47, 48, 51
  mediation, 90, 93, 95, 96, 99
Qurdūs b. al-Ḥārith b. Mālik, 198–9
Quṭayᶜa, 84
Qutayba b. Muslim, 120, 136, 140–1, 171–2, 177, 179–80, 182, 183, 186, 187
Quthum b. ᶜAbbās, 120

Rabbān b. Ḥulwān, 175
Rabīᶜa (tribal grouping), 3, 38, 182, 186, 211n
  in Basra, 80, 86, 93–4, 96, 98, 99, 146, 147, 148, 153
Rabīᶜa b. Muhrib al-Ghāmidī, 39
Rabīᶜa b. Nājid al-Azdī, 103
Rabīᶜa b. Ziyād, 149
Rabinjan, 170
Radamān, 31
Rajāʾ b. Ḥaywa al-Kindī, 138
Rāmhurmuz, 127
Rasan, 28
al-Rasheed, Madawi, 155–6
Rāshid b. ᶜAbd al-Raḥmān al-Azdī, 71
Rashīd b. ᶜAmr al-Jadīdī, 173
Rashid, Hossein, 82
Rāsib, 85–6, 138
Rāsil, 173
Rawāḥa, 185
al-Rawas, Isam, 49
Rawḥ b. ᶜAbd al-Muʾmin, 144
Rawḥ b. Ḥātim al-Hamdānī, 201
Rawḥ b. Ḥātim al-Muhallabī, 132, 155, 167n
al-Rawwād b. al-Muthannā al-Azdī , 196, 198, 210
Rayḥāna bt. Abī al-ᶜĀṣ b. Umayya, 82
Raysūt, 51
Rayy, 143, 154, 173, 176, 208
Razīn b. Jābir, 196, 208–9
Retsö, Jan, 25–7, 151
Ridda, Wars of the, 5, 14, 38, 46, 48, 49, 53–5, 56, 75, 118
Rihan, Mohammad, 5
Rishahr, 81
Rizām, 39
Robertson Smith, W., 1, 10
Robin, Christian, 7, 27–8, 37
Robinson, Chase, 194, 195, 197, 199–200, 201, 204
Ruʾba b. al-Makhbul, 85
Rubkha b. Ḥārith b. ᶜĀʾīdh, 51
Rufayda, 91
al-Ruqād b. Ziyād al-ᶜAtakī, 128, 132–3
al-Rūr, 173
Rustāqubādh, 137
Rutbil of Sijistān, 150

Sabāʾ, 26, 31–2, 37
Ṣaᶜb b. Duhmān, 40